AF726078

The Political Economy of Energy Subsidy Reform

DIRECTIONS IN DEVELOPMENT
Public Sector Governance

The Political Economy of Energy Subsidy Reform

Gabriela Inchauste and David G. Victor, Editors

WORLD BANK GROUP

© 2017 International Bank for Reconstruction and Development / The World Bank
1818 H Street NW, Washington, DC 20433
Telephone: 202-473-1000; Internet: www.worldbank.org

Some rights reserved

1 2 3 4 20 19 18 17

This work is a product of the staff of The World Bank with external contributions. The findings, interpretations, and conclusions expressed in this work do not necessarily reflect the views of The World Bank, its Board of Executive Directors, or the governments they represent. The World Bank does not guarantee the accuracy of the data included in this work. The boundaries, colors, denominations, and other information shown on any map in this work do not imply any judgment on the part of The World Bank concerning the legal status of any territory or the endorsement or acceptance of such boundaries.

Nothing herein shall constitute or be considered to be a limitation upon or waiver of the privileges and immunities of The World Bank, all of which are specifically reserved.

Note that the International Institute for Sustainable Development (IISD) has copyright over chapter 4 (by Christopher Beaton, Lucky Lontoh, and Matthew Wai-Poi) of the work. Notwithstanding, The World Bank has permission to include this chapter in the work and make it publicly available under the CC BY 3.0 IGO license. See note on the first page of the chapter.

Rights and Permissions

This work is available under the Creative Commons Attribution 3.0 IGO license (CC BY 3.0 IGO) http://creativecommons.org/licenses/by/3.0/igo. Under the Creative Commons Attribution license, you are free to copy, distribute, transmit, and adapt this work, including for commercial purposes, under the following conditions:

Attribution—Please cite the work as follows: Inchauste, Gabriela, and David G. Victor, Editors. 2017. *The Political Economy of Energy Subsidy Reform*. Directions in Development. Washington, DC: World Bank. doi:10.1596/978-1-4648-1007-7. License: Creative Commons Attribution CC BY 3.0 IGO

Translations—If you create a translation of this work, please add the following disclaimer along with the attribution: *This translation was not created by The World Bank and should not be considered an official World Bank translation. The World Bank shall not be liable for any content or error in this translation.*

Adaptations—If you create an adaptation of this work, please add the following disclaimer along with the attribution: *This is an adaptation of an original work by The World Bank. Views and opinions expressed in the adaptation are the sole responsibility of the author or authors of the adaptation and are not endorsed by The World Bank.*

Third-party content—The World Bank does not necessarily own each component of the content contained within the work. The World Bank therefore does not warrant that the use of any third-party–owned individual component or part contained in the work will not infringe on the rights of those third parties. The risk of claims resulting from such infringement rests solely with you. If you wish to reuse a component of the work, it is your responsibility to determine whether permission is needed for that reuse and to obtain permission from the copyright owner. Examples of components can include, but are not limited to, tables, figures, or images.

All queries on rights and licenses should be addressed to World Bank Publications, The World Bank Group, 1818 H Street NW, Washington, DC 20433, USA; e-mail: pubrights@worldbank.org.

ISBN (paper): 978-1-4648-1007-7
ISBN (electronic): 978-1-4648-1008-4
DOI: 10.1596/978-1-4648-1007-7

Cover art: © Petar Hadzi-Boskov / The World Bank Art Program. The work is titled "Exit From Disorder" (1997) (monotype, PN473168). Used with the permission of the artist and the World Bank Art Program. Further permission required for reuse.
Cover design: Debra Naylor, Naylor Design, Inc.

Library of Congress Cataloging-in-Publication Data has been requested.

Contents

Box

Figures

Maps

Tables

Foreword

Untargeted price subsidies could easily be construed as one of the most expensive and most regressive fiscal policies in low- to middle-income countries. In fact, public expenditure on subsidies often exceeds the entirety of these countries' social safety net expenditures many times over, making this a critical area of reform that can reap important benefits for social welfare and macroeconomic and fiscal stability. In some cases, the energy subsidy bill is enormous—straining countries' fiscal capacity, skewing the distribution of income away from the poor, and perpetuating large distortions in economic activity toward capital-intensive and environmentally damaging activities. In these places, no other single policy failure is as consequential as subsidies. Although there is ample evidence of the unfavorable fiscal and benefit incidence of subsidies, the economic arguments on behalf of fiscal sustainability and equity are often not enough to allow for reforms to take hold.

Why are subsidies so difficult to reduce? And when governments have eventually managed to reduce subsidies, what disrupted the political equilibrium that gave rise to them in the first place? Relatively few World Bank reports provide a political economy perspective on this issue. Instead, most of the work on subsidies has focused on their sectoral efficiency, fiscal sustainability, or distributional impacts. Even so, most do point to the critical role of political economy in subsidy reform.

This volume was initiated at the request of World Bank country teams working in countries considering energy subsidy reforms. Their main complaint was that although they understood the macroeconomic, fiscal, and distributional reasons for recommending a reform, they had difficulty in providing examples of the political economy circumstances that might allow reforms to take place. The request was to provide an in-depth account of the timing and sequencing of countries that had successfully reformed energy subsidies—and to do so within a broader political economy context. Observing the political economy climates of governments that have grappled with subsidy reform provides a rich source of learning for other countries with comparable political climates. Instead of drawing up a prescriptive road map for reform, the idea was to derive lessons and to point to the circumstances that enabled reforms to take place.

The team assembling this volume reached out for expertise outside the Poverty and Equity Global Practice. First, to a colleague with expertise on the determinants of political incentives to pursue economic development, Philip Keefer (who helped to put together the conceptual framework at the concept note stage), and then to David Victor, professor of political science at the University of California, San Diego. Subsequently the composition of all the country teams contributing to this volume has been a mix of macroeconomists as well as poverty, social development, and energy specialists who have benefited greatly from collaboration with global and country-level experts.

We hope that the experiences presented in these case studies will benefit not only World Bank teams but also development practitioners and policy makers anywhere who are considering reforms.

Ana Revenga
Senior Director
Poverty and Equity Global Practice
The World Bank

Acknowledgments

This book was cofunded by the Poverty and Equity Global Practice (GP), the Multi-Donor Trust Fund for Poverty and Social Impact Analysis (PSIA), and the United Nations Development Programme/World Bank Energy Sector Management Assistance Program (ESMAP).

The team was led by Gabriela Inchauste (task team leader and lead economist, Poverty and Equity GP) under the guidance of Ana Revenga (senior director, Poverty and Equity GP) and Carlos Silva-Jauregui (lead economist, Poverty and Equity GP). Members of the team and their chapter-specific tasks were as follows:

We received insightful suggestions and advice from Philip Keefer, Vivi Alatas, Ramesh Ramankutty, and Roberto Senderowitsch, who served as peer reviewers for the final version of this volume. We are also very grateful to colleagues from the World Bank for their comments at various stages in developing the concept note and the drafts and presentations of the book. In particular, a special thanks to Phil Keefer for vital assistance in crafting the analytical framework used in this study and to Linda Wong for exceptional research assistance. For comments and discussions and many other forms of assistance, we thank Sudeshna Ghosh Banerjee, Kathleen Beegle, Mcdonald Benjamin, Oscar Calvo-Gonzalez, Thomas Flochel, Rohit Khanna, Caterina Ruggeri Laderchi, Tania Meyer, Vasco Molini, Edmundo Murrugarra, Ambar Narayan, Sameer Shukla, Bipul Singh, Paolo Verme, and Ruslan Yemtsov. We are also very grateful to Mary A. Anderson for editing the manuscript and to Vanessa Jarnes for formatting the many figures and tables in the volume. For excellent administrative support, we thank Nelly Obias and Indiana Taylor.

We also thank the many country authorities, development partners, and civil society organizations that provided their time during the research of each case study—they are thanked specifically in each chapter.

About the Authors

Sheila Addo is the head of planning and research in the Planning, Pricing and Research Unit of the National Petroleum Authority in Ghana. Her research interest and focus is on policy formulation and implementation as well as the commercial, social, and regulatory impacts of public policy, especially in the petroleum downstream industry. She has contributed to the feasibility analysis, development, implementation, and monitoring and evaluation of numerous downstream policies in Ghana. Addo holds a master's degree in agricultural economics from the University of Ghana, Legon.

Morgan Bazilian is lead energy specialist in the World Bank's Energy and Extractive Industries Global Practice. With more than two decades of experience in the energy sector, his work has ranged from international relations to systems analysis, infrastructure investment, market regulation, governance, and security. He holds a doctorate in energy analysis and was a Fulbright Fellow. He has published widely in the peer-reviewed literature, and is a member of the World Economic Forum's Global Advisory Council on Energy, a Fellow at the Center for Global Energy Policy at Columbia University, and a research associate at Cambridge University. Previously he worked on energy issues at the United Nations, and was the deputy chief executive officer of the Irish National Energy Agency. He also served as the European Union's lead negotiator on low-carbon technology at the UN climate negotiations.

Christopher Beaton is a research officer with the Global Subsidies Initiative (GSI) of the International Institute for Sustainable Development (IISD). His primary research interest is fossil fuel subsidies, including fossil fuel subsidy identification, estimation, and impact assessment, as well as how best to plan and implement subsidy reform. From 2014 to 2015, his portfolio at the GSI included managing a program of research and outreach focused on Indonesia. He has collaborated with a wide range of organizations, including the Asian Development Bank; the United Nations Development Programme/World Bank Energy Sector Management Assistance Program (ESMAP); the German Agency for International Cooperation (GIZ); the United Nations Environment Programme (UNEP); the World Bank; and national research institutes in countries including Bangladesh,

India, Indonesia, Nigeria, the Philippines, Thailand, and Vietnam. The GSI is dedicated to better understanding the impacts of subsidies on sustainable development and, where necessary, how subsidies can be reformed. Its comprehensive body of work on this topic is freely available on its website (http://www.iisd.org/gsi), including political economy analysis but also work on a wide range of other issues, such as producer subsidies and linkages with gender, climate change, and renewable energy.

Andrea Gallina is senior governance specialist in the Public Service and Performance Unit for Latin America and the Caribbean region at the World Bank. His research interests include political economy of policy reforms, social accountability, and social participation. He has published in academic volumes and peer-reviewed journals in the areas of the political economy of innovation and technical change, the political economy of the Euro-Mediterranean economic integration, and the role of migration for local development. His operational work at the World Bank covers the areas of anti-corruption, citizen engagement, and coalition building for reforms. Before joining the Bank, he was associate professor at the Department of Society and Globalization at Roskilde University in Denmark, where he coordinated several collaborative international research projects and publications. Gallina holds a doctorate in social sciences from Roskilde University and a master's degree in political sciences from the University of Rome La Sapienza.

Gabriela Inchauste is a global lead on the distributional impact of fiscal and social policies for the Poverty and Equity Global Practice of the World Bank and a lead economist in the Europe and Central Asia region. Her recent work includes comprehensive assessments of the distributional impact of fiscal policies; ex ante analysis of the distributional impacts of policy reforms; and diagnostics to better understand the channels through which economic growth, labor market opportunities, and public policies can lead to poverty reduction. Before joining the Bank, she was a senior economist at the Inter-American Development Bank and the International Monetary Fund, where she contributed to operational and analytical activities in numerous countries on topics including macroeconomic forecasting, public expenditure policy, poverty and social impact analysis, fiscal and debt sustainability analysis, and subsidy reform. Inchauste holds a doctorate in economics from the University of Texas at Austin.

Yusuf Mansur is the Minister of State for Economic Affairs in Jordan and has worked in economic policy, trade, antitrust, competitiveness, and local economic development. Previously, he served as deputy chief commissioner of the Aqaba Special Economic Zone; as chief executive officer (CEO) of EnConsult, a regional economic consulting firm based in Jordan; as CEO of the Jordan Agency for Economic Development; as CEO of the Jordan Investment Board; as resident representative of the United Nations Development Programme (UNDP) in

Kuwait; and as director general of the Jordan Telecom Regulatory Commission. After receiving his doctorate in economics from the University of Oklahoma, he taught at Texas A&M University, Mu'ta University (Jordan), Talal Abu-Ghazaleh (TAG) Graduate Business School (Jordan), and the University of Jordan. He has published several books and more than 70 technical papers. When not employed in the public sector, he works as a consultant, educator, and columnist.

Samuel Oguah is a power engineer with six years of professional experience in the utility sector in West Africa, where he worked for both the public generation and transmission companies in Ghana. He undertook numerous assignments relating to feasibility studies, power system planning, contract management, and engagement with the Ministry of Energy and the West Africa Power Pool. He maintains a strong focus on Ghana's energy sector. Before joining the World Bank's Energy and Extractive Industries Global Practice, he worked with the Bank's Climate Policy and Finance Department for nearly two years, focusing on sustainable energy systems and various climate-related issues, including accounting for externalities in the energy sector. In his current position, Oguah is focusing on power systems operations, planning, and regulatory aspects (including transmission regulation, integration of renewables regulations, and smart grids).

Miguel Eduardo Sánchez is senior economist in the World Bank's Macroeconomics and Fiscal Management Global Practice, with experience in economic policy dialogue in a number of Latin American and Southeast Asian countries. He previously worked for the Spanish Institute for Foreign Trade as trade and investment analyst, both in Madrid and Ankara. He holds a master's degree in political economy of development from the SOAS (School of Oriental and African Studies), University of London, and a doctorate in economics from Universidad Autónoma de Madrid. His research interests include subnational fiscal policy, political economy, and foreign direct investment in developing economies. He has published several works on these topics and is a reviewer of academic journals, including the *Journal of International Business Studies* and the *European Journal of Political Economy*.

Umar Serajuddin is a Senior Economist at the Development Data Group (DECDG) of the World Bank. He leads the socioeconomic and demographic data team at DECDG and is closely involved with the Bank's Sustainable Development Goal monitoring initiatives. He has also worked as a poverty expert in the South Asia and the Middle East and North Africa regions of the World Bank. Serajuddin holds a doctorate in economics from the University of Texas at Austin and has published several works on poverty, inequality, and social protection–related topics.

David G. Victor is a professor of international relations at the School of Global Policy and Strategy and director of the Laboratory on International Law and

Regulation (ILAR) at the University of California, San Diego. Previously Victor was a professor at Stanford Law School, where he taught energy and environmental law. He is an internationally recognized leader in research on energy and climate change policy as well as energy markets. His research focuses on regulated industries and how regulation affects the operation of major energy markets. He has a dual understanding of the science behind climate change and how international and domestic public policy work. Victor's 2011 book, *Global Warming Gridlock: Creating More Effective Strategies for Protecting the Planet,* explains why the world hasn't made much diplomatic progress on the problem of climate change and explores new strategies that would be more effective. Victor is a leading contributor to the Intergovernmental Panel on Climate Change (IPCC), a United Nations–sanctioned international body with 195 country members.

Matthew Wai-Poi is a Senior Economist in the Poverty and Equity Global Practice of the World Bank, where he leads the analytical work program on poverty and inequality in Indonesia. His work includes research on urban poverty, the middle class, and top incomes, and he is the lead author of *Indonesia's Rising Divide,* a recent flagship report on inequality. He led the technical assistance to the Indonesian government on developing a national targeting system for social assistance and holds a PhD in economics from Columbia University.

Abbreviations

ADESS	Social Subsidies Administration (Dominican Republic)
BDC	bulk distribution company
BLSM	Bantuan Langsung Sementara Masyarakat (temporary cash transfer program, Indonesia)
BLT	Bantuan Langsung Tunai (unconditional cash transfer program, Indonesia)
CDEEE	Dominican Corporation of State Electricity Companies
DPR	People's Representative Council (Indonesia)
EDEs	electrical distribution companies (Dominican Republic)
ENIGH	National Household Survey of Income and Expenditure (Dominican Republic)
FDI	foreign direct investment
GDP	gross domestic product
GLSS	Ghana Living Standards Survey
HOI	Human Opportunity Index
IMF	International Monetary Fund
KIP	Indonesia Smart Card
KIS	Indonesia Healthy Card
KSKS	Prosperous Family Saving Card (Indonesia)
LPG	liquefied petroleum gas
MGO	marine gas oil
NDC	National Democratic Congress (Ghana)
NEPCO	National Electric Power Company (Jordan)
NGO	nongovernmental organization
NPA	National Petroleum Authority (Ghana)
NPP	New Patriotic Party (Ghana)
OECD	Organisation for Economic Co-operation and Development
OPEC	Organization of the Petroleum Exporting Countries
PBU	Price Build Up (petroleum price schedule, Ghana)
PDI-P	Indonesian Democratic Party of Struggle

PLD	Dominican Liberation Party
PLN	State Electricity Company (Indonesia)
PRA	Blackout Reduction Program (Dominican Republic)
PRD	Dominican Revolutionary Party
PSIA	Poverty and Social Impact Analysis
SEIC	Secretary of State for Industry and Commerce (Dominican Republic)
SIUBEN	Single Beneficiary Selection System (Dominican Republic)
TOR	Tema Oil Refinery (Ghana)
UPPF	Unified Petroleum Price Fund (Ghana)

CHAPTER 1

Introduction

Gabriela Inchauste and David G. Victor

Overview

Every year governments spend vast sums of resources subsidizing the consumption of energy products, with many perverse effects. The resources spent on subsidies divert public budgets from other purposes such as investments in education and infrastructure. Energy consumption subsidies, although often intended to benefit the poor, are typically regressive as the bulk of the benefits accrue to those with the highest levels of consumption—those at the top of the income distribution. Subsidy programs also distort energy markets by encouraging excessive consumption overall while shifting demand toward subsidized products and away from those products whose pricing better reflects real market conditions.

These problems are widely known, yet the total level of subsidy remains high. Consumer and producer subsidies were estimated at 0.7 percent of global gross domestic product (GDP) in 2013 (Coady et al. 2015). That's because subsidies, for all their distortions to the function of government and energy markets, are often extremely popular politically. Consumer-facing subsidies usually begin as a price stabilization policy, typically in the form of price controls, and organized consumer groups around the world have credibly demonstrated they will mobilize—even to the point of riot—when the price of essential products rises to unacceptable levels.

Subsidies that begin small with noble, well-focused purposes to ensure price stability can become entrenched. The presence of a subsidy attracts supportive interest groups that mobilize politically to press for larger, more permanent subsidies. As a result, removal or redirection of the subsidy becomes harder. Indeed, the problem of energy subsidies isn't one of expert knowledge about their perverse effects. It is, rather, a problem of political economy.

This study explores the political economy of energy subsidy reform. For years, especially in the 2000s when energy prices have been high, this topic has been central to many political agendas. In 2009, the Group of 20 (G-20) advanced and emerging market economies called for a phaseout of inefficient fossil fuel subsidies in all countries, and the G-20 reaffirmed this in 2012 (IMF 2013b).

The experience with reform is highly varied. Currently as many as 27 countries are already reforming fossil fuel subsidies. In addition to subsidy reform, 40 countries and over 20 subnational jurisdictions now apply or have scheduled the introduction of a carbon price, and another 26 are actively considering one (Klevnäs, Stern, and Frejova 2015). Despite many failures at reform, there have also been striking successes. All told, subsidies today are US$117 billion per year lower than they would have been without recent reforms (IEA 2015).

Indeed, a study on the political economy of energy subsidy reform is particularly relevant today because the steep decline in most energy commodity prices over the past two years has created an opportunity for reformers (CFR 2015; Klevnäs, Stern, and Frejova 2015). Lower prices for crude oil and products have meant that the subsidy needed to sustain retail price controls is much smaller. Indeed, in some countries, the continuation of price controls set in the era of high global prices means that, in effect, schemes that used to create subsidies are now raising the local cost of energy products relative to global markets.[1] For commodity exporting countries in particular, low prices have created massive fiscal pressure on governments, which in turn has created urgent needs for reform.

In short, many political leaders have seized these reform opportunities. What should be learned from their experiences? And how can reformers remove and reframe subsidies in ways that are politically durable—so that the problem of subsidies does not reappear when world market prices rise again?

Relatively few World Bank reports provide a political economy perspective on energy subsidy reform. Most of the work by Bank teams on subsidies has focused on the sectoral efficiency, fiscal sustainability, optimal policy design, or distributional impacts of subsidies. For example, a recent internal stocktaking of analytical reports on energy subsidies by Bank teams over the past 10 years found that only a quarter of them undertake some analysis of the political economy of reforms. It is widely known that political economy is central to energy subsidy reform—a point made in an array of diverse studies (Beaton et al. 2013; Victor 2009). Yet, to date, most of the literature on energy subsidies has not engaged with political economy needs in a structured, detailed manner.

Case Study Selection

Starting from a political economy perspective, we look in depth at four countries—the Dominican Republic, Ghana, Indonesia, and Jordan—that display wide variation in the motivations and strategies for reform. In each case we describe the reform implementation process, including the timing and sequencing of events, the communication strategy, and the rollout of mitigating measures.

Our sample includes countries that have focused reform on petroleum products as well as those that have tried to address electricity subsidies. The sample includes net oil importers (the Dominican Republic, Ghana, and Jordan) as well as an oil exporter (Indonesia, for part of its history) and a country that recently found and began exporting oil (Ghana). The sample includes countries that were under pressure to reform from outside funders as well as those where reform emerged, to a larger degree, from within (such as Indonesia). And although we look at just four countries, we have been able to observe a much larger number of varied experiences with reform. That's because these four countries, all told, reflect over 30 distinct experiences with reform (as listed and described in annex 1A). Those episodes of reform are the unit of analysis in this study.

This study focuses in depth on four countries rather than, more thinly, on a larger sample because the reform process is to some degree specific to every national circumstance. Indeed, one of the reasons that no simple textbook for subsidy reform has emerged is that the local details matter enormously and vary by country, by market, by fuel type, and by the political organization of the relevant interest groups. The factors relevant in political economy are highly complex and difficult to study without detailed case study analysis.

We have also selected four countries where energy subsidies are an important part of the state budget and thus where we were likely to observe reform efforts. That, of course, introduces a bias in our study by focusing on settings where subsidies lie at the center of political debate. However, these countries are representative of the many nations that have large subsidies—nations that, as a group, are at the crux of the subsidy reform problem globally.

Indeed, worldwide, these four countries are not extreme cases. None of these countries had subsidies amounting to more than a couple of percentage points of GDP. In contrast, there are cases around the world where energy subsidies amount to more than 10 percent of GDP (the Islamic Republic of Iran, Turkmenistan, Uzbekistan, República Bolivariana de Venezuela, and Zimbabwe) (IMF 2015b).

Of course, there are other countries where energy subsidies do not figure so centrally—for example, today's Chile, China, or Mexico. In those countries, the politics of subsidy reform are less urgent but might also unfold in ways that differ from the patterns revealed here because subsidies are less acutely contested politically. Although there is evidence that subsidy reform is working in some instances, many nations (along with the four discussed here) continue to struggle with energy subsidies and their reform.

Each case study is designed to be readable on its own so that reformers and other policy makers can see what has been tried in context. They can see how well-intentioned reforms have been stymied by inattention to political forces—or derailed by exogenous events. And they can see how crafty reformers have taken advantage of windows of opportunity that arise from their own creation as well as from the vagaries of markets and politics.

The studies are aimed, as well, at students of the political economy of energy policy—a field that has emerged as professors and practitioners have learned that technocratic understanding of the energy system is not enough for policy makers. What's needed in the field and in the classroom is a fuller picture of how the science of the best policy is deployed through both the science and the art of what is politically possible.

Literature Review

To complement that in-depth analysis, we have also examined the larger, voluminous literature on energy subsidies and reform. That literature includes studies that look broadly at the experience with reform.[2] It also includes a large number of studies on diverse country experiences with reform.[3] We are mindful, as well, that the prospects for reform also hinge on how nations organize their national energy industries—often relying on state-owned firms and on the reform of those institutions, for which there are large literatures as well.[4]

The extant literature has suggested many possible alternative triggers for reform, including growing fiscal pressures or a fiscal crisis (Schneider and Heredia 2003; Tomassi 2003); imitation of other reforming countries (García-Zamor and Khator 1994; Toonen 2001); and donor pressure (Therkildsen 2000).

Some analytical literature also has described the obstacles to reform, including low capacity to commit or deliver complex public goods in place of subsidies (Pritchett and de Weijer 2010; Strand 2013); clientelism (Kitschelt and Wilkinson 2007; Van de Walle 2003); fear of mass unrest or violence should subsidies be removed (Cox, North, and Weingast 2013; North et al. 2007); and perverse or misaligned electoral institutions (Armijo, Biersteker, and Lowenthal 1994; Bueno de Mesquita et al. 2004; Keefer 2011).

Analytical Framework of Political Economy

To create a structure so that the details of each country did not overwhelm our ability to compare across cases, we have relied on a simple framework that lies at the core of most studies of political economy. It is well known that when the gains from political action can flow to a highly concentrated set of actors, those beneficiaries will often organize into a special interest group to express and seize those benefits through the political process. Meanwhile, when the benefits and costs of a policy are broadly diffused across many diverse stakeholders, it is often difficult to organize those stakeholders into a politically influential force. The simple framework we have adopted—which looks at the size of benefits from subsidy policy that flow to special interests, to citizens, or to both—has been widely discussed within the field of political economy for half a century.[5]

Political scientists and economists have extended those ideas about the political roles of organized special interest groups in many directions. For example, one branch of research has shown how different types of political leadership emerge depending on the organization of the "winning coalition" of interests needed for leaders to stay in power (Bueno de Mesquita et al. 2004). In some political systems, those winning coalitions consist of very small groups organized around obtaining policies that serve their narrow special interests. In other systems—notably, well-functioning democracies—political leaders must appeal to broad segments of the society, and thus policy tends to be organized around generating broad benefits, such as from investment in public goods. In clientelistic systems, political leaders appeal to their voters by providing material goods in return for electoral support (Stokes 2009). Indeed, the field of comparative politics has

Table 1.1 Dimensions of Subsidy Policy Benefits

		Benefits to the broader public	
		Large	*Small*
Benefits to special interests	**Large**		
	Small		

shown how different types of political systems—from presidential to parliamentary democracies to autocracies—can be understood through the lens of how political benefits are organized and delivered to interest groups and voters (Acemoglu and Robinson 2006; Cheng and Haggard 1999; Lijphart 1999; Moe and Caldwell 1994; Stepan 2001).

Our simple framework suggests that it is useful to look at subsidy and its reform across two dimensions: the extent to which concentrated or diffuse benefits flow to the (a) general public versus (b) special interest groups. The real world is more complex, of course, but this two-dimensional framework (table 1.1) offers a solid starting point for political economy analysis.[6] We will show its value in explaining, for example, why political leaders succeed and fail at overcoming well-organized groups with entrenched interests—a task that is often essential to successful subsidy reform.

Main Lessons

While highly varied, the cases presented here suggest six main observations and lessons.

Energy Subsidies Often Follow a Life Cycle

Across the four countries we study, subsidies usually began as price stabilization policies mainly designed to reduce exposure to price volatility for low-income consumers. In none of the countries did the policy makers who created these programs actually understand in detail who would benefit from the subsidies nor whether other risk mitigation policies might address price volatility more effectively. Subsidies were a mechanism readily at hand because they usually took the form of price controls implemented within an economy where the government already controlled many prices. Other mechanisms, such as targeted cash transfers to the poor, or other policies aimed at mitigating risk were not available.

Initially, the costs of those policies were small and not particularly visible. With time and continued public expenditure, however, interest groups emerged that favored those subsidies. In none of the cases we examine were those interest groups principally formed around serving the poor, but in most of the cases those interest groups became formidable opponents to reform.

Over time, subsidies swelled in size and political power. The costs of these subsidies, by contrast, commanded less political attention because they were less tangible and highly diffused across the society. For example, within the framework shown in table 1.1, the subsidy benefits typically moved from the lower-right corner (small benefits to both citizens and special interests) to the upper-left corner (large benefits to both citizens and special interests). Reforms, when successful, either shifted the subsidies back to the lower-right corner or removed them altogether.

Understanding the life cycle of subsidies is important because when a subsidy is created it is rarely clear when (and whether) the policy will emerge to become a political juggernaut. Once the costs of that policy are visible, reform is not readily available.

Awareness of patterns in the life cycle of subsidy reforms also draws attention to the fact that subsidy reform is usually a process, not a single event. The political forces that create and entrench subsidies arise over long periods of time and become interlocked with a country's politics. Reversing or redirecting those forces takes time and experimentation—leading, often, to reform failures as well as successes.

Subsidy Reform Strategies Vary Because the Underlying Political Economy Problems Vary

When benefits are concentrated, satisfying (or isolating) interest groups with alternative policies is important. When benefits are diffuse, it can be much harder to identify and manage the political coalition needed for reform. Communication with diverse stakeholders about the costs of existing subsidies and the opportunities for reform can be a central element of effective energy subsidy reform. Although every case is different, the most difficult tasks for reformers have come in two varieties, depending on *who* has benefited most from subsidies: (a) mitigating opposition from special interest groups, or (b) credibly compensating the broader public for the reduction or removal of subsidies. Therefore, successful reforms begin with an understanding of which political economy problem the reformers must solve.

One type of political challenge concerns subsidies that generate benefits for highly concentrated interest groups with few benefits for the broader public. These are classic cases of special interest politics and draw directly from the iconic logic of political economy. For example, passenger transportation unions in the Dominican Republic are so powerful that the media have named them "los dueños del país" (the owners of the country).

In such cases, the central task for reformers involves inoculating themselves against the political power of the special interests—or satisfying the interest groups with some alternative policy they prefer even more. In the Dominican Republic, the replacement of the generalized subsidy for liquefied petroleum gas (LPG) with a targeted transfer was possible because of the inclusion of a sister program benefiting drivers of LPG-fueled taxicabs. In addition, the president issued a decree awarding monthly quantities of diesel to the major (and most powerful politically) public and cargo transport unions (as further discussed in chapter 2).

The other type of political challenge is very different and probably much harder for policy makers to address—when the beneficiaries of the subsidy are large in number and highly diffused in the public. (Special interest groups may also benefit.) For instance, the broad public gained substantially from the subsidy program in Indonesia. Even poor and vulnerable households, who benefited relatively less from total spending on subsidies, found that the benefits gained were relatively large as a percentage of their incomes (see chapter 4). Similarly, in Jordan, the wealthiest quintile received three times more in fuel subsidies on average than the poorest quintile, but the amount of kerosene and LPG subsidies for poorer income groups was relatively high as a percentage of their expenditures (Atamanov, Jellema, and Serajuddin 2015). In these settings, the benefits from the subsidy are *visible* to the broader public. That public also bears the costs because the subsidy scheme is financed by the state budget, but those costs are much less visible.

In these settings, the central task for reformers is to make a credible offer to the public that the removal of visible benefits will deliver new yet currently invisible gains. Reformers must find a way not only to make that promise credible but also to communicate to the public what they are doing. Thus, many of the studies in this book find that communication is a central element of effective energy subsidy reform.

Governments Vary in Their Capacity to Implement Politically Difficult Energy Subsidy Reforms

These studies echo a finding in much of political economy research about the importance of government leadership and strength as conditions for the adoption of innovative policy reforms (see, for example, Acemoglu and Robinson 2006). When government is not confident of its power, there are strong disincentives to adopt policies that could embolden opponents and be seen as evidence of political failure. Leaders who are politically weak or governments that are poorly administered or ineffective in delivering services have few resources to credibly offer (nor penalties to credibly threaten) to special interest groups that might block reforms.

In such settings, the government may also be unable to credibly convince the general public that subsidy reforms will lead to better outcomes—especially if those outcomes are uncertain and far in the future. For instance, in Indonesia, Suharto was able to increase gasoline prices by 385 percent in 1982 at a time when public political activities outside the general election period were restricted and political activities below the district level were prohibited. However, once the 1997–98 Asian Financial Crisis hit, the Suharto regime was politically much weaker. In that weakened context, Suharto's announcement of a 70 percent increase in gasoline prices proved to be the "missing piece" that shifted public opinion away from seeing him as a good leader surrounded by bad advisors and toward viewing him as one of the speculators and corrupt businessmen who had caused the economic disaster.

The ensuing protests culminated in Suharto's stepping down and the transition to democracy, as further discussed in chapter 4.

For many political theorists, political weakness is a virtue. A hallmark of many democratic systems, for example, is a government that is reflective of voter interests rather than one that empowers political leaders with their own independent policy ambitions. But, as many scholars in comparative politics have noted, structurally or cyclically weak government can impede the process of political consolidation while making other hard policy choices effectively impossible (for example, Linz and Stepan 1996). In none of the cases presented in this volume did governments adopt politically challenging reforms at a time when political leaders had relatively low levels of confidence in their ability to retain power.

Governments find the confidence for reform from many sources, and the studies in this volume point to three in particular: crisis, political strategy, and reform strategy.

Crisis. As many studies have already shown, big reforms often occur during crisis. That's because a crisis can radically increase the credibility of reformers: there are no other options if government has already exhausted local policy options and is turning to the International Monetary Fund (IMF) and other outside lenders for support. Crisis is usually a driving force for reform among the many cases where countries have quickly adopted radical reforms—such as in the Islamic Republic of Iran, which removed one of the world's largest energy subsidy regimes as the government faced fiscal crisis from the cost of covering rapidly growing oil product imports (Guillaume, Zytek, and Farzin 2011; Hassanzadeh 2012).

Often these crises take the form of a macroeconomic shock. Some crises, however, are more specific to the energy industry. For instance, from 2006 to 2012, public opinion in the Dominican Republic became increasingly negative concerning the government's efficiency in terms of its ability to promote democratic principles, improve security, reduce poverty, and fight against corruption—making it one of the countries with lowest perceived efficiency in Latin America (see chapter 2). Under these circumstances, it is not surprising that the exposure of corruption scandals linked to the head of the electricity company led to street protests. Suddenly, the political cost of *not* reforming the subsidized electricity program became larger than the costs of reform.

Political strategy. When governments have few rivals—either because they are well organized themselves or because their rivals have been vanquished—the political confidence needed for reform may be readily at hand. For instance, in Indonesia, newly elected President Yudhoyono was able to increase prices in 2005 partly because his main opposition party had suffered heavy losses in the elections, and partly because he was adept at bringing a number of parties into his governing coalition. However, the same president failed to increase prices after his reelection in 2012, partly because he could not consolidate political support (see chapter 4). Government leaders know this and, where possible, adjust the political difficulty of the policies they pursue to their political capabilities.

Reform strategy. This volume also makes the case that governments can engineer reform strategies such that they minimize the political resources needed while maximizing the degree of reform. We further discuss this "reform engineering" below.

It is common to note that there are windows of opportunity for reformers. Many studies about reform in the past year have pointed to the drop in energy prices as one such window (for example, Kojima 2016). Our studies suggest that is true and that the political windows of opportunity can open in many ways that are often unpredictable (Kingdon 1995). Those windows can open both when prices are low (because the cost of reforms is low) and when prices are high (because the cost of failure to reform is high).

The role of political confidence as a crucial factor in the timing of reform has been identified in many other studies as well. Studies that have observed governments that shift between periods of political strength and weakness have been able to document the phenomenon carefully. For example, in Thailand, the government has fluctuated in its policy between deregulating and reintroducing subsidies (IISD and GSI 2013). Thai leaders who must face heavily contested democratic elections favor subsidies. When they are ousted, military-backed rulers remove the distortions. This pattern repeated in 2013 with a new era of military control. The chairman of the state-owned oil company—formerly the energy minister appointed after the 2006 military coup—asked the junta to use its new power to remove fuel subsidies (Bloomberg News 2014). Massive reforms soon followed (Platts 2015).

Improvements in Social Protection Systems Are Critical to the Success of Reforms

When designing this study we expected that each case study would centrally focus on the size and allocation of costs and benefits of reform. Although we found that to be true, a more central finding concerns the importance of the government's administrative capacity to design and implement better-targeted social assistance. Where energy subsidies are intended to help the poor, simply removing them is not a viable option for reformers. Cutting expensive and poorly targeted subsidies must go hand in hand with credible policies to introduce better mechanisms for social protection.

Early in the life cycle of most of the subsidies discussed in this book, we see the problem that governments lack the administrative tools needed to design and implement better-targeted social assistance programs. Energy subsidies are very expensive ways to benefit the poor, but from the perspective of policy makers, they may be better than no social assistance program at all.

Each case study examines how the subsidy policy allocates benefits by income class. In nearly every case, subsidies provide slightly larger benefits (relative to income) to the poor than to the rich. Yet the total amount of subsidy that flows to the middle class and wealthier segments of society is much larger than what gets spent on the poor. In Indonesia, for example, half of all petroleum subsidies flows to the wealthiest 20 percent of the population (figure 1.1, panel a). However, the value of energy subsidies is actually greater for poorer households

Figure 1.1 Distributive Impact of Fuel Subsidies in Indonesia

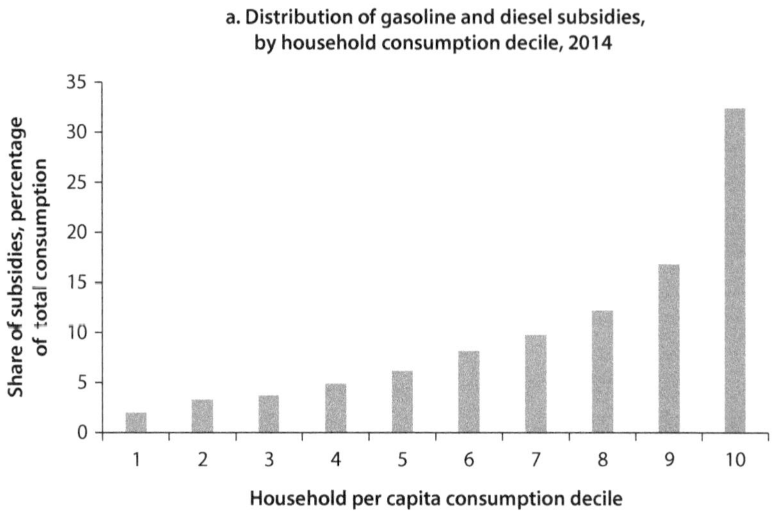

Sources: National Socioeconomic Survey (SUSENAS) of the Central Statistics Agency (Badan Pusat Statistik, BPS), Indonesia, http://microdata.bps.go.id/mikrodata/index.php/catalog/SUSENAS; World Bank calculations.
Note: Household per capita consumption deciles are after spatial adjustments for purchasing power. The subsidy value each year is estimated as the difference between the regulated price of subsidized gasoline and diesel and the retail price of nonsubsidized gasoline and diesel. This subsidy is applied uniformly to each liter of consumption, because the data do not break out household consumption of subsidized and nonsubsidized fuel. This may lead to a slight overstatement of the subsidy for the richest households, which are slightly more likely to use nonsubsidized gasoline because of its higher octane rating.

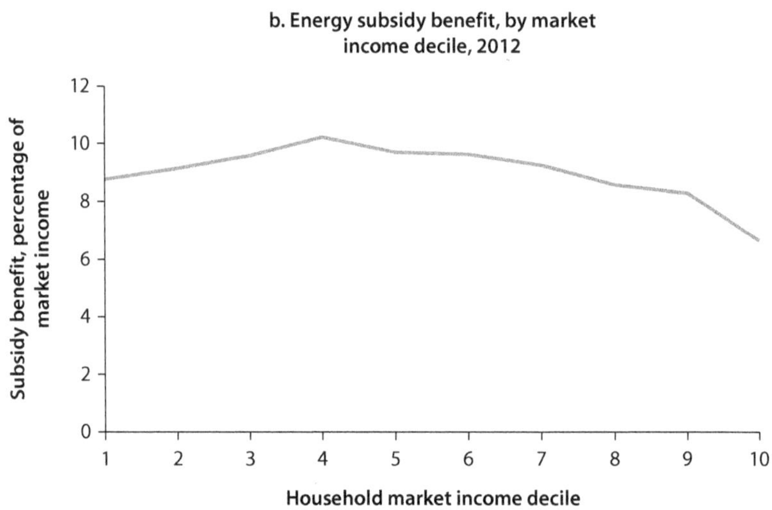

Sources: National Socioeconomic Survey (SUSENAS) of the Central Statistics Agency (Badan Pusat Statistik, BPS), Indonesia, http://microdata.bps.go.id/mikrodata/index.php/catalog/SUSENAS; Indonesia MoF and World Bank 2015.
Note: Chart includes all energy subsidies (including gasoline, diesel, kerosene, liquefied petroleum gas [LPG], and electricity), of which gasoline and diesel make up around two-thirds. "Market income" refers to total current income before direct taxes: the sum of gross (pretax) wages and salaries, capital gains, consumption of own production, imputed rent for owner occupied housing, and private transfers.

than for richer households as a share of their market incomes (figure 1.1, panel b). Similarly, before electricity subsidy reform in the Dominican Republic, the amount benefiting the richest 10 percent of the population was 17 times higher than the portion benefiting the poorest 10 percent, but electricity subsidies made up a higher share of the income of the poor than that of higher-income groups (see chapter 2).

In none of these cases do reformers remove poorly targeted, broad-based subsidies without first laying the groundwork for a better system of social assistance—a process that often takes years and often includes administrative and technological innovations (such as smart cards and extensive data collection) that make it feasible to target cash transfers to the individuals and households that would gain the most from social assistance. In some cases, these capabilities to adopt improved social assistance programs arose independently of the energy subsidy system (as in the Dominican Republic and Indonesia). In other settings, the need for energy subsidy reforms partly spurred the need to develop these systems (as in Jordan). Either way—fortuitously accidentally or intentionally—the process of building and implementing a social assistance system that effectively targets the poor is a long-term process, implying that the politicians who will eventually benefit from having these systems in place may not be the same ones who get them going.

Where governments have shifted spending from broad-based consumer subsidy programs to better-targeted programs, they have typically achieved overall savings. Unsurprisingly, the size of the savings depends on the degree of reform. For example, the 2002 reforms in Indonesia were estimated to have saved around 2.5 percent of GDP, while the compensation package was reported to have cost only around 0.2 percent of GDP (see chapter 4).

Where governments have been worried about political survival, the cost savings, at least initially, have been smaller. For example, the 2013 subsidy cuts in Indonesia were estimated to have saved around 0.4 percent of GDP, while the compensation package was reported to have cost around 0.3 percent of GDP, for a net savings of 0.1 percent of GDP.

In the countries we have studied, these alternative means of delivering social assistance came in part from a political commitment. But a central factor in explaining their creation is the empowerment of technocrats who designed and tested the schemes—often using the latest technology such as smart cards and micropayment schemes, which are less vulnerable to corruption.

These Studies Reveal Many Examples of Active "Reform Engineering"

Some of the episodes of reform involve governments tinkering with prices to solve tactical problems—such as a hole in the state budget that opens when price controls create a subsidy that turns out to be more expensive than planned. But the most interesting cases involve governments that take a strategic approach to the challenges of political economy. In these settings, fixing energy subsidies is central to the governments' missions of retaining political power and of reorganizing how the government delivers benefits to the population.

There is no textbook for this type of "reform engineering," but some of the central elements include the following:

- *Creating the capacity to implement alternative policies*. As noted above, one of the main explanations for successful energy subsidy reform lies with the creation of alternative mechanisms for targeting benefits more efficiently. Without demonstrable improvements in the administrative capacity to deliver quality social services, subsidy reforms will have only modest effects.
- *Depoliticizing tariffs*. One of the striking findings in this study is that even when governments try to reform subsidies they often find themselves drawn into subsidy politics. That's because most governments regulate prices with the intention of stabilizing prices, not necessarily intending to create subsidies. However, price controls exert a powerful gravitational force on politics. Both incumbents and their challengers know that government has the capacity to control prices, and when political opportunities arise, that capacity can't be ignored. A key for reformers is to visibly remove that capacity and thus remove price manipulation as an instrument of politics.
- *Building credibility*. The more benefits that subsidies deliver to well-organized interest groups or visibly to an electorate, the harder it is for government to reform. That's because reform involves costs—or fears of costs—that powerful interest groups won't tolerate. For example, in Bolivia, President Morales had to rescind a move to eliminate fuel subsidies in early 2011 when widespread unrest and the threat of a nationwide transport strike ensued (*Wall Street Journal* 2011). The result was a change in policy that led to an increase in subsidy expenditures from 0.9 percent of GDP in 2010 to 2 percent of GDP in 2014 (IMF 2015a, table 4). Reform engineers find ways to make shifts in the way benefits are delivered credible. For example, in Ghana, the government negotiated a trigger point with the local commercial vehicle transport union to prevent sporadic, unjustified increases in transport fares in 2012. It was agreed that transport fares would go up by one-third of the fuel price increases but only when cumulative fuel prices within the year exceeded 10 percent (see chapter 3).

The Findings Have Mixed Implications for the Current Period of Low Oil Prices

For oil exporting countries, low prices have created an impetus for reform. Other studies have looked more closely at the sheer size of fiscal pressure that these countries now face (IMF 2015c). From our study, it is easy to see that these governments, having few alternatives to reform, will probably adopt big reforms. That was the situation that Indonesia faced as its oil exports dwindled and the country became a net oil importer: crude oil production has been in decline since 1995, while gas production has plateaued in recent years. This has led to increasing reliance on costly imported oil and oil products. Today, Indonesia is ranked 22nd globally in crude production and 29th in crude reserves (see chapter 4). Globally, the process of energy policy reform in major oil exporting nations is, at this writing, already under way—from Brazil to Mexico to the Persian Gulf nations.

For oil importing countries, on the other hand, the decline in oil prices is harder to assess as a factor in reform. What is clear is that the total subsidy size has declined for the simple reason that local price caps are less expensive to maintain when global prices fall. And that has made it easier for reformers to adopt market pricing. For example, Ghana removed government control of petroleum product prices by taking advantage of the downward trend in international prices in 2015 (see chapter 3).

What's not clear is what happens when global prices rise again. In countries that have not adopted reform engineering—in particular, countries that have not credibly removed government from the business of setting prices—it could prove extremely easy to reverse course.[7]

Chapter Structure

This chapter unfolds over seven sections, including this introduction. The next section examines the varied reasons for energy subsidy reforms, because understanding the motivation for reform helps to reveal the political forces at work. Subsequently, "What Is Subsidy Reform?" discusses the varied types of reforms that affect the energy sector. The "Analytical Framework" section presents the political economy framework used to organize this study, including several hypotheses suggested by the framework. "A Political Economy Analysis of the Onset, Evolution, and Reform of Subsidy Regimes" shows what our chosen framework reveals about the "life cycle" of a subsidy and its reform. "Case Study Selection" briefly describes some methodological issues, such as case study selection, that are important to understanding the full content of this project as well as the contents of each of the country-specific chapters. The "Conclusion" section briefly summarizes the findings already highlighted previously.

Why Reform?

Why do reformers take on the very difficult task of altering energy subsidies—a task nearly always fraught with large political costs and risks? The studies in this book suggest that three basic logics drive reform—often with multiple motivations evident at once. Here, we describe the three in terms of their political impetus, in the order of their importance in driving reform: fiscal strain on the government, the burdens imposed on influential interest groups, and inefficient delivery of benefits to the poor. Interestingly, this ordering—starting with fiscal strains on government and ending with the need to better target policies for the poor—runs exactly opposite to the order of priority that most social policy analysts follow when advocating for energy subsidy reform.

Fiscal Strain on the Government

Political leaders, when they are in power, need to manage subsidy costs because their constituents evaluate them by looking, in large part, to the performance of government. And energy subsidies can create large costs to the government, increasing fiscal strain.

All four of these country studies reveal that political leaders often ignore the need for energy subsidy reform as long as subsidies don't generate highly visible costs. But reform is harder to avoid when costs explode, as in the following examples (in order of occurrence):

- *In the Dominican Republic*, the economy was buffeted in 2008–09 by rising oil prices and the international economic crisis—two exogenous events that ballooned the cost of the subsidy while also diminishing the country's tax base. These events resulted in unsustainable fiscal costs that created immense pressure on the government to plug its budget holes through LPG subsidy reform.
- *In Jordan*, similarly, the 2012 subsidy reform was spurred by an unsustainable primary fiscal deficit, a decline in reserves, and an external current account deficit of 12 percent of GDP.
- *In Indonesia*, the government was on course for a budgetary crisis in November 2014 when it implemented a fuel price hike because the previous budget had not allowed for higher-than-planned expenditure on fuel subsidies.
- *In Ghana*, petroleum subsidies caused serious liquidity challenges, motivating the price deregulation reform in 2015—a task made politically easier by the collapse in world oil prices.

Major fiscal crises are a clear example where leaders face no option but change. However, sudden reforms may themselves also constitute shocks that endanger their ultimate success. In the aftermath of the 1997–98 Asian Financial Crisis, energy subsidy reforms in Indonesia that had long been discussed in the government were suddenly a necessity—in part because of conditions set by the IMF and other external lenders (Beaton and Lontoh 2010). In the midst of crisis, rather than following the intended gradual subsidy phaseout strategy, the government announced sudden price increases of 25 percent for kerosene, 60 percent for diesel fuel, and 71 percent for gasoline (IMF 2013a). Violent protests and insurgency against the Suharto regime, in power since the 1960s, followed (Røsjø 2014). As noted earlier, these political pressures helped catalyze Suharto's removal from office the next year, in 1998, and taught all subsequent Indonesian leaders about the dangers of shocks in the form of energy subsidy reforms (see chapter 4).[8]

Fiscal Crises from Exogenous Shocks

Sometimes these fiscal crises can be triggered by exogenous shocks, including oil price movements that are essentially unpredictable. In Jordan, government reformers were forced to change policies when they faced two severe exogenous shocks during the 2010–12 period (see chapter 5):

- *Oil prices rose* after a lull following the 2008–09 global financial crisis. Between 2010 and 2012, these exogenous price rises multiplied the cost of subsidies by a factor of eight (from 0.4 percent of GDP in 2010 to 3.1 percent of GDP in 2012).
- *Sabotage shut down the Arab Gas Pipeline* in early 2012, cutting off a primary source of fuel for Jordan's power grid. The repeated attacks were part of the political convulsions that spread across the region in the wake of the Arab Spring. With gas no longer available, Jordan turned to burning more-expensive fuel oil for power.

Fiscal Crises from Less-Visible Subsidy Costs

In addition to the visible fiscal costs, political leaders also discovered many less-visible costs from large subsidy programs. Among those costs is the need for unexpected, rapid changes in political and industrial priorities. Because many governments subsidize energy by regulating prices, they, in effect, offer a subsidy of unknown public cost. Some entity—whether the government as a whole, importing firms, or state-owned enterprises—sits between the global price for energy commodities (which can fluctuate extensively) and the nationally regulated price. When the global price changes quickly and national prices are reset more slowly, that mediating entity bears the huge, unexpected increase in expenses that suddenly appears.

In Indonesia, for instance, fuel subsidies increased from 0.8 percent of GDP in 2009 to 2.1 percent of GDP in 2011 as international crude prices increased from US$44 per barrel in 2009 to US$107 per barrel in 2012 (see chapter 4). Similarly in Ghana, the established price mechanism used historical import prices, leading to unsustainable subsidies such that over 30 percent of the oil importers' working capital was locked up in unpaid subsidies (see chapter 3).

These less-visible costs from subsidy policies accrue not just to government but also to organizations that are connected and exposed to government action. Notably, when subsidies become unexpectedly large, many governments play a shell game to hide and shift the cost. Energy firms (suppliers and traders), including state-owned firms, are particularly exposed because they often operate under soft budget constraints (Victor and Heller 2007; Victor, Hults, and Thurber 2012).

In Ghana, for example, the state-owned Tema Oil Refinery (TOR) was left exposed to the cost of price controls because it imported crude oil at world prices but sold its products at regulated price levels. When prices changed quickly, holes in TOR's budget would appear—making it impossible for the firm to plan orderly investments and even basic operations. For instance, following elections in 2008, the winning party followed through on a campaign promise to reduce energy prices. That promise, along with higher global oil prices, led by February 2009 to a debt of unreimbursed subsidy costs so large that it forced TOR to suspend operations. In turn, the cost of this debt rippled through the larger economy because other important entities could not clear payments (Laan, Beaton, and Presta 2010). Moreover, at no time during the period covered in our case study did TOR come close to meeting its operating capacity given its lack of liquidity due to the subsidy debts on its books. Consequently, to cover demand, the government needed to encourage additional private sector imports of finished products as well as increased production from a private sector refinery.

In sum, across all four of these countries, the biggest episodes of reform were mainly triggered by the appearance of large, visible costs to government. But in many of the cases, reformers kept working on energy subsidy reform even after the visible costs diminished because they sought to reduce the less-visible costs as well—particularly the inability to set reliable priorities because (a) exogenous shocks in global energy markets could suddenly increase the cost of subsidy, and (b) subsidy policy was prone to political distortions that disproportionately harmed incumbents.

Burdens Imposed on Powerful Interest Groups

Across these four countries we have observed, mainly, that subsidies create large benefits for well-organized interest groups while less-organized groups (such as taxpayers) suffer. That is the standard prediction of the most basic political economy models of collective action and group behavior (Wilson 1973). But subsidies can also create visible costs to organized groups—notably when those groups have alternative policy priorities that would gain from liberating public funds through energy subsidy reform.

For example, in Ghana, the bulk distribution companies (BDCs)—the private companies that import most of the fuel used in the country—have been stuck periodically with huge financial losses as a result of government arrears in payment of subsidies. The BDCs have consequently lobbied strongly in favor of reform. Similarly, there are groups that have poverty reduction at the top of their agenda and can heavily influence political decisions through advocacy or aid, including civil society organizations, consumer interest groups, political pressure groups, nongovernmental organizations (NGOs), and development partners (see chapter 3).

Inefficient Benefit Delivery to the Poor

Most notably, general consumption subsidies are inefficient ways to benefit the poor. For example, in the Dominican Republic before the 2008 reform, the amount of LPG subsidies benefiting the richest 10 percent of the population was at least five times the amount benefiting the poorest 10 percent (see chapter 2). The standard logic looks, instead, to benefits that are targeted directly to the poor—ideally in the form of direct transfers to income that poor households can then decide how best to allocate.

The literature on energy subsidies is replete with analysis showing how subsidy mechanisms are usually very poor ways to target benefits to the poor (Coady et al. 2006). A United Nations Environment Programme (UNEP) study in the early 2000s found that in the Islamic Republic of Iran, the wealthiest income group received 78 times the gasoline subsidy received by the lowest-income group. And in urban areas, the highest-income group received 42 times the diesel subsidy received by the lowest-income group. Such disparities were less pronounced for subsidies of other energy products that are more disproportionately used by the poor, such as kerosene and LPG (UNEP 2003).

Following this logic, some countries have tried to make energy consumption subsidies more efficient by improving how they are allocated. In South Africa, for example, a system of targeted electricity subsidies has led some locales to try to allocate costly subsidies just to the poorest households (Christensen et al. 2015; Davidson and Mwakasonda 2009; Howells et al. 2006; Vagliasindi 2012; Winkler 2006). Other countries have created smart card systems for allocation (Vagliasindi 2012).

The best practices, however, lie with direct income transfers. For instance, in the Dominican Republic, a system of smart cards and strong central administration was in place in 2008, enabling the government to reform its LPG subsidy by targeting direct cash transfers to roughly the poorest 40 percent of the population (see chapter 2).

Improved social policy goes hand in hand with policies designed to make markets more effective in allocating resources within the society. These four country studies confirm what has long been known in the study of subsidies: below-market costs encourage overconsumption of subsidized products as well as distortionary efforts by consumers to switch toward subsidized products. In Indonesia, for example, large differences in fuel costs affected motorists' choice of vehicles (chapter 4, figure 4.8).

More generally, the literature has noted that below-market energy prices can lead to excessive energy intensity in an economy and can harm productivity (Cornillie and Fankhauser 2004; Hang and Tu 2007). They can also lead to higher emissions of energy-related pollutants, which is why many studies identify energy subsidy reform as a strategy for controlling emissions that often has large "co-benefits" for societies (Fattouh and El-Katiri 2012; UNEP 2008; Victor 2011).

Interestingly, when economic and social policy analysts write about energy subsidies, they usually start their discussion with this last of the three major motivations for subsidy reform. They focus on the potential for much better social policy by retargeting subsidies to worthier purposes and through greater use of market forces to allocate resources within society. Yet when a history of energy subsidy reform is viewed through the lens of political economy, the order is reversed: the main drivers are the impacts that are more immediate to government leaders, starting with the need to address fiscal crises. These problems generate more powerful forces for reform because they are harder for political leaders to ignore: they directly implicate the functioning of government and generate greater political accountability for leaders.

What Is Subsidy Reform?

What is our dependent variable—reform—when it comes to energy subsidies? Most of the literature on energy subsidies and reform answers this question narrowly: reform is a policy that changes the size and allocation of a subsidy.

Indeed, the work on this volume began by examining reform under that definition. As a practical matter, that has meant focusing in particular on government regulation of wholesale or retail prices for energy-related products. We will call these *pricing reforms*.

Pricing Reforms

As detailed in annex 1A, each of the four case studies has included several rounds of pricing reforms—usually guided, at least loosely, by a philosophy that links the goals of reform to the level of prices. In all four of the countries, that philosophy has involved treating different fuels differently—usually with lower prices for fuels that tend to be consumed by lower-income groups and by politically well-connected groups. In Jordan, for example, LPG is vitally important for the poor and thus a central element of the country's energy subsidy scheme; diesel and gasoline, by contrast, tend to be consumed by populations that are wealthier and less sensitive to fuel prices.

As the work proceeded, however, it became clear that at least three other kinds of reforms are also important: *institutional*, *informational*, and *complementary reforms*.

Institutional Reforms

In addition to direct reform of pricing mechanisms, most of the observed episodes of reform included institutional reforms. Those include reforms to pricing mechanisms—notably the removal of ad hoc government control over prices and a shift to pricing mechanisms that are more automatic or even full reliance on markets for pricing. Institutional reforms have also included reorganization of *how* subsidies are paid—for example, shifting from systems in which a state-owned enterprise acts as intermediary between imports and in-country sales to one where the government pays direct cash transfers.

These institutional reforms matter because they alter the ways that political forces are mobilized and influence policy. When the pricing mechanism is ad hoc, the politics of price and subsidy focus on government leaders and their challengers. When the mechanism is more independent, the opportunities for direct political manipulation are weakened.

In the Ghana case study, a shift to an automatic price mechanism in which local prices would float in closer proportion to world prices—even though all cross-subsidies were not removed—helped to depoliticize the process of setting retail prices (see chapter 3). Ghana's new National Petroleum Authority—an institution whose governing board includes government officials, trade union and company representatives, experts, and some NGO representatives rather than just government itself—was created to monitor reforms that have kept domestic prices in line with international prices (Crawford 2012). The recent reform is a complete removal of government's role in the establishment of prices (price deregulation), taken in an environment of falling oil prices. Whether it survives in a context with less-convenient global price trends remains to be seen and could potentially depend on whether other governance and social protection measures have been taken to safeguard the independence of the price-setting mechanism.

Beyond the countries examined in this study, we note that the literature has examples of other countries that have relied heavily on the political benefits of delegating these controversial decisions to automatic mechanisms or independent authorities. In Tanzania, energy subsidy reform has included a large role for a specialized regulatory agency that administers licenses, manages regulations, and also keeps the public informed about prices and reviews the proper functioning of the market (such as concerns about price collusion practices). Kenya and South Africa instituted similar policies to regularly publish prices (Alleyne 2013).

Institutional reforms that lead to more predictable policy environments may also ease the process of transition and make it easier for firms and politicians to focus on long-term investments and policy strategies. In Brazil, the government began the process of liberalizing the energy market in the 1990s—in tandem with an economywide effort to shift from state-controlled capitalism to more-liberal development strategies. Facing opposition from interest groups, the government built public support by promising lower prices and improved services to consumers while also stretching out the reform process. Its hope was that the improved efficiency from a liberalized market would help keep prices low (IMF 2013a).

The order in which Brazil chose products for subsidy removal depended on the political difficulty of the sectors involved. The first products to lose subsidies, in 1993, were those consumed by politically weak stakeholders: asphalt, lubricants, and products mainly used by firms. Next was gasoline for final consumers in 1996, LPG for final consumers in 1998, and finally diesel in 2001. Subsidies for ethanol producers and the suppliers of equipment and services to the national oil company, Petrobras, remained until the end of the liberalization program in 2002. Subsidies for fuel to supply the thermal power plants in Amazonia, a politically sensitive region, remained for 10 years until 2012 (IMF 2013a).

And once the government revoked Petrobras's monopoly over the sector in 1995, it created an independent—and soon highly regarded—National Petroleum Agency (Agência Nacional do Petróleo, ANP) to oversee deregulation efforts, restructure the sector, and manage the auctioning of oil fields for exploration (de Oliveira 2012). Although the ANP's main mission was not to oversee subsidy policy, it—along with other independent agencies such as a similar body created for the electric power sector—made it much harder for the government to reverse course on reforms even when they became politically inconvenient later (de Oliveira 2007). That did not eliminate political interference in energy markets—a point underscored by recent scandals at Petrobras—but it did lead to a more predictable policy environment.

Informational Reforms

In addition to institutional changes, about one-third of the reform episodes examined in this study involve active efforts to increase the flow of certain information.

These informational reforms can, in some settings, alter what is politically feasible. In effect, information can make interest groups aware of benefits that might flow to them if they were better organized politically. Put differently, the provision of information can reduce the transaction costs for political organization and make the political economy of some policy reforms easier to manage.

In Ghana's reforms, for example, wider availability of information probably made it easier for think tanks such as the IMANI Center for Policy & Education to document how the government has manipulated petroleum pricing and the allocation of subsidies in ways that have harmed the poor—insights that, in turn, helped to strengthen the coalition of reformers, including those outside the country seeking reform, such as the IMF.[9]

Informational reforms can also play important roles in convincing stakeholders to consent to giving up a benefit they have in hand (a subsidy) in exchange for some better outcome (lower tax burdens and better-functioning energy markets) in the future. When Ghana shifted to a more automatic pricing mechanism, it also made details on how prices were calculated much more transparent—and thus harder to politicize as well as to reverse by future governments (Laan, Beaton, and Presta 2010). In contrast, efforts to reform subsidies in Jordan have been impeded by the fact that, as measured in opinion surveys, the public knew little about subsidy policy and was wary about related reforms (see chapter 5).

Complementary Reforms

Finally a wide array of complementary reforms show up in about one-third of episodes examined (annex 1A). Some of these involve investments in human or physical capital, and others involve allowing price increases in the transport sector, among other types. What these reforms have in common is that they complement or substitute for subsidies in ways that help reformers reduce the size of subsidies and improve their allocation. In some way these are all actions that can lead to greater social legitimacy of the reform process, which is critical for its political sustainability.

In all of the cases examined in this volume, there is a "pendular" tendency in reform formulation and implementation. Even when progress has been made in implementing the right reforms, it has been challenging to make these reforms more permanent. One important element of this is the capacity of societies to define reform agendas that come as the result of legitimate processes, for which technical legitimacy is only one part of the picture. Each of our studies looks at how these complementary reforms shift what is possible in the realm of energy subsidy reforms.

The importance of interlocking reforms is hardly unique to the cases we examine here. For instance, after Gabon raised gasoline and diesel fuel prices by 26 percent in 2007, it also instituted these complementary reforms (Alleyne 2013):

- The National Social Guarantee Fund (CNGS) resumed cash payments to the poor while conducting a new and improved census of lower-income households.

- The CNGS increased assistance to single mothers and funding to microcredit programs helping women in rural areas.
- Households that consumed below a threshold of electricity and water got it for free, up to a limited quantity.
- School enrollment fees were waived for public schools, and textbooks were free for primary school.
- Investment to expand rural health services, electrification, and the drinking water supply were accelerated.
- The public transport network was expanded.

The IMF team that studied the experience in Gabon has looked to other African countries such as Mozambique and Nigeria and found similar patterns—that social programs generally, not just those linked to energy, were expanded to offset the harm to poor families when energy subsidies are reduced or redirected (Alleyne 2013).

Analytical Framework

To help focus the political analysis in each study, we did two things. First, we selected a sample of countries that was designed to offer a diversity of experiences with reform. All else equal, partially controlled diversity offers the prospect of identifying some relationships between causes and effects. By working with a small number of countries—and thus controlling for many country factors—the identification of cause-and-effect patterns offers the prospect of research findings that might be applicable more generally to other countries and circumstances. We discuss that sampling further in another section below.

Second, we began each case study with a common, simple model of political economy that focused the case study authors on the goal of understanding how the size and allocation of costs and benefits might affect policy design and outcomes. That framework, the topic of this section, offers a starting point for identifying general patterns in the incidence of energy subsidies as well as opportunities for reform.[10]

The framework we use is based on the most fundamental maxim from the study of political economy: policies arise to serve well-organized interests at the expense of the general welfare (Wilson 1973). We have applied this idea to roughly characterize energy policies in a country as offering (a) either substantial or relatively few benefits to well-organized special interests, and (b) either substantial or relatively few benefits to citizens at large. This yields four case categories:

- *Case 1:* Both special interests and citizens derive large benefits.
- *Case 2:* Special interest benefits are large, and citizen benefits are small.
- *Case 3:* Citizen benefits are large, and special interest benefits are small.
- *Case 4:* No one gains significant benefit.

Table 1.2 Characterizing Subsidy Policy Benefits: Basic Framework

Beneficiary type and benefit size	*Citizen benefits are large*	*Citizen benefits are small*
Special interest benefits are large	Case 1	Case 2
Special interest benefits are small	Case 3	Case 4

Table 1.1 showed the basic logic; it is reproduced here showing the case numbers, which correspond to the types listed above (table 1.2). For each type of case, the proposed framework provides some theoretical intuition on the circumstances that could lead to an energy subsidy reform being more (or less) likely.[11] We turn to each of these hypotheses below.

Case 1: Large Benefits to Both Special Interests and Citizens

Case 1 implies large fuel subsidies, such as in countries where retail prices are low for all users even when global prices are high. Large users benefit exceptionally, but average citizens also see a significant contribution to their household budgets.

The theoretical intuition is that such cases of massive energy subsidies exist because citizens cannot act collectively to pressure government to adopt different policies that might be less costly or have higher net benefits. Moreover, well-organized special interests fear that a change in policy will harm their interests. Each depends on the support of the other for the benefits, and neither will support lowering benefits for the other. Governments tolerate this situation because leaders gain electoral and other benefits from the subsidy and are not forced to deal with the cost.

Based on this intuition, we began this project with theoretical expectations that reform in this case would be more likely when some or all of these conditions are present:

- Government can make a credible commitment to citizens and interest groups that policy reforms will leave them better off. Solving this credibility problem may require having alternative programs in place that are designed for endurance and timed such that new benefits flow in tandem with the loss of benefits from energy subsidies.
- Citizens develop greater capacity to mobilize in their own collective interests—for example, when they are made aware of the costs of broad-based subsidies and the potential for improved welfare outcomes from better use of those expenditures.
- Special interests find it more difficult to mobilize, in effect reducing the political cost to government of reforming subsidies. For example, special interest groups might become disorganized for some reason, or government might find different ways to satisfy their core aims.
- The costs of providing benefits rise sharply (for example, if world fuel prices skyrocket).

- Governments face a general fiscal or balance-of-payments stringency, with energy subsidies being a large part of the problem.
- External pressure changes the political equilibrium, such as when donors or lenders have exceptional leverage.

In contrast, reform is *not* likely under the following conditions:

- Governments fear mass mobilization and protest by the public in response to removal of subsidies.
- Governments change or elections are introduced, because the underlying problem of making a credible commitment to reform remains the same (unless a more credible party or politician replaces a noncredible incumbent).
- Governments promise to replace energy subsidies with cash transfers to average citizens, since average citizens do not believe that these transfers are credible unless they are supported by special interests.

Case 2: Large Benefits to Special Interests, Small Benefits to Citizens

Case 2 arises when prices are high for households and low for industrial users. For example, in the Dominican Republic large consumers can purchase electricity directly from generators, rather than having to go through the distribution companies, leading to large savings relative to households.

The theoretical intuition is that such a policy exists when citizens have little ability to advance their collective interests, while organized lobbies are powerful. Subsidies would then flow to special interests to the extent that the well-organized interest groups can exercise leverage on the government—such as when there are family or party ties, or when the interest groups command a vital part of the economy (for example, transport). As a general rule, we expect that subsidies of this type arise and persist because they benefit a particularly small fraction of the population or their costs are not large enough to have substantial, broad-based impacts on the functioning of the economy and the public budget. The benefits to the citizenry as a whole may be small or, more likely, citizens generally pay diffused costs while special interests gain concentrated benefits. As such, these are iconic cases expected from the logic of political economy.

Based on this intuition, we expected at the outset of this project that reform would therefore be more likely when some or all of these conditions are present:

- Governments can credibly provide special interest groups with alternative benefits that better meet their interests.
- Citizens develop greater capacity to mobilize in their own collective interests.
- The government changes, and special interests no longer have a large influence within the successor government.
- Fuel prices skyrocket (making the total cost of the special interest subsidy more visible), or governments otherwise face the general need for fiscal stringency.
- External pressure changes the political equilibrium.

In contrast, reform is *not* likely under the following conditions:

- The subsidy remains small and thus neither attracts broader public attention nor drains the public budget.
- The special interest groups remain well organized.

Case 3: Small Benefits to Special Interests, Large Benefits to Citizens

Case 3 generally involves subsidies that are intended exclusively to benefit most households. These might be low prices for fuel used predominantly by households (such as kerosene) and less by organized firms (such as diesel). In these settings, citizens are well organized enough to demand subsidies from the government—perhaps because governments, seeking electoral advantage, brandish subsidies as a way to curry broad-based political favor.

The theoretical intuition behind Case 3 is that subsidies can offer visible political advantages that political leaders might want to use broadly. Leaders, for example, might need to appeal to large, lower-income segments of the electorate to retain power. They might fear mass uprising from energy price shocks or other events that the public might view as failures of government. Leaders in this setting might lack alternative mechanisms that could target subsidies more efficiently. For example, if benefiting the poor is electorally important, a government may nonetheless use broad-based energy subsidies because it lacks the capacity to implement targeted cash transfers or other better alternatives. The poor, for example, may be organized into parties and be pivotal voters—such as when social solidarity is high or when "social altruism" is inspired by specific, rather than general, consumption needs of the poor.

A standard political economy framework would suggest that Case 3 is rare. Normally, political economy involves well-organized groups obtaining benefits for themselves while the broader public interest is harmed (Case 2). However, we consider Case 3 (and find evidence that such cases exist) because there may be settings where politicians are more attentive to delivering broad benefits while special interest groups are little involved. Those groups may see few benefits for themselves from pursuing such subsidies—perhaps because they do not believe such policies can be sustained. Put differently, these cases might be called "populist political economy" in logic.

Reductions in these subsidies, we expected at the outset of this project, would be more likely when some or all of these conditions are present:

- The poor are no longer pivotal to the electoral success of a government. For example, parties that oppose redistribution may come to power in response to ideological shifts or the perceived poor performance of redistribution policies.
- Government can credibly offer alternative policies to some or all of the citizenry.
- Government may create direct cash transfers or other programs that allow it to administer alternative systems for transferring benefits to the poor.

- The costs of the subsidies rise, such as when international fuel prices rise or subsidized energy leads to substantial increases in consumption.
- Politicians' beliefs change about the "special" nature of energy, and redistributive policies shift to more-efficient transfers.
- External pressure changes the political equilibrium, such as when donors with exceptional leverage become important to a government's political survival or other exogenous shocks require a change in the public budget.

In contrast, reform is *not* likely under the following conditions:

- The subsidy remains small enough not to trigger the need for reform.
- Governments fear mass mobilization and protest by the public in response to removal of subsidies.
- Special interests emerge that, along with the broader public, lobby for continuation of the subsidy (that is, entrenching the subsidy into Case 1).
- Governments continue to perceive that the benefits from the subsidy are crucial to their political survival.

Case 4: Few Benefits to Either Special Interests or Citizens

In Case 4, no interest group, organized or general, benefits exceptionally from two classes of energy policies. In one class, subsidies are simply low or nonexistent. In the other class—more interesting and reflective of energy policies in several countries—policy is intended to stabilize fuel prices in an "actuarially fair" manner (higher prices charged in "good times" fully offset the costs of subsidies in "bad times"), permitting consumption smoothing by average citizens. These "ideal" stabilization policies have a second-order effect on consumer welfare but will insulate governments against political shocks. Large users, with greater capacity to hedge against fuel price changes, may not even receive second-order benefits.

Such policies leave the domain of Case 4—and become examples of other ideal case types—under two circumstances. First, prices rise more than anticipated, depleting the stabilization fund built up when prices were low. In this setting, the subsidy policy moves to one of the other cases, depending on the size and distribution of benefits. Second, stabilization funds can only survive if no arbitrage is enforced between subsidized and full-price markets. If special interests can manipulate access to the fund when world prices are high and domestic prices (because of the fund) are low, then Case 2 applies.

The theoretical intuition in this case is that stabilization policies would persist unless they fall out of the domain of Case 4 and into one of the other cases. Moreover, they would persist until parties with a pro-market ideology come to power. Note that when ideological parties are present, citizen mobilization is more likely to be high; if so, Cases 3 and 4 are more likely to prevail. Hence, the ideological shifts associated with changes in government are more likely to matter in these cases.

For Case 4, "reform" should be a largely empty set. There may be reforms in the special setting of stabilization funds—so that funds are properly sized and targeted.

But overall, Case 4 is a setting when subsidy is low and the need for reform is small. There is no need to redirect an inefficient subsidy to a more efficiently targeted policy. There is no need to overcome entrenched special interest groups.

A Political Economy Analysis of the Onset, Evolution, and Reform of Subsidy Regimes

The studies in this project use the framework presented above for two purposes. First, the framework suggests a set of iconic types of subsidies. These are "ideal types" in the sense of theory; in the real world, any particular subsidy might have elements of more than one of these types. But they are a starting point for understanding the array and strength of the interest groups that might favor or oppose any particular subsidy. Each of the case studies examined in this project has identified multiple examples of energy subsidies and then analyzed the underlying size and allocation of costs and benefits to place them on tables 1.1 and 1.2.

The second purpose of this framework is to understand how political interests can be reorganized so that a subsidy can be shifted from one box to another. Reform involves a situation where that process of shifting is led by policy, and all of the case studies in this project examine those policies closely.

Although this project focuses on policy, we note that there are also some examples of shifting for purely exogenous reasons. In all the countries that use price controls as the means of delivering subsidies, the big rise in oil prices in the 2000s shifted subsidies that might have been located in the lower-right corner. It moved them west if the pricing scheme was designed to keep fuels used by particular special interests within a certain band. The big rise in global prices, even as those local prices did not follow, led to a radical expansion in the size of the subsidy. For example, changes in international prices led to an increase in generalized fuel subsidies in the Arab Republic of Egypt to 5–7 percent of GDP between 2010 and 2012, and back down to 3 percent of GDP in 2014 (Kojima 2016). In other settings, a pricing regime designed to affect all fuels led to a shift in subsidy that moved northwest. For example, in Indonesia the rapid rise in world oil prices meant that most domestic users of fuels enjoyed a rapidly larger subsidy.

Our particular focus is policy-driven shifts in subsidies. There is no single strategy for policy reform, but the purpose of a political economy framework is to illuminate how the policy process is affected by organized interest groups and by the functioning of government.

The Life Cycle of a Subsidy Regime

The cases in this project also suggest some general patterns in the emergence of subsidies and in the varied policy reform efforts. We will call those patterns the "life cycle" of a subsidy regime (figure 1.2).

Subsidies often begin with modest purposes at modest levels, as shown in the lower-right corner. In the classic political economy framework, well-organized interest groups would realize that a scaling up of those small subsidies would

Figure 1.2 Life Cycle of a Subsidy Regime

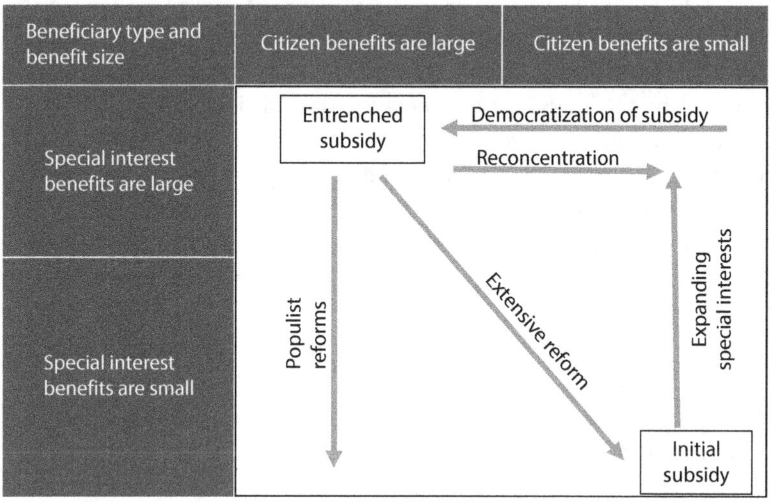

be to their advantage. As a result, the subsidy regime moves north. Standard political economy models would predict that north-moving subsidy to be a stable outcome—an iconic example of special interest politics.

For example, the importance of political power is revealed by how big variations in the world energy markets intersected with democratic politics in Ghana. By the time world prices began to decline in July 2008, fuel prices had become a hot campaign issue for the upcoming elections at the end of that year. Promises to maintain low fuel prices by the main opposition party, the National Democratic Congress (NDC), proved to be effective. The NDC won the election and reduced fuel taxes. By March 2009, Ghana's fuel prices were more than 45 percent lower than those in neighboring countries, leading to a surge in consumption and smuggling of fuel out of the country (Laan, Beaton, and Presta 2010).

In our study, however, we see many examples of subsidies that do not remain in the northeastern corner. Instead, the subsidy is democratized for reasons anticipated earlier in the "Analytical Framework" section. Special interests realize the benefits from a large subsidy. But political leaders—often goaded by the opposition or animated by fears of losing power—also realize the benefits of providing a broad-based subsidy. The subsidy regime thus shifts west and becomes deeply entrenched.

In several instances, we find examples of political leaders who, fearful of losing political support, extended subsidy regimes that had been more narrowly targeted to ones that generated large, broad-based benefits to most of the public. These are the most difficult cases for reformers because they lead to the highest costs and are animated by political forces—a combination of leaders who fear the loss of broad-based public support and organized special interest groups that oppose any reduction of the subsidies.

So far, we have focused on policy reforms that make subsidy regimes worse from the standpoint of public policy—by shifting subsidies north and west. Now we look at the types of reform that may follow by focusing on reforms that emanate from the most-entrenched, hardest-to-reform regimes.

Reformers might focus on reentrenching the subsidy regime—moving from a very costly broad-based subsidy to one designed to be politically more efficient because it is catering to a smaller number of well-organized interest groups. Many of the energy subsidy reforms in this project include examples of this. Jordan's 2008 energy subsidy reforms, for example, did not fix the problem of subsidy overall, but they did reconcentrate subsidies back to a slightly smaller base of beneficiaries. Similarly, the LPG reform in the Dominican Republic targeted benefits to the poor and to some extent to the powerful transport sector, leading to an overall fiscal savings.

Reformers have also done things that are quite unexpected within the standard political economy framework. They have shifted subsidies from the northwest corner (Case 1) to the south (Case 3)—removing special benefits while preserving broad-based benefits. This kind of "populist" reform is evident in several of the reform episodes in Ghana, for example. Leaders, keen to retain public office and fearful of swings in the sentiment of the electorate, have found it difficult to reform broad-based subsidies, yet have been willing to allow the costs of subsidies to flow against well-organized interest groups, such as industry and even the state-owned refinery. Groups that should (within a standard political economy framework) be extremely aware of their interests and highly organized to advance them in the public policy process found themselves disadvantaged compared with the democratic logic of political survival.

The most challenging cases of reform—called "extensive reform" in figure 1.2—involve a shift from the northwest (Case 1) back to the southeast (Case 4). In this project, we see no examples of such extensive reform except when linked to other social reforms. Taking on well-organized special interests as well as dismantling visible public benefits is a task that few leaders would be willing to undertake unless they could demonstrate some countervailing benefits.

Indeed, we found few examples from around the world of this kind of extensive reform in the absence of countervailing policy reforms. One of the few examples may be the large reduction in subsidies by the newly installed military government in Thailand in 2015—an action that was feasible because the coup's assertion of political power vanquished any serious political opponents (Platts 2015).

Other Significant Elements of Subsidy Regimes

The power of a simple framework is that it focuses starkly on a few important factors. Nonetheless, simplicity necessarily sacrifices richness. As shown earlier, table 1.1 and figure 1.2 omitted many important elements that explain the onset, evolution, and reform of subsidy regimes. Here we suggest three that merit closer attention.

Visible versus Invisible Benefits

First, as the Indonesia case study makes especially clear, it is important to distinguish between *visible* and *invisible* benefits from subsidies. The standard, simplified political economy framework has not focused on the visibility of policy benefits and costs because most political economy analysis has focused on other factors—namely, the ability of concentrated special interests to organize themselves politically and exploit the less-organized mass public (Olson 1965; Peltzman 1976). The case studies in this project reveal many examples of that—notably when governments try to change subsidy policies in ways that affect well-organized and politically powerful transport unions.

A fuller analysis, however, would look in more detail at the broad-based political support for subsidies. Leaders use subsidies because they are convenient (if expensive) ways to deliver visible public benefits. Not surprisingly, leaders unsure of their tenure are more prone to favor broad-based subsidies than are those who are confident they can make unpopular decisions and remain in power.

A missing ingredient in understanding the political attractiveness of broad-based subsidies is whether the public understands the costs of those policies and the benefits and legitimacy of alternative approaches. All of the examples of successful extensive reform involved active communication with the public about the purpose of the reforms. In Indonesia, the recently elected government began that communication campaign during the election—thus lowering the political cost of shifting subsidy policies since the newly empowered government was implementing a widely known campaign promise when it cut back broad-based subsidies. And during the transition from the old government to the new, leaders of both parties found ways to split the political cost of removing these expensive subsidies (see chapter 4). In terms of our political economy framework, these strategies increased the visibility of the otherwise invisible broad-based benefits of energy subsidy reform. In so doing, they changed how the public calculated the merits of subsidies—from a pure stream of benefits to a stream of benefits with even larger costs.

The importance of visibility is probably particularly high for broad-based subsidies because highly diffused, nonexpert voters may be unaware of how subsidy policy affects the larger health of the economy as well as distortions to political behavior. By contrast, well-organized interest groups—such as energy traders, transport unions, or fishermen (who use a great deal of fuel for their boats)—are probably much better informed about their calculus of special interest.

Distinctions among Special Interests

A second extension to the framework here would involve more clarity about the concept of "special interests" than shown earlier in table 1.1 and figure 1.2. We use the standard political economy approach to understanding those interests: what's "special" about them is that they are groups organized to advance a particular self-interest rather than the broader public interest. In standard analysis of public policy, special interests are seen as pernicious forces in politics, and the larger aim of serving the public interest involves taming special interests and channeling their influence in ways that serve broader public purposes. Doing that is hard because, according to the standard political economy framework, special interest groups know who they are and tend to be well organized politically because the benefits from collective action are concentrated within their special realms.

However, not all special interests act against the public interest. In all four of these case studies, we see efforts to organize policies intended to generate benefits for a particular special interest: the very poor. This is a group whose political influence is often latent, although some of the case studies discuss interest groups that are active and organized with the goal of advancing the interests of the poor—for example, development NGOs. In all of the cases where external funders (such as the international financial institutions) become active, those funders often included protection of the interests of the poor as part of their conditions for offering financial and other support.

The Role of Institutions

A third extension to the framework concerns the role of institutions. Most of the field of political economy analysis looks not simply at the size and allocation of interest groups but also at how those interests are organized and expressed (Peltzman 1976; Wilson 1973). That is affected by many factors related to the broader political and social organization of a country.

Particularly important to the study of how interests get organized and expressed is the role of institutions, such as political institutions, that set the rules and expectations for how individual interests aggregate into forces that influence public policy. Institutions lie at the center of research on political economy. The four case studies point, in particular, to the importance of various institutional factors: government decision-making authority, constitutional and legal constraints, the modes by which governments intervene in the economy, and the organization of civil society.

Allocation of government decision-making authority. There is a long history of studying how different kinds of political systems affect policy outcomes. Presidential systems with strong legislatures that share authority for making and overseeing legislation have many more veto points, for example, than consolidated autocracies in which leaders have unified control (Bueno de Mesquita et al. 2004; Hammond 2005; Moe and Caldwell 1994).

Our studies have examined these factors by looking at two dimensions of political power. One is how political leaders are accountable to their electorate—such as voters or elites within the society. In all four of the case study countries, as is true generally in the world, these mechanisms have become more democratic, which has expanded the breadth of the principals who ultimately choose and replace leaders.

The other dimension is shared authority—the extent to which leaders can manipulate the policies that determine the level of subsidy through their own actions (for example, executive decisions) versus whether they must share power, such as when subsidies are an integral part of a national budget that the legislature and the head of government determine through some joint action. As a general rule, strong leaders have been more willing and able to control subsidies than weaker ones.

Determinations by the courts and legal system. A particularly important strand of research in political economy and comparative politics in recent decades has concerned the role of the legal system. This new focus reflects, in part, the massive legal reforms in many countries—mainly to create a more professional and independent judiciary (Shetreet and Deschênes 1985).

Few of the case studies in this project, however, focus much on the courts. Plausibly, that is because most energy subsidy policies are matters of legislative and executive discretion. They do not raise larger constitutional questions of control over policy and the expanse of power of the executive and legislative branches. One exception is Indonesia, where the Constitutional Court decided that the government must play a role in determining fuel pricing as part of its constitutional social obligations, creating a difficult space for policy making because any new automatic pricing system may be ruled illegal by a constitutional challenge, and pricing reforms more generally could be legally challenged with this precedent (see chapter 4).

In addition, a productive line of future research might also look at administrative reforms, such as the ability of the government to create tax exemptions. Many countries, as part of larger political reforms, also create more-independent bureaucracies overseen by systems of administrative law. Those systems, channeled in the right direction, could favor certain kinds of subsidy reform as well as replacement of subsidies by other administrative systems that better target benefits to the poor.

Interventions by the state. Another major theme in political economy is that states are organized in very different ways and perform very different functions in their economies and political systems (Pierson 1998). Where the state is large, the potential gains from political influence are huge as well. A growing number of studies in comparative political economy have also focused on channels of influence—such as clientelism—that don't necessarily flow through the state. In these cases, even a large crisis is insufficient to dislodge the influence of special interests.

The studies in this volume were not explicitly designed to examine state size and administrative organization. However, we were attentive to *how* the state intervened in energy markets—including through control over state-owned enterprises that play a central role in many energy markets. For instance, before 2001, Ghana's Tema Oil Refinery (TOR) was charged with setting fuel prices at "affordable" levels, which created huge subsidy debts on its books that continued to plague its finances well into the next decade (see chapter 3). Similarly, the state-owned distribution company in the Dominican Republic provides electricity subsidies, with large losses resulting from financial, technical, and operational losses, as well as losses from previously contracted power purchase agreements and a social program to facilitate access by the rural poor (see chapter 2).

Organization of civil society. Finally, political economy is influenced heavily by the ways—outside the state—that forces within a society become organized. Our studies have shown that labor and industrial unions play a major role as vehicles for organizing energy-related interests, particularly large energy consumers such as private transportation companies or large oil importers.

Also important in some of our cases is the role of civil society groups in organizing and expressing otherwise latent social interests in energy policy, such as the impact of energy policies on income and development of the very poor.

We list these four institutional factors as elements that have appeared generally in the literature of political economy, and we have illustrated how they have played out in our case studies. However, our study was not designed to investigate these factors exhaustively; doing so would require a large sample selected explicitly to obtain variation on these institutional factors.

Case Study Selection

This section summarizes the selection of the sample of four countries. In addition to ensuring regional representation, access to informed counterparts, and enough variation in the depth and scale of reforms, the countries were selected with an eye to three main factors:

- *Significant role of energy subsidies.* That raised the odds that in the sample we would be observing politically difficult—and thus informative—efforts to alter policies over time and with exogenous changes in the markets for fuels. Among the countries in Southeast Asia, energy subsidies are particularly large in Indonesia, where they account for about 18 percent of government spending (OECD 2015). Subsidies are also quite substantial in Malaysia and Thailand, and, in the three countries, reforms have been discussed and attempted several times but have generally met with public protests (OECD 2015).
- *Many episodes of reform.* Most importantly, we selected a sample that would include a large number of distinct efforts to alter subsidy policies—what we call "episodes" of reform. These episodes are the unit of analysis in our project. Across four countries and about two decades of efforts to create and adjust energy subsidy policies, we observe over 30 episodes of reform, as detailed in annex 1A.
- *Variation in the iconic political economy cases.* The sample represents a variety of cases and dynamics within the political economy framework adopted at the beginning of the project (shown earlier in table 1.1). Variation in the cases would lead to variation in reform attempts and, in turn, variation in the outcomes from reform.

In creating this sample, we were mindful that there is always a trade-off between sample size and the depth of analysis that is possible. The existing literature reflects two extremes. At one extreme are studies that look at energy subsidies across large fractions of the world economy—in some cases, essentially all nations.

That literature has offered a compelling big picture of the size of subsidies and the scale of the challenge for reform. At the other extreme are the many individual case studies—a literature that is large and rich with insight. Our niche is to offer the richness of detailed case studies within a common structure so that a more general set of insights might be drawn from the sample.

Each case study begins with an overview of the country's political and economic structure to set a foundation for understanding the political economy of the decision-making process. From there, the studies detail the history of subsidies, starting with the original motivations for the subsidies and proceeding with how those motivations have evolved with markets and politics. The bulk of each study examines the many episodes of reform.

Conclusions

In 2009 the leaders of the G-20 made the elimination of energy subsidies a central element of their policy platform. Since then, little systematic follow-up has occurred to progress toward that goal. Within countries, however, there have been many different national efforts to cut subsidies, including some notable successes. Those active policy reforms, along with the big decline in global oil prices, have brought energy subsidies to their lowest levels in several years (IEA 2015). During the diplomatic process leading to the 2015 United Nations Climate Change Conference, many countries also indicated they were planning to adopt reforms and adjustments to a large array of national policies that influence emissions—including reforms of energy subsidy policies.

The problems with energy subsidy reform have been known for a long time. The resources spent on subsidies could be devoted to many other important social purposes. And the politics of subsidy create distortions—at times, huge ones—with harmful effects on political systems as well as on energy markets. Yet, for many countries, fixing the problems of energy subsidies has not been easy. Energy subsidy reform is, mainly, a challenge of political economy.

This volume looks at the political economy of energy subsidy reform systematically. Beginning with a framework drawn from the core insights of political economy, it identifies iconic cases of energy subsidy based on the size and allocation of costs and benefits. The next chapters focus on four countries for in-depth application of that framework. Each of these countries has a history of large energy subsidies and thus poses, for reformers, important real-world challenges. Each has also undergone a series of reform efforts. All told, across the four countries there have been about 30 episodes of reform—with huge variation in the types of reforms undertaken and in the success of outcomes.

A primary finding is that the most successful reforms nearly always involve a large amount of political engineering: active efforts by policy leaders to identify the political forces that created energy subsidies in the first place and then to redirect or inoculate those forces. Among other things, such political engineering has allowed governments to avoid or blunt the political force of well-organized clientelist interest groups. In some cases, the process of reform has benefited, as well, from fortuitous exogenous shocks—such as the sudden drop in global prices that has made it easier for reformers to remove price controls without fearing a consumer backlash.

Most interesting, perhaps, is that energy subsidies often follow a life cycle. They begin with noble goals, such as helping to smooth out price fluctuations to protect the poor, but evolve in ways that inflate their cost and make reform politically difficult. One pattern evident across each of these cases is that breaking that life cycle has required the creation of alternative mechanisms for delivering benefits to the poor—notably cash transfers. Policy makers have, in most cases, created these programs in response to pressures and opportunities unrelated to the problem of energy subsidy. But once in place, the opportunity to adopt much more efficient social policy has made other reforms, including energy-related reforms, possible.

The news about reform is hardly all good. However, the four cases presented here suggest that the ability of reformers to tackle energy subsidies has been increasing with time and effort. That suggests that reforms put into place during the current period of low energy prices have a decent chance of remaining in place when prices rise again.

Annex 1A Episodes of Subsidy Reform

Table 1A.1 Subsidy Reform Episodes, Chronologically by Country, in the Four Case Study Countries

No.	*Country*	*Year*	*Type of reform*[a]	*Outcome of reform*
1	Dominican Republic	2000	pricing, institutional, informational	LPG prices are equalized, without respect to use, to RD$13 per gallon. Consumers are to receive LPG subsidy by submitting a coupon at specific packing plants. One coupon would be valid for a gallon of LPG. Each week, the plants would present a bill with the total number of coupons it collected to the Targeting Unit.
2	Dominican Republic	2001	institutional	The LPG subsidy program is transferred to the Social Cabinet's jurisdiction.
3	Dominican Republic	2001	pricing, institutional, informational	The Blackout Reduction Program (Programa de Reducción de Apagones, or PRA) is passed, targeting electricity subsidies on a geographical basis. Businesses move to areas covered by the program. Regulatory reform for the electricity sector is also passed, but institutional weaknesses and legal inconsistencies remain.
4	Dominican Republic	2003	pricing	A presidential decree increases the price of LPG for all users to RD$25 per gallon.
5	Dominican Republic	2008	pricing, institutional, informational, complementary	Bonogas, a program for poor households and cab drivers, replaces the previous subsidy system.
6	Dominican Republic	2009	pricing	Electricity tariffs are increased by 6.4 percent.
7	Dominican Republic	2010	pricing, institutional, informational, complementary	PRA is dismantled and replaced by means-test-based Bonoluz, for the poorest consumers to claim a subsidy for the use of the first 100 kilowatt-hours.

table continues next page

Table 1A.1 Subsidy Reform Episodes, Chronologically by Country, in the Four Case Study Countries *(continued)*

No.	*Country*	*Year*	*Type of reform*[a]	*Outcome of reform*
8	Ghana	2001	pricing, institutional	Establishment of an automatic adjustment formula is based on import parity and full cost recovery.
9	Ghana	2002	pricing, institutional	Fuel price now includes a debt service charge called the Tema Oil Refinery (TOR) Debt Recovery Levy to pay for the accumulated subsidy debt to TOR. Price hikes by the end of 2002 cause the government to abandon the automatic adjustment in the face of heavy citizen resistance.
10	Ghana	2003	pricing	In January, prices are adjusted upward by 90 percent to achieve full cost recovery. The reimplementation of the automatic adjustment formula includes a "K" factor this time around to account for TOR's inefficiencies. A public outcry causes a downward adjustment as the government faces general elections in 2004.
11	Ghana	2004	pricing, informational, complementary	A Poverty and Social Impact Analysis (PSIA) is launched, and the results cause a removal of subsidies, redirecting the savings into social protection programs such as improved access to quality health care and education for the worse-off in society.
12	Ghana	2005	institutional	The National Petroleum Authority (NPA) is established as the downstream regulator and custodian of the automatic adjustment formula. The Unified Petroleum Price Fund is established to ensure equal prices of petroleum products throughout the country.
13	Ghana	2006	institutional	A price stabilization fund is introduced to pay marketers for subsidies on LPG, kerosene, and premix.
14	Ghana	2012	complementary	A transport fare formula is established with transport operators. The government negotiates a trigger point for increasing transport fares in response to fuel price increases. Commercial vehicle transporters are to increase transport fares by a third of the fuel price increase, if the cumulative increase in fuel prices exceeds 10 percent. This is based on the condition that all other factors in the transport fare model have also changed. For instance, insurance and spare parts costs should have also increased substantially. Agitations from labor unions, coupled with anticipation of general elections in December, cause a 20 percent reduction of the increase implemented in January.
15	Ghana	2013	complementary	The Rural LPG Promotion Program is launched to encourage the use of LPG as an alternative fuel in rural areas to prevent deforestation.
16	Ghana	2014	pricing	Subsidy levels are reduced drastically. A Special Petroleum Tax (a 17.5 percent value added tax on petroleum products) is introduced in November.
17	Ghana	2015	pricing, informational, complementary	The latest reform, price deregulation, is implemented after heavy lobbying from bulk distribution companies (BDCs), oil financing banks, and the NPA due to the heavy government indebtedness to the industry.

table continues next page

Table 1A.1 Subsidy Reform Episodes, Chronologically by Country, in the Four Case Study Countries *(continued)*

No.	*Country*	*Year*	*Type of reform*[a]	*Outcome of reform*
18	Ghana	2016	pricing, institutional	The Energy Levies Act is implemented in January, causing a 28–30 percent increase in prices. Civil society, labor unions, and transport operators protest and dialogue with the government for various types of compensation. This price increase, however, has not affected the latest reforms as the oil marketers have been allowed to pass through the increase fully to the pump.
19	Indonesia	1983–96	pricing	Under the Suharto regime and after the oil boom, Indonesia undergoes a period of deregulation, renewed liberalization (in reaction to falling oil prices), and rapid export-led growth. The level of corruption at all levels of government bureaucracy is an increasing concern. From 1990, Indonesian fuel demand grows on average by about 7 percent per year.
20	Indonesia	1998	pricing	The government announces large price increases for fuel and electricity. The price of kerosene increases by 25 percent, diesel fuel by 60 percent, and gasoline by 71 percent. Subsidy cuts trigger protests over the ensuing weeks from thousands of students in the cities of Medan, Bandung, and Yogyakarta, which devolved into general rioting.
21	Indonesia	1999	pricing	The aviation fuel subsidy is removed.
22	Indonesia	2000	pricing	Price of gasoline is raised by 15 percent, diesel by 9 percent, and kerosene by 25 percent. The increases are followed by violent demonstrations but are not reversed.
23	Indonesia	2001	pricing, institutional	A new Oil and Gas Law is introduced that provides a legal basis for moving away from the subsidy regime, and it abolishes Pertamina's monopoly over the downstream sector, opening it up to entry by other players. Efficient, competitive pricing of petroleum fuels is to be supervised by BPH Migas. The subsidies for diesel and marine fuel for industrial and sea transport sectors are removed. Fuel prices for large industry, which represented about 23 percent of the market, are increased to 50 percent of the international market price. Indonesia introduces a semiautomatic fuel pricing system for subsidized automotive gasoline and diesel products for the industry, transportation, and fishery sectors. Gasoline prices are raised by 26 percent and diesel by 50 percent.
24	Indonesia	2002	pricing, institutional	A presidential decree reduces fuel subsidies in phases, aiming to set gasoline prices at 100 percent and diesel at 75 percent of the international market price, within certain bounds, for both household and industrial users. Student demonstrations take place in the city of Makassar, with smaller protests also taking place in Jakarta, Surabaya, Denpasar, Manado, and Bandung.
25	Indonesia	2003	pricing	Attempted price increases in 2003 are hotly opposed. Diesel prices are increased by only 6.5 percent instead of the originally planned 21.9 percent.

table continues next page

Table 1A.1 Subsidy Reform Episodes, Chronologically by Country, in the Four Case Study Countries *(continued)*

No.	*Country*	*Year*	*Type of reform*[a]	*Outcome of reform*
26	Indonesia	2005	pricing, institutional, informational, complementary	The government increases fuel prices in March and again in October by an average of 29 percent and 114 percent, respectively, reducing the Indonesian state budget deficit by US$4.5 billion in 2005 and by US$10 billion in 2006. A presidential decree announces that the remaining fuel subsidies are to be phased out but does not specify a time frame. In October, prices are raised to international market levels for industry, and the government rolls out the first payment in a cash transfer scheme targeted at poor households (Direct Cash Assistance, or BLT), worth US$30 per household.
27	Indonesia	2008	pricing, institutional, informational, complementary	Fuel prices are increased on average by 28.7 percent. The BLT is used again to compensate poor households.
28	Indonesia	2012	pricing	The government attempts to increase the prices of subsidized gasoline and diesel, but this is prevented following a vote on the issue in parliament.
29	Indonesia	2013	pricing, institutional, informational, and complementary	The price of gasoline is increased from Rp 4,500 (US$0.41) per liter to Rp 6,500 (US$0.59) per liter, a 44 percent increase; and the price of diesel from Rp 4,500 (US$0.41) per liter to Rp 5,500 (US$0.50) per liter, a 22 percent increase. This is combined with a Rp 29.1 trillion package of compensation mechanisms targeted at low-income households, including a temporary cash transfer, a basic infrastructure program, and expansions of the Poor Student Education Support (BSM) program, the Hopeful Family Program (PKH) conditional cash transfer, and the Rice for the Poor (Raskin) program.
30	Indonesia	2014	pricing	Subsidized gasoline prices increase from Rp 6,500 to Rp 8,500 (US$0.52 to US$0.7) per liter, and diesel prices increase from Rp 5,500 to Rp 7,500 (US$0.44 to US$0.62) per liter.
31	Indonesia	2014	pricing	President Joko Widodo announces the removal of subsidized gasoline and the introduction of a "fixed" price for subsidized diesel at Rp 1,000 (US$0.08) below the market price. Because of falling international oil prices, the immediate impact is for the price of subsidized gasoline to decrease from Rp 8,500 (US$0.68) to Rp 7,600 (US$0.61) per liter, while the price of subsidized diesel is lowered from Rp 7,500 (US$0.60) to Rp 7,250 (US$0.58) per liter. In the Revised State Budget 2015, the allocation of state funds to fuel subsidies falls by just over Rp 211 trillion (US$16.9 billion), equal to over 10 percent of all originally planned government expenditure in 2015.
32	Jordan	2005	pricing, institutional, informational, complementary	The government implements a three-year strategy for the elimination of energy subsidies starting in 2005. The price increases are dramatic: gasoline prices increase by around 10 percent, while fuel oil for power and industry increase by 33 percent and 59 percent, respectively. These increases, however, do not prevent the subsidies from increasing as oil prices in international markets continue to rise. Consequently, the government decides to raise prices again in the same year.

table continues next page

Table 1A.1 Subsidy Reform Episodes, Chronologically by Country, in the Four Case Study Countries *(continued)*

No.	*Country*	*Year*	*Type of reform*[a]	*Outcome of reform*
33	Jordan	2008	pricing, institutional, informational, complementary	The government decides to remove almost all energy subsidies, resulting in price increases ranging from 16 percent for gasoline to 76.5 percent for LPG. To ensure that domestic prices are aligned with international markets, the government establishes a committee comprising members from the Ministry of Energy and Mineral Resources, Ministry of Finance, and the Jordan Petroleum Refining Company to set the price on a monthly basis based on a formula to reflect international prices and freight allowance. During this period, the government increases the minimum wage and provides a salary increase as well as a one-time bonus to low-paid government employees.
34	Jordan	2012	pricing, institutional, informational, complementary	Prime Minister Ensour announces fuel subsidy reform. Fuel subsidies are fully eliminated, resulting in price increases.

Note: LPG = liquefied petroleum gas. RD$ = Dominican pesos. Rp = Indonesian rupiah.
a. "Pricing reform" refers to government regulation of the wholesale or retail prices of energy-related products, including policies that change the size or allocation of a subsidy. "Institutional reform" refers to pricing *mechanisms*, notably the removal of ad hoc government control over prices and shifting to more-automatic pricing mechanisms (such as formulas) or even full reliance on markets for pricing. Institutional reforms have also included reorganization of how subsidies are paid—for example, shifting from systems in which a state-owned enterprise acts as intermediary between imports and in-country sales to one where the government pays direct cash transfers. "Informational reform" refers to active efforts to increase the flow of information to increase interest groups' and citizens' awareness of how a policy change would be beneficial to them. "Complementary reform" refers to reforms that complement or substitute for subsidies in ways that help reformers to reduce the size of subsidies and improve their allocation.

Notes

1. See, for example, the case of India (MoF, Government of India 2015).
2. That literature, while large, notably includes Beaton et al. (2013); Coady et al. (2015); Clements et al. (2013); IEA (2014, 2015); IMF (2015b); Kojima (2013, 2016); UNEP (2003); Vagliasindi (2012); and WEF (2013).
3. For example, in the Arab world (Boersma and Griffiths 2016; Fattouh and El-Katiri 2012); in Brazil (de Oliveira and Laan 2010); in China (Zhang and Qin 2015); in Egypt (Abouleinein, El-Laithy, and Kheir-El-Din 2009); in India (Clarke 2015; TERI and IISD 2012); in Latin America and the Caribbean (Di Bella et al. 2015); in the Middle East and North Africa (Fattouh and El-Katiri 2015; Hassanzadeh 2012; Sdralevich et al. 2014); in Southeast Asia (Beaton and Lontoh 2010; Bridel and Lontoh 2014; IISD and GSI 2013); and in Sub-Saharan Africa (Alleyne 2013; James 2014).
4. For example, on state-owned oil companies, see McPherson (2003) and Victor, Hults, and Thurber (2012). On the special issues of electricity reform, see Besant-Jones (2006) and Victor and Heller (2007).
5. For more about the foundations of the framework, see Olson (1965), Peltzman (1976), and Stigler (1971). For its application to modern studies of political systems, see Wilson (1973).
6. We are deeply indebted to Phil Keefer, who proposed this analytical framework.
7. See Kojima (2016) for a recent review following the decline of oil prices in 2014 and their subsequent rise in 2015.

8. Similar experiences with loss of political power after an attempt to reform subsidies abound across the world.
9. The IMANI Center for Policy & Education, for example, documented that US$80 million of the US$110 million in government LPG subsidies intended for rural communities instead went to urban areas (Boahen 2015).
10. This framework was developed by Phil Keefer in 2014 as part of the concept note for this volume. See appendix A.
11. This theoretical intuition served as a first step in the development of each case study, including the set of hypotheses that were then tested by case study authors. Details of the conceptual framework with which this project began are available in appendix A.

References

Abouleinein, S., H. El-Laithy, and H. Kheir-El-Din. 2009. "The Impact of Phasing Out Subsidies of Petroleum Energy Products in Egypt." Working Paper 145, Egyptian Center for Economic Studies, Cairo.

Acemoglu, D., and J. Robinson. 2006. "Economic Backwardness in Political Perspective." *American Political Science Review* 100 (1): 115–31.

Alleyne, T. 2013. *Energy Subsidy Reform in Sub-Saharan Africa: Experiences and Lessons.* Washington, DC: International Monetary Fund.

Armijo, L., T. Biersteker, and A. Lowenthal. 1994. "The Problem of Simultaneous Transitions." *Journal of Democracy* 5 (4): 161–75.

Atamanov, A., J. Jellema, and U. Serajuddin. 2015. "Energy Subsidies Reform in Jordan: Welfare Implications of Different Scenarios." Policy Research Working Paper 7313, World Bank, Washington, DC.

Beaton, C., I. Gerasimchuk, T. Laan, K. Lang, D. Vis-Dunbar, and P. Wooders. 2013. *A Guidebook to Fossil-Fuel Subsidy Reform for Policy-Makers in Southeast Asia.* Report for the Global Subsidies Initiative of the International Institute for Sustainable Development, Geneva.

Beaton, C., and L. Lontoh. 2010. *Lessons Learned from Indonesia's Attempts to Reform Fossil-Fuel Subsidies.* Report of the Global Subsidies Initiative and International Institute for Sustainable Development, Geneva.

Besant-Jones, J. E. 2006. "Reforming Power Markets in Developing Countries: What Have We Learned?" Energy and Mining Sector Board Discussion Paper 19, World Bank, Washington, DC.

Bloomberg News. 2014. "PTT Chief Urges Thai Junta to End Fuel Subsidies." July 16. http://www.bloomberg.com/news/articles/2014-07-16/ptt-chief-urges-thai-junta-to-end-fuel-subsidies-southeast-asia.

Boahen, S. K. 2015. *Deregulation Will End Petro Politics and Satisfy Ghana's IMF Deal on Fuel Subsidies.* Energy & Environment Issue Report 00123 (April 23), IMANI Center for Policy & Education, Accra. http://www.imaniafrica.org/2015/04/23/deregulation-will-end-petro-politics-and-satisfy-ghanas-imf-deal-on-fuel-subsidies/.

Boersma, T., and S. Griffiths. 2016. *Reforming Energy Subsidies: Initial Lessons from the United Arab Emirates.* Research report for the Energy Security and Climate Initiative, Brookings Institution, Washington, DC.

Bridel, A., and L. Lontoh. 2014. *Lessons Learned: Malaysia's 2013 Fuel Subsidy Reform.* Research Report, Global Subsidies Initiative and International Institute for Sustainable Development, Geneva.

Bueno de Mesquita, B., A. Smith, R. Siverson, and J. Morrow. 2004. *The Logic of Political Survival.* Cambridge, MA: MIT Press.

CFR (Council on Foreign Relations). 2015. *Fuel Subsidy Reform: Insights from a CFR Workshop.* Summary report of fuel subsidy reform workshop, CFR, Washington, DC.

Cheng, T.-J., and S. Haggard. 1999. "Democracy and Deficits in Taiwan: The Politics of Fiscal Policy 1986–1996." In *Presidents, Parliaments, and Policy*, edited by S. Haggard and M. McCubbins, 183–228. New York: Cambridge University Press.

Christensen, J. M., G. A. Mackenzie, L. Nygaard, and M. B. Pederson. 2015. *Enhancing Access to Electricity for Clean and Efficient Energy Services in Africa.* Copenhagen: UNEP DTU (Technical University of Denmark) Partnership.

Clarke, K. 2015. *Diesel Subsidy Reform in India: Lessons Learned.* Research Report, Global Subsidies Initiative, and International Institute for Sustainable Development, Geneva.

Clements, B., D. Coady, S. Fabrizio, S. Gupta, T. Alleyne, and C. Sdralevich, eds. 2013. *Energy Subsidy Reform: Lessons and Implications.* Washington, DC: IMF.

Coady, D. P., M. El Said, R. Gillingham, K. Kpodar, P. Medas, and D. Newhouse. 2006. "The Magnitude and Distribution of Fuel Subsidies: Evidence from Bolivia, Ghana, Jordan, Mali, and Sri Lanka." Working Paper 06/247, International Monetary Fund, Washington, DC.

Coady, D., I. W. H. Parry, L. Sears, and B. Shang. 2015. "How Large Are Global Energy Subsidies?" Working paper WP/15/105, International Monetary Fund, Washington, DC.

Cornillie, J., and S. Fankhauser. 2004. "The Energy Intensity of Transition Countries." *Energy Economics* 26 (3): 283–95.

Cox, G., D. North, and B. Weingast. 2013. "The Violence Trap: A Political-Economic Approach to the Problems of Development." Working paper, Hoover Institution, Stanford University, Stanford, CA.

Crawford, G. 2012. "Ghana's Fossil-Fuel Subsidy Reform." Case Study 09, Institute of Development Studies, Brighton, U.K.

Davidson, O., and S. Mwakasonda. 2009. "Electricity Access for the Poor: A Study of South Africa and Zimbabwe." *Energy for Sustainable Development* 8 (4): 26–40.

de Oliveira, A. 2007. "Political Economy of the Brazilian Power Industry Reform." In *The Political Economy of Power Sector Reform: The Experiences of Five Major Developing Countries*, edited by D. G. Victor and T. C. Heller, 31–75. Cambridge: Cambridge University Press.

———. 2012. "Brazil's Petrobras: Strategy and Performance." In *Oil and Governance: State-Owned Enterprises and the World Energy Supply*, edited by D. G. Victor, D. R. Hults, and M. C. Thurber, 515–56. Cambridge: Cambridge University Press.

de Oliveira, A., and T. Laan. 2010. "Lessons Learned from Brazil's Experience with Fossil-Fuel Subsidies and their Reform." Paper for the Trade, Investment and Climate Change Series, Global Subsidies Initiative and International Institute for Sustainable Development, Geneva.

Di Bella, G., L. Norton, J. Ntamatungiro, S. Ogawa, I. Samake, and M. Santoro. 2015. "Energy Subsidies in Latin America and the Caribbean: Stocktaking and Policy Challenges." Working paper WP/15/30, International Monetary Fund, Washington, DC.

Fattouh, B., and L. El-Katiri. 2012. *Energy Subsidies in the Arab World.* Arab Human Development Report Research Paper Series, United Nations Development Programme, New York.

———. 2015. "A Brief Political Economy of Energy Subsidies in the Middle East and North Africa." Oxford Institute for Energy Studies (OIES) Paper: MEP 11, University of Oxford, U.K.

García-Zamor, J.-C., and R. Khator, eds. 1994. *Public Administration in the Global Village.* Westport, CT: Praeger.

Guillaume, D., R. Zytek, and M. R. Farzin. 2011. "Iran—The Chronicles of the Subsidy Reform." Working paper WP/11/167, International Monetary Fund, Washington, DC.

Hammond, T. H. 2005. "Veto Points, Policy Preferences, and Bureaucratic Autonomy in Democratic Systems." In *Politics, Policy, and Organizations: Frontiers in the Scientific Study of Bureaucracy*, edited by G. Krause and J. Meier, 73–103. Ann Arbor, MI: University of Michigan Press.

Hang, L., and M. Tu. 2007. "The Impacts of Energy Prices on Energy Intensity: Evidence from China." *Energy Policy* 35 (5): 2978–88.

Hassanzadeh, E. 2012. "Recent Developments in Iran's Energy Subsidy Reforms." Policy Brief, Global Subsidies Initiative and International Institute for Sustainable Development, Geneva.

Howells, M., D. G. Victor, T. Gaunt, R. J. Elias, and T. Alfstad. 2006. "Beyond Free Electricity: The Cost of Electric Cooking in Poor Households and a Market-Friendly Alternative." *Energy Policy* 34 (17): 3351–58.

IEA (International Energy Agency). 2014. *World Energy Outlook 2014.* Paris: Organisation for Economic Co-operation and Development and IEA.

———. 2015. *World Energy Outlook 2015.* Paris: Organisation for Economic Co-operation and Development and IEA.

IISD and GSI (International Institute for Sustainable Development and the Global Subsidies Initiative). 2013. *A Citizens' Guide to Energy Subsidies in Thailand.* Geneva: IISD.

IMF (International Monetary Fund). 2013a. "Case Studies on Energy Subsidy Reform: Lessons and Implications." Supplement to *Energy Subsidy Reform: Lessons and Implications*, edited by B. Clements, D. Coady, S. Fabrizio, S. Gupta, T. Alleyne, and C. Sdralevich. Washington, DC: IMF.

———. 2013b. "Reforming Energy Subsidies: Summary Note." Summary note, IMF, Washington, DC.

———. 2015a. *Bolivia: 2015 Article IV Consultation—Press Release; Staff Report; and Statement by the Executive Director for Bolivia.* Country Report 15/334. Washington, DC: IMF.

———. 2015b. "Counting the Cost of Energy Subsidies." *IMF Survey Magazine*, July 17. http://www.imf.org/external/pubs/ft/survey/so/2015/NEW070215A.htm.

———. 2015c. *Saudi Arabia: Selected Issues.* Country Report 15/286. Washington, DC: IMF.

Indonesia MoF (Ministry of Finance) and World Bank. 2015. "Taxes and Public Spending in Indonesia: Who Pays and Who Benefits?" Working Paper 101667, World Bank, Jakarta.

James, L. M. 2014. *Recent Developments in Sudan's Fuel Subsidy Reform Process.* Research Report, Global Subsidies Initiative and International Institute for Sustainable Development, Geneva.

Keefer, P. 2011. "Collective Action, Political Parties, and Pro-Development Public Policy." Policy Research Working Paper 5676, World Bank, Washington, DC.

Kingdon, John W. 1995. *Agendas, Alternatives, and Public Policies*. New York: HarperCollins College Publishers.

Kitschelt, H., and S. Wilkinson, eds. 2007. *Patrons, Clients and Policies: Patterns of Democratic Accountability and Political Competition*. Cambridge: Cambridge University Press.

Klevnäs, P., N. Stern, and J. Frejova. 2015. "Oil Prices and the New Climate Economy." Briefing paper for The New Climate Economy project of the Global Commission on the Economy and Climate, London and Washington, DC.

Kojima, M. 2013. "Petroleum Product Pricing and Complementary Policies: Experience of 65 Developing Countries since 2009." Policy Research Working Paper 6393, World Bank, Washington, DC.

———. 2016. "Fossil Fuel Subsidy and Pricing Policies: Recent Developing Country Experience." Policy Research Working Paper 7531, World Bank, Washington, DC.

Laan, T., C. Beaton, and B. Presta. 2010. "Strategies for Reforming Fossil-Fuel Subsidies: Practical Lessons from Ghana, France and Senegal." Paper in the series, "Untold Billions: Fossil-Fuel Subsidies, Their Impacts and the Path to Reform," Global Subsidies Initiative and International Institute for Sustainable Development, Geneva.

Lijphart, A. 1999. *Patterns of Democracy: Government Forms and Performance in Thirty-Six Countries*. New Haven, CT: Yale University Press.

Linz, J. J., and A. Stepan. 1996. *Problems of Democratic Transition and Consolidation: Southern Europe, South America, and Post-Communist Europe*. Baltimore, MD: Johns Hopkins University Press.

McPherson, C. 2003. "National Oil Companies: Evolution, Issues, Outlook." In *Fiscal Policy Formulation and Implementation in Oil-Producing Countries*, edited by J. M. Davis, R. Ossowski, and A. Fedelino, 184–203. Washington, DC: International Monetary Fund.

Moe, T. M., and M. Caldwell. 1994. "The Institutional Foundations of Democratic Government: A Comparison of Presidential and Parliamentary Systems." *Journal of Institutional and Theoretical Economics* 150 (1): 171–95.

MoF (Ministry of Finance), Government of India. 2015. "From Carbon Subsidy to Carbon Tax: India's Green Actions." In *Economic Survey 2014–15*, 122–28. Vol. 1. MoF, Government of India.

North, D., J. Wallis, S. Webb, and B. Weingast. 2007. "Limited Access Orders in the Developing World: A New Approach to the Problems of Development." Policy Research Working Paper 4359, World Bank, Washington, DC.

OECD (Organisation for Economic Co-operation and Development). 2015. "Economic Outlook for Southeast Asia, China, and India 2015: Special Supplement—March 2015." Supplement to *Economic Outlook for Southeast Asia, China, and India 2015*, OECD, Paris.

Olson, M. 1965. *The Logic of Collective Action: Public Goods and the Theory of Groups*. Cambridge, MA: Harvard University Press.

Peltzman, S. 1976. "Toward a More General Theory of Regulation." *Journal of Law and Economics* 19 (2): 211–40.

Pierson, C. 1998. *Beyond the Welfare State? The New Political Economy of Welfare*. 2nd ed. Malden, MA: Blackwell Publishers.

Platts. 2015. "Thailand Keeps Up Energy Price Reform Momentum, Raises Compressed Natural Gas Prices." February 2. http://www.platts.com/latest-news/natural-gas/singapore/thailand-keeps-up-energy-price-reform-momentum-26997553.

Pritchett, L., and F. de Weijer. 2010. "Fragile States: Stuck in a Capability Trap?" *Background paper for World Development Report 2011: Conflict, Security, and Development*. Washington, DC: World Bank.

Røsjø, M. J. 2014. "The Adverse Effects of Fossil-Fuel Subsidies in Indonesia." Master's thesis, Department of Economics, University of Oslo.

Schneider, B. R., and B. Heredia, eds. 2003. *Reinventing Leviathan: The Politics of Administrative Reform in Developing Countries*. Miami: University of Miami North-South Center Press.

Sdralevich, C., R. Sab, Y. Zouhar, and G. Albertin. 2014. *Subsidy Reform in the Middle East and North Africa: Recent Progress and Challenges Ahead*. Washington, DC: International Monetary Fund.

Shetreet, S., and J. Deschênes, eds. 1985. *Judicial Independence: The Contemporary Debate*. Dordrecht, Netherlands: Martinus Nijhoff Publishers.

Stepan, A. 2001. *Arguing Comparative Politics*. New York: Oxford University Press.

Stigler, G. J. 1971. "The Theory of Economic Regulation." *The Bell Journal of Economics and Management Science* 2 (1): 3–21.

Stokes, S. C. 2009. "Political Clientelism." In *The Oxford Handbook of Comparative Politics*, edited by C. Boix and S. C. Stokes, 604–27. Oxford: Oxford University Press.

Strand, J. 2013. "Political Economy Aspects of Fuel Subsidies: A Conceptual Framework." Policy Research Working Paper 6392, World Bank, Washington, DC.

TERI and IISD (The Energy and Resources Institute and International Institute for Sustainable Development). 2012. *A Citizens' Guide to Energy Subsidies in India*. Geneva: IISD.

Therkildsen, O. 2000. "Public Sector Reform in a Poor, Aid-Dependent Country, Tanzania." *Public Administration and Development* 20 (1): 61–71.

Tomassi, M. 2003. "Crisis, Political Institutions, and Policy Reform: The Good, the Bad, and the Ugly." Leitner Working Paper 2003-01, Yale University, New Haven, CT.

Toonen, T. A. J. 2001. "The Comparative Dimension of Administrative Reform: Creating Open Villages and Redesigning the Politics of Administration." In *Politicians, Bureaucrats and Administrative Reform*, edited by G. Peters and J. Pierre, 183–201. London: Routledge.

UNEP (United Nations Environment Programme). 2003. *Energy Subsidies: Lessons Learned in Assessing Their Impact and Designing Policy Reforms*. Geneva: UNEP.

———. 2008. *Reforming Energy Subsidies: Opportunities to Contribute to the Climate Change Agenda*. Report commissioned by the Division of Technology, Industry and Economics, UNEP, Geneva.

Vagliasindi, M. 2012. *Implementing Energy Subsidy Reforms: Evidence from Developing Countries*. Directions in Development Series. Washington, DC: World Bank.

Van de Walle, N. 2003. "Presidentialism and Clientelism in Africa's Emerging Party Systems." *Journal of Modern African Studies* 41 (2): 297–321.

Victor, D. G. 2009. "The Politics of Fossil-Fuel Subsidies." Paper in the series, "Untold Billions: Fossil-Fuel Subsidies, Their Impacts and the Path to Reform," Global Subsidies Initiative and International Institute for Sustainable Development, Geneva.

———. 2011. *Global Warming Gridlock: Creating More Effective Strategies for Protecting the Planet*. New York: Cambridge University Press.

Victor, D. G., and T. C. Heller, eds. 2007. *Reforming Electric Power Markets in Developing Countries: Politics, Law and Institutions*. Cambridge: Cambridge University Press.

Victor, D. G., D. Hults, and M. Thurber. 2012. *Oil and Governance: State-Owned Enterprises and the World Energy Supply*. Cambridge: Cambridge University Press.

Wall Street Journal. 2011. "Bolivia Restores Subsidies for Fuel." January 3. http://www.wsj.com/articles/SB10001424052748703820904576058071716311988.

WEF (World Economic Forum). 2013. *Lessons Drawn From Reforms of Energy Subsidies*. Report, World Economic Forum, Geneva.

Wilson, J. Q. 1973. *Political Organizations*. Princeton, NJ: Princeton University Press.

Winkler, H., ed. 2006. *Energy Policies for Sustainable Development in South Africa: Options for the Future*. Rondebosch, South Africa: Energy Research Centre, University of Cape Town.

Zhang, S., and X. Qin. 2015. *Lessons Learned from China's Residential Tiered Electricity Pricing Reform*. Research Report, Global Subsidies Initiative and International Institute for Sustainable Development, Geneva.

CHAPTER 2

The Dominican Republic: From Generalized to Targeted Subsidies

Andrea Gallina, Gabriela Inchauste, Pavel Isa, Catherine Lee, and Miguel Sánchez

Introduction

Subsidies, including energy subsidies, could easily be construed in many developing countries as a fiscal tool that is not only expensive but also one that benefits the better-off to a greater extent. Having started initially as a way to protect households from price fluctuations, public expenditures on energy subsidies are often many times larger than all social safety net expenditures combined, making this a critical area of reform that can reap important benefits for social welfare and macroeconomic and fiscal stability. Despite ample evidence that these subsidies typically benefit the better-off in much greater proportion than the poor, the technical arguments often do not suffice to enable the removal of these subsidies. In particular, reform is especially difficult in the face of antireform coalitions formed by powerful interest groups. Under which circumstances, then, can reforms of this nature take place?

This chapter presents the case of the Dominican Republic, which, over the past decade, achieved a shift from generalized to targeted energy subsidies. We focus on the 2008 reform of liquefied petroleum gas (LPG) subsidies and the 2009 reform of electricity subsidies. Reform was particularly beneficial in an oil-importing country like the Dominican Republic, whose challenges include high fuel costs for local consumption and electricity generation as well as a fiscal system characterized by low revenue collection and thus limited fiscal space to conduct social policies.[1]

The Dominican Republic confronted large fiscal losses in the electricity sector because of inefficiencies in distribution and low prices. All citizens benefited, in one way or another, from the low prices, as did numerous special interests. Starting in 2008, the country undertook a number of reforms that, in the end, had a modest effect on the fiscal losses, reduced some of the benefits to citizens, and kept intact most of the benefits for special interests.

Historical Overview

Energy subsidies have been a long-standing problem in the Dominican Republic. By the 1990s a history of policies to provide the population with cheap LPG and electricity—combined with poor governance, lack of investment, and mismanagement—had left the country with large, untargeted LPG subsidies and inefficient, loss-making electricity utility companies (Moya Pons 1998).

The government kept LPG prices low, seeing them as important for household budgets. Meanwhile, electricity subsidies resulted from tariffs that were not based on the cost associated with efficient provision. At the same time, a great deal of electricity was supplied effectively for free because of widespread theft of electricity; fraud in metering and billing; poor bill collection; and the free, albeit rationed, supply of electricity to unmetered consumers (World Bank 2014b). Together, these subsidies accounted for about 3.2 percent of gross domestic product (GDP) in 2007—a substantial share of the government budget. Electricity accounted for the dominant share—about 1.2 percent of GDP (Vagliasindi 2012).

To address the problems in the electricity sector, between 1998 and 1999 the government unbundled the vertically integrated Dominican Electricity Corporation (the sole sector player in the 1990s) into two generation companies and three electrical distribution companies (EDEs), all of which were privatized.[2] However, the sector remained plagued by (a) a tradition of illegal connections and nonpayment of bills (less than 60 percent of all energy provided was paid for through tariffs); (b) the government's unwillingness to adjust tariffs to fully reflect changes in fuel prices and the exchange rate; and (c) inadequate fiscal resources to cover the resulting gap between costs and revenues.

An adverse oil shock in 2002 highlighted system deficiencies and, as a result, two of the EDEs (EdeNorte and EdeSur) were renationalized amid continuous blackouts. To try to instill a culture of electricity invoice payment, a Blackout Reduction Program (Programa de Reducción de Apagones, or PRA) established a geographic subsidy in allegedly poor areas, but this effort created a series of perverse incentives that resulted in businesses moving to those areas.

Despite these long-standing problems, the government has passed several rounds of energy subsidy reforms (big or small) in the aftermath of a deteriorating fiscal situation. First, after a severe domestic financial crisis in 2003–04, the government passed measures to cut the fiscal deficit in half. Consequently a deficit that amounted to almost 9 percent of GDP for the consolidated public sector in 2003 shrank to about 4.5 percent of GDP in 2008, and the public debt-to-GDP ratio was reduced by almost half, from about 56.8 percent in 2003 to 38.1 percent in 2008 (GODR 2004; IMF 2011).[3]

In 2005, the government renewed its commitment to reform by increasing tariffs and strengthening efforts to reduce line losses, improve targeting of subsidies, expedite fraud detection, improve management of power supply rationing (by rewarding areas where collections are higher), and reduce the costs of electricity generation (GODR 2005). The strategy envisaged stabilizing the electricity supply, a necessary condition to improve collection rates. To this end, the government aimed to satisfy about 70 percent of the daily electricity demand. Throughout 2005–07 the government intended, in principle, to allow electricity prices to fluctuate in line with international oil prices and the exchange rate. However, it did not commit to eliminate subsidies, but rather committed to reduce "nonpriority spending" if electricity prices became temporarily lower than the reference prices and additional transfers to the electricity sector were needed (GODR 2007).

In 2008, a sharp increase in oil prices made the sheer size of subsidies untenable. The government spent 2.75 percent of GDP on electricity subsidies in 2008, or about US$1.2 billion. Although these generalized subsidies were progressive in relative terms (the subsidy for poorer income groups being high relative to their share of income), they were not progressive in absolute terms (the amount benefiting the richest 10 percent of the population being at least five times that benefiting the poorest 10 percent). If these resources had been allocated each year as transfers to the poor (about 750,000 families), each family would have received US$130 a month, more than enough to eliminate extreme poverty (IMF 2010). However, it was also clear that the removal of subsidies without a mitigating program would be especially hard on the poor, because subsidies constituted a larger share of their incomes.

The government of President Leonel Fernández, elected in early 2008, adopted a massive reform in response to the following series of internal and external shocks:

- High international food and oil prices combined with four tropical storms that seriously disrupted agricultural production during the first half of 2008.
- Rising domestic inflation was met with contractionary monetary policy, which reduced economic activity.
- In late 2008, the economy began to experience the effects of the global economy slowdown, especially in its main trading partner, the United States.

To combat the adverse effects of these shocks, the government increased food assistance expenditures as well as subsidies for energy and public transport, which, combined with falling revenues from reduced economic activity, led to an increase in the fiscal deficit (IMF 2010).

Given the difficulties in continuing to finance the deficit, the government embarked on a program to reduce the primary deficit and improve the quality of expenditures by removing LPG subsidies for all but low-income households, using a scheme called Bonogas.[4] The Bonogas cash transfer program, targeted to the poorest 40 percent of households, replaced a generalized LPG subsidy in 2008. The introduction of Bonogas led to significant savings: the LPG subsidy had averaged 0.5 percent of GDP from 2004 to 2008, while the cost of Bonogas amounted to 0.13 percent of GDP in 2009 (ADESS 2016; Vagliasindi 2012).

Similarly, in 2009, the government replaced the PRA with a means-tested electricity subsidy called Bonoluz. The fiscal savings from Bonoluz were more limited than those from Bonogas: the PRA subsidy amounted to an estimated 0.3 percent of GDP in 2008, while Bonoluz had a cost of around 0.08 percent of GDP in 2013 (ADESS 2016; Vagliasindi 2012).

Objectives and Structure

As part of the volume's wider effort to learn from experiences with energy subsidy reforms around the world, this case study aims to document the economic, political, and distributional circumstances that allowed these reforms to take place. In particular, it documents the details of the reform process—including its design, passage, and implementation—and shows how the Dominican Republic's political economy affected those policy choices. In contrast to other studies that have tended to focus normatively on the need for subsidy reform, the objective is to document *how* reforms took place, thus enabling other countries considering reform to learn from others' experiences. In addition, this case study seeks to analyze the political dynamics that enabled reform despite opposition from the "losers" of the reform. For this purpose, we follow the framework proposed in chapter 1 of this volume to enable a coherent description of the political economy of reform.

The rest of the report is structured as follows: The next section describes the country context, including the Dominican Republic's economic, poverty, and equity environment as well as the political conditions at the time of the reforms. The subsequent sections provide detailed accounts of the gas and electricity subsidy reforms, including their fiscal and distributional impacts. Using the proposed framework, the chapter then analyzes the conditions and political dynamics that allowed the reforms to take place, including the roles of different stakeholders. The final section summarizes the findings and several aspects of the unfinished reform agenda. Annex 2A provides a timeline of main political events, while annex 2B provides a detailed sequence of subsidy reforms.

Country Economic and Political Context

Economic Growth

As in most of Latin America, the 1980s in the Dominican Republic were marked by economic turmoil, stemming from large fiscal deficits coupled with monetary expansion that led to inflationary pressures. In turn, inflation exacerbated the distortions created by extensive price controls. An overvalued domestic currency, combined with extensive foreign exchange restrictions and high trade barriers, dampened export growth and foreign investment. Attempts to implement stabilization programs were short-lived because of a lack of fiscal discipline, partly on account of sizable losses in public enterprises.

By 1990, the economic crisis led the government to adopt a comprehensive economic program that included price liberalization, fiscal consolidation, and devaluation of the exchange rate (IMF 1999). Since then, strong and sustained economic growth have characterized the past two decades. The Dominican Republic has become the second-fastest-growing economy in the region, growing by 5.7 percent per year in 1995–2013 (compared with the 5.9 percent achieved by Panama, the region's top economic performer). Overall, real GDP growth rate in the Dominican Republic exceeded the average growth of the Latin America and Caribbean region in 16 out of the 22 years spanning the 1990–2011 period. Average incomes increased by 51 percent in the 1990s and by another 45 percent in the following decade.[5]

After a period of rapid and stable economic growth during most of the 1990s and early 2000s, the economy contracted in 2003 (by –0.3 percent), leading to a sharp spike in poverty in the wake of a domestic financial crisis precipitated by a major bank failure, which led to rapid currency depreciation and inflation (figure 2.1). These economic shocks reverberated throughout the political system, leading to a wave of broader policy reforms, including those on systemic risks and financial assets (2004); a tax reform (2004); and new planning, budgeting, and procurement laws (2006), among others.

The economy recovered in 2005 and grew even faster than during the precrisis period. Although the global financial crisis, particularly the recession in the United States, slowed down the Dominican economy in 2008 and 2009, growth remained positive in both years (5.2 percent in 2008 and 3.4 percent in 2009) and well above the Latin America and Caribbean region as a whole. Growth bounced back in 2010, expanding by 7.8 percentage points, and slowed down again in 2011, 2012, and 2013 (by 4.5, 3.9, and 4.1 percentage points, respectively) in a context of weakening internal demand. More recently, gold exporting and construction have been among the strongest contributors to economic growth.

Poverty and Inequality Reduction

Despite this stellar growth performance, poverty has not fallen in the Dominican Republic as it has elsewhere in the region. In fact, poverty has increased in the country over the past 10–15 years. The official extreme poverty rate in 2013 was 10 percent, higher than in 2000 (8.1 percent). Meanwhile, the moderate poverty rate increased from 32 percent to 41 percent between 2000 and 2013, mostly because of the long-lasting effects of the 2003–04 financial crisis, which brought 1.7 million people into poverty.[6] By comparison, moderate poverty rates in Latin America and the Caribbean fell from 43 percent in 2000 to 23 percent in 2014.[7]

Unsurprisingly, growth incidence curves show that incomes fell sharply during the crisis period, particularly for those in the third and fourth income deciles (figure 2.2, panel b).[8] However, this decline came on the heels of falling incomes for the poor in the early 2000s (figure 2.2, panel a). Strong economic growth during the postcrisis period benefited the poor but just moderately (figure 2.2, panel c).

The positive but relatively slow increase in the incomes of people below and slightly above the poverty line is consistent with a period of robust economic

Figure 2.1 Economic Growth and Poverty Trends in the Dominican Republic

a. GDP trends, 1991–2013

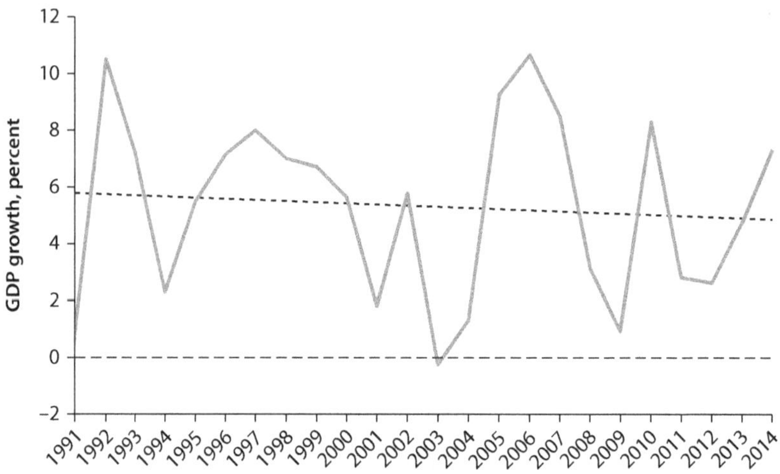

Source: World Development Indicators Database.

b. GDP growth and poverty headcount, 2000–12

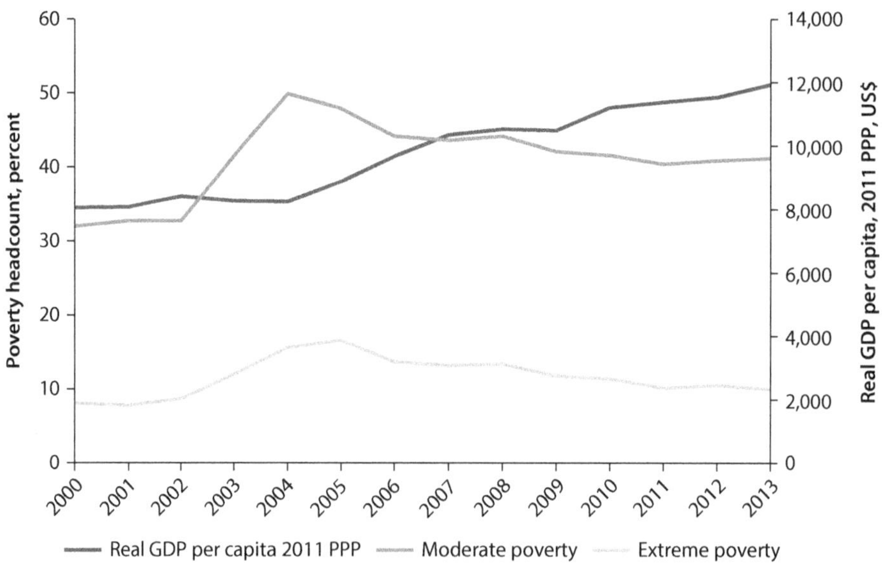

Sources: GDP data from World Development Indicators Database; poverty rates from MEPyD 2014.
Note: PPP = purchasing power parity. Poverty rates correspond to national official measures. "Extreme poverty" refers to per capita incomes that are insufficient to purchase the minimum caloric requirement for adequate nutrition. "Moderate poverty" refers to per capita incomes that are insufficient to purchase a basic basket of food and nonfood goods and services.

Figure 2.2 Growth Incidence Curves of Income per Capita

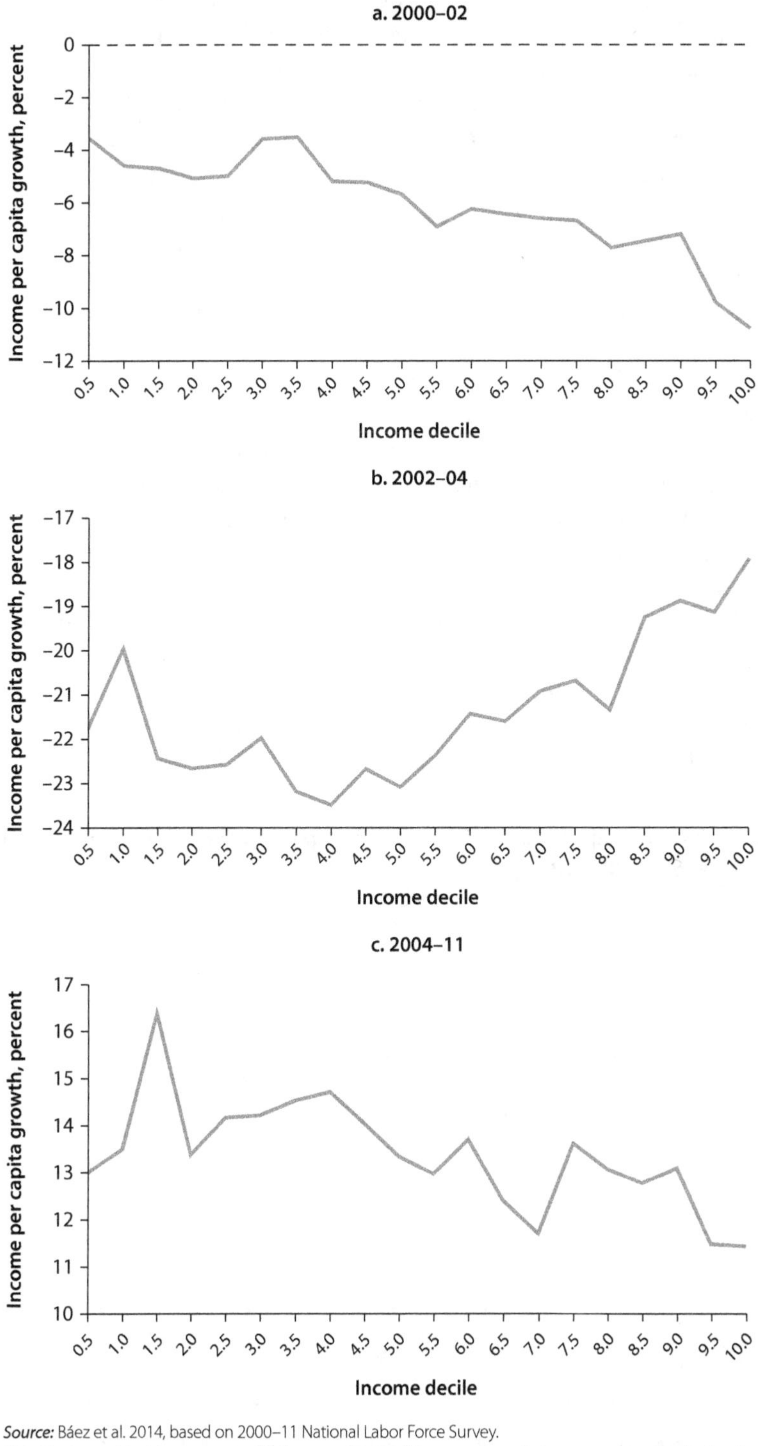

Source: Báez et al. 2014, based on 2000–11 National Labor Force Survey.
Note: The growth incidence curves plot the growth rate of income per capita between two points in time for each decile of the distribution to illustrate how the gains of economic growth—or the losses of economic recessions—were distributed across the population.

growth that nonetheless has brought only modest poverty reduction. Only recently, between October 2013 and October 2014, has moderate poverty incidence fallen, by an estimated 5 percentage points, to 36 percent of the population. This notable decrease is partly attributed to increases in construction and agriculture employment generated by a series of public spending efforts (building of 18,000 classrooms, programs to support productivity in rural areas, and other projects). In addition, there were changes in family composition and increases in labor force participation, employment, and real wages (Báez et al. 2014).

However, except during the economic crisis period, income growth at the bottom of the distribution was faster than at the top of the distribution during most of the decade, illustrated by the moderate decline in measured income inequality (figure 2.3). Nevertheless, the pace of this improvement in inequality was slower than in the rest of the region, in part because of the strong reversal during the 2003–04 crisis period.

Beyond income measures of poverty and inequality, access to basic services continues to be a challenge, although such access has expanded over the past decade. The Human Opportunity Index (HOI) measures how equitably opportunities are distributed among different subgroups depending on personal circumstances (such as birthplace wealth, race, or gender). Increases in access to circumstance-specific disadvantaged groups have contributed to the improvement of the HOI in the Dominican Republic. For instance, school enrollment is close to universal (table 2.1). However, at this pace, it could take the country almost 30 years to universalize the opportunities captured in the HOI. This is similar to the amount of time it would take for Central America (36 years) to do

Figure 2.3 Income Inequality in the Dominican Republic Relative to Latin America and the Caribbean Region, 2000–13

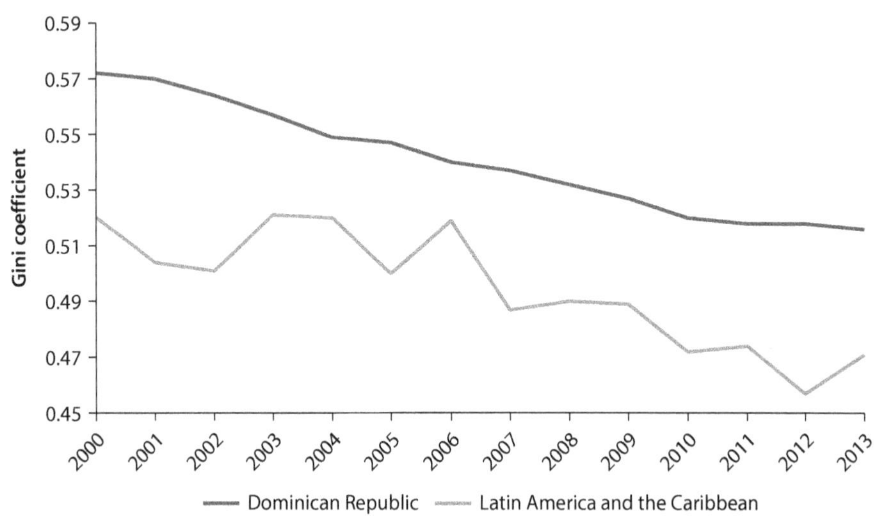

Source: World Bank LAC Equity Lab, http://www.worldbank.org/en/topic/poverty/lac-equity-lab1/overview.
Note: Gini coefficients, based here on income per capita, measure the inequality of income distribution. A value of 0 indicates full equality, and 1 indicates maximum inequality.

Table 2.1 HOI for Education, Safe Water and Sanitation, Housing, and Assets Ownership in the Dominican Republic, 2000–11

	Education		*Safe water and sanitation*		*Housing*	*Assets*
Year	*Enrollment*	*Sixth grade on time*	*Water*	*Sanitation*	*House with hard floor*	*Asset ownership*
2000	97	43	61	37	87	62
2004	98	56	64	44	92	59
2011	96	68	61	55	95	62

Source: Báez et al. 2014, based on National Workforce Surveys of 2000, 2002, 2004, and 2011.
Note: HOI = Human Opportunity Index, the coverage rate of opportunities adjusted for equity of distribution among different subgroups based on circumstances.

the same but well above the Latin American and Caribbean region, which is projected to achieve this objective in approximately 24 years (Báez et al. 2014).

Fiscal Policy

Thus the Dominican Republic has grown rapidly compared with its peers yet has done less in providing benefits for the country's poorest. Part of the explanation for this outcome lies with the country's fiscal policy, which limits the government's ability to provide sufficient access to and quality of public goods and services.

The fiscal system in the Dominican Republic is characterized by both low revenue collection and lack of progressivity. For example, the country's tax revenues averaged 13.8 percent of GDP between 2000 and 2014 (figure 2.4, panel a). By comparison, the regional average was 20.5 percent in 2012.[9]

A total of five tax reforms over the past nine years have been unable to systematically address the low tax burden, particularly through more direct taxes. Notably, tax expenditures (subsidies delivered through the tax code as deductions, exclusions, or other preferences) amount to around 6.7 percent of GDP. Two-thirds of these consist of value added tax (VAT) exemptions on spending for education, health, transportation, and certain food products. However, exemptions accruing to special economic zones also represent about 1 percentage point of GDP in forgone revenue collections. The complex political economy of reform in these two areas has probably blocked the formulation of deeper tax reforms (World Bank 2014b).

The low level of public revenues, along with budget rigidities, constrains the fiscal space to implement social policies and provide more and better public goods. In fact, until recently, the Dominican Republic had one of the lowest relative expenditures on education in Latin America and the Caribbean, measured either as a share of GDP or as total government expenditures. In education, the high enrollment rates combined with low public spending have led to overcrowding and serious quality concerns, although the new administration has increased budgeted education expenditures from 2.25 percent of GDP in 2012 to 4 percent of GDP in 2013 through 2015 (MINERD 2014). Public spending on health has also increased in recent years but remains low in the Dominican Republic as a share of GDP per capita (2.9 percent), much lower than the regional average (3.4 percent) in 2014.[10]

Figure 2.4 Central Government Revenues and Expenditures in the Dominican Republic

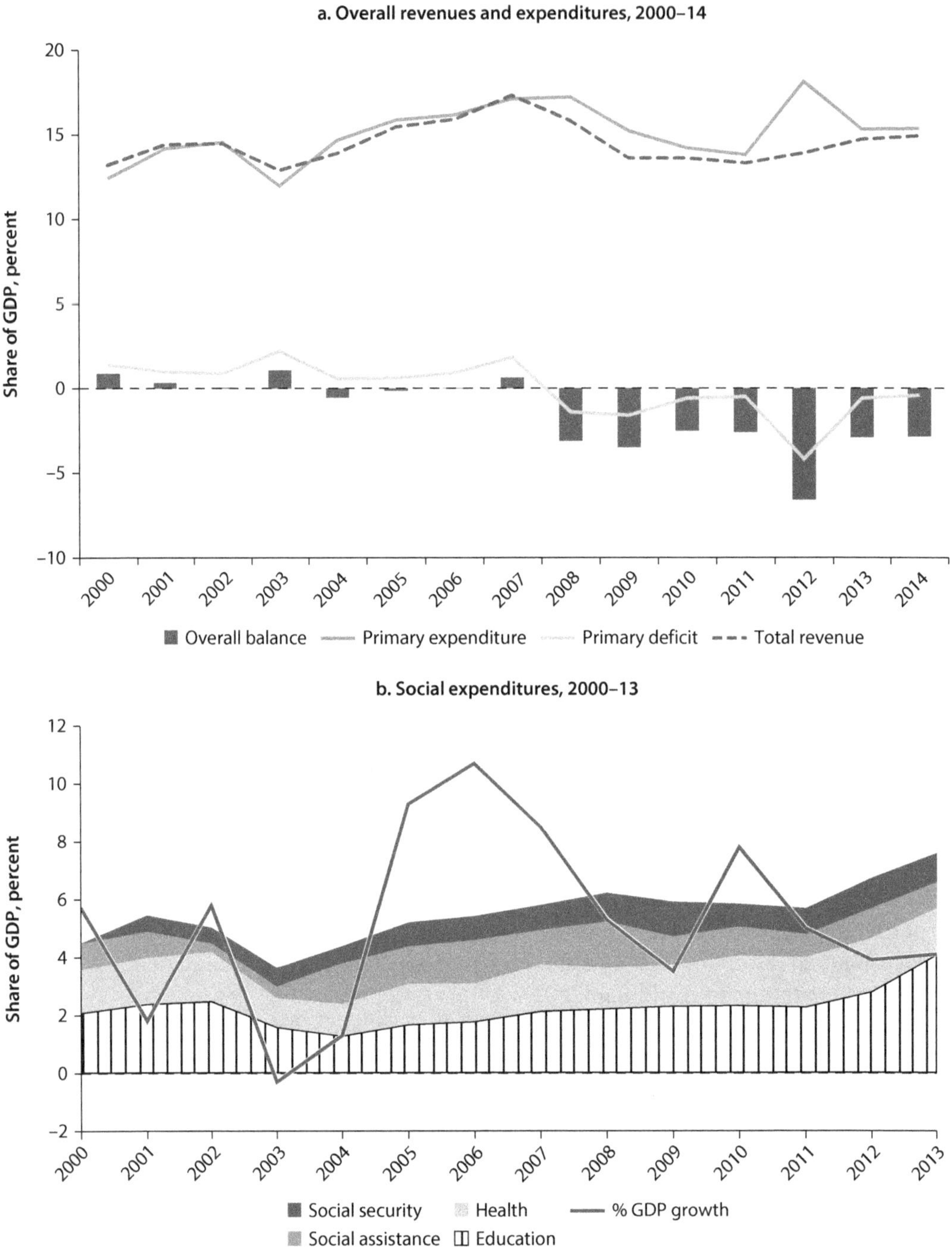

Sources: World Bank, based on data from the Ministry of Economy, Planning and Development; Integrated Financial Management Information System (SIGEF); and Central Bank of Dominican Republic.

Further complicating matters on the expenditure side, during recent election years the government has tended to adopt looser fiscal policies in an effort to win broader political support. This expansion of public investment has usually been directed to transportation infrastructure. During the election years of 2008 and 2012, economic expenditures (mainly energy, transportation, and communications) were 50 percent higher than the average in nonelection years (figure 2.5).

In this context of limited fiscal space, energy subsidies—of which the dominant share goes to electricity—have been a strain. Electricity sector transfers reached 1.8 percent of GDP in 2012, equivalent to triple the budget for social transfers, the entire budget on public health, or two-thirds of the spending on education that year (World Bank 2014a).

Political System and Clientelism

The political system in the Dominican Republic has historically been defined by the strong concentration of power in the executive branch. The president's power derives from both constitutional norms and political party organization. The Dominican Constitution gives the president ample powers of appointment, public resource allocation, and legislation. In addition, Dominican presidents have traditionally played a leading role in their political parties, giving them a great deal of added control over the legislature and local government.

Figure 2.5 Government Spending as a Share of GDP in the Dominican Republic, by Category, 2008–14

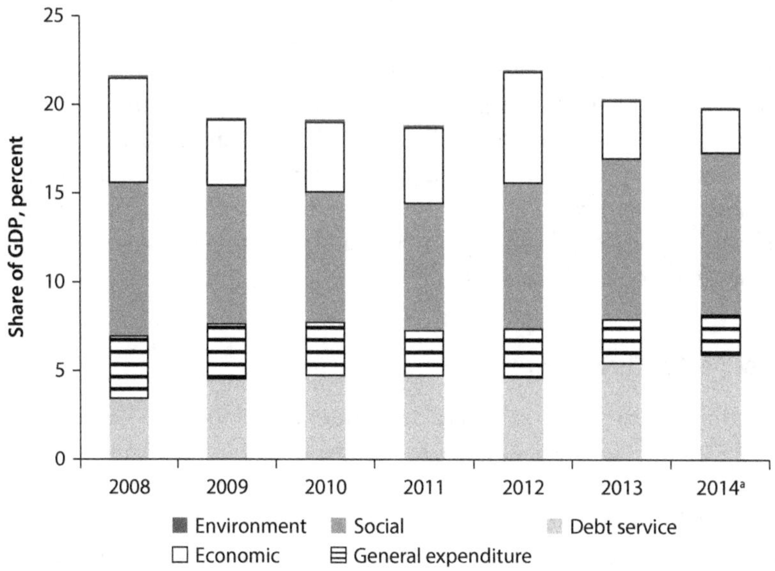

Sources: World Bank, based on data from the Integrated Financial Management Information System (SIGEF), Ministry of the Treasury, and Central Bank of Dominican Republic.
Note: "Social" expenditures include education; health; sports, recreation, and culture; social security; social assistance; and housing and urban development.
a. 2014 data are estimates.

In spite of the existence of at least two dozen political parties, the Dominican Republic is a de facto two-party system: two major parties, the Dominican Liberation Party (PLD) and the Dominican Revolutionary Party (PRD) have garnered more than 80 percent of the votes in the past four elections.[11] One important attribute of the Dominican political system is its lack of ideological differentiation since both parties can occupy any position in the political spectrum depending on the issue. Formally, the PRD is affiliated with the Socialist International, but an analysis of both electoral programs shows only minor ideological differences between the parties (World Bank 2014b).

Political parties in the Dominican Republic have among the lowest level of programmatic orientation in Latin America, along with those of six other countries in the region (Rufín et al. 2014). In fact, as documented in Ardanaz, Scartascini, and Tommasi (2010), the competition by strong parties on clientelistic grounds results in low quality of public policies in the Dominican Republic relative to other countries in the region. The Dominican Republic ranks first in the clientelism scale in Latin America (Morgan, Espinal, and Seligson 2010). About 20 percent of an interviewed sample in 2010 confirmed that a candidate or a party had offered them something in exchange for political support (World Bank 2014b). In one global study, the Dominican Republic is rated as one of the three most clientelistic countries in the world, together with Mongolia and Senegal (Kitschelt and Kselman 2011).

As for the political influence of institutional special interests, none of the major parties has strong links to unions or other organized popular groups. The exception is the transport unions, particularly those traditionally aligned with the PRD such as Fenatrano (the most powerful, whose affiliates transport 2 million of the 3 million passengers per day in Santo Domingo); Conatra (whose passengers are more suburban); and Fenatrado. In terms of entrepreneurial interests, there is an economic divide between large, family-owned importing and mainly commercial conglomerates and a more fragmented manufacturing sector concentrated in two main cities (Santiago and Santo Domingo). There is a historical alliance between leading politicians and prominent business elites (mostly large, family-owned conglomerates).[12]

Energy Sector Overview

The Dominican Republic is largely dependent on imported oil, natural gas, and coal.[13] In 2008, 68 percent of electricity generation was based on oil, 15 percent on coal, 12 percent on natural gas, and only 5 percent on hydro and biofuels. By 2012, oil-based electricity generation had declined to 53 percent, while natural gas accounted for 25 percent, coal for 17 percent, and hydro and biofuels for 5.7 percent.[14]

This dependence on imported fuels has meant that the energy sector has historically faced the challenge of passing the effects of world market fluctuations on to its consumers, particularly when it comes to electricity and LPG. The latter had special treatment until 2008, with the government fixing its retail price at below-market rates while fluctuations for imported fuels have been passed through to consumers for all other hydrocarbons.

The electricity sector has traditionally been even harder to reform. In 2012, the Dominican Republic had 98 percent electricity coverage, ranking it above the Latin American average (96.4 percent).[15] However, widespread blackouts and brownouts effectively reduce this coverage. Moreover, because tariffs have traditionally been held down to appease political constituents, the government has largely absorbed fluctuations in international fuel prices.

This fiscal problem has been compounded by several domestic issues. First, electricity generation depends on imported fuel, primarily oil, which has been expensive and volatile in price. Second, hiring practices in the state-owned electricity companies have not been responsive to company needs, leading to a bloated sector where corruption has thrived. Third, many customers, including major government agencies, do not pay regularly for their electricity, either because customers fail to pay invoiced amounts or because energy delivered to end users is never invoiced because of fraud, theft, or lack of metering and customer registration (Manzetti and Rufín 2006). Despite multiple attempts at reform, the electricity sector, particularly the distribution companies, have continued to sustain high losses that have led to large explicit and implicit subsidies.

The following two sections examine the origins, challenges, revisions, and impacts of LPG and electricity subsidies and the attempts to reduce them in recent years. The focus is particularly on the process of reform, detailing how proponents campaigned, convened, compromised, mitigated, and timed changes in LPG and electricity prices, with varying degrees of success.

Reform of LPG Subsidies

History of LPG Subsidies

As mentioned earlier, the Dominican government exercised extensive price controls during the 1980s, including controls on petroleum prices. Economic reform beginning in 1990 corrected the prices, leading to increases of 200–300 percent. The newly imposed petroleum tax (equaling the difference between the state-controlled retail price of various fuels and the sum of their ex-refinery price and a distributor's margin) helped to improve the Dominican fiscal position between 1990 and 2000. Although the ex-refinery price varied directly with international oil prices and changes in the official exchange rate, the retail prices for petroleum products were seldom adjusted; therefore, a decline in world prices boosted the revenue to the government and distributors. However, this structure left the fiscal position of the government susceptible to large swings in revenue.

In addition to these distortions that applied generally to all petroleum products, additional policies distorted the price of LPG, a fuel the government deemed an important consumption good of the Dominican household. On this logic, the state-controlled retail price for propane gas was kept lower than world prices (IMF 1999). Indeed, the distinction between LPG and other fuels was featured during the economic reforms put in place by President Leonel Fernández in 1996, when the government began distinguishing between the price of LPG for domestic use (RD$6 per gallon) and LPG for industrial, commercial, or vehicular use (RD$10 per gallon, later raised to RD$13 per gallon in 1999).[16]

Special treatment of LPG continued to be a feature of energy policy in the Dominican Republic until 2008, despite a series of attempted reforms (for a timeline, see annex 2B). First, following the 2000 presidential election, in which the opposition PRD led by President Hipólito Mejía came to power, the new government put forward a package of fiscal reforms, including a new hydrocarbons tax law that converted the previous system of fuel price differentials into an array of specific excise taxes linked to the consumer price index.[17] Administrative discretion was thus removed, and retail prices started being revised weekly in line with wholesale prices. This change became effective for all fuels except LPG. In fact, the new hydrocarbons tax law mandated that, to protect household budgets, the executive branch provide a direct subsidy to families to buy LPG for domestic uses. The law mandated that the subsidy always remain at least as large as it was at the time the law was passed. Despite the law's focus on protecting household budgets, LPG prices for domestic, industrial, and commercial purposes were equalized to RD$13 per gallon.[18]

At the same time, the state also made its first attempt to target LPG subsidies through a coupon distribution program.[19] However, this effort ended prematurely and abruptly because of corruption allegations involving the Ministry of Industry and Commerce. During this effort, the overall LPG subsidy program was transferred to the Social Cabinet[20]—an administrative move that proved important later because the Social Cabinet's administrative capabilities made feasible a more targeted subsidy program.

Next, in 2003, the president decreed that the price of LPG would be fixed at RD$25 per gallon for the end consumer.[21] The announced decision was that all exchange-rate risk would be borne by the government and would not discriminate by the consumer's level of income or type of use. Unfortunately, the 2003–04 Dominican financial crisis devalued the currency by more than 100 percent. At world market prices, LPG would have cost more than RD$50 per gallon, more than twice the price fixed by government.

Renewed reform efforts followed the 2004 election that returned Leonel Fernández to power. By the end of his first month in office, his administration eliminated the LPG subsidy for consumers who used more than 100 pounds, including industrial users, hotels, and restaurants.[22] This represented less than 20 percent of consumption, as most users of LPG were small consumers, small companies, and public transportation.

Importantly, the reform also announced that a targeting mechanism would be put in place to provide the subsidy exclusively to low-income households. This reform was not implemented until the end of 2008, but two important measures did take place quickly: (a) regular publication of the prices of subsidized and unsubsidized LPG; and (b) fixed reimbursement, instead of a fixed price, so that, starting in June 2005, RD$17.35 was compensated per gallon, thus passing market price fluctuations and exchange rate risk on to the consumer.

The Bonogas LPG Reform

Although reforms had been approved in the early 2000s, little effort was made to implement them. That situation became untenable by 2008, when international oil and gas prices rose sharply. Fiscally, this rise in world prices left the government responsible for a large and growing subsidy burden. Importantly, genuine reform had become politically more palatable given the availability of a more robust social protection system that could credibly target poor households.

Shortly after the reelection of President Fernández in May 2008, the executive branch announced in September that it would fully remove the generalized subsidy and instead target LPG subsidies to poor households. The objective was to focus the subsidy on roughly the poorest 40 percent of the population and public transport drivers, thus preventing price increases for poor passengers (Díaz 2013). These two purposes were translated into parallel programs—one for households (Bonogas-Hogares) and the other for transport drivers (Bonogas-Choferes).

Targeting Poorer Households: Bonogas-Hogares

Targeting became the responsibility of the Social Cabinet,[23] which in 2005 had launched a social safety net called Solidaridad, largely in response to the 2003 economic crisis.[24] The presence of Solidaridad gave the Social Cabinet the information and the administrative capacity needed to implement a targeted subsidy scheme. In 2004, by executive power, the government created a Social Subsidies Administration (ADESS) within the Social Cabinet to unify the management of social subsidies, which would come to include the new LPG subsidy targeted to low-income households, Bonogas-Hogares.

The implementation of Bonogas depended crucially on the existence of mechanisms to target and distribute these and other nationwide social transfers to households. Among these mechanisms, both established in 2004–05, were the Solidaridad debit card and the Single Beneficiary Selection System (SIUBEN), a national database of low-income households. SIUBEN contains information on nearly 60 percent of all households in the country and uses an objective proxy means test to help achieve transparency, equity, and efficiency in the allocation of public resources.[25] Today SIUBEN provides a registry with the full names of beneficiaries, identification numbers, and addresses for each of the following programs (Gámez, Cheston, and Coudouel 2011):

- Eating Is First (Comer es Primero)
- School Attendance Incentive (Incentivo a la Asistencia Escolar, ILAE)
- National Council of Elderly Persons (Consejo Nacional de la Persona Envejeciente, CONAPE)

- National Health Insurance (Seguro Nacional de Salud)
- Bonogas-Hogares subsidy for the domestic use of cooking gas (LPG)
- Bonoluz-Hogares subsidy for household electricity (further discussed below)

The initial SIUBEN database was created from the government's First Socioeconomic Study, which surveyed 1.2 million households comprising 4.4 million individuals (56 percent of the population) in 2004–05 (Gámez, Cheston, and Coudouel 2011). The survey was implemented in selected geographical areas that displayed high levels of poverty.[26]

In addition, SIUBEN allows for continuous, on-demand household enrollment, facilitated through decentralized Regional Technical Units. When SIUBEN receives a request, staff visits the household to administer a survey, enters the information into the registry, and applies a proxy means test to determine the household's poverty status (Gámez, Cheston, and Coudouel 2011). In addition to direct requests from households, SIUBEN works with a network of community organizations that present requests on behalf of households they serve. The ADESS website offers a portal for individuals to look up their Solidaridad status, as well as detailed statistics on the subsidies such as the number of beneficiaries per program for each province.[27] A telephone helpline was also set up to answer any questions regarding the status of, or amount on, one's Solidaridad card.

Based on the information in SIUBEN to identify beneficiaries, the conditional cash transfer program Solidaridad was developed to provide efficient, reliable, and transparent identification and payment of beneficiaries for multiple social targeted programs via a smart card. The Solidaridad card was backed by Visa and issued by four financial institutions selected by a public tender. Card distribution points were identified and verified for feasibility by ADESS field staff. In May 2005, in parallel with the Social Cabinet's development of the SIUBEN, ADESS initiated nationwide distribution of the Solidaridad card, assisted in each locality by provincial governments and religious groups.[28] By the end of 2005, the government had delivered 196,226 cards, and by the end of 2006, a total of 216,152 cards had been distributed in various districts of the country (ADESS 2016).

A total of 833 *colmados*, or neighborhood shops, were identified for the Social Supply Network (RAS), a network of private businesses where the social subsidies could be spent for goods and services with a swipe of the Solidaridad card. This number increased to 1,233 by 2006. All participating shops were required to undergo technological renovation necessary to implement the Solidaridad payment system and attend a seminar on the rules and procedures of the program. These steps not only aided the implementation of Solidaridad but also helped to modernize these small businesses' operations.[29]

The system of central administration, smart cards, and shops laid a foundation for better administration of targeted subsidy schemes that, fortuitously, was already in place when the government decided in 2008 to reform its LPG subsidy. Bonogas-Hogares targeted roughly the poorest 40 percent of the population in 2008—twice the number of Solidaridad beneficiaries.[30]

These households would receive RD$228 per month, an amount calculated to cover average household consumption of six gallons per month at a market rate of RD$38 per gallon at the time. The inclusion of the lower-middle class was viewed as an important mechanism for appeasing those households, which do not consume much LPG in any case. The middle class never did protest the passage of the Bonogas-Hogares reform, because it was part of a large pro-poor program with clear targeting mechanisms and because of their low levels of collective action. It should also be noted that, for the middle class, the financial implications were not significant. A middle-class family would buy a 100-pound tank every 2.5 months; thus the difference between subsidized and unsubsidized prices (RD$38) would not amount to much for middle-class standards.[31]

Appeasing Transport Groups: Bonogas-Choferes

Even though the middle class did not strongly oppose the idea of reform, one group of stakeholders did: those who depended on providing transportation for their livelihood. Politically, the replacement of the generalized LPG subsidy with Bonogas-Hogares was ultimately possible because of the inclusion of a sister program named Bonogas-Choferes, which would benefit drivers of taxicabs fueled by LPG.[32]

Passenger transportation unions in the Dominican Republic were, and remain, so powerful the media has dubbed them "los dueños del país" (the owners of the country). It became inevitable and necessary that the Social Cabinet gain the buy-in of the "transportistas," who would be hurt by the removal of the LPG subsidy. In this regard, the head of the Social Cabinet and even President Fernández personally attended several meetings with the transport groups to discuss the reforms. As further described below, the transport unions ultimately received significant compensation in the process of LPG reform.

Although all the major transport unions insisted that they be the direct recipients of the subsidy, the Social Cabinet feared mischanneled benefits and insisted on construction of an official database of legally registered drivers that would list vehicles, plate numbers, and routes. From this database individual drivers would be selected. To be eligible, beneficiary drivers would need to have valid identity documents, a vehicle recorded in the database of the Internal Revenue Service, and registration with one of the existing public transport routes supervised by the Land Transport Technical Office (OTTT), the Santiago City Council, or the Metropolitan Transit Authority (AMET). Unions could demand the inclusion or exclusion of a beneficiary but would need to have the backing of one of these three entities.

Based on consumption of six gallons of LPG per day at a market price of RD$38 per gallon, the monthly subsidized value of Bonogas-Choferes would be RD$3,420 per driver.[33] This amount was determined in 2008 by the Social Cabinet in conjunction with the Ministry of Finance and the Ministry of Industry and Commerce. Initially, about 21,719 drivers registered for Bonogas-Choferes, of whom 14,640 were deemed eligible. As of December 2012, the program covered 15,936 drivers (ADESS 2009, 2016).

The effect of removing the generalized LPG subsidy was further mitigated by the practically simultaneous passage of a generalized diesel subsidy.

President Fernández issued a decree awarding monthly quantities of diesel to major public and cargo transport unions as well as to companies in free trade zones to assist with the generation of thermal energy.[34] The volume of the diesel subsidy received by different unions is determined by the Ministry of Industry and Commerce. The distribution of diesel is at the discretion of union leaders among drivers within a union.

Subsequent additional executive decrees in 2011 removed the consumption tax on petroleum derivatives (those passed in the early 2000s) for transport unions' confederations that directly acquire fuels and then supply them to individual drivers (usually at a premium).[35] This benefit is capped at a monthly consumption of 3 million gallons. Although originally this benefit was supposed to expire after three months, it was repeatedly extended.

In 2012, the diesel subsidy was broadened to include natural gas, extending the benefit to power generation.[36] Meanwhile, the subsidy has subsidized roughly 30 percent of all diesel consumption, without any targeting feature. As of December 2012, the transport confederations were receiving 3 million gallons of diesel per month tax-free. The confederations also benefited from other measures at the time of the removal of the generalized LPG subsidy, such as the exemption from tariffs on imported vehicles. Unfortunately, the cost of these tax expenditures has not been quantified.

Impact of the Bonogas Reform

Fiscal Impact

Even with all of the concessions to the transport unions, the LPG subsidy reform of 2008 appears to have benefited the Dominican fiscal situation. In the last quarter of 2008, when Bonogas was implemented, the average monthly expenditure on the LPG subsidy amounted to RD$249 million—a saving of RD$606.4 million or 71 percent from the monthly average in the first three quarters (when the LPG subsidy was still generalized). The LPG subsidy had averaged 0.5 percent of GDP from 2004 to 2008; since 2009, this figure has been 0.13 percent of GDP (Díaz 2013), as shown in figure 2.6.

For its part, the generalized diesel subsidy had incurred a fiscal cost of RD$1.5 billion (0.07 percent of GDP) by December 2011, subsidizing mostly urban, suburban, touristic, or freight transporters. Although this was more than twice the amount spent on Bonogas-Choferes (0.03 percent of GDP) and comparable in size to the RD$1.9 billion spent on Bonogas-Hogares (0.09 percent of GDP), the changes resulted in a net savings in the fiscal accounts—from 0.5 percent of GDP spent on LPG subsidies in 2008 to a total cost for the compensatory programs of less than 0.2 percent by the end of 2011 (ADESS 2016; Vagliasindi 2012). Thus the combined LPG reform and associated compensation to the transport unions (such as the diesel subsidy) provided a net fiscal saving.

Distributional Impact

Before Bonogas. To calculate the benefit incidence of the generalized gas subsidies before Bonogas, we use the 2007 National Survey of Income and

Figure 2.6 Public Spending on Untargeted LPG Subsidies and Bonogas in the Dominican Republic, as a Share of GDP, 2004–12

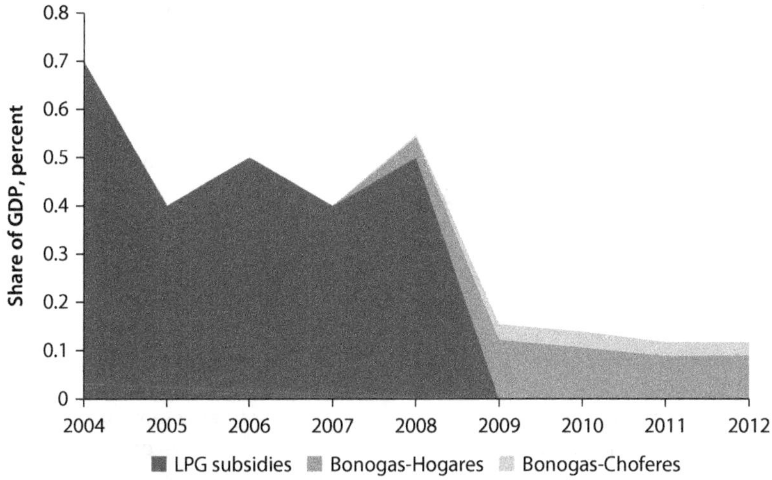

Sources: ADESS 2016; Vagliasindi 2012.
Note: LPG = liquefied petroleum gas. Bonogas-Hogares (Bonogas-Home) is an LPG subsidy targeted to the poorest 40 percent of households. Bonogas-Choferes (Bonogas-Driver) is an LPG subsidy targeted to eligible urban transport drivers. The government replaced a generalized LPG subsidy with the targeted Bonogas subsidies in 2008.

Expenditure (ENIGH), which has information on household gas expenditures and quantity purchased in the month before the survey. The results show that the generalized subsidy benefits were concentrated at the top of the income distribution, where consumption is the greatest. Indeed, the benefit to the richest 10 percent of the population was at least five times the benefit to the poorest 10 percent (figure 2.7, panel b). However, the amount of subsidy for poorer income groups was high relative to their share of income. (This is shown by a concentration curve for subsidies that is above the Lorenz curve of income distribution in figure 2.7, panel a).[37] These results show that the removal of subsidies without a mitigating program would be especially hard on the poor, because subsidies constituted a larger share of their incomes (figure 2.7, panel a).

After Bonogas. Although Bonogas was introduced in 2008, a year after the 2007 ENIGH, we can also simulate the post-Bonogas incidence as if it had existed in 2007. To simulate the distribution of subsidies after Bonogas, we assumed that all households meeting the eligibility criteria received the subsidy if they bought gas. We kept constant the gallons purchased by each household in 2007 and assumed that all households had paid the official nonsubsidized price that was valid when they were surveyed. The Bonogas subsidy was RD$280 per household, but households that did not purchase gas in the month previous to the survey were assigned no subsidy even if eligible.

Figure 2.7 Concentration of Income and Gas Subsidies in the Dominican Republic before Bonogas, 2007

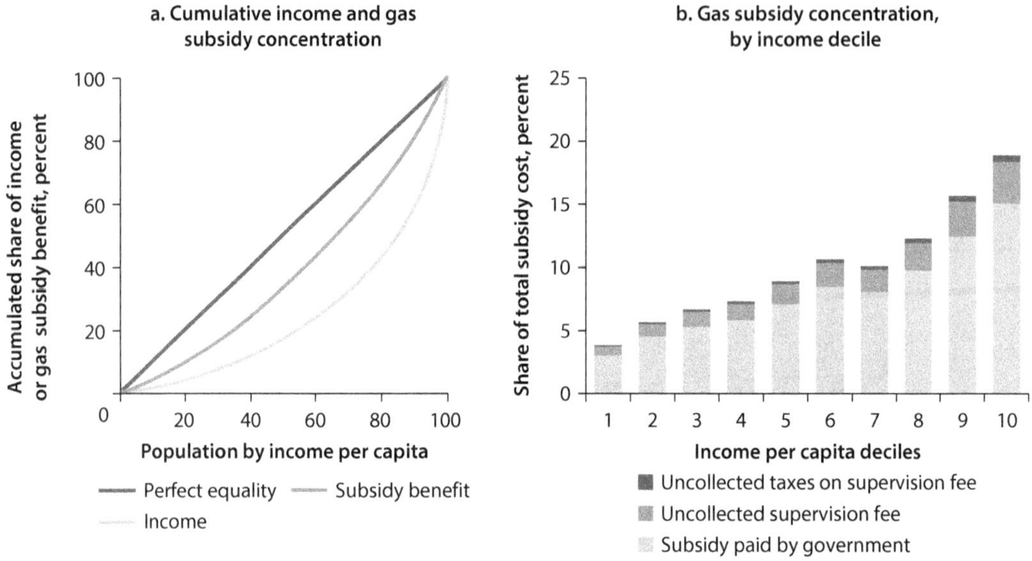

Source: Estimates based on 2007 National Household Survey of Income and Expenditure (ENIGH).
Note: Figure orders households from poorest (left) to richest (right) by net incomes per capita (after taxes) but before transfers. "Bonogas" refers to a liquefied petroleum gas (LPG) subsidy targeted to the poorest 40 percent of households, which replaced a generalized LPG subsidy in 2008.

In contrast to the generalized subsidy, Bonogas was progressive in absolute terms (figure 2.8). Bonogas is not only a larger share of income for lower income groups, as shown by a concentration curve above the Lorenz curve of income distribution, but it also lies above the 45-degree perfect equality line, indicating that a larger share of total spending on Bonogas is targeted to the poor (figure 2.8, panel a). In fact, when we simulate the benefits of the reform, we find that 49 percent of all spending on Bonogas was targeted to the bottom 40 percent of the income distribution (figure 2.8, panel b).

Bonogas-Choferes and Diesel Subsidies. It is difficult to quantify the distributional impact of Bonogas-Choferes and the new diesel subsidies because data on the incomes of drivers or passengers are not available. However, observers largely suspect that both populations belong to the middle to lower-middle class. Although policy makers have discussed targeting the Bonogas-Choferes subsidies to public transport passengers, they have deemed such a change to be too logistically challenging.

Impact on LPG Use

The supply of LPG below market prices creates significant distortions given that LPG is a good substitute for other fuels. Before 2008, when the LPG subsidy remained generalized, the proportion of LPG fuel consumption had been rising, particularly with the adaptation of vehicles to be LPG-compatible. After the subsidy targeting began in 2008, the proportion of LPG use relative to other fuels ceased to grow (figure 2.9).

Figure 2.8 Concentration of Income and Gas Subsidies in the Dominican Republic after Bonogas, 2007

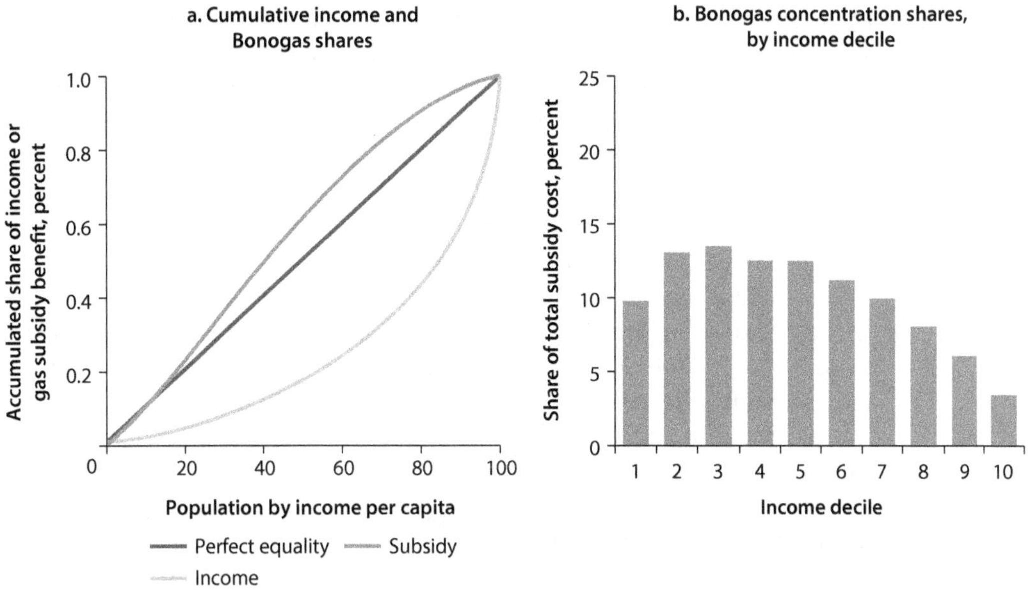

Source: Estimates based on 2007 National Household Survey of Income and Expenditure (ENIGH).
Note: Figure orders households from poorest (left) to richest (right) by net incomes per capita (after taxes) but before transfers. "Bonogas" refers to a liquefied petroleum gas (LPG) subsidy targeted to the poorest 40 percent of households, which replaced a generalized LPG subsidy in 2008.

Figure 2.9 LPG Consumption in the Dominican Republic, 2003–13

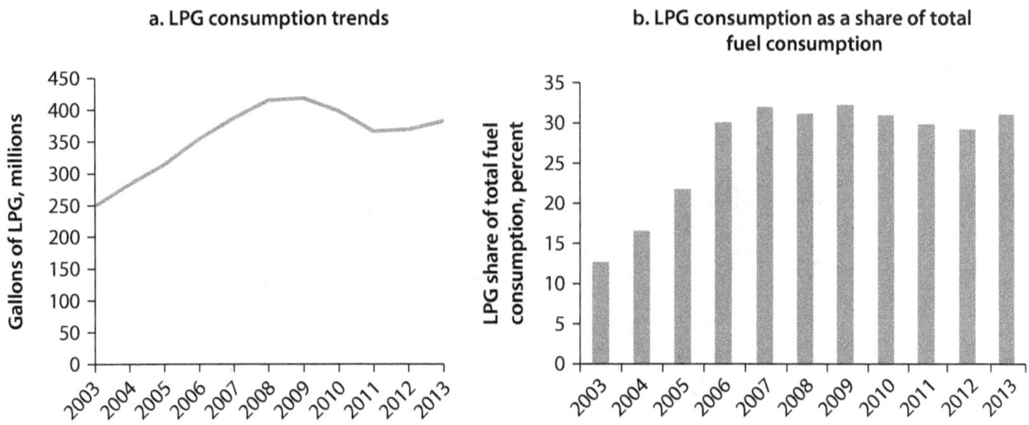

Source: Ministry of Industry and Commerce monthly fuel consumption statistics (accessed March 24, 2014), http://www.mic.gob.do/direcciones/hidrocarburos/estadísticas/consumo-de-combustibles.aspx.
Note: LPG = liquefied petroleum gas.

Reform of Electricity Subsidies

The largest and most difficult to reform aspect of the Dominican energy system is the electricity sector. Historically, poor performance and high fiscal costs for the government have characterized the sector. Blackouts are relatively common; technical losses as well as underbilling and theft in electricity distribution are well above the Latin American average (Jiménez, Serebrisky, and Mercado 2014). The government has covered these losses with large, opaque, and poorly targeted subsidies to the sector.[38] At their peak, electricity subsidies amounted to 2.7 percent of GDP in 2008 (figure 2.10).

This section focuses on two attempts to reform the electricity sector: the Blackout Reduction Program (PRA), initiated in 2001, and the Bonoluz program, implemented in 2009. The PRA was a geographically targeted program that was not successful because of its design and the perverse incentives it created. In contrast, Bonoluz built on the success of Bonogas and was better administered, yielding better results.

Notably, however, the overall impacts of the Bonoluz reforms have been minimal in terms of reducing total electricity subsidies and redirecting them to those who would benefit most. Hampering the reform's effectiveness have been the sector's complexity and the fact that most losses are due to underbilling, largely because of the overall poor performance and highly political management that has historically characterized the sector.

Figure 2.10 Public Expenditures on Electricity Subsidies and Bonoluz in the Dominican Republic, 2004–12

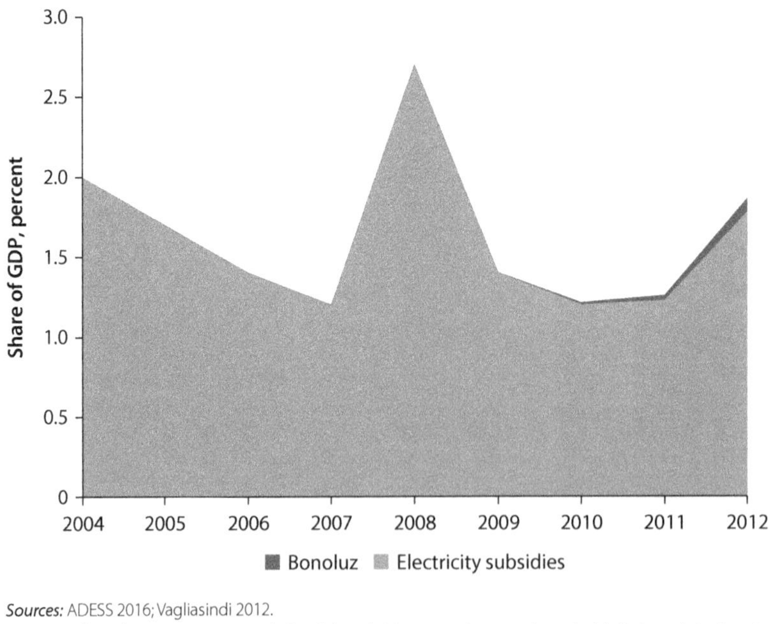

Sources: ADESS 2016; Vagliasindi 2012.
Note: Bonoluz refers to a means-tested electricity subsidy targeted to poor households that was introduced in 2009. Bonoluz replaced the government's geographically targeted Blackout Reduction Program.

History of Electricity Subsidies

At the end of the 1980s, after decades of state control, the Dominican electricity system showed deficiencies in production, processing, and final energy use. Power depended on imported oil products, which accounted for 95 percent of all fuel sources for electricity generation in 1989.[39] In that same year, the electricity deficit was approximately 20 percent of electricity demand (World Bank 1991). In fact, electricity outages between 1984 and 1988 cost the Dominican economy an estimated 4 percent of GDP per year (USAID 1995). Generation, transmission, and distribution of electricity were part of a state monopoly managed by the Dominican Electricity Corporation (CDE), which operated at a significant financial deficit and could not invest in greater generation capacity.

Despite increasing calls for reform, it was not until 1997 that the General Public Enterprise Reform Law was passed, whereby the government opened the electric sector to private participation.[40] The government divided CDE into seven separate enterprises: two generation companies, a hydroelectric generation company, a transmission company, and three distribution companies (EDEs, one for each region).[41] In addition, the government created the Dominican Corporation of State Electricity Companies (CDEEE), the holding company owning the stock of each of these companies.

Private participation was opened up in two ways: First, there was a tender for 49 percent of the stock of the two largest generation plants, along with their management. Second, there was a tender for 49 percent of stock in the three distribution companies, which were regional monopolies, along with their management. The CDEEE, and therefore the Dominican government, kept 100 percent of the stock of the transmission company and the hydroelectric generation plant.

When privatization finally occurred in 1999, oil prices were at their lowest level in decades, and oil products accounted for 88 percent of total electricity generation sources.[42] However, from that year onward, prices increased rapidly. In 2000, energy sector institutions took measures to cushion the effect of fuel price growth on electricity rates by establishing a cap rate for final users, promising to subsidize the losses to distribution companies. By the end of 2000, the government had established a subsidy for fuels used in electricity generation. The cost of these subsidies continued to increase, generating strong fiscal pressure on the government and financial stress on companies participating in the electricity market, which typically had to wait long periods for the government to actually pay for the subsidized amounts.

Distribution was always the most critical part of the sector because this is where most of the losses occurred. These included technical losses, due to the poor state of the existing network, as well as nontechnical losses from electricity that was delivered but not paid for.[43] Together, these losses reached nearly 40 percent of total energy purchased by the distribution companies.

As in other developing countries, the main problem in the commercialization of electricity was in densely populated urban areas on the periphery of major cities. These areas are characterized by high poverty rates and precarious housing and public service infrastructure, including low investment in electricity distribution networks. These factors, combined with a large number of illegal connections, led to large financial losses.

These areas were a major challenge for the distribution companies for two reasons: First, because users have relatively low levels of consumption, collection efforts render low returns, particularly since significant investment is needed to rehabilitate or expand distribution networks to regularize thousands of users and convert them into clients. Second, there is strong resistance to payment in these areas because the service is so precarious. Indeed, these are areas where widespread blackouts are commonplace and electricity is available only a few hours a day. Moreover, the poor state of the networks often led to electrocution accidents, which in turn led to hostile attitudes toward any electric company worker aiming to charge for the use of electricity. These problems made it difficult to provide the security needed for electric workers and for meters.

The Blackout Reduction Program

To temporarily address these problems, the government created the Blackout Reduction Program (PRA) in November 2001. Before forcing the distribution companies to face the challenge of charging for electricity in these areas, the government decided to support the newly established private management by identifying a set of neighborhoods across the country that clearly had collection problems. In these neighborhoods, the government would finance 75 percent of electricity consumption, and the distribution companies would collect the remaining 25 percent. In effect, this amounted to a geographically targeted subsidy.

To implement the PRA, a total of 368 neighborhoods in urban areas of the largest cities were identified.[44] To make the subsidy effective, the distribution companies separated the circuits of these preidentified areas and installed meters for electricity provided to each neighborhood. Based on the value of energy provided to each of these neighborhoods, the state committed to pay 75 percent of this value to the distribution companies. To target the subsidy to households, distribution companies estimated the consumption of businesses in PRA neighborhoods and began charging them a fixed estimated amount.[45]

Despite these efforts, the PRA subsidies generated a set of incentives that ultimately led to higher losses for the distribution companies and public finances (Actis 2014; Díaz 2013):

- The distribution companies had incentives to provide electricity to PRA circuits given that they had a guaranteed 75 percent payment without any billing costs. This also served as an incentive to increase the number of PRA neighborhoods.
- Users had incentives to move to PRA areas, particularly small businesses that could tap the electricity of their noncommercial neighbors.
- Users in PRA neighborhoods had incentives to increase their electricity use because they faced no penalties for overconsumption.

Simultaneously, the government promoted joint efforts with community organizations to improve collections through public awareness campaigns about the need to ensure the financial sustainability of the service. It also aimed to improve service delivery by both reducing blackouts and providing greater certainty in the timing of these blackouts.

In 2003, when the financial crisis hit, the PRA was already in effect. The strong devaluation of the Dominican peso that followed hit households hard, leading to a large increase in poverty, as described earlier. In the absence of a safety net, the government introduced several measures to combat the economic crisis, including two that had a direct impact on the electricity sector: first, a new electricity tariff regime under which distribution companies could no longer adjust tariffs to recover increases in energy prices; and second, a system of subsidies to compensate distributors for the difference between what they charged their customers and what they were legally entitled to receive (Harper and Fernández 2010).

Therefore, despite the incentives for distribution companies to provide electricity to PRA neighborhoods, the amount of energy directed to those neighborhoods did not significantly increase: between 2004 and 2009, it averaged about 1.1 megawatt-hours per year, or about 10.9 percent of total energy provided nationwide (table 2.2).

However, these statistics may simply reflect that increased demand in PRA areas was not matched by higher supply but rather by greater rationing and more blackouts. Moreover, energy losses in PRA neighborhoods during this period were close to 90 percent (table 2.2). Average collections paid for only 9.2 percent of energy delivered, much lower than the targeted 25 percent. These were technical losses due to both poor wiring and nontechnical losses related to very few meters.[46] Between 2004 and 2009, the government ended up repurchasing the

Table 2.2 Electricity Supply and Losses in PRA Neighborhoods, Dominican Republic, 2004–09

	Energy to PRA neighborhoods			*Losses in PRA neighborhoods*		
Year	*MWh*	*Share of total energy nationwide (%)*	*Share of paid energy delivered to PRA neighborhoods (%)*	*Share of unpaid energy delivered to PRA neighborhoods (%)*	*Share of total sector losses from PRA neighborhoods (%)*	*PRA subsidies (US$, millions)*
2004	960,040	11.3	7.6	92.4	25.2	—
2005	1,008,691	10.5	7.2	92.8	21.2	95.51
2006	1,168,341	11.1	7.4	92.6	21.8	145.10
2007	1,237,362	11.2	10.3	89.7	23.1	158.17
2008	1,251,747	11.1	10.8	89.2	24.9	153.68
2009	1,157,991	10.4	11.7	88.3	25.5	163.09
Total	n.a.	10.9	9.2	90.8	23.6	715.55

Sources: Data from the Dominican Corporation of State Electrical Companies (CDEEE) and Central Bank of Dominican Republic.
Note: PRA = Blackout Reduction Program, which subsidized electricity provision to selected lower-income, urban neighborhoods. n.a. = not applicable. — = not available. MWh = megawatt-hours. "Losses" refers to technical losses (electricity entering the network that does not reach end users because of transmission or distribution system issues) as well as nontechnical losses (electricity delivered but not billed or paid for).

three distribution companies because of their poor financial condition.[47] However, it is important to note that losses in PRA neighborhoods only made up about 24 percent of the losses of the sector (table 2.2), pointing to the fact that most of the problem did not result from nonpayment by poor households but rather from delivery of electricity that was never charged for or never paid for by regular clients.

Other Electricity Subsidies

In addition to the PRA, as of the end of 2008, the electricity sector received various other subsidies:

- *Direct subsidies to distributors to cover financial losses.* The government's objective with this subsidy was to maintain a socially acceptable level of electricity provision. The losses of the distribution companies were due to
  - The precarious state of the distribution network (technical losses);
  - The cost of energy provided but not billed or paid for, because of illegal connections, absence of meters, or fixed billing based on underestimated consumption;[48]
  - The cost of energy provided but not billed or paid for by public institutions that the government's executive branch designated as untouchable (*no-cortables*), including public schools, hospitals, and other public facilities;
  - The differences between (a) the cost of electricity purchases from the power purchase agreements (PPAs) still held by the Dominican Corporation of State Electrical Companies (CDEEE) (San Felipe and San Pedro de Macorís Electricity Company); and (b) the price at which CDEEE sells this electricity to the EDEs; and
  - Exceptionally high staffing and operating expenditures by regional standards.
- *A tariff structure that did not make up for the cost of provision.* Although the tariff structure is supposed to be revenue-neutral for the distributors, in practice it was not, because the consumption blocks above 700 kilowatt-hours per month could not completely cross-subsidize those below that level of consumption.
- *Rural subsidies.* Distribution networks were extended or isolated systems created to facilitate electricity access for the rural poor.

By 2008, when international oil prices spiked, this system had generated an unsustainable situation where the generation and distribution bill continued to grow and the government could not pay for the difference, which led to increased interruption of services and widespread public protests. In this context of fiscal constraints, social discontent, increased poverty, and private sector dissatisfaction with the government, subsidy reform gained momentum.

Subsidies in PRA neighborhoods averaged about US$155 million per year between 2005 and 2010, even when oil prices increased in 2008 (figure 2.11). As a whole, transfers from the public sector budget to the electricity sector have exceeded 1 percent of the Dominican GDP every year since 2005; in 2008,

Figure 2.11 Total Electricity Subsidies Relative to PRA Subsidy, the Dominican Republic, 2005–10

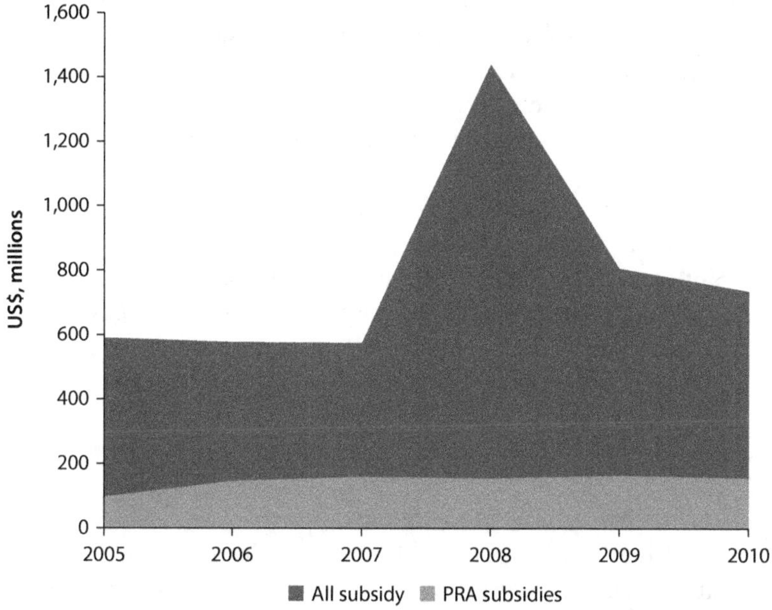

Sources: ADESS 2016; Vagliasindi 2012.
Note: PRA = Blackout Reduction Program, which subsidized electricity provision to selected lower-income, urban neighborhoods.

the spike in world oil prices raised this figure to 2 percent of GDP (as noted earlier; see figure 2.10). It is difficult to identify which of the subsidies listed above is the most important, since, in practice, the government doesn't issue the transfers separately but as a lump sum to CDEEE, which then allocates the funds to the EDEs.

Distributional Impact of Subsidies under the PRA

According to the 2007 ENIGH, when the PRA was in effect, 83 percent of total electricity subsidies were directed at nonpoor households (Actis 2014). Among those households with meters, 94 percent of the benefits were delivered to nonpoor households. Among the households with fixed rates (without meters), the nonpoor absorbed 91 percent of the subsidy. Finally, among the households with neither meters nor fixed tariffs, 77 percent of subsidies went to the nonpoor. That the poor were not the largest beneficiaries of subsidies should come as no surprise given the following (Actis 2014; Díaz 2013):

- The generalized subsidy given to distribution companies to cover their losses benefited the largest consumers the most: the richest 10 percent of the population captured 45 percent of this subsidy.

- The subsidy for households with consumption of less than 700 kilowatt-hours also benefited nonpoor households. In particular, almost no poor households consumed more than 300 kilowatt-hours. Moreover, 44 percent of the beneficiaries of this cross-subsidy were in the seventh, eighth, and ninth deciles of the income distribution. The ninth decile received 27 percent of the benefits, while the poorest decile received only 14.3 percent.
- Most households with fixed rates and those without a meter were nonpoor.

Despite the overall failure of the PRA program to reduce costs, ensure the viability of the distribution companies, and improve service delivery, it was the first attempt to instill a culture of payment in the electricity sector. Moreover, anecdotal evidence indicates that the joint initiatives by the government, the distribution companies, and community organizations led to some positive results in some neighborhoods, particularly in neighborhoods with high social capital where the efforts were perceived to be aiming to address multiple community issues.[49]

The Reform Process: From PRA to Bonoluz

In 2008, the large increase in fuel prices caused electricity subsidies to rise to 2.7 percent of GDP, which was fiscally unsustainable. As a result, in May 2009, the government ordered the targeting of the PRA, further restricting the subsidy to the poor.[50] In August 2009, at the government's request, the Inter-American Development Bank and the World Bank prepared an action plan to support comprehensive sector reform (IDB 2009; World Bank 2009). The plan served as a basis for the government's own plan, presented in December 2009.[51] The plan proposed the adoption of corrective measures in seven main areas (rates, subsidies, losses, management, trust funds, institutional framework, and investments) to be addressed simultaneously and comprehensively. For their part, the international financial organizations supported implementation of the reforms through their own budgetary resources (IDB 2013).

The electricity sector reforms had the following main objectives:

- Provide reliable service to all clients
- Eliminate untargeted subsidies
- Diversify generation away from a high dependence on fossil fuels
- Achieve a long-term viable energy sector

The reforms increased consumer tariffs (from their already high levels), reformed the tariff mechanism, and increased income-based targeted subsidies to poor clients under a new program (Bonoluz), which replaced the old geographically targeted (and poorly implemented) PRA program. Overall, the reforms aimed to generate the correct incentives for households to rationally consume energy, for distribution companies to comply with their function as the commercial managers of the system, and for the "users" of the system to formalize their contractual situations with the distribution companies.

Although the PRA subsidy was only a fraction of the total electricity subsidy, the government focused on its reform because (a) it was not benefiting the poor and most vulnerable groups, and (b) the savings that reform could generate would help to reduce the sector's overall fiscal burden.

Notably, a PRA-related corruption scandal in mid-2009 accelerated the reform effort. The media reported that the executive vice president of the CDEEE had employed a large number of his family members. In addition, the former manager of the PRA, Marcos Lara, and two of his deputies were dismissed and indicted for embezzlement of funds (Benzán 2012; *Diario Libre* 2009; Soto and López 2009). This scandal offered a political window of opportunity: the conviction of the CDEEE head triggered the reform process as the government sought to distance itself from the scandal, leading to a change in the CDEEE leadership and a new approach. A new decree eliminated the PRA, and the Social Cabinet was ordered to design a targeted cash transfer program, Bonoluz, to compensate poor households for the removal of PRA subsidies.

As in the case of Bonogas, Bonoluz used the SIUBEN to identify poor households residing in PRA neighborhoods. By the end of 2009, close to 200,000 households in PRA neighborhoods were identified as poor. In addition, the SIUBEN identified another 600,000 poor households outside of PRA neighborhoods. Bonoluz is a targeted cash transfer to cover consumption of the first 100 kilowatt-hours per month, while the client would need to pay for any consumption above that amount. The program used the Solidaridad card already being used for Bonogas and set the same eligibility criterion as for Bonogas.

The new transfer constitutes an improvement over the PRA, because it ensured a more targeted use of public resources. In tandem with the Bonoluz reforms, the government raised the general electricity tariff by 12 percent and changed the structure of the tariff system so that households consuming more than 300 kilowatt-hours per month were no longer cross-subsidized, down from the original threshold of 700 kilowatt-hours per month (Vagliasindi 2012).

Implementation of Bonoluz

The transition from the PRA program to Bonoluz was implemented in two phases. First, all customers in PRA areas had to become regular customers, which would require installing meters and improving the network. Second, Bonoluz was implemented, benefiting only qualifying households in PRA neighborhoods. Given the public hostility to any intervention from the distribution companies, achieving these objectives required a coordinated effort among several government institutions (CDEEE, the Social Cabinet's technical coordination unit, ADESS, the superintendent of electricity, the superintendent of police, and the Ministry of Finance) consisting of several steps (GCPS 2010):

1. *A community awareness campaign.* The government needed to communicate what it intended to do, describe what was planned, and improve service. A cadre of social workers to be deployed at the community level was trained to ensure that the same message was being consistently delivered.

2. *Rehabilitation of electrical lines.* This effort included ensuring the availability of electricity on public streets and main roads, and prevention of electrical accidents through small repair and maintenance work.
3. *Promotion of electricity conservation.* The distribution companies often held neighborhood meetings, sports events, contests, and prizes promoting electricity conservation.
4. *Introduction of Bonoluz.* The government identified eligible households in PRA areas to receive the Bonoluz cash transfer.

In summary, the government attempted to ensure that social outreach and better service delivery preceded any collection attempts, the introduction of meters, or other changes. For areas where new meters were not possible, there was a new survey of household appliances to estimate and assign a fixed tariff. For some pilot areas, prepaid meters were introduced, and the distribution companies began to guarantee electricity service 24 hours a day, seven days a week, wherever collection rates exceeded 85 percent.

The clearest result of the reform effort was the increase in the number of registered clients for the distribution companies. Once the Bonoluz program began, the total number of registered electricity users increased from 1.4 million in December 2009 to more than 2.2 million in 2012 (figure 2.12).

Figure 2.12 Numbers of Registered EDE Clients and Bonoluz Beneficiaries, the Dominican Republic, 2009–14

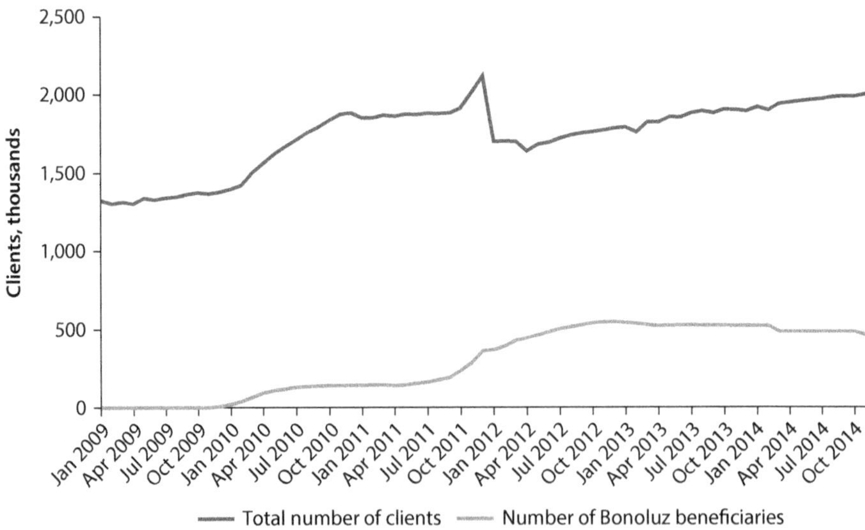

Source: CDEEE, various years.
Note: EDE = electricity distribution company. The peak shown in the total number of EDE clients in November–December 2011 resulted from a registration error, which was corrected in January 2012. Bonoluz is an income-based cash transfer program targeted to poor households that covers consumption of the first 100 kilowatt-hours per month. Bonoluz replaced the geographically targeted Blackout Reduction Program (PRA) starting in late 2009.

However, there is still room for improvement. Census figures showed that the Dominican Republic had 2.9 million households in 2012, implying that more than 600,000 households were not registered clients. Even assuming that the number of households without service increased from the 160,000 identified in 2007, this still leaves room for improvement in identifying households that consume electricity but are not registered clients.

Moreover, the difficulty in charging for electricity consumption is still very much a problem to the extent that many households are not metered. Many informants noted that the PRA seems to continue invisibly.[52] Given the transaction costs in disconnecting and reconnecting clients in these neighborhoods, clients are not metered, do not pay for electricity, and are not disconnected from the service.

Fiscal Impact

The cost of the PRA subsidy was estimated at around US$150 million (or 0.3 percent of GDP) in 2008 (noted earlier in figures 2.10 and 2.11). In contrast, the cost of Bonoluz in 2013 was about US$55 million (or 0.08 percent of GDP), according to ADESS (2016). Additional fiscal savings came from eliminating the PRA program structure (including 800 staff), as the administration of Bonoluz has been consolidated within ADESS.

The transition from PRA to Bonoluz has helped to achieve some fiscal savings, since Bonoluz expenditures are a fraction of total energy subsidies relative to the PRA program (figure 2.13, panel a). However, these savings are small relative to the size of central government transfers to the electricity sector, which continue to be a heavy fiscal burden.[53] In turn, electricity sector transfers are about a third of overall current transfers (figure 2.13, panel b).

Moreover, fuel price increases in 2010–11 were not matched by comparable increases in tariffs, so that any savings from the dismantling of the PRA was outweighed by the increase in generalized subsidies to the distribution companies to cover their continued losses (figure 2.14).

Distributional Impact

The 2004 and 2007 ENIGH surveys have information on electricity expenditures and quantity purchased by households in the month before the survey. Combining this information with the tariff structure, Díaz (2013) calculates the incidence of the cross-subsidy, the generalized subsidy, and the PRA program before Bonoluz implementation.

Before Bonoluz, the generalized subsidies (to the distribution companies to cover losses) and the cross-subsidies (to all households consuming less than 700 kilowatt-hours per month) were not progressive in absolute terms. The amount of the generalized subsidy benefiting the richest 20 percent of the population was nearly three times the amount benefiting the poorest 20 percent (figure 2.15, panel b).

In relative terms, however, the distribution of electricity subsidies was progressive. As Díaz (2013) argues, all electricity subsidies made up a higher share of the

Figure 2.13 Electricity Sector Subsidies and Other Government Transfers, the Dominican Republic

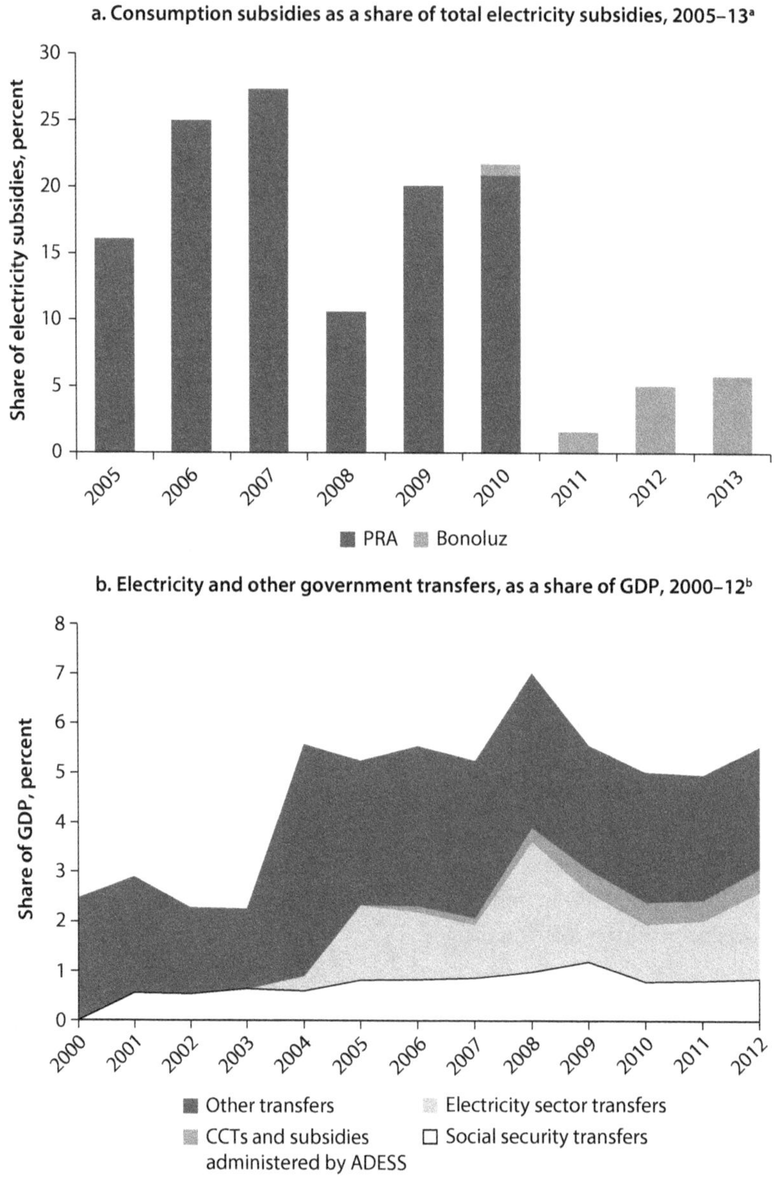

Sources: World Bank estimates based on data from the Integrated Financial Management Information System (SIGEF) and Central Bank of Dominican Republic.

a. PRA = Blackout Reduction Program, which subsidized electricity provision to selected lower-income, urban neighborhoods from 2001 to 2010. Bonoluz is an income-based cash transfer program targeted to poor households that covers consumption of the first 100 kilowatt-hours per month. Bonoluz replaced the geographically targeted Blackout Reduction Program starting in late 2009.

b. CCT = conditional cash transfers, including Bonoluz. ADESS = Social Subsidies Administration. "Other transfers" includes general government transfers to state-owned enterprises among others.

Figure 2.14 Electricity Sector Subsidy and Oil Price Trends, the Dominican Republic, 2000–13

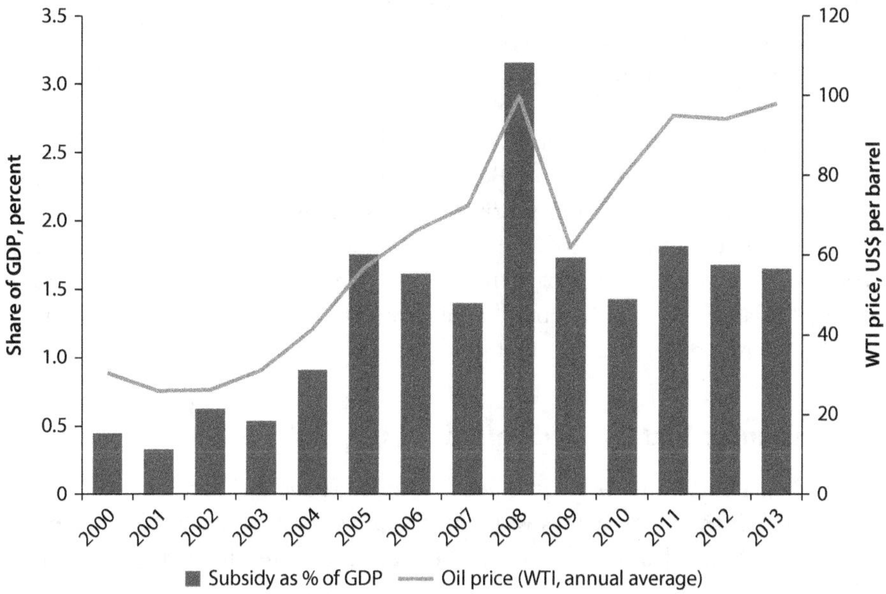

Source: World Bank estimates based on data from the Integrated Financial Management Information System (SIGEF), Dominican Corporation of State Electricity Companies (CDEEE), and Central Bank of Dominican Republic.
Note: WTI = West Texas Intermediate, a grade of crude oil used as a pricing benchmark.

Figure 2.15 Concentration of Income and Electricity Subsidies before Bonoluz, by Income Decile, the Dominican Republic

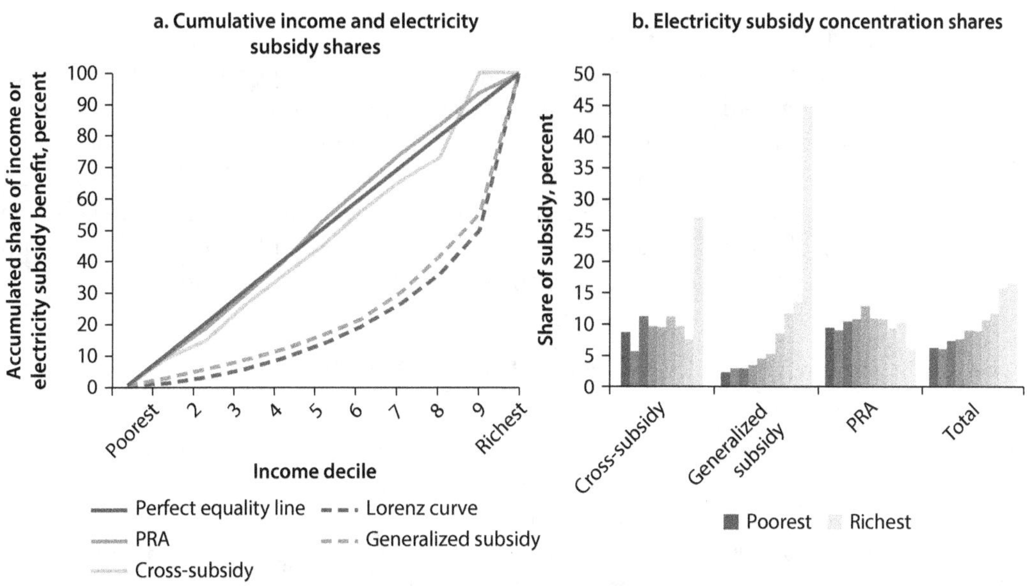

Sources: Díaz 2013, based on 2004 National Household Survey of Income and Expenditure (ENIGH).
Note: PRA = Blackout Reduction Program, which subsidized electricity provision to selected lower-income, urban neighborhoods from 2001 to 2010. Bonoluz is an income-based cash transfer program targeted to poor households that covers consumption of the first 100 kilowatt-hours per month; it replaced the geographically targeted PRA starting in late 2009. The "cross-subsidy" refers to a subsidy for all households consuming less than 700 kilowatt-hours per month. The "generalized subsidy" was given to electricity distribution companies to cover their losses.

income of poorer income groups than of the higher income groups. (This is shown in a concentration curve for subsidies that is above the income Lorenz curve in figure 2.15, panel a.) Moreover, in effect, the richest decile mostly subsidized the ninth decile with the cross-subsidy. In contrast, the PRA program largely benefited the middle class.

Given the lack of data after the Bonoluz reform, the best we could do to simulate the distributional impact of Bonoluz would be to use the 2007 ENIGH. Because the Bonoluz eligibility criterion was essentially the same as for the Bonogas program, it is safe to assume that the distribution of Bonoluz resources was similar to those for Bonogas. If so, as shown earlier in figure 2.8, Bonoluz provides a larger share of income for lower income groups, and a larger share of total spending on Bonoluz is targeted to the poor.

Circumstances That Enabled Reforms

The Bonogas and Bonoluz reforms led to a small reduction in total energy subsidies, although the fiscal savings were limited. As shown earlier in figures 2.6 and 2.10, total savings from Bonogas and Bonoluz amounted to slightly more than 0.3 percent of GDP by 2011, mostly on account of Bonogas. Bonogas replaced an untargeted LPG subsidy with a targeted cash transfer and more-limited diesel subsidies. Bonoluz overall has been less successful, however, largely because it did not tackle the main elements leading to the large losses in the distribution companies—namely the large technical and nontechnical losses outside of PRA areas, including those due to the cost of energy provided but not billed or paid for.

Characterizing the Reforms

Using the framework proposed in chapter 1, one can roughly characterize energy policies according the size of the benefits they offer to concentrated "special interests" versus the benefits that are more broadly diffused to citizens at large. This framework yields a range of possibilities—shown in tables 2.3 and 2.4 along with a mapping of the varied LPG and electricity policies in the Dominican Republic. In what follows, we document the conditions that allowed for the 2008–09 reforms to take place, following the hypotheses established by the adopted framework.

Table 2.3 Characterizing LPG Subsidy Benefits in the Dominican Republic

Beneficiary type and benefit size	*Citizen benefits are large*		*Citizen benefits are small*
Special interest benefits are large	**Case 1** LPG subsidies in the Dominican Republic before reforms	→ / ↓	**Case 2** Bonogas-Choferes in the Dominican Republic after reforms
Special interest benefits are small	**Case 3** Bonogas-Hogares in the Dominican Republic after reforms		**Case 4**

Note: LPG = liquefied petroleum gas. Bonogas-Hogares (Bonogas-Home) is an LPG subsidy targeted to the poorest 40 percent of households. Bonogas-Choferes (Bonogas-Driver) is an LPG subsidy targeted to eligible urban transport drivers. The government replaced a generalized LPG subsidy with the targeted Bonogas subsidies in 2008.

Table 2.4 Characterizing Electricity Subsidy Benefits in the Dominican Republic

Beneficiary type and benefit size	*Citizen benefits are large*	*Citizen benefits are small*
Special interest benefits are large	**Case 1** → Electricity subsidies in the Dominican Republic under PRA	**Case 2** Electricity subsidies in the Dominican Republic after Bonoluz reforms
Special interest benefits are small	**Case 3**	**Case 4**

Note: PRA = Blackout Reduction Program, which subsidized electricity provision to selected lower-income, urban neighborhoods. Bonoluz is an income-based cash transfer program targeted to poor households that covers consumption of the first 100 kilowatt-hours per month. Bonoluz replaced the geographically targeted PRA starting in late 2009.

LPG Reform Analysis

Before the LPG reform process, the Dominican Republic had large generalized benefits but no particular targeting of the LPG subsidy to special interests—a scenario closest to Case 1 (upper-left corner) (table 2.3). However this equilibrium moved closer to Case 3 after the reforms for Bonogas-Hogares, and closer to Case 2 for Bonogas-Choferes. According to the framework, an equilibrium described in Case 3 exists when social solidarity increases (possibly because of the 2003–04 financial crisis) and when "social altruism" is inspired by specific, rather than general, consumption needs of the poor. By the end of the Bonogas-Hogares reform process, the political equilibrium around LPG subsidies was closer to Case 3. However, Bonogas-Choferes mostly benefits transport unions; thus that policy is closer to Case 2.

Electricity Reform Analysis

The electricity subsidy reforms only applied to a small portion of the overall electricity subsidy, which mostly did not affect large interest groups. The Dominican Republic's electricity subsidies came closest to Case 1—with large benefits to special interest groups such as entrepreneurs who moved to the PRA areas, as well as large benefits to the public as a whole in the form of a generalized subsidy (table 2.4). In this equilibrium, neither citizens nor vested interests believe government promises to continue to provide benefits into the future.

To the extent that Bonoluz allowed for some reform, it was to reduce the share of benefits to nonpoor citizens living in PRA areas, which comes closest to Case 2. However, the bulk of energy subsidies persist because large benefits to special interest groups persist, including to large industrialists who can buy directly from the generating companies rather than having to go through the distribution companies. Not surprisingly, this setting continues to prove to be fiscally expensive.

The Role of Economic Crises

The framework described in chapter 1 predicts that reform is more likely at a time of impending crisis because a crisis allows for a political realignment that often includes taking on special interest groups. In particular, subsidy reform is more likely under Case 1 if the following conditions hold:

- The costs of providing benefits rise sharply.
- Governments face general fiscal stringency, *and* energy subsidies are a large fraction of government spending.
- External pressure changes the political equilibrium.

In 2003–04 the Dominican Republic experienced the largest banking crisis in the region (measured as the value of nonperforming assets as a percentage of GDP), plunging 1.4 million people into poverty (Báez et al. 2014). The government reacted by passing comprehensive legislation providing for financial prudence and Central Bank restructuring. However, the effect of the 2003 crisis—and its large impact on poverty—forced the government to visibly improve its social safety net, seen as critical to prevent voters' spontaneous rejection of the incumbent at the ballot box. Following the 2003–04 crisis, economic and social cabinets were formed to design programs that were both economically and socially desirable.

Just five years later, in 2008–09, the country was buffeted by rising oil prices and the international economic crisis. The rate of GDP growth dropped from 9.5 percent in 2007 to 3.5 percent in 2009. The Bonogas and Bonoluz programs were fostered by the unsustainable fiscal costs from the international rise in prices in 2008 and a politically tinged desire to increase transfers to the poor.

Although the idea of targeting LPG subsidies to the poor had been considered in 2004, the rise in energy prices made generalized subsidies truly unsustainable by 2008, when a safety net was already in place that would enable targeting. Moreover, confronted with a common position on the part of the international financial institutions (the Inter-American Development Bank, International Monetary Fund, and World Bank), the government had little option but to adopt some of the proposed reforms and thus give up some political control over the sector in exchange for valuable financial support.

The 2008 increase in energy prices precipitated a significant shift in LPG policy but not in electricity policy. This is consistent with industrial users continuing to have privileged access to prices below cost-recovery levels, the weakness of citizen mobilization, and close links between political leaders and industrialists. (These connections allow industrialists to dispense with citizen-industrialist alliances to cement the credibility of their policy privileges—and enable them to be the last to bear the brunt of fiscal adjustment.)

The Role for Citizen Mobilization

According to the framework, subsidies are likely to persist in Case 1 when citizens generally have limited ability to defend their collective interests. Indeed, recent research on the Dominican Republic shows that only 5.4 percent of the country's population participate in protests—among the lowest percentage in the region (Rufín et al. 2014).[54]

Citizens are instead prone to seeking individual solutions to problematic or missing public goods and services—among them, heavy reliance on domestic generation of electricity,[55] digging of own wells to get running water at home, reporting of car accidents to private companies rather than to police, use of generators and inverters at home to compensate for irregular electricity provision, and use of private services for health and education (Sánchez and Senderowitsch 2012). Even among the poorest 20 percent of the population, almost 13 percent of households send children to private schools (a high percentage given that those families are living below the poverty threshold) (Rufín et al. 2014).

However, worsening circumstances could lead to a serious decline in support for the government such that, independent of the challenger's identity, the incumbent could lose. Under this scenario, reforms are more likely to take place if citizens develop greater capacity to mobilize in their own collective interests.

By the late 2000s, the political situation in the Dominican Republic reflected such worsening circumstances:

- Support for the government declined as the multiple financial crises in the mid-to-late 2000s exacerbated disillusionment. Only 15 percent of respondents to the 2010 Latinobarómetro survey thought the government was ruling on behalf of the whole population, the lowest percentage in the entire region (World Bank 2014b).[56]
- Citizens had a high perception of corruption and considered the quality of public services to be poor. The 2010 Latinobarómetro survey found that only 28 percent of the population believed that public policies improved living conditions (World Bank 2014b).
- Citizen ratings of government efficiency regarding its ability to promote democratic principles, improve security, reduce poverty, and fight corruption eroded significantly between 2006 and 2012, making the Dominican Republic one of the countries with lowest perceived efficiency in Latin America (Espinal, Morgan, and Seligson 2013).

Under these circumstances, the mid-2009 scandals linked to the management of CDEEE led to street protests, which added to pressure for his removal. Suddenly, the political cost of *not* reforming exceeded the costs of reform. This explains the reform of the PRA program in favor of Bonoluz.

The Role of Stakeholder Involvement

The government took steps to ensure the political viability of the reform efforts. Both the LPG and PRA reforms included a communication strategy that centered on the fiscal costs of these subsidies and the fact that they were not reaching the poorest. The communication outreach was coupled with a concerted effort to include stakeholders at the table and negotiate with them, supported not only by analytical work advocating reform but also by a series of quick surveys and focus groups that helped decision makers decide on the timing and the political viability of the reforms.

In the case of the LPG subsidy reform, risk mitigation efforts included the introduction of Bonogas-Choferes and the introduction of diesel subsidies for the companies transporting goods. In the wake of the 2008 global economic crisis, the government called for a national dialogue, inviting unions, civil society, and political parties to participate. In addition, among the several meetings with stakeholders, the president participated in negotiations with transport leaders. During these consultations, transport unions negotiated diesel subsidies in addition to the Choferes program. With the drivers on board, the (already paying) middle class was less likely to resist the reform.

In the case of the PRA reform, the risk mitigation efforts included the introduction of small-works programs to improve the network as well as a concerted effort to include stakeholders in the reform process.

The Role of Administrative Feasibility and Competence

The framework predicts that the Case 3 equilibrium (large citizen benefits and small special interest benefits)—relevant to LPG subsidies in the Dominican Republic—would be more likely when politicians change their beliefs about the "special" nature of energy and shift redistributive policies to more-efficient transfers. In the case of LPG, subsidies were broadly available but small (amounting to 0.7 percent of GDP in 2004) and not preferentially targeted to political clients. Thus, the critical ingredient, in addition to the crisis, was a growing consensus that untargeted generalized subsidies were disproportionately benefiting richer households. Perhaps more importantly, however, the availability of an effective targeting mechanism allowed the reform to take place.

The establishment of SIUBEN and the existence of a well-functioning Solidaridad program made the implementation of targeted subsidies feasible for the first time. Note that Solidaridad, with its electronic identification and payment system, removed the need to hire many government personnel and therefore did not require a burdensome behavioral or institutional change.

In contrast, given the scale of the problems in the electricity sector, better electricity performance will take more time and will be harder for politicians to take credit for. Moreover, true electricity subsidy reform would require convincing politically important stakeholders who could cripple the incumbent's ability to mobilize votes. In fiscal terms, this is certainly the case: subsidies to the electricity sector far exceed those to the Bonogas and Bonoluz programs.

An Unfinished Agenda

A few key features of the Dominican Republic's subsidy reform programs could improve. Perhaps most notably, there is no way to ensure that the existing clientelistic relationships don't become further entrenched through the receipt of cash transfers or other benefits. For example, national identification cards openly indicate party affiliation, which raises the question of whether households are being targeted for Bonogas-Hogares and Bonoluz exclusion or inclusion based on their political affiliation.

Indeed, some observers see cash transfers as an additional tool in the existing political machinery, even if the Solidaridad program, Bonogas, and Bonoluz have significantly improved targeting of generalized subsidies.[57] Focus groups with community leaders revealed that although the original data collection involved in assembling the registry of Solidaridad beneficiaries was free of political interference, the allocation of the Solidaridad cards has not been completely freed from political interference.[58] In particular, some neighborhood political leaders suggested to beneficiaries that if they did not attend political party meetings or vote in a certain way, they were in danger of losing their Solidaridad cards.[59]

Although the share of Solidaridad beneficiaries belonging to each political party was more or less equal at first, there has been an increase in the share of beneficiaries belonging to the incumbent party (PLD) (Espinal, Morgan, and Seligson 2013). Moreover, some community leaders say that Bonogas and Bonoluz have divided their communities between beneficiaries and nonbeneficiaries and therefore have served to demobilize citizens from demanding better services.[60] In addition, "route managers" of transport unions now determine who drives a particular route and provide key information for the database of drivers from which Bonogas-Choferes beneficiaries are selected.[61]

Conclusions

This chapter has discussed the reforms of two energy subsidies in the Dominican Republic, namely the LPG subsidy reform in 2008 and the electricity subsidy reform in 2009–10. Both reforms aimed to improve the targeting of price subsidies toward needy households while reducing the impact on the fiscal accounts. The study has documented the details of the reform process, including its design, passage, and implementation—and has shown how those policy choices were affected by political economy factors. For this purpose, we followed the framework presented in chapter 1 to enable a coherent description of the political economy of reform.

The reform effort in the Dominican Republic serves as a useful case study for three main reasons:

- It is an oil-importing country and, as such, is extremely vulnerable to international price fluctuations.
- It has relatively low revenues, making the allocation of resources especially important.
- It has a political system characterized by clientelism rather than ideology.

Under these circumstances, subsidy reform has been especially difficult. It has required a combination of circumstances for reform, including impending financial crises, the availability of a targeting mechanism, a window of opportunity created by corruption scandals, and concerted efforts by the administration to communicate and consult with politically powerful stakeholders.

Despite the advances in subsidy policy in the Dominican Republic, there is still a large unfinished agenda. Reforming the energy subsidies has led to a small reduction in total energy subsidies by dismantling an untargeted LPG subsidy and replacing it with a targeted cash transfer and more-limited diesel subsidies.

As for the electricity reform, although some savings have resulted from dismantling the geographically targeted subsidy in favor of a means-tested subsidy, the overall reform has been less successful than the LPG reform because it did not tackle the large losses in the distribution companies due to nonpayment, theft, and waste.

Annex 2A Political Chronology of the Dominican Republic

Table 2A.1 Major Political Events in the Dominican Republic, 1821–2016

Year(s)	*Event(s)*
1821–43	In 1821, the Dominican Republic gains independence from Spain but is soon thereafter invaded by Haitian leader Jean-Pierre Boyer, uniting the island for the next 22 years.
1844	On February 27, 1844 (Dominican Independence Day), Juan Pablo Duarte executes a bloodless coup in Santo Domingo. During the next 16 days all of the eastern towns announce their decision to separate from Haiti.
1844–65	General Pedro Santana Familias and Buenaventura Báez Mendez dominate the political scene. In 1861 Santana agrees to the annexation of the Dominican Republic by Spain. However, on March 3, 1865, the annexation is annulled and Spain withdraws its soldiers following a fight for restoration.
1865–78	Political turmoil dominates this period. An attempt to gain U.S. statehood fails in a U.S. Senate vote.
1879–82	Two dominant parties—the Azules and the Rojos—emerge. For the next three years the Azules control the government.
1882–99	General Ulises Heureaux comes to power. He retains power through fraudulent elections and army control. Heureaux borrows vast sums from U.S. investors at high interest rates. He also replaces the National Bank with the U.S.-owned and operated San Domingo Improvement Company. Heureaux is assassinated in July 1899.
1900–05	Soon after Heureaux's death, the Dominican Republic could not repay its debts. The U.S. government intervenes by taking control of the customs houses in 1905, guaranteeing repayment of all loans.
1905–11	Ramón Cáceres is elected president. He sets up the railway, improves the postal service, installs telegraph lines, rebuilds docks, funds new schools, and constructs highways. He increases export taxes on Dominican sugar to pay for public improvements, which angers plantation owners. Cáceres is assassinated in 1911.
1911–16	Various revolutions follow Cáceres's death. U.S. President Woodrow Wilson, concerned about U.S. national security, threatens to send marines if elections are not held. Juan Isidro Jimenes is elected president but is soon impeached by the Dominican Congress. The United States offers support, and although Jimenes only requests weapons, the U.S. Marines are sent in.
1916–24	The Dominican Republic comes under U.S. control for eight years. In particular, the Americans control the budget. The American troops leave by 1924, because Woodrow Wilson is no longer in power, World War I is over, and the United States is considerably less concerned with the Dominican Republic's strategic importance.
1924–30	President Horacio Vásquez has a progressive government, building roads that create access to the countryside, schools, and irrigation and sanitation services.

table continues next page

Table 2A.1 Major Political Events in the Dominican Republic, 1821–2016 *(continued)*

Year(s)	*Event(s)*
1930–61	Rafael Leónidas Trujillo, chief of the National Police (which later became the National Army), forces Vásquez to resign. Trujillo holds an election in which he is the sole candidate. Trujillo rules the Dominican Republic with an iron fist from 1930 until his assassination in 1961. Trujillo uses his government to amass a personal fortune by establishing monopolies that his family controlled. Trujillo carries out programs of public works and construction. He also presses for industrial progress, and scores of factories are opened. Agricultural production improves and the economy flourishes.
1962–66	President Joaquín Balaguer is in office at the time of Trujillo's assassination. Elections are organized. In 1962 Juan Bosch Gaviño is elected but is toppled in a military coup in 1963. Bosch and a group of supporters who called themselves the Constitutionalists take to the streets and seize the National Palace. To reinstate order, 24,000 U.S. soldiers were ordered to the Dominican Republic until new elections were held in 1966.
1966–78	Balaguer defeats Bosch in national elections. Balaguer purges the military and uses the National Police to curtail nonmilitary opposition. His reelections in 1970 and 1974 are mostly accomplished through intimidation. The economy expands rapidly, benefiting from favorable world prices for sugar. However, by the late 1970s, plunging sugar prices and rising oil costs bring the Dominican economy to a standstill.
1978–86	Silvestre Antonio Guzmán of the Dominican Revolutionary Party (PRD), founded by Bosch, defeats Balaguer in the elections. Public works programs are brought to a halt, and the administration borrows heavily from abroad. Guzmán's popularity diminishes rapidly. Salvador Jorge Blanco is elected in 1982. Soon after comes the debt crisis, and the Dominican Republic enters an agreement with the International Monetary Fund (IMF). Macroeconomic and structural measures are put in place, and slowly the economy picks up and inflation is brought under control.
1986–96	Balaguer is reelected for a fifth term. He runs his government like a dictatorship, intimidating political rivals. He reverses the adjustment program under Blanco, leading to a sharp depreciation of the peso and annual inflation of 60 percent. By 1990, 900,000 Dominicans move to New York, fleeing the economic situation. Balaguer rigs the 1990 and 1994 elections. However, in 1994 the military threatens to intervene, and the United States and other governments pressure the Dominican Republic. Balaguer agrees to cut his last term short and hold elections 18 months later.
1996–2000	Leonel Fernández of the Dominican Liberation Party (PLD), also founded by Bosch, wins the presidency. He presides over strong economic growth, privatization, and structural reform.
2000–04	Hipólito Mejía becomes president. The events of September 11, 2001, and the ensuing slowdown in the world economy take a toll on economic growth. In 2003, failures of three large banks due to fraud and mismanagement lead to a banking crisis.
2004–12	Leonel Fernández is elected in 2004 and 2008, serving two consecutive terms.
2012	Danilo Medina (PLD) wins narrowly with 51.2 percent of votes (versus Hipólito Mejía, who garnered 47 percent) in May. He institutes sweeping fiscal reform, including restructuring the electricity sector and raising the sales tax, food tax, and gasoline prices. Large protests result. He also implements an increase in education spending to 4 percent of GDP and promotes increased rural finance and expands state procurement for small and medium enterprises. His allies amend the constitution to allow him to run again in 2016.
2016	The next executive and legislative elections are scheduled (delayed by two years to sync with the presidential election).

Sources: Jaramillo and Sancak 2007 and World Bank.

Annex 2B Timeline of Recent Energy Subsidy and Related Political Events in the Dominican Republic

Table 2B.1 Energy-Related Events and Subsidy Reform Efforts in the Dominican Republic, 1990s–2016

Year	*Event*
Early to mid-1990s	The electricity sector, previously solely in the hands of the state-owned, vertically integrated Dominican Electricity Corporation (CDE), addresses capacity shortages through power purchasing agreements with independent power producers that signed contracts to supply the CDE as the single buyer of energy.
1994	The Secretary of State for Industry and Commerce (SEIC) fixes the price of liquefied petroleum gas (LPG).
1994	The presidential election of Joaquín Balaguer is widely considered fraudulent, criticized internationally and protested at home.
1996	Joaquín Balaguer is finally dethroned after three decades of on-and-off presidency. Leonel Fernández of the Dominican Liberation Party (PLD) takes his place, with the support of urban, middle-class groups.
1997	The Secretary of State for Industry and Commerce (SEIC) for the first time distinguishes between the price of LPG for domestic use (fixed at RD$6 per gallon) and for industrial, commercial, or vehicular use (fixed at RD$10 per gallon).
1997	A new, legitimate Supreme Court is named by means of an open process.
1999	The industrial, commercial, and vehicular use price of LPG rises to RD$13 per gallon.
1999	The government auctions 50 percent of shares in newly formed power generation and distribution entities to private investors. Unfortunately, in the absence of well-defined law, agents' activities are regulated by contracts and executive decrees lacking legal weight. The privatization fails to attract sufficient investment.
2000	Hipólito Mejía of the populist Dominican Revolutionary Party (PRD) is elected president in May and begins his rule in August.
Late Aug. 2000	LPG prices are equalized, without respect to use, to RD$13 per gallon. Consumers are to receive the LPG subsidy by submitting a coupon at specific packing plants. One coupon would be valid for a gallon of LPG. Each week, the plants would present a bill with the total number of coupons it collected to the Targeting Unit.
Nov. 2000	Congress passes a law stating: "The Executive Power will provide a direct subsidy to families for the purchase of LPG for domestic use in order to protect the budget of Dominican households. This subsidy *will never be less than the present*" and "LPG for domestic, industrial, and commercial use will have the same maximum price for purchase in the plant to the consumer."
2001	The LPG subsidy program is transferred to the Social Cabinet's jurisdiction.
2001	The Blackout Reduction Program (PRA) is passed, targeting electricity subsidies on a geographical basis. Businesses move to areas covered by the program. Regulatory reform of the electricity sector is also passed, but institutional weaknesses and legal inconsistencies remain.
2003	A presidential decree fixes the price of LPG for all users to RD$25 per gallon.
2003	The peso devaluates by more than 100 percent. The market price of LPG rises to more than RD$50 per gallon. Fuel prices further rise as a result of the Iraq war. The government does not adjust the electricity tariff for residential customers' first blocks (up to 700 kilowatt-hours) and creates a stabilization fund to cover the difference.
Late 2003	Violent protests break out against rising prices and power cuts.

table continues next page

Table 2B.1 Energy-Related Events and Subsidy Reform Efforts in the Dominican Republic, 1990s–2016 *(continued)*

Year	*Event*
2004	Leonel Fernández is elected president for a second time in May and begins mandate in August.
Late Aug. 2004	LPG subsidy reform is passed. The subsidy becomes targeted to low-income households and is eliminated for industrial, hotel, and restaurant use as well as any consumption over 100 pounds. Instead of fixing the price, the reimbursement becomes fixed. Starting in June 2005, RD$17.35 was compensated per gallon. Prices of subsidized and unsubsidized LPG would be published regularly. An exclusive targeting mechanism for low-income households was to be in place by 2005, but in practice this does not occur until 2008.
2005	The Solidaridad conditional cash transfer (CCT) program is launched.
2007	The Dominican Republic enters a free trade agreement with the United States and Central American nations.
2008	Incumbent Leonel Fernández is reelected.
Sept. 2008	Bonogas, a program for poor households and cab drivers, replaces the previous subsidy system. For households in extreme poverty, moderate poverty, or the lower-middle class: based on an average consumption of six gallons per month, at the market rate of RD$38 per gallon at the time, the monthly consumption subsidy is RD$228 per household. For drivers: based on an average consumption of six gallons per day, the monthly subsidy amounts to RD$3,420.
Oct. 2008	The SEIC establishes a single price for LPG.
2009	The global economic crisis results in another fiscal crisis, but the World Bank, International Monetary Fund, and Inter-American Development Bank help the country to ride it out. Electricity tariffs are increased by 6.4 percent.
May 2010	After the most recent legislative election, the governing party (PLD) retains power.
2010	Electricity subsidy reform is passed. Electricity tariffs are increased by 12 percent, and the consumption ceiling below which electricity is subsidized falls from 700 kilowatt-hours per month to 300 kilowatt-hours per month. The PRA is dismantled and replaced by the means-test-based Bonoluz program, under which the poorest consumers can claim a subsidy for the first 100 kilowatt-hours of consumption.
May 2012	In the most recent presidential election, Danilo Medina (PLD) wins narrowly with 51.2 percent of the votes (Hipólito Mejia garnering 47 percent); he begins rule in August.
2012	The fiscal deficit climbs from 2.6 percent of GDP in 2011 to 6.8 percent in 2012.
Nov. 2012	Sweeping fiscal reform is passed, including restructuring of the electricity sector and increases in sales tax, food tax, and gasoline prices. Large protests result.
2016	The next executive and legislative election is scheduled (delayed by two years to sync with the presidential election).

Note: White rows designate political events. Rows with darker background colors designate events relevant to energy subsidies.

Notes

1. The country's tax revenues averaged 13.8 percent of gross domestic product (GDP) between 2000 and 2014, well below the regional average of 20.5 percent. Tax revenue come from the "Fiscal Sector" database of the Central Bank of Dominican Republic, http://www.bancentral.gov.do/estadisticas_economicas/fiscal/. GDP data come from OECD (2015).

2. Pursuant to the Law of Reform of Public Companies (No.141-97).
3. Some of this debt reduction was due to debt restructuring (GODR 2004).
4. The Bonogas program included Bonogas-Hogares (Bonogas-Home) for poor households and Bonogas-Choferes (Bonogas-Driver) for collective transportation.
5. Data on GDP and income growth from the World Development Indicators Database, http://data.worldbank.org/data-catalog/world-development-indicators.
6. The poverty headcount data were calculated according to the government's official poverty measurement methodology, which resulted from the work of a technical poverty committee created by the government and comprising several national and international institutions. "Extreme poverty" refers to per capita incomes that are insufficient to purchase the minimum caloric requirement for adequate nutrition. "Moderate poverty" refers to per capita incomes that are insufficient to purchase a basic basket of food and nonfood goods and services. For further detail, see Báez et al. (2014).
7. Regional poverty headcount data, based on a "moderate poverty" line of US$4 per person per day (2005 PPP), are from the Socio-Economic Database for Latin America and the Caribbean (SEDLAC), http://sedlac.econo.unlp.edu.ar/eng/.
8. Growth incidence curves plot the growth rate between two points in time of the welfare measure (income or consumption) for each percentile of the baseline distribution (for instance, using household surveys), thus examining how the gains of economic growth—or the losses of economic recessions—are distributed across the population.
9. Tax revenue come from the "Fiscal Sector" database of the Central Bank of Dominican Republic, http://www.bancentral.gov.do/estadisticas_economicas/fiscal/. GDP data come from OECD (2015).
10. Data from the World Development Indicators Database.
11. The recent split of the PRD into two parties— namely the Majority Revolutionary Party (PRM) and the Dominican Revolutionary Party (PRD)—has created a new landscape.
12. Interviews with World Bank staff knowledgeable about the reforms. All interviews were conducted in confidentiality, and the names of interviewees are withheld by mutual agreement.
13. Energy data come from the Inter-American Development Bank's Energy Database, http://www.iadb.org/en/topics/energy/energy-database/energy-database,19144.html.
14. "Electricity Generation and Losses by Source," Inter-American Development Bank (IDB) Energy Database, http://www.iadb.org/en/topics/energy/energy-database/energy-database,19144.html?view=v15.
15. Data from the World Development Indicators Database.
16. Secretary of State for Industry and Commerce (SEIC) Resolution Nos. 3897 and 309-99.
17. Law 112-00 of January 2000.
18. Secretary of State for Industry and Commerce (SEIC) Resolution No. 141-00.
19. The coupon distribution program was to function as follows: Consumers could submit a coupon (each valid for a gallon of LPG) at specific packing plants. The plants would present a weekly bill, with the total number of coupons it collected, to the Targeting Unit.
20. Presidential Decree No. 537-01.

21. Presidential Decree No. 249-03.
22. Presidential Decree No. 1068-04.
23. The Vice President of the Republic is officially the coordinator of the Social Cabinet.
24. *Solidaridad* is a conditional cash transfer (CCT) program that provides eligible families with about US$75 every three months if they comply with certain conditions, including the school enrollment and attendance of all household children and regular health checkups for children under the age of five years ("Progresando con Solidaridad" website, Government of the Dominican Republic, http://www.solidaridad.gov.do).
25. SIUBEN was modeled after Colombia's SISBEN (Social Program Beneficiary Identification System).
26. The geographical areas were selected according to the National Poverty Map, which was developed in 2004 with World Bank assistance on the basis of the 2002 Census and the 2002 Demographic and Health Survey (Gámez, Cheston, and Coudouel 2011).
27. For more information, see the ADESS website: http://www.adess.go.dr.
28. These included the Social Pastoral of the Catholic Church, the Social Service of Dominican Churches, and the Pontifical Catholic University.
29. Authors' interview with Ramón González Paulino (current administrator), Ángel Melo Feliz, Matilde Chaves, Eddy Gomera García, Carlos Ricardo, and María Lugo-Silverio of ADESS, February 2014.
30. The objective was to target households in SIUBEN's socioeconomic priority categories P1, P2, and P3 (based on the government's Quality of Life Index, or ICV). P1 corresponded to extreme poverty (ICV less than 37.5), P2 to moderate poverty (ICV between 37.5 and 54.5), and P3 to the lower-middle class (ICV between 54.5 and 61) (Yepes and Subran 2010).
31. Interview with Susana Gámez, former coordinator of the Social Cabinet, February 13, 2014.
32. Many of the *públicos*—the Dominican Republic's informal taxicabs—run on gas, not gasoline.
33. Interviews with Director General of Hydrocarbons Rafael López and Ramón Abreu Beato of the Permit Office of the Ministry of Industry and Commerce, March 2014.
34. The free trade zones received exemptions from taxes levied on natural gas and fuel oil. Because such taxes are not suitable for transfer, the diversion of this benefit was not a concern.
35. Presidential Decree Nos. 183-11, 362-11, 523-11, and 626-11.
36. Presidential Decree No. 265-12.
37. A transfer whose concentration curve lies everywhere above the Lorenz curve is globally progressive in relative terms. A transfer whose concentration curve lies everywhere above the diagonal (that is, the per capita transfer decreases with income) is globally progressive in absolute terms. For a full discussion on defining the progressivity of taxes and transfers, see Duclos and Araar (2006). Figure 2.7, panel a, orders households by their net incomes (incomes after taxes) but before transfers. Similar results were obtained using the Lorenz curve of household per capita consumption, which is akin to measuring disposable income, that is, income after taxes and direct cash transfers. These results are available upon request.

38. For a complete review of the electricity sector, see IDB (2009) and World Bank (2009). Rufín and Zucchini (2010) and Vagliasindi (2012) also provide a great political economy perspective of these reforms.
39. "Electricity Generation and Losses by Source," Inter-American Development Bank's Energy Database, http://www.iadb.org/en/topics/energy/energy-database/energy-database,19144.html?view=v15.
40. The Law of Reform of Public Companies (No. 141-97) allowed the privatization or "capitalization" of state companies in the electricity sector, thus dismantling the vertical integration that had been part of the state-owned electricity company since 1955.
41. The two generation companies are Empresa de Generación Eléctrica Haina (EGE Haina) y Empresa de Generación Eléctrica Itabo (EGE Itabo). The hydroelectric generation company is Empresa de Generación Hidroeléctrica Dominicana (EGEHID). The transmission company is Empresa de Transmisión Eléctrica Dominicana (ETED). The three distribution companies (EDEs, one for each region) are Empresa de Distribución Eléctrica del Este (EdeEste), Empresa de Distribución Eléctrica del Sur (EdeSur), y Empresa de Distribución Eléctrica del Norte (EdeNorte).
42. "Electricity Generation and Losses by Source," Inter-American Development Bank's Energy Database, http://www.iadb.org/en/topics/energy/energy-database/energy-database,19144.html?view=v15.
43. Technical loss of electricity represents the difference between the amount of electricity that enters the network and the amount delivered to end users, reflecting the degree of productivity of transmission and distribution systems (Jiménez, Serebrisky, and Mercado 2014).
44. Díaz (2013) reports that there were 482 PRA neighborhoods by 2008, implying a 30 percent increase in the areas covered by the PRA program between 2002 and 2008. He also argues that 58 percent of the users in PRA neighborhoods corresponded to a single distribution company (EdeEste)—a concentration that may point to the arbitrary nature of PRA neighborhood designations toward the late 2000s since the region served by EdeEste is not necessarily poorer than the others.
45. The authorities estimated energy consumption based on a survey of electric appliances used in each household.
46. Some informants mentioned that the newly privatized distribution companies did not have investment plans to improve the network system, which is a prerequisite for the effective commercialization of electricity (authors' interviews with Ministry of Finance officials, March 2014).
47. The government repurchased EdeNorte and EdeSur in 2004 and EdeEste in 2009.
48. The 2007 ENIGH found 1.1 million irregular connections, representing 47 percent of users in the country. Similarly, 442,000 clients (19.4 percent of all users) either had no meter or paid a fixed amount, and 1.3 million users claimed they paid either irregularly or not at all for electricity (Actis 2014).
49. Authors' interviews with community leaders in the Guachupita neighborhood, March 2014.
50. Presidential Decree No. 108-49.
51. Presidential Decree No. 421-09.
52. Interviews with Magín Díaz and José Luis Actis of the Ministry of Finance and with the Dominican Public Policy Observatory of the Autonomous University of Santo Domingo, February 2014.

53. The central government compensates the electricity sector for, among other things, technical losses, commercial losses, a cross-subsidy implicit in the electricity tariff, and a portion for investment.
54. People living in the north and the south of the country are more likely to participate in protests than those living in Santo Domingo National District (Rufín et al. 2014).
55. People often opt to generate their own electricity even though, in 2007, the monthly cost associated with a power inverter (off-grid diesel electricity generator) was RD$2,362.96 (US$60), far more than the average electricity bill of RD$896.09 (US$24) (Rufín et al. 2014).
56. Latinobarómetro is an annual public opinion survey that involves some 20,000 interviews in 18 Latin American countries, representing over 600 million people. Latinobarómetro Corporation, a nonprofit NGO based in Santiago de Chile, is solely responsible for the production and publication of data (Latinobarómetro website, accessed January 26, 2006, http://www.latinobarometro.org).
57. Interview with Edwin Croes and Fernando Peña of the Dominican Centre for Public Policy (ODPP), Autonomous University of Santo Domingo, February 2014.
58. Interview with Edwin Croes and Fernando Peña of the Dominican Centre for Public Policy (ODPP), Autonomous University of Santo Domingo, February 2014. Also see Báez (2012).
59. Interview with Edwin Croes and Fernando Peña of the Dominican Centre for Public Policy (ODPP), Autonomous University of Santo Domingo, February 2014. For similar reporting, see Peña (2013).
60. Interview with focus group of community leaders led by Barrio Alternativo, February 2014.
61. Interviews with Director General of Hydrocarbons Rafael López and Ramón Abreu Beato of the Permit Office of the Ministry of Industry and Commerce; Cristina Matos and Hector Mojica of the Technical Office for Ground Transportation (OTTT); and Ramón Cabrera of the City of Santiago, March 2014.

References

Actis, José Luis. 2014. "Evaluación de los Subsidios en las Tarifas Eléctricas Residenciales en la República Dominicana" [Assessment of Subsidies in Residential Electricity Tariffs in the Dominican Republic]. Paper, Pontificia Universidad Católica Madre y Maestra, Santiago, Dominican Republic.

ADESS (Social Subsidies Administration). 2009. *Memorias Administradora de Subsidios Sociales (ADESS) 2004–2008*. Santo Domingo: ADESS.

———. 2016. *Subsidios Otorgados por Año y Mes* [*Subsidies Granted by Year and Month*]. Statistical report, Santo Domingo: ADESS.

Ardanaz, Martín, Carolos Scartascini, and Mariano Tommasi. 2010. "Political Institutions, Policymaking, and Economic Policy in Latin America." Working Paper 158, Inter-American Development Bank, Washington, DC.

Báez, Javier E., Luis Felipe López-Calva, Andres Castañeda, and Ali Sharman. 2014. "When Prosperity Is Not Shared: The Weak Links between Growth and Equity in the Dominican Republic." LAC Opportunities for All study, World Bank, Washington, DC.

Báez, Patricia. 2012. "La insolidaridad de la Tarjeta Solidaridad en los campos de Bayaguana" [Lack of Solidarity of the Solidaridad Card in the Fields of Bayaguana].

Video report, *Acento* (Santo Domingo), May 9. https://www.youtube.com/watch?v=aX09ATn4HxM.

Benzán, Ramón Cruz. 2012. "Condenan a 4 años de prisión al ex director del PARA por desfalco de RD$50 millones" [Former PRA Director Sentenced to Four Years in Prison for Embezzling RD$50 Million]. *Listin Diario*, May 15. http://www.listindiario.com/la-republica/2012/5/14/232386/Condenan-a-4-anos-de-prision-al-ex-director-del-PRA-por-desfalco.

CDEEE (Dominican Corporation of State Electricity Companies). Various years. *Report on Electricity Sector Performance*. http://www.cdeee.gob.do/transparencia/estadisticas-institucionales.

Diario Libre. 2009. "Radhamés Segura admite emplea a familiares en la CDEE" [Radhamés Segura Admits Employing Family at CDEEE]. July 1. http://www.diariolibre.com/noticias/radhams-segura-admite-emplea-a-familiares-en-la-cdeee-MKDL205669.

Díaz, Magín. 2013. "Análisis de Políticas Públicas en Rep. Dominicana: Los Casos del Subsidio Generalizado al Gas Licuado de Petróleo y del Subsidio Geográfico a la Electricidad." Fundación Global Democracia y Desarrollo (FUNGLODE), Universidad de Salamanca, Spain.

Duclos, Jean-Yves, and Abdelkrim Araar. 2006. *Poverty and Equity: Measurement, Policy, and Estimation with DAD*. New York: Springer and International Development Research Centre.

Espinal, Rosario, Jana Morgan, and Mitchell A. Seligson. 2013. *Cultura política de la democracia en República Dominicana, 2012: Hacia la igualdad de oportunidades* [*Political Culture of Democracy in the Dominican Republic: Toward Equal Opportunities*]. Country report, Washington, DC: U.S. Agency for International Development (USAID). http://www.vanderbilt.edu/lapop/dr/DR_Country_Report_2012_V3_revised_W.pdf.

Gámez, Susana, Timothy Cheston, and Aline Coudouel. 2011. "The SIUBEN Targeting System." In *Improving the Quality of Public Expenditure in the Dominican Republic*, edited by Ximena Fernandez Ordonez, Khattri Nidhi, Pedro Arizti, John Mario González, and Patricia Rogers, 39–42. Working Paper 71472, Washington, DC: World Bank.

GCPS (Office for Coordination of Social Policy). 2010. *Manual Procesos Operativos Desmonte del PRA e Implantación de BonoLuz*. Operations manual, Santo Domingo: GCPS.

GODR (Government of the Dominican Republic). 2004. "Dominican Republic—Letter of Intent, Supplementary Memorandum of Economic Policies, and Technical Memorandum of Understanding." Letter of Intent of the Government of the Dominican Republic, Santo Domingo, January 23. http://www.imf.org/external/np/loi/2004/dom/01/index.htm.

———. 2005. "Dominican Republic: Letter of Intent, Memorandum of Economic and Financial Policies, and Technical Memorandum of Understanding." Letter of Intent of the Government of the Dominican Republic, Santo Domingo, January 14. http://www.imf.org/external/np/loi/2005/dom/011405.pdf.

———. 2007. "Dominican Republic: Letter of Intent, Memorandum of Economic and Financial Policies, and Technical Memorandum of Understanding." Letter of Intent of the Government of the Dominican Republic, Santo Domingo, January 31. http://www.imf.org/external/np/loi/2007/dom/013107.pdf.

Harper, James, and Andrés Fernández. 2010. *The Dominican Republic's Electricity Industry: A Sector that Generates Attractive Yields*. Research report, BCP Securities LLC, Greenwich, CT.

IDB (Inter-American Development Bank). 2009. "Dominican Republic Gets $500 Million Loan from the IDB." Press release, October 21. http://www.iadb.org/en/news/news-releases/2009-10-21/dominican-republic-gets-500-million-loan-from-the-idb,5802. html.

———. 2013. "Country Program Evaluation: Dominican Republic 2009–2013." Document RE-453-1, Office of Evaluation and Oversight, IDB, Washington, DC.

IMF (International Monetary Fund).1999. *Dominican Republic: Selected Issues*. Country Report 99/117, Washington, DC: IMF.

———. 2010. *Dominican Republic: Staff Report for the 2009 Article IV Consultation and Request for a Stand-By Arrangement; Supplement to the Staff Report and Staff Statement; Public Information Notice and Press Release on the Executive Board Discussion*. Country Report 10/135, Washington, DC: IMF.

———. 2011. *Dominican Republic: Second and Third Reviews Under the Stand-By Arrangement and Request for Waivers of Applicability—Staff Report; Staff Supplement; Informational Annex; Press Release on the Executive Board Discussion*. Country Report 11/71, Washington, DC: IMF.

Jaramillo, L., and C. Sancak. 2007. "Growth in the Dominican Republic and Haiti: Why Has the Grass Been Greener on One Side of Hispaniola?" Working Paper 07/63, International Monetary Fund, Washington, DC.

Jiménez, Raúl Alberto, Tomás Serebrisky, and Jorge Mercado. 2014. "Power Lost: Sizing Electricity Losses in Transmission and Distribution Systems in Latin America and the Caribbean." IDB Monograph 241, Inter-American Development Bank, Washington, DC.

Kitschelt, H. P., and D. M. Kselman. 2011. "Do Institutions Matter For Parties' Electoral Linkage Strategies?" Paper presented at the 2011 Annual Meeting of the American Political Science Association, Seattle, WA, September 1–4.

Manzetti, Luigi, and Carlos Rufín. 2006. "Private Utility Supply in a Hostile Environment: The Experience of Water, Sanitation and Electricity Distribution Utilities in Northern Colombia, the Dominican Republic and Ecuador." Sustainable Development Department Best Practices Series, IFM-142, Inter-American Development Bank, Washington, DC.

MEPyD (Ministry of Economy, Planning and Development, Dominican Republic). 2014. "Actualización de las estimaciones oficiales de pobreza monetaria en la Republica Dominicana" [Updating Official Estimates Monetary Poverty in the Dominican Republic]. Study by the Advisory Unit of Economic and Social Analysis (UAAES), MEPyD, Santo Domingo.

MINERD (Ministry of Education, Dominican Republic). 2014. "Consideraciones sobre el presupuesto 2015" [Considerations on Budget 2015]. Office of Educational Development Planning and Financial Programming, MINERD, Santo Domingo.

Morgan, J., R. Espinal, and M. Seligson. 2010. "Political Culture of Democracy in the Dominican Republic, 2010: Democratic Consolidation in the Americas in Hard Times." Study by the Latin American Public Opinion Project (LAPOP), AmericasBarometer, and Vanderbilt University, Nashville, TN.

Moya Pons, Frank. 1998. *The Dominican Republic: A National History*. Princeton, NJ: Markus Wiener Publishers.

OECD (Organisation for Economic Co-operation and Development). 2015. "Revenue Statistics in Latin America: Dominican Republic (Edition 2015)." Tax Statistics database, OECD, Paris. http://www.oecd-ilibrary.org/taxation/data/oecd-tax-statistics_tax-data-en.

Peña, Gustavo Olivo. 2013. "Margarita hace politiquería con la tarjeta Solidaridad." *Acento* (Santo Domingo), February 14. http://acento.com.do/2013/politica/48020-margarita-hace-politiqueria-con-la-tarjeta-solidaridad-reportaje-de-la-lupa/.

Rufín, Carlos, and Davide Zucchini. 2010. *Political Economy of Policy Reform Study: The Dominican Republic's Electricity Sector.* Consultant's report, Washington, DC: World Bank.

Rufín, C., D. Zucchini, M. E. Sánchez, and R. Senderowitsch. 2014. "The Dominican Republic: Moving from Exit to Voice—Shifting Incentives in the Power Sector." In *Problem-Driven Political Economy Analysis: The World Bank's Experience*, edited by Verena Fritz, Brian Levy, and Rachel Ort, 91–118. Washington, DC: World Bank.

Sánchez, Miguel E., and Roby Senderowitsch. 2012. "The Political Economy of the Middle Class in the Dominican Republic: Individualization of Public Goods, Lack of Institutional Trust, and Weak Collective Action." Policy Research Working Paper 6049, World Bank, Washington, DC.

Soto, Paolah, and Luis López. 2009. "Otro que cae: Radhamés Segura y su huacal en la CDEE." *Ahiequeprende.com*, June 27. http://ahiequeprende.com/2009/06/27/otro-que-cae-radhames-segura-y-su-huacal-en-la-cdee/.

USAID (U.S. Agency for International Development). 1995. *Environmental Assessment for the Dominican Republic Power Sector.* Report for the Dominican Republic National Energy Commission and USAID/ Santo Domingo, Dominican Republic.

Vagliasindi, Maria. 2012. *Implementing Energy Subsidy Reforms: Evidence from Developing Countries.* Directions in Development. Washington, DC: World Bank.

World Bank. 1991. *Dominican Republic: Issues and Options in the Energy Sector.* Report 8234, Washington, DC: World Bank.

———. 2009. "Dominican Republic: World Bank Approves US$300 Million to Support Social Sectors and Public Finance." News Release 2010/144/LAC, November 17.

———. 2014a. "Dominican Republic–Public Expenditures Management and Financial Accountability Review." Unpublished manuscript, World Bank, Washington, DC.

———. 2014b. *Rentas o reformas? La economía política del desarrollo en República Dominicana* [*Patronage or Reform? The Political Economy of Reform in the Dominican Republic*]. Institutional and Governance Review, Report 91312, Washington, DC: World Bank.

Yepes, T., and L. Subran. 2010. "Simulation of the Impact of Conditional Cash Transfer Programs on Health and Education." Poverty Social Impact Analysis, World Bank, Washington, DC.

CHAPTER 3

Ghana: Lessons Learned, New Strategies

Sheila Addo, Morgan Bazilian, and Samuel Oguah

Introduction

Several papers have explored the political economy aspects of Ghana's energy and natural resources sectors, including those of oil and gas (Obeng-Odoom 2015); mining (Nyame and Grant 2014); electricity planning (Abdul-Salam and Phimister 2016); and timber (Hansen and Lund 2011). Nor is there any shortage of literature on the political economy of postcolonial states (Bernstein 2015; Bezemer, Bolt, and Lensink 2014; Fisher Onar, Liu, and Woodward 2014; Power 2009; Yufanyi Movuh 2012).

In contrast, this chapter specifically examines recent aspects of subsidy reform in Ghana through a political economy lens. Its focus is the set of reforms in the petroleum sector since about 2001. Although a rich, ongoing set of issues is being addressed in the power sector, those issues are beyond the scope of this brief analysis.

Despite a series of subsidy reforms in Ghana since 2001, they have not been sustained because of inconsistency in implementation. Reforms have often been suspended after the executive branch intervened in the full pass-through of world prices to domestic prices. Meanwhile, subsidy programs have caused tremendous fiscal strain on the government. Past subsidy reform processes were not sustained for many reasons, among them the lack of an adequate mitigation strategy that could help sustain automatic price increases, lack of stakeholder consultation, poor communication, and lack of clearly defined roles.

Despite the evidence that many types of subsidies cause economic harm, it is often difficult for governments to remove subsidies, especially in developing countries (Kojima 2016). Ghana is no different. Petroleum pricing has repeatedly been on the campaign agenda during election years. The decision to adjust pump prices has often been at the discretion of the executive and in many instances has undermined past reform efforts. There is also genuine concern that reducing subsidies will affect the poor. Although this is true, it is widely known that reforms often benefit the wealthy far more than the poor and there are better options for supporting the poor and vulnerable.

Various governments have attempted different approaches, including a complete removal of subsidies, redirection into other petroleum products and nonpetroleum sectors, and more recently a full liberalization of prices. Results of these reform attempts have been mixed, but to a large extent reforms have proved to be unsustainable.

Over the long term, Ghanaian reform has been incremental, but across any one- or two-year period, governments have either cut or increased subsidies by up to 50 percent or more. A central puzzle in this case study is: what explains the large swings in subsidies? On the one hand, short horizons and susceptibility to populist promises seem to have allowed for sudden big increases in subsidies. On the other hand, weak popular resistance has led to cuts when a crisis forces subsidies back down again.

This study presents a thorough analysis of petroleum subsidy reform strategies in Ghana, with a critical look at their development, objectives, and the political influences and impacts of those reforms from the perspective of government, the general public, and key interest groups.[1] In contrast to other studies, the objective is to document *how* reforms took place, thus enabling other countries pursuing reform to learn from others' experiences. For this purpose, the framework presented in chapter 1 of this volume is followed to enable a coherent description of the political economy of reform. It forms part of a wider effort to learn from experiences with energy subsidy reforms around the world.

The study will focus on the reform efforts in 2001, 2002, 2004–05, and 2011 because they introduced key changes to petroleum pricing policies in attempts to remove subsidies. The subsidies largely benefited citizens (understood as the population at large), and reforms in these periods were triggered by increasingly significant fiscal deficits caused by growing consumption and a weakening of the local currency. This study will also show that the removal of subsidies was often hampered by various governments' inclination to focus on electoral gain because of elections associated with the multiparty political system.

In 2007, Ghana discovered oil in commercial quantities and started full-scale production in 2011. Despite being an oil-producing country, Ghana's total proven and potential oil reserves are relatively small, making the country a net importer of petroleum products.[2] On average, about 5 percent of the annual consumption is exported to the neighboring landlocked countries such as Burkina Faso and Mali. The Tema Oil Refinery (TOR)—the principal refinery in the country—has a capacity of 45,000 barrels per day,[3] but because of operational challenges rarely meets that capacity and contributed just 4 percent of national consumption in 2014.

Petroleum product prices in Ghana are set at import parity based on full cost recovery of investments made along the supply chain. This has been the basis of an adjustment formula introduced in 2001 as part of an effort to deregulate markets for petroleum products. Although that pricing policy has been in place for a long time, it has not been fully implemented because the executive branch of government has repeatedly intervened, in the face of soaring world market prices, to stabilize costs for fear of political backlash from the general public and the political opposition.[4]

The formula also used historical exchange rate quotes from the Bank of Ghana (BoG), implying that, with the depreciation of the local currency (the cedi), some substantial foreign exchange losses to importers would be created. These losses occurred and persisted despite provisions to compensate for foreign exchange losses in the country's petroleum products Price Build Up (PBU) schedule. The differential in product pricing, as well as the foreign exchange loss bills, was put at the doorstep of government, causing either huge budget deficits or (usually unbudgeted) subsidies payable by the government. Arrears in the payment of these subsidies have caused shortages of petroleum products, with important impacts on overall macroeconomic performance.

In July 2015, Ghana started to implement price deregulation with the objective of removing government control from prices and potentially addressing the challenges that price regulation has caused in the industry. Subsequently, in January 2016, some tax reforms were also applied in petroleum product pricing. Implementation strategies of the latest reforms include timing of implementation, improved communication to the public, more active stakeholder engagement, and the use of state-owned enterprises for implementation.

The rest of the report is structured as follows: The next section describes the country context, including Ghana's political, economic, poverty, and equity environment. The subsequent "Reform of Subsidies" section details the petroleum subsidy reforms, including their fiscal and distributional impacts. "Circumstances That Enabled Reforms," using the proposed framework, then analyzes the circumstances and political dynamics that allowed the reforms to take place, including lessons learned and the roles of different stakeholders. The final section summarizes the findings and discusses the prospects for success of the latest reforms. Annex 3A provides a chronology of main political events; annex 3B, a list of Ghana's poverty reduction initiatives; annex 3C, a chronology of subsidy reforms; and annex 3D, the factors making up Ghana's petroleum pricing formula.

Country Political and Economic Context

Political System

Ghana was the first country to gain independence from British Colonial Rule in Sub-Saharan Africa in 1957, and had an estimated population of about 27.4 million at the end of 2015 (UNDESA 2015). The government is established in the framework of a democratic republic, with a president elected by the people as head of state. The constitution establishes Ghana as a unitary republic with sovereignty residing in Ghanaians.

After independence, democratic elections were conducted in 1957, 1969, 1979, 1992, and every four years since then—most recently in 2012, with another general election due in November 2016.[5] Ghana runs a multiparty system with two major political parties: the ruling National Democratic Congress (NDC) and the current opposition, the New Patriotic Party (NPP). Executive authority is established in the Office of the Presidency together with the Council of State, an advisory body to the president. The multiparty system in Ghana has created a competitive political environment that has put a premium on leaders' ability to demonstrate tangible benefits for voters. This environment has contributed to the use of executive intervention in the pass-through pricing mechanisms for petroleum products—intervention that, in turn, has contributed significantly to the failures of past reforms.

Since its return to a multiparty system more than two decades ago, Ghana has made major strides toward consolidating its democratic achievements.[6] The progress in electoral politics since 1992 has been impressive. Elections have been held peacefully and in a generally acceptable manner. This success has been attributed to factors such as innovative constitutional provisions, effective electoral management, consensus among political actors, the crucial role of civil society organizations and the media, and mass participation in elections, with 60–80 percent voter turnout (Frempong 2008).

The country's history and electoral provisions have contributed toward the achievement of an effective democratic political system (Zounmeou 2009). The Parliament of Ghana is vibrant and, despite inherent challenges and the dominance of the two leading political parties, has created the avenue for debate and vigorous legislative activity. Ghana is constantly ranked among the top three countries in Africa for freedom of the press and freedom of speech (Freedom House 2016). The broadcast media are the strongest, with radio being the most far-reaching medium of communication.

The Constitution of Ghana requires every president to present a national development program to Parliament within two years of being in office.[7] Over the years, the coordinated programs for social and economic development have been developed with the full participation of both the private and public sectors, using evidence-based policy making to the extent possible.[8] These programs have also served as a guide for donor support and external interventions. In most cases, successor programs have proceeded from where the predecessor programs left off.

The structure of institutions and political power in Ghana consist of the executive, legislative (Parliament), and judicial branches, as follows (Abdulai 2009):

- *Executive.* Executive power resides in the president, who is the head of state, the commander-in-chief of the armed forces, and the head of government. The president appoints 10–19 ministers to form a cabinet and helps to determine the government's policies.
- *Legislative.* Parliament is the second arm of power, headed by a speaker and made up of elected members from all the constituencies of Ghana. They are the lawmakers and representatives of the people.
- *Judicial.* The judiciary, headed by the chief justice and consisting of superior courts and lower courts, is responsible for upholding the rule of law in the country.

Other groups that heavily influence political decisions in the country, either through advocacy or through aid, include civil society organizations, consumer interest groups, political advocacy groups, nongovernmental organizations, and development partners.

Economic Growth

Ghana is endowed with rich mineral resources and a thriving agricultural sector, which contributed 24 percent of gross domestic product (GDP) in 2014 (GSS 2015). Since independence, successive governments have developed and pursued several programs to accelerate the growth of the Ghanaian economy and raise living standards.

In many ways, Ghana has made tremendous progress toward these goals, as detailed later in the chapter. Still, the economy had major challenges to overcome. Ghana aims to become an upper-middle-income economy by 2020 through the development of its population's knowledge and skills (NDPC 1994). An important requirement for government-driven programs to work is good fiscal health, which is often compromised by high subsidies in the energy sector.

Macroeconomic Development

Ghana has experienced strong macroeconomic growth since 1984, attributable to liberal economic policies as well as substantial receipts of foreign aid and foreign direct investment (Alagidede, Baah-Boateng, and Nketiah-Amponsah 2013). Real GDP growth between 2009 and 2014 peaked at 15 percent in 2011, largely driven by oil revenue in that year. By 2014, however, growth had declined to the level of 2009 (figure 3.1).

Over the same period, the largest contributor to GDP has been the services sector followed by agriculture and industry (MoF 2015). Despite an increase in

Figure 3.1 Real GDP Growth in Ghana, 2009–14

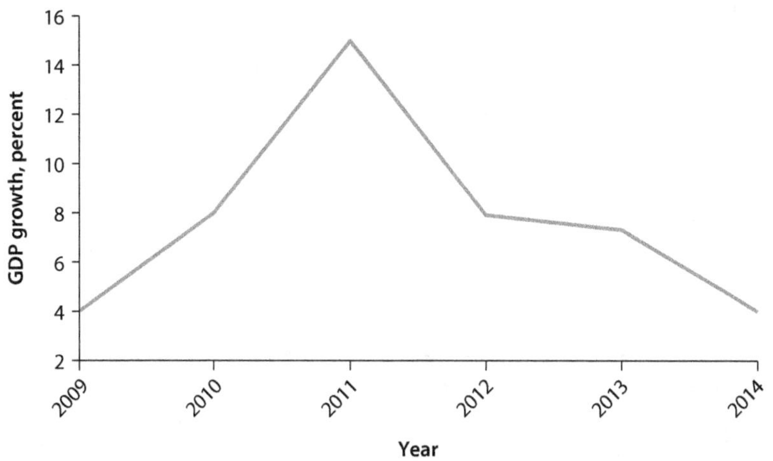

Source: GSS 2015.

Figure 3.2 Fiscal Balance in Ghana, 2009–14

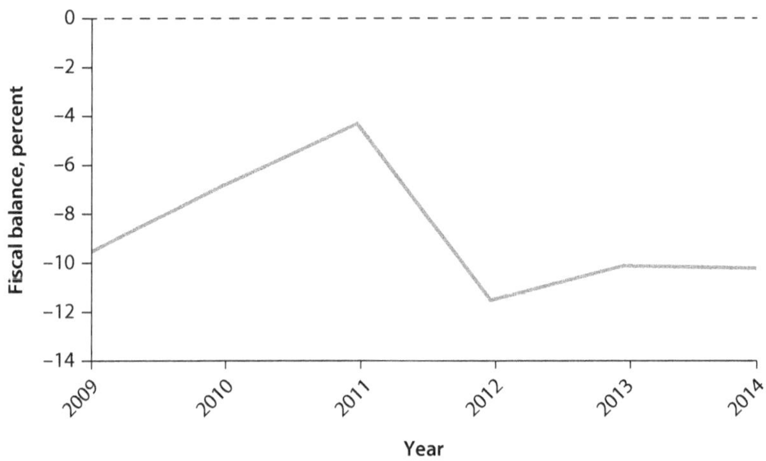

Source: Ministry of Finance 2015 Provisional Fiscal Data, http://www.mofep.gov.gh/fiscal-data.

revenue from oil production, a swelling wage bill and overruns in current spending offset higher revenue, leading to double-digit fiscal deficits in 2012–14 (figure 3.2), putting Ghana's fiscal, external, and debt positions on an unsustainable path (IMF 2015).

Despite the slowdown in Ghana's economic growth, which saw a decline from 4 percent in 2014 to 3.7 percent in 2015, it is expected that the economy will rebound to a growth rate of 5.8 percent in 2016 and 8.7 percent in 2017. This follows implementation of initiatives to resolve the power crisis as well as policies aimed toward consolidation of macroeconomic policy (AfDB, OECD, and UNDP 2016).

Fiscal, Monetary, and Financial Policies

Ghana has relied heavily on external and domestic debt instruments to finance its rising deficits (figure 3.2) (IMF and World Bank 2015). As a result, the country's debt-to-GDP ratio has consistently been on the rise from 2009 to 2015. The highest increase in gross public debt as a percentage of GDP occurred in 2012 (a rise of 10 percentage points in a single year) because of increased expenditure typical of election years in the country. The rapidly rising public debt resulted in significantly higher interest payments, constraining other priority spending.

The external position weakened through mid-2014, given lower external financing, as it became difficult to roll over bonds held by nonresidents and large outstanding letters of credit for oil imports needed to be cleared. This led to large capital outflows, low net international reserves in the third quarter, and a sharp depreciation in the exchange rate. International reserves reached critically low levels alongside a 31 percent year-on-year depreciation of the cedi at the end of 2014 (IMF 2015).

Figure 3.3 Recent Inflation and Currency Depreciation Rates in Ghana

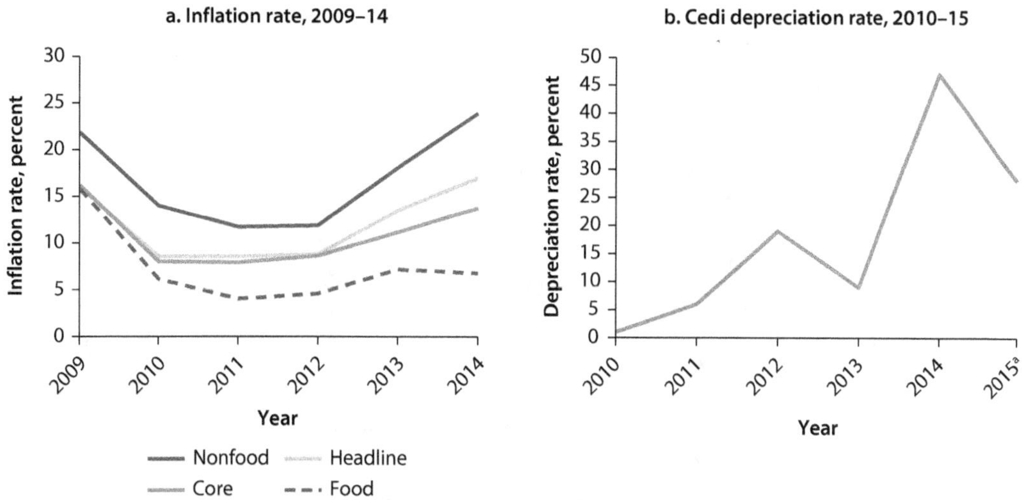

Source: Based on Ghana Statistical Service data, http://www.statsghana.gov.gh/.
Note: "Headline Inflation" is a measure of the total inflation within the economy. "Core inflation" is a measure of inflation excluding transitory or temporary price volatility.

Source: Based on Bank of Ghana data, https://www.bog.gov.gh/index.php.
a. 2015 estimates as of third quarter 2015.

As the large depreciation passed through to domestic prices of imported products, inflation increased substantially above the BoG's target, moving from single digits in 2010–12 to 17 percent in 2014 (figure 3.3, panel a). The resulting increase in nominal interest rates weighed down growth and the real incomes of most households. Recognizing that policies were not bringing the expected results, the government in August 2014 asked for the International Monetary Fund's (IMF) support to help with policy adjustment, restore market confidence, and revive Ghana's transformation agenda (IMF 2015).

Poverty and Inequality Reduction

Poverty

Ghana has seen a significant reduction in headcount poverty rates between 1990 and 2012 (GSS 2014). According to the United Nations Development Programme, the country is the first Sub-Saharan African country to have achieved the United Nations' Millennium Development Goal 1 of halving extreme poverty by 2015.[9]

Overall poverty rates have declined significantly in recent years (from 52.7 percent in 1991 to 21.4 percent in 2012), while extreme poverty declined even more quickly (from 37.6 percent in 1991 to 9.6 percent in 2012), as shown in figure 3.4. Ghana's performance compares well with that of other countries in Sub-Saharan Africa. In 2012, the poverty rate in Ghana was less than half the African average of 43 percent, a substantial improvement over 1991, when it had been only 10 percent lower than the African average (Molini and Paci 2015).[10]

Figure 3.4 Poverty Rates in Ghana, Selected Years

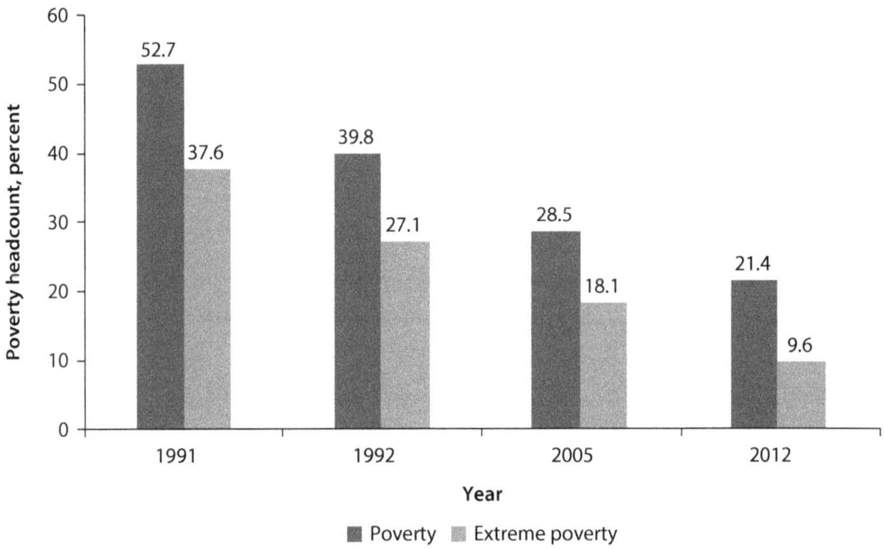

Source: Molini and Paci (2015), based on Ghana Living Standards Survey (GLSS) Rounds 3–6, Ghana Statistical Service (GSS).
Note: "Poverty" refers to the share of the population with consumption (per adult equivalent) below the value of a minimum basket of food and nonfood items, based on the Ghana Statistical Service (GSS) 1999 poverty line of ₵370.89 per adult equivalent per year in 2005 prices, which remained in effect until 2013. "Extreme poverty" refers to the "food poverty line," that is, the share with consumption below the value of a minimum basket of food (₵288.47 per adult equivalent per year in 2005 prices). Use of the 1999 poverty line does not appear to have unduly affected the 2012 poverty rate, which is estimated at 21.4 percent, compared with the official rate of 24.3 percent based on the GSS's revised (2013) poverty line of ₵1,314 per adult equivalent per year (equivalent to about US$1.83 per person per day) in the January 2013 prices of the Greater Accra region (Molini and Paci 2015).

Progress has gone beyond the reduction of consumption poverty. Ghana has also substantially improved various nonmonetary indicators of poverty. For example, infant mortality declined from 57 deaths per 1,000 live births in 1998 to 41 in 2014, and under-5 mortality declined by more than half. Fertility is also decreasing, which has led to a reduction in the dependency ratio (Molini and Paci 2015).

Inequality

In contrast to the progress in poverty reduction, Ghana is becoming an increasingly unequal country. Inequality in household consumption has widened considerably between the poorest and the richest, particularly between 1998 and 2005. In 1991, consumption per capita in the top decile of the distribution was five times greater than in the bottom percentile. By 2012, the gap had widened to nearly seven times, and the Gini index rose from 37.5 to 40.8 (Molini and Paci 2015). However, Ghana still compares favorably with other African countries; its Gini coefficient is still below the median and one of the lowest compared with rapidly growing African countries (Molini and Paci 2015).

Much of the increase in inequality reflects increased regional disparities, although within-region inequalities are also pronounced. Poverty and inequality have decreased in all regions except the Eastern Region and the Upper East,

Upper West, and Northern Regions.[11] Poverty has increasingly become concentrated in rural areas and in the northern part of the country, and one out of three poor people lives in a rural area—an increase from one out of five in 1991 (Molini and Paci 2015).

The Reform of Subsidies

Energy Sector Overview

Petroleum

Ghana began production of crude oil in 2010 and hit full capacity in 2011. Since then, the commodity has served as a major source of revenue to support the national budget (MoF 2015). The Ghana National Petroleum Corporation (GNPC) is mandated as the national oil company to lead exploration activities in the country. Estimated oil in place at Ghana's currently producing Jubilee oil field is about 600 million barrels, and current crude oil production from Ghana's Jubilee oil field is about 105,000 barrels per day (Kosmos Energy 2016).[12]

In 2013, crude oil exports accounted for about 19 percent of Ghana's total merchandise exports, corresponding to a total value of more than US$3 billion (UN 2015). GNPC forecasts crude oil production to peak in 2020 at 236,000 barrels per day (figure 3.5), offering greater prospects for oil revenue in the country.[13]

Figure 3.5 Projected Oil Production in Ghana, 2016–36

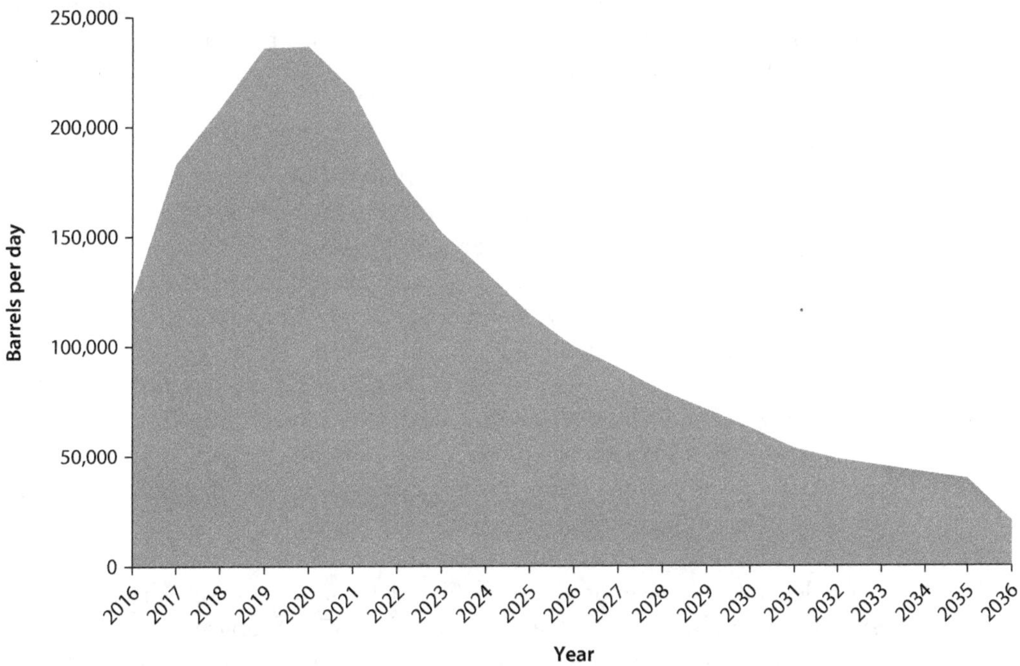

Source: Based on interviews and data from Ghana National Petroleum Corporation.

Its crude oil production capacity notwithstanding, the country imports about 3.39 million metric tons of refined products per year (mainly gasoline, diesel, and liquefied petroleum gas [LPG]) and consumes about 3.27 million metric tons per year.[14]

The state-owned TOR is the country's principal refinery and has a capacity to refine 45,000 barrels per day into all the downstream products consumed in the country.[15] In addition, a privately owned minirefinery (with capacity of about 22,000 barrels per day) supplies gas oil and fuel oil.[16]

Total consumption of petroleum products has reached about 70,000 barrels a day. This means that, at full capacity, the refineries' combined production would fall short of national consumption by only about 4 percent. However, TOR has been operated well under capacity since 2007 because of aged equipment needing refurbishment and because of significant indebtedness from unfunded state subsidies to domestic petroleum products. In 2014, the refinery supplied less than 10 percent of consumption. The shortfall in supply has been filled by private sector companies called bulk distribution companies (BDCs). Given TOR's low availability, crude oil from the Jubilee field is exported rather than refined at TOR, and crude oil is usually imported from Nigeria to be refined at TOR.[17]

In addition to its crude oil reserves, the country has a healthy reserve of associated and nonassociated gas, currently producing about 100 million standard cubic feet per day. A natural gas processing plant of 150 million standard cubic feet capacity, located at Atuabo in the Western Region, has been commissioned and currently supplies about 70 million standard cubic feet per day of processed gas to the Volta River Authority (Ghana's major power generation company, and solely owned by the government).[18] The plant also produces 300 metric tons per day of LPG, mainly for domestic consumption, out of potential production of about 550 metric tons per day.[19]

Electricity

While not central to this chapter, it is important to briefly cover the power sector. Like the petroleum sector, electricity provision has presented challenges in the sustainable implementation of meticulously planned reform processes. Until 2015, both power and petroleum issues were handled under the same ministry. Electricity supply is plagued with commercial losses from unmetered supply and illegal connections. Also undermining the utilities' financial health are longstanding debts by government ministries, departments, and agencies as well as poorly targeted and administered rural electricity subsidy programs.

Hydroelectricity is Ghana's primary power source, providing 55 percent of generation, while thermal energy provides 45 percent. The Electricity Company of Ghana currently contributes 75 percent of the country's installed generation capacity of nearly 2,925 megawatts, with the remaining 25 percent contributed by independent power producers.[20] Electricity tariffs are subsidized, and the state-owned utilities are unable to recover the costs of service provision. Ghana exports power to neighboring Togo and also has an agreement to export power to, or import power from, Côte D'Ivoire to balance demand (GRIDCo 2014).

Until early 2015—when the Ghana Gas Processing Plant (GPP) began commercial operations to process raw gas from the Jubilee field into lean gas for power production—the main source of fuel for power production was imported light crude oil and imported gas from Nigeria via the West African Gas Pipeline. Even with the GPP supplying an average of about 70 million standard cubic feet per day, imported fuel remains a substantial source for power generation. Disruptions to the gas supply from Nigeria have forced greater reliance on imported crude oil and thus substantially increased the cost of electricity generation, leading to large subsidies in the power sector (Kojima 2016).

On the other hand, population growth, rural electrification, and industrial expansion have led to an increase in power demand; demand has grown by about 6.5 percent per year since 2001, with average annual growth of 10 percent recorded from 2010 to 2013 before the recent energy crisis. Ghana's electricity access rate is among the highest in Sub-Saharan Africa, and demand has steadily increased to 13 terawatt-hours, with peak demand of 2,061 megawatts in 2014 (Energy Commission 2015).

Poor hydrology, inadequate fuel supply for thermal generation, and unplanned outages have resulted in major supply deficits since 1997 (CEPA 2007). The deficits have prompted power rationing or load shedding every year. The energy crisis worsened recently in 2014, causing a major constraint to development (USAID 2015). The power crisis costs the country US$2.2 million daily and US$686.4 million annually, translating to about 2 percent of GDP (Ackah 2015).

The Public Utilities Regulatory Commission (PURC) is responsible for regulating the price of electricity in Ghana. So far, the government has not made a major move toward privatization of electricity.

Subsidy Reform Overview

Electricity and petroleum subsidies have been commonplace in the country from 1991 as a result of failed attempts at both electricity and petroleum subsidy reforms. Because of pressure from political interest groups and the general public, attempts to reform both sectors have not been successfully sustained.

Petroleum subsidy reforms have been going on for two decades, using strategies including establishment and activation of an automatic adjustment formula as well as product cross-subsidization. The most recent reforms (since July 2015) have seen the removal of government control over petroleum product prices—the most ambitious reform strategy ever implemented in the sector. The latest reform has introduced competition among the country's oil marketing companies, which has ultimately benefited consumers through lower and competitive pump prices. The reform, helped by falling world crude oil prices, is expected to avoid over US$500 million in annual foreign exchange losses and over ₵1 billion (US$250 million) in annual subsidy bills (NPA 2015).

Despite the current success of the latest petroleum subsidy reform program in Ghana, it is important to observe whether these reforms will remain in place when world prices begin to swing upward again. It is therefore necessary to analyze the behavior of Ghanaian policy makers throughout the reform decision-making process as well as throughout the implementation of the various reforms.

This subsection examines the various reforms that have been implemented in the petroleum sector, focusing particularly on the circumstances that allowed the subsidy reforms to take place given the economic, political, and distributional background at the time. The subsection begins with a description of the petroleum sector, describes and analyzes the history of subsidies, and finally describes the various subsidy reforms that have been implemented in the country.

The Petroleum Sector

Ghana's downstream petroleum subsector existed before independence in 1957, and the sector has grown and diversified over the years. Deregulation has been the main policy objective, with three main targets: (a) decentralization of product imports and supply, (b) decentralization of infrastructure provision and management, and (c) removal of government control over prices. Since 1996, the supply of petroleum products has been improved such that TOR is no longer the main source. Since 2006 the private sector has been licensed to build and operate infrastructure, and in 2001 an automatic price adjustment formula was developed with the ultimate aim of removing government control of prices.

Products consumed in Ghana are classified into foreign and domestic products, depending on the type of end user. Foreign products comprise jet fuel; diesel to the mining sector; and marine gas oil (MGO), which is diesel sold to the oil rig (on the Jubilee field) and foreign vessels. These products have been fully deregulated since 2009 and have extra margins on their prices to aid in paying for subsidies for domestic products. Domestic products include gasoline; diesel; LPG (a composition of propane and butane); premix fuel (a fuel blend for two-stroke fishing boat engines, transportation on Lake Volta, and automated cocoa spraying machines); MGO (for local vessels and internal water transportation by leisure boats and fishing activities); and residual fuel oil for powering industry machinery.

Total consumption of petroleum products has grown by about 42 percent between 2010 and 2015, with the most significant growth in 2012, mainly due to a cyclical increase in expenditure associated with infrastructure development, as is typical in election years.[21] However, consumption of certain products declined over the period: fuel oil, for example, declined sharply (by 64 percent), although this product accounts for only a tiny fraction of the country's total petroleum product demand (figure 3.6). This shift away from fuel oil is mainly due to a shift by industries toward LPG to power their machines, in turn partly due to the efficient and cleaner nature of LPG, LPG's lower cost, and the unreliable nature of TOR fuel oil supply. MGO local and kerosene declined by about 47 percent and 84 percent, respectively, because of a gradual removal of the subsidy on both products since 2012 as well as a supply rationing process on kerosene conducted by the National Petroleum Authority (NPA) in 2012.[22]

Ghana's petroleum subsidies can be quantified using the price-gap approach. Domestic prices are set against an international reference price, and the gap is

Figure 3.6 Petroleum Product Consumption in Ghana, 2010–15

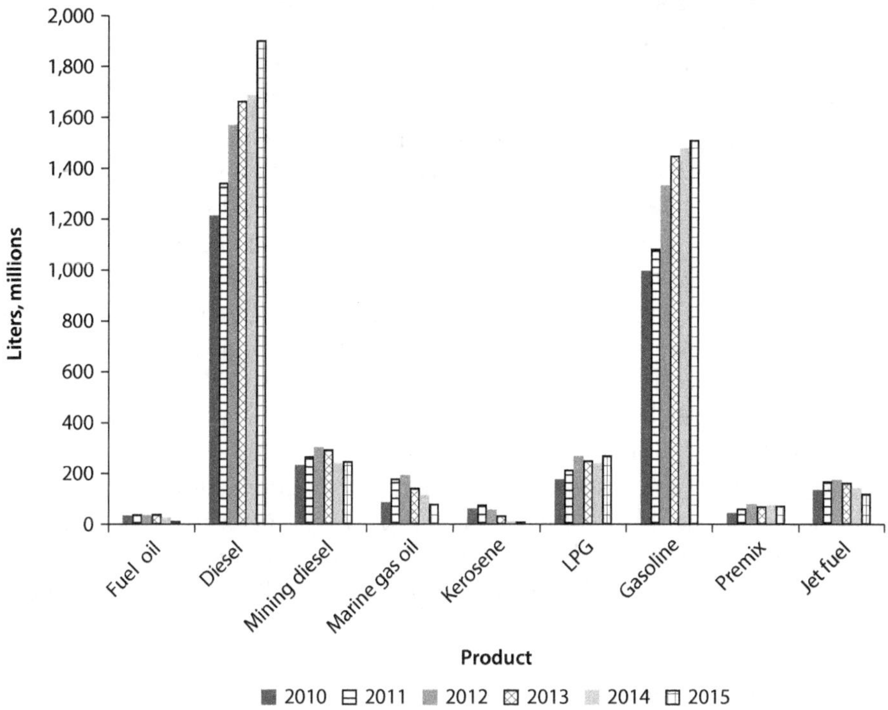

Source: National Petroleum Authority database, http://www.npa.gov.gh.
Note: LPG = liquefied petroleum gas. Premix is a low-octane gasoline fuel blend largely used for fishing boat motors.

adjusted for political and policy purposes. This approach has allowed policy makers to use prices to advance a variety of policy goals, but it has also meant that the subsidy regime is constantly exposed to the volatility of international prices. Historically, the National Petroleum Tender Board (a committee at the then Ministry of Energy and Mines) was responsible for petroleum product pricing until the NPA, an independent regulatory body, was created to take over in 2005 by an Act of Parliament (Act 691).

The NPA's objective is to regulate, oversee, and monitor activities in the petroleum downstream industry as well as to establish a Unified Petroleum Price Fund (UPPF). The NPA has operated various subsidy regimes from partial subsidy to cross-subsidies. The extent of the subsidy regime implemented depended heavily on the political will of the government at the time in response to agitations from special interest groups such as civil society, the opposition political party, labor unions, commercial vehicle transporters, and the general public.

Before 2012, kerosene was heavily subsidized, and diesel was sometimes illegally adulterated with kerosene to increase profit margins (Kojima 2016). This caused revenue loss to the state, first in misapplied subsidies as well as unpaid taxes. A reduction in the kerosene subsidy, coupled with an NPA quality control program called the Petroleum Products Marking Scheme, saw a significant drop (about 67 percent) in kerosene consumption in 2014; it was expected to have dropped by another 17 percent in 2015. Consumption of aviation turbine kerosene (ATK) suffered from the extra margin placed on its price to help pay for the subsidies on domestic products, which makes the ATK prices higher than in most Sub-Saharan African countries. Therefore, airlines prefer to load as much fuel as they can before landing in Accra and then only top up in Accra—a practice that has caused a 10 percent decline in ATK consumption.[23]

Premix fuel (a low-octane gasoline fuel largely used by fishermen for their outboard motors) is heavily subsidized to support the fishing industry; users of the product also have strong political influence. Part of the premix subsidy goes into developmental projects in the various landing beach communities, where premix distribution to fishermen is centralized. Consumption of MGO foreign (gas oil sold to foreign vessels and oil rigs) increased by 170 percent between 2010 and 2015, the biggest jump (500 percent) occurring in 2011 when Ghana began substantial commercial production of oil.

Consumption of the three most widely consumed products—gasoline, gas oil, and LPG—increased between 2010 and 2015 by 52 percent, 57 percent, and 53 percent, respectively. This is mainly attributable to economic growth and increasing use of LPG in industries as well as in smaller commercial vehicles (taxis) (NPA 2015).

History of Petroleum Subsidies and Pricing Reforms

2001: Automatic Adjustment Formula and Cross-Subsidy. Before 2001, when an automatic adjustment formula was established for petroleum product prices, TOR set prices based on production costs or import costs. After the cost basis was determined, final prices were then set with heavy subsidization for most fuels—in an effort to ensure "affordable" fuel and encourage economic growth. Subsidies were fairly manageable then, until a combination of increased volumes and the weakening cedi resulted in huge subsidy debts on TOR's books.

In June 2001, an automatic price adjustment formula—the petroleum products PBU schedule—was established based on a buildup of costs at import parity from northwestern European countries. This was done to ensure that petroleum product prices reflected full cost recovery at import parity as well as to prevent absorption of TOR inefficiencies as costs in petroleum product prices. The formula was supposed to be activated to reflect on domestic prices when there was a 2.5 percent variance between the weighted value of products using current domestic prices and the value using import parity pricing (CEPA 2003). Another key feature of the formula was a social policy objective to ameliorate the impact of petroleum product prices on the poorer segment of society, hence the implementation of cross-product subsidization.

For example, gasoline prices in the same year were increased by about 61 percent to generate the revenues needed to limit the price increases of fuels that are important to low-income populations: kerosene, diesel, and LPG. This scheme was based on the Ghana Living Standards Survey IV (GLSS IV), which showed that gasoline consumption accounted for a higher share of expenditure in high-income households while identifying kerosene as a product used in low-income households (GSS 2000). Diesel was not directly used by the poor, but its indirect impacts on the poor were large because diesel was the main fuel widely used for commercial transportation of people, goods, and food from the hinterlands.

Diesel was also extensively used in the agricultural sector through mechanization. LPG was considered for cross-subsidization for environmental reasons—the ultimate aim being to encourage the use of LPG in place of wood fuels for cooking and heating in the poorest households. A cross-subsidy levy of 5 pesewas per liter of gasoline has been charged for years, with negative levies for all other fuels.

Two key elements helped build the rationale for the choice of gasoline for product cross-subsidization: First, gasoline is a product that is widely consumed by the middle- to high-income classes in Ghana. Second, at the time this decision was made, the volumes of gasoline consumed were far higher than the combined volumes of the other products, making it easy to levy gasoline consumption to cross-subsidize all other products whose consumers were mainly seen as lower-income earners.

Today, however, the positive levy on gasoline is no longer enough to cross-subsidize all other fuels given the increase in consumption volumes of subsidized products. For example, in 2015, the government's net revenue from cross-subsidy levies was a deficit of ₵3.6 billion (2.9 percent of estimated 2015 GDP), with diesel making up the largest loss (table 3.1). Because of the obsolete nature of the cross-subsidy—and after substantial lobbying by the NPA—Parliament in December 2015 passed the Energy Levies Act (Act 899), which, among other measures, repealed the cross-subsidy levy from the petroleum products PBU schedule.

2002: TOR Debt Recovery Levy. In March 2002, the petroleum pricing formula was adjusted to accommodate a petroleum debt service charge called the TOR Debt Recovery Levy. Parliament approved this adjustment solely to manage the TOR debt (CEPA 2003). TOR, being the major petroleum product supplier at the time, had accumulated debt from previously unpaid subsidies since 1996,

Table 3.1 Net Impact of Cross-Subsidies in Ghana, 2015

Measurement	*Fuel oil*	*Diesel*	*MGO*	*Kerosene*	*LPG*	*Premix*	*Gasoline*
Consumption (million liters except LPG in kilograms)	13	1,900	36	133	275	73	1,508
Cross-subsidy levy (pesewas per liter)	−1.39	−2.70	−6.23	−4.84	−18.40	−0.36	5
Cross-subsidy revenue (cedis, millions)	−18	−5,127	−226	−643	−5,057	−26	7,540
Total cross-subsidy losses (cedis, millions)	−11,098						
Total cross-subsidy revenue (cedis, millions)	7,540						
Net cross-subsidy (cedis, millions)	−3,558						

Source: National Petroleum Authority database, http://www.npa.gov.gh.
Note: MGO = marine gas oil. LPG = liquefied petroleum gas. Premix is a low-octane gasoline fuel blend largely used for fishing boat motors.

and by 2002 the debt had reached levels that threatened TOR's continuous operation. The debt service charge at that time was estimated to be 95 percent of the cedi value of international price windfalls from November to December 2001, and it was supposed to be applied throughout 2002.

Even though some industry observers lauded the idea of making current consumers pay for the previously enjoyed subsidy, the rise in prices that came from the automatic mechanism led the government to abandon the automatic adjustment by the end of 2002 for fear of voter backlash. Depreciation in the exchange rate should have led to higher local prices, but the government did not allow the pass-through of world market prices to domestic prices, thereby further increasing the debt on TOR.

In January 2003, prices were increased by 90 percent to achieve full cost recovery at import parity while reflecting world market prices—a reimplementation of the automatic adjustment formula, this time with a "k" factor to reflect the inefficiencies of TOR relative to similar refineries abroad (CEPA 2003). The change also included the institution of a Parliament-approved TOR Debt Recovery Levy in the price. However, this brought about stiff, widespread opposition among the general public, civil society organizations, and the NDC (the main opposition party).

Faced with general elections in 2004, the government backed away from full adjustment and reduced prices. The result was that subsidies substantially increased, as did the potential debt that would accrue to TOR. In the late 2000s, the TOR debt was diversified, not only because of subsidies but also because of the company's failure to meet its financial obligations to both its crude oil suppliers and its bankers. As of December 2015, the value of the TOR debt was about US$580 million.

2004–05: Post-PSIA Reforms. Petroleum subsidy reforms in 2004 marked the turning point, as the government concluded that the subsidy in place was not viable. This laid the foundation for subsequent subsidy reforms and the price deregulation nine years later, which would ultimately become the best approach to date.

The unsustainability of the subsidy regime caused the government to launch a Poverty and Social Impact Analysis (PSIA) for petroleum products in 2004. The study was steered by a committee drawn from universities, the government, and the GNPC (Coady and Newhouse 2006). The PSIA showed that petroleum subsidies benefited citizens who were better off. Following the assessment, prices were increased by 50 percent in February 2005 to liberalize prices.

Although trade unions opposed the price hikes, the policy was generally accepted, and there were no large-scale demonstrations against the increase (Bacon and Kojima 2006). In the same year, the NPA was established and began setting ceiling prices at import parity benchmarking as a continuation of the 2001 reforms. The composition of the NPA board reflects a representation of both special interests and citizens.[24]

As an extension of both the 2001 and 2004 reforms, a UPPF was also established in 2005 to equalize petroleum product prices throughout the country by harmonizing transport charges. A UPPF levy was imposed on each fuel (currently 9 pesewas per liter). The ex-refinery differential, which operated like a price stabilization fund, was introduced in the last quarter of 2006 to pay fuel marketers for underrecovery of costs for selling kerosene, LPG, and premix.

The formula also used historical exchange rate quotes from the BoG, implying that the depreciation of the local currency (the cedi) had created some substantial foreign exchange losses to importers. Foreign exchange losses are estimated as the difference between (a) the cedi-to-U.S. dollar exchange rate that the NPA allows in the petroleum products PBU schedule, and (b) the actual exchange rate used to settle the letters of credit to import the products. These exchange losses can be as high as 24 percent of the cost of importing a standard cargo size of 33,000 tons.

In October 2007, price reviews increased from once a month to twice a month to reflect more-current international prices. Further price adjustments, however, were suspended between May and November of 2008 because of high energy and food prices that year. Moreover, the 2008 general elections were not spared from petroleum politics: then-candidate John Atta Mills described President John Kufuor's administration as insensitive toward the plight of Ghanaians, his criticism centering on a heavy tax component of local petroleum product prices. After attaining victory, Mills and his party, the NDC, promised Ghanaians a further reduction in fuel prices. Subsequently, the frequency of price adjustments fell sharply beginning in 2009, along with a continuous reduction in taxes.

Figure 3.7 shows the trend of petroleum product prices in Ghana. Gasoline prices were the highest, partially because of the cross-subsidization policy. LPG prices were consistently low from 1990 to 1996, reflecting the long-running campaign to switch from the use of wood fuels (Kojima 2016).

Figure 3.7 Local Pump Prices in Ghana, 1990–2015

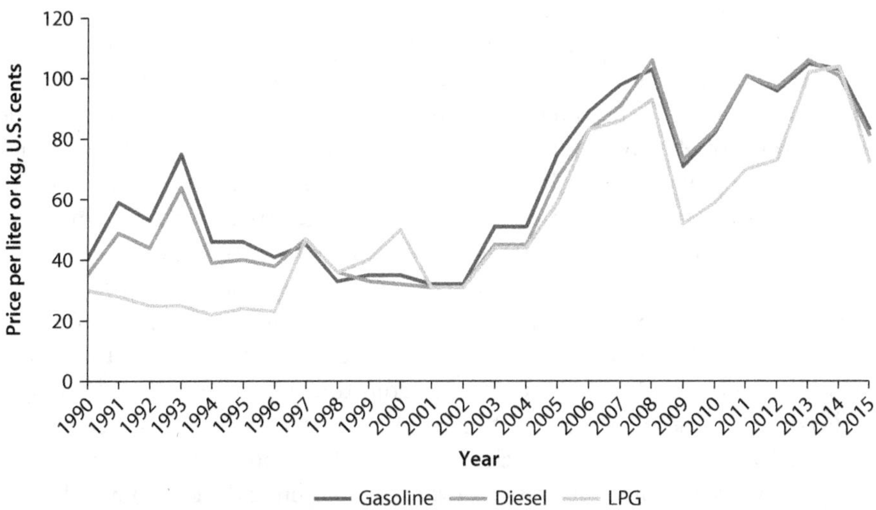

Source: National Petroleum Authority database, http://www.npa.gov.gh.
Note: LPG = liquefied petroleum gas. kg = kilogram. Gasoline and diesel prices are per liter; LPG prices are per kilogram.

Infrequent price adjustments have sometimes been followed by sharp price increases. In June 2009, prices were increased by 30 percent across the board for all fuels to reduce subsidies. There were no price adjustments in 2010.

2011–14: Toward Price Deregulation. Although the seeds of successful subsidy reform were planted in 2004, it was not until December 2011 that Ghana finally began an unreversed process to cut fuel subsidies. Several of these adjustments tended to be large. For instance, in January 2011, prices were increased by 25–30 percent except for kerosene and premix, whose prices were not changed because of the subsidies' target beneficiaries: fishing and rural communities.

At the same time, foreign exchange losses compounded. Although the PBU formula incorporated some foreign exchange loss provision (of about US$10 per metric ton for gasoline and diesel and about US$14 per metric ton for LPG), the rate of cedi depreciation overran the allowed compensation in 2011, creating significant foreign exchange losses. The difference in product pricing as well as the foreign exchange loss bills were borne by the government and increased the fiscal deficit. Delayed payment of these subsidies also challenged the liquidity of importers, leading to shortages of petroleum products. Between June 2011 and December 2013, foreign exchange losses were valued at US$397 million (22 percent of 2013 GDP).[25]

Given these losses, fuel prices increased by about 20 percent on January 1, 2012. About the same time as the 2012 price adjustment, the government negotiated a trigger point with the local commercial vehicle transport union to prevent sporadic, unjustified increases in transport fares. It was agreed that transport fares would go up by a third of the fuel price increase only when cumulative fuel price increases within the year exceeded 10 percent. This increase was also upon the condition that other variables in the transport fare formula had changed; for instance, vehicle insurance and spare parts costs must also have increased significantly.

The NPA cited increases in crude oil prices and the depreciation of the cedi as the major reasons for the subsidy cuts. The cuts came as Ghana faced budget deficits and increasing pressure from the IMF to remove the subsidies, which the IMF contended were not effective in directly aiding the poor and promoted corruption and smuggling. Worker groups such as the Ghanaian Trade Union Congress and other types of pressure groups promised to call indefinite nationwide strikes, and partially in response to this, the government in early February 2012 reduced the price increase by 20 percent. The reduction was also fueled by the ruling government's need to win political points during the ongoing 2012 general election campaign.

Since 2012, the government has made inconsistent attempts to further remove subsidies, with less-frequent price adjustments. The premix subsidy was reduced from close to 70 percent to a maximum of 50 percent in a negotiation with the landing beach committees, which have deep-rooted political affiliations with the two key political parties and therefore command significant influence on potential voters. The kerosene subsidy was reduced drastically to remove the long-standing economic incentive to adulterate it with diesel. The savings from the removed subsidy were redirected toward improving the government solar lamp project (to help villagers replace kerosene lamps with sustainable lighting) as well as the rural electrification project to reduce the need for kerosene for power in rural areas, where mostly low-income earners live.

Not until February 2013 did the government adjust fuel prices again, including a 15 percent increase for kerosene, 20 percent for gasoline and diesel, and 50 percent for LPG. In the same year, government launched the Rural LPG Promotion Program to reduce reliance in rural areas on wood fuels and kerosene for cooking as well as to reduce wood-fuel-related respiratory illness.

In the last large price increases, in July 2014, prices of most fuels rose by 22–27 percent except for fuel oil and LPG, whose prices rose by 16 percent. In November 2014, the Special Petroleum Tax (a value added tax of 17.5 percent of the ex-depot price of petroleum products)[26] was implemented in the PBU schedule as a source of government revenue. This tax resulted in a marginal 3 percent increase in pump prices.[27]

The gaps in price, which indicate the level of subsidy at each point in time, are shown in figure 3.8. The period with the highest subsidy was in 2012—a general election year in Ghana (figure 3.8, panel a). Premix fuel remains the product with the highest subsidy, reaching 70 percent in 2012. In 2015, all subsidies were removed from all products except for premix fuel, whose subsidy (close to 40 percent) was maintained for two major reasons: First, users of premix fuel are local fishermen who have strong political lobbying power in the country. Second, fishing is vital to the livelihoods of people along the 550 kilometer coastline, and most fishing communities are rural and poor. There are therefore several community development programs for these communities, and the cost is built into the premix subsidy.

The highest annual subsidy growth (278 percent) occurred between 2010 and 2011, and the lowest (–68 percent) was between 2012 and 2013, when major increases adjusted the prices to levels equivalent to world prices (figure 3.8, panel b). With the 2015 reforms, subsidies have stopped growing; with growth of –2 percent in 2015, they are essentially flat.

More recently, on January 1, 2016, the government implemented changes in the PBU, as required by passage of the Energy Levies Act of 2015. A new Energy Debt Recovery Levy was introduced to contribute toward the TOR debt recovery, mitigate the BDCs' foreign exchange loss, and increase infrastructure support to the power sector. The cross-subsidy levy (a levy on gasoline and a subsidy on all other products) had become obsolete because the shift in consumption volumes was removed. An exploration levy, which was meant to finance the activities of the GNPC, was also repealed.

At the same time, a Road Fund Levy aimed at financing maintenance and improvement of road infrastructure was increased from 7 pesewas per liter to 40 pesewas per liter. The Energy Fund Levy, which finances the activities of the Energy Commission (policy advisors to the Ministry of Power and Ministry of Petroleum), was increased from 0.05 pesewa per liter to 1 pesewa per liter. Finally, a price stabilization and recovery margin levy of 12 pesewas per liter was

Figure 3.8 Petroleum Subsidy Trends in Ghana, 2010–15

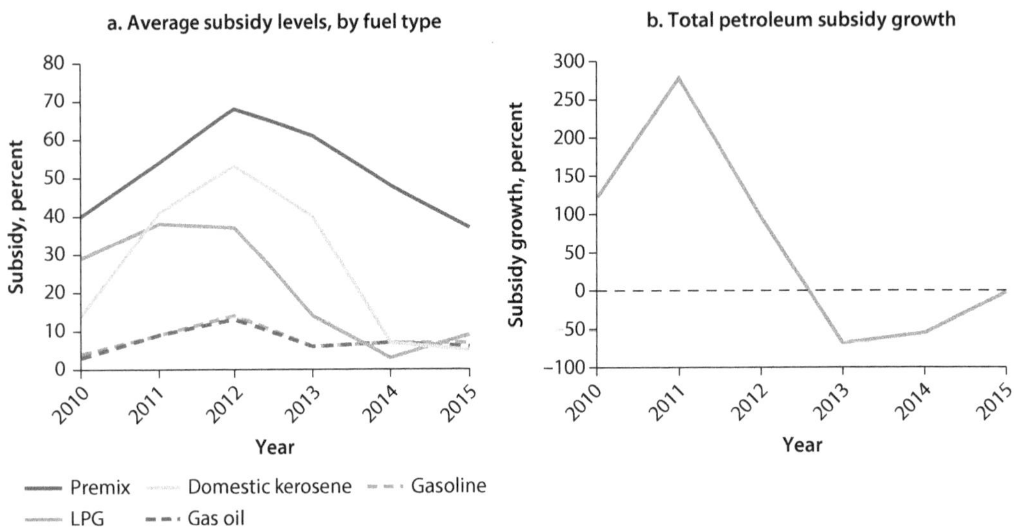

Source: Interviews with, and data from, National Petroleum Authority officials.
Note: LPG = liquefied petroleum gas. Premix is a low-octane gasoline fuel blend largely used for fishing boat motors.

introduced to pay for the premix fuel subsidy and to create a buffer fund to pay for any future subsidies government intends to apply.

The price effect of the price deregulation was a 28–30 percent increase in domestic fuel prices. This increase, occurring at a time when world prices are falling significantly, meant that a full pass-through price without the new levies would have resulted in a 5 percent reduction in prices. Politically, the opposition NPP and civil society did not receive this increase well. At the same time, electricity and water tariffs also went up by over 50 percent, and a new tax law was implemented that required Ghanaians to pay more taxes.[28]

Key labor unions in the country have begun negotiations with the government over wage and salary increases amid threats of a strike. Commercial transport operators are also negotiating with the government amid threats to increase local transport fares. And pressure groups are demanding a reduction in fuel prices, otherwise threatening court actions and nationwide demonstrations.

2015–Present: Price Deregulation. Unpaid subsidies, coupled with the slide of the cedi, caused the main interest groups—the banks and the BDCs—to lobby the executive heavily. As part of the IMF program of fiscal consolidation, the IMF directed that all subsidies be either budgeted for or removed (IMF 2015). Hence on July 1, 2015, petroleum product prices were deregulated in the most ambitious petroleum subsidy reform ever attempted in Ghana. The reform implementation included the following key strategies:

- *Timing of implementation* to ensure a minimal impact at the pump from subsidy removal and private sector pricing. As such, the downward trend of international prices was considered in choosing a deregulation commencement date of July 1, 2015. On that date, average crude oil prices were about US$58 per barrel—a drop of 88 percent from the 2013 average (US$109 per barrel) and 71 percent from the 2014 average (US$99 per barrel).

- *Stakeholder consultation and engagement*, given that the NPA was going to relinquish its price-determining role to the private sector-dominated industry participants for the first time since 2005. It was necessary to (a) train stakeholders on the pricing formula, and (b) appeal to them not to quickly increase margins—a move that could make the whole deregulation process unpopular and cause a reversal by government.
- *Communication* of the impact of subsidy, the existing government indebtedness to the BDCs, and the fact that subsidies were resulting in smuggling and adulteration of petroleum products. The general public, civil society, and consumer interest groups were sensitized to understand the need for a drastic subsidy reform. It was also communicated that the IMF program had a zero tolerance for subsidies.
- *Strategic use of state-owned oil supply chain actors*—including the Bulk Oil Storage and Transportation Company (BOST), Go Energy (a BDC), and Ghana Oil Company (GOIL, an oil marketing company)—to drive competition toward lower pump prices, especially in the first six months of price deregulation. This was to prevent the private sector players from forming a cartel or creating any price-induced artificial shortages.

Although these four strategies have ensured the success of price deregulation so far, it will be important to observe the performance of the reform programs when world prices begin to rise. Because of the PBU structure as well as the guidelines given to the industry, it is expected that prices will be fairly passed on without any unfair or illegal margins by the marketers. The government is also likely to allow a pass-through of the prices because of the ongoing fiscal consolidation and austerity policies being implemented under the IMF Extended Credit Facility.[29]

Impact of Reforms

Economic Impact

The latest reform was feasible largely because international oil prices declined, and it is intended to bring about keen competition among oil marketers such that more competitive prices are offered to the citizens and processes are in place to prevent cartelization. The NPA estimates that, without price deregulation, 2015 subsidies on petroleum products would have reached ₵1.5 billion (1.2 percent of estimated 2015 GDP) by the end of December 2015. Foreign exchange losses from June 2011 to June 2015 were estimated at ₵3.9 billion.[30] Considering that funds were needed for other developmental projects in health, agriculture, and infrastructure, among other priorities, the subsidy savings represent huge fiscal progress for the government.

Moreover, the petroleum subsidy had consistently locked up over 30 percent of the BDCs' working capital, constraining them from importing to augment TOR's shortfall, which had exceeded 70 percent in 2011.[31] This situation caused a shortage or near-shortage of petroleum products every year, especially toward the last quarter. Removal of subsidies means that BDCs can set competitive prices at full cost recovery, thus improving their ability to supply petroleum products. Industry players are becoming much more efficient both in finding sources for products and in determining their market margins.

Distributional Impact

Based on household expenditure data in the GLSS VI (GSS 2014), the NPA in 2015 established (based on 2014 prices) that the bottom 20 percent of the population spend nearly 5 percent of their household budget on fuel, while the top 20 percent spend over 14 percent of their budget on fuel (table 3.2). Rural households spend 1.9 percent of their consumption budget on petroleum products and transportation, whereas urban households spend 2.84 percent (NPA 2015).[32]

The same study observed that the top household income quintile (richest 20 percent) benefited from petroleum subsidies three times more than the bottom quintile (poorest 20 percent), and in 2014 only 1 percent of LPG subsidies benefited the bottom 20 percent (table 3.3). This confirms that subsidies, even though targeted at the poorer segment of society, always benefit the richer

Table 3.2 Share of Household Budget Spent on Fuel in Ghana, by Income Quintile, 2015

percentage of total consumption

Expenditure type	*1 (bottom 20%)*	*2*	*3*	*4*	*5 (top 20%)*
LPG	0.01	0.07	0.11	0.27	0.35
Kerosene	0.12	0.14	0.13	0.10	0.06
Gasoline or diesel	0.90	0.91	0.91	1.09	2.78
Transportation	3.80	4.53	5.14	5.93	11.21
Total	4.83	5.65	6.29	7.39	14.39

Source: NPA 2015.
Note: LPG = liquefied petroleum gas.

Table 3.3 Distribution of Subsidy Benefits in Ghana, by Household Consumption Quintile, 2014

percentage of total benefits

Expenditure type	*1 (bottom 20%)*	*2*	*3*	*4*	*5 (top 20%)*
LPG	1.1	8.6	13.9	33.2	43.2
Kerosene	22.7	25.5	24.1	17.6	10.1
Gasoline or diesel	13.7	13.8	13.8	16.6	42.1
Total	13.9	14.3	14.3	17.0	40.5

Source: NPA 2015.
Note: LPG = liquefied petroleum gas.

Table 3.4 Direct Impact of Fuel Price Increases in Ghana, by Household Income Quintile, 2014
percentage of total household consumption

Expenditure type	*1 (bottom 20%)*	*2*	*3*	*4*	*5 (top 20%)*
LPG	0.01	0.08	0.13	0.31	0.41
Kerosene	0.20	0.22	0.21	0.15	0.09
Gasoline or diesel	1.35	1.37	1.36	1.64	4.16
Transportation	5.70	6.80	7.71	8.90	16.81
Total	7.26	8.47	9.41	11.01	21.47

Source: NPA 2015.
Note: LPG = liquefied petroleum gas.

segments because of richer households devote a higher share of their expenditure to petroleum products (NPA 2015).

By implication, fuel price increases or subsidy reductions affected urban households more than rural households, with the exception of kerosene, which is a major fuel used in the rural areas that lack electricity as a power source. The proportion of household budgets spent on kerosene in rural areas is 0.13 percent, while in the urban areas it is 0.06 percent (NPA 2015). Similarly, the direct impact of fuel price increases was larger for households in the top 20 percent of the distribution than those at the bottom (table 3.4).

Although the richest households benefit the most from subsidies, poorer households, particularly in urban areas, do benefit from them as well. Between September 2013 and December 2014, fuel prices increased by more than 50 percent, while electricity tariffs increased by more than 150 percent. Because fuel is an important intermediate good, this increase in prices also had important indirect welfare impacts through higher prices throughout the economy. Clementi, Molini, and Schettino (2016) estimate a 5 percentage point increase in poverty as a result of these direct and indirect price increases, putting an additional 1.3 million individuals into poverty. They also estimate that the extreme poverty headcount rate (persons living on less than ₵792, or about US$205, per adult equivalent per year) rose by about 2 percent (from a baseline of 8.54 percent).

Circumstances That Enabled Reforms

To explain the context of the reforms and petroleum pricing policies in Ghana, the various reforms will be analyzed using the conceptual framework developed for the broader study. According to the framework, to identify the features of the political system that must change to enable reform, we must first understand (a) why the government had preferred the particular distribution of benefits embedded in the policies, and (b) why it had been politically desirable to achieve those distributional objectives through subsidies as opposed to other types of programs.

Why Did the Government Prefer Subsidies?

The subsidies that existed before the 2001 reforms largely benefited both the citizens and vested interests. The subsidies were not particularly targeted at any special interest or the citizens. The government employed subsidies to avoid price shocks to citizens. A key feature of all reforms has been a social policy objective to ameliorate the impact of petroleum product prices on the poorer segment of society (for example, through cross-subsidization of the products most used by the poor: kerosene and LPG). However, the evidence does not match the objectives, because the wealthy benefited more than the poor from the subsidies.

Both imperfect citizen information and the lack of government credibility contribute to a political preference for inefficient subsidies. Most citizens judge the government's performance by the cost of living. Therefore, to avoid political backlash from price shocks beyond their control, the government holds petroleum prices to mask these shocks. Cash transfers could serve the same purpose, but their impact is more retrospective because citizens will feel the price shock before being compensated for it. Relative to cash transfers, subsidies are also easier to administer and can be quickly implemented, and thus they are preferable to the government (Bacon and Kojima 2006).

To educate Ghanaian citizens, the government used the results of the 2004 PSIA to launch a series of public awareness campaigns through the media to explain the justification for the price increase (IMF 2013). Among these efforts, the minister of finance launched a public relations campaign with a broadcast explaining the need for the price increases and announcing measures to mitigate their impact. A series of interviews with government officials and trade union representatives followed. The Ministry of Energy and Petroleum also ran newspaper advertisements that included charts showing that Ghana's fuel prices were the lowest in West Africa after Nigeria's.

The money saved by not paying subsidies was then redirected to transparent, easily monitored social support programs including immediate elimination of fees at primary and junior secondary schools, a program to improve public transport, the allocation of extra funds for primary health care in Ghana's poorest areas, and an increase in funds to a rural electrification scheme (WEF 2013). Despite the efforts, automatic adjustments were again halted and subsidies built up once more.

Characterizing the Reforms

Using the framework for political economy analysis of subsidy reforms presented in chapter 1, one can characterize energy policies according to the size of the benefits they offer to concentrated special interest groups versus the benefits that are more broadly diffused to citizens at large. This framework yields a range of possibilities—shown in table 3.5 along with a mapping of the subsidy policies in Ghana.

Case 1: Large Special Interest and Citizen Benefits

The subsidies that existed before the 2001 reforms (when the automatic adjustment formula was established) largely benefited both citizens and special interests.

Table 3.5 Characterizing Subsidy Policy Benefits in Ghana

Beneficiary type and benefit size	*Citizen benefits are large*	*Citizen benefits are small*
Special interest benefits are large	**Case 1** Pricing policies before 2001 reforms	**Case 2** n.a.
Special interest benefits are small	**Case 3** Post-2001 pricing policies, including cross-subsidy policy 2004 price reforms after PSIA Subsidies before 2015 price deregulation	**Case 4** n.a.

Note: n.a. = not applicable in the case of Ghana; PSIA = Poverty and Social Impact Analysis.

Under these conditions, reforms are likely when (a) the costs of subsidies rise; (b) there is a general fiscal constraint, and energy subsidies are a large fraction of government spending; or (c) external pressure compels the government to take action.

As it happened, rising international prices and the costs of providing subsidies triggered the 2001 reforms. In 2002, TOR's growing debt and its spillover into the petroleum sector prompted action once more, leading to introduction of the TOR levy and a resumption of price adjustments. Foreign exchange losses also contributed to fiscal pressure on the government, triggering renewed reform efforts.

Case 3: Small Special Interest Benefits and Large Citizen Benefits

The cross-subsidy policy at the beginning of implementation was designed such that gasoline users were levied to pay for the subsidies on the other products. This was consistent with Case 3 of the framework until consumption volumes changed and the levy no longer sufficed to subsidize consumption of the other products. All other reform policies after 2001 have also maintained an element of subsidies meant to reduce impacts on the poor, thus placing these policies more under Case 3 wherein special interests get few of the benefits and citizens get most of the benefits.

The post-PSIA reforms of 2004 mainly benefited the education and health sectors because of a redirection of the petroleum subsidy into these sectors to reduce poverty. Low income earners, especially in the rural areas, were targeted as beneficiaries.

Similarly, in the 2005 reforms (including establishment of the NPA and the UPPF to better regulate prices), resources previously used for subsidies were redirected to provide other social support programs. Likewise, in the 2011 reforms, the subsidy was redirected into solar lamp projects, a continuation of the rural electrification scheme, and the rural LPG promotion program.

Despite these early improvements, subsidy policy in Ghana has repeatedly drifted back to an equilibrium closer to Case 1. Although the subsidies were identified as being ineffective, the power of the vote restrained the government from total deregulation. Even the cross-subsidy policy eventually presented little benefit to both citizens and gasoline users as it moved into a net negative balance in 2003. Citizens benefited largely from lower domestic prices while the BDCs and oil financing commercial banks faced persistent liquidity constraints. In 2014, about 30 percent of the BDC working capital was locked up in government subsidy debts, and these debts were in reality carried on the books of the oil financing banks as credit to the BDCs. Both groups, being strong lobbyists of political interests, contributed significantly to the reform that led to the 2015 price deregulation.

As noted earlier, the framework predicts that reform is more likely to happen when, among other things, the costs of providing benefits rise sharply; governments face general stringency, with energy subsidies being a large fraction of government spending; and external pressures change the political equilibrium. In the case of Ghana, all three conditions applied. World price hikes from 2007 to 2013 informed the various reforms that were implemented.

It was not only price underrecoveries that led to the 2015 price deregulation but also the accumulated losses from cedi depreciation. The cedi depreciated by about 181 percent between 2009 and 2015. The petroleum price formula had used historical exchange rate quotes from the BoG, creating substantial foreign exchange losses to importers as the cedi depreciated.

The latest reform was also heavily influenced by the government's fiscal consolidation and austerity program under the IMF, which made no provision for petroleum subsidies in the latest fiscal consolidation program. The BDCs and oil financing commercial banks also lobbied heavily to facilitate the reforms because of the subsidies' negative impact on their business.

Lessons Learned

Subsidies are intended to cushion the poor but are ineffective in doing so. For instance, as of 2014 in Ghana, people within the top 20 percent income bracket benefited three times more from subsidies than did those in the bottom 20 percent, and the bottom 20 percent received only 1 percent of LPG subsidies (NPA 2015). Moreover, subsidies have grave fiscal and macroeconomic implications.

However, subsidy reforms require significant political will because social and political tensions are likely to derail such reforms. Political will, in this case, involves the formulation of a subsidy policy that relies on nongovernmental financing of subsidies—strategies such as cross-subsidization, price smoothing schemes, and price stabilization levies. They could also include programs to eliminate subsidies, instead delivering social assistance to the vulnerable through direct transfers. These policies are more sustainable while providing fiscal relief, enabling the government to concentrate on the supply of social and economic infrastructure.

Ghana's experience with subsidy reforms has taught the importance of the following:

- *Use of research and evidence-based decision making.* Ghana used the results of the GLSS IV to make its 2001 decisions on cross-subsidization. In addition, the results of the 2004 PSIA concerning petroleum products helped the government to decide upon subsidy reforms while also bolstering its case for the reforms in communications to the general public.

- *Communication and stakeholder engagement.* A good communication strategy helped the 2005 subsidy reforms to succeed. The Ministry of Finance used the PSIA results to drive communication, helping in the delivery of the reform message. Heavy stakeholder consultation, driven by the NPA, also strengthened the latest reform. The stakeholders consulted and engaged included the cabinet as well as parliamentary subcommittees on Energy and Mines and the parliamentary committee on subsidiary legislation (both types of committees including a good mix of NDC and NPP members). Industry players were consulted and involved in the planning stage, and civil society, consumer watch groups, and the general public were educated extensively about price deregulation.
- *Evidence of failure.* A major factor that helped in the success of the latest reforms is the evidence available to all that previous subsidy regimes had failed, with negative implications such as smuggling, adulteration, and fiscal strain. For example, under a regulated pricing regime, the government (through the BoG) had the obligation to supply foreign currency for oil imports—a bill that amounted to about US$3.6 billion a year, which was over 50 percent of the country's reserves in 2014 and 2015. Oil import bills alone significantly contributed to the cedi depreciation.
- *Free-market competition for industry players.* The latest reforms in Ghana, which removed government control over petroleum product prices, enabled the free market to operate efficiently to provide competitive prices to consumers.
- *Support of state institutions to create an enabling environment.* The latest Ghana reforms utilized state-owned institutions to ensure a buffer of petroleum product supply at market prices, thus ensuring that consumers were not unduly taken advantage of by the private sector under the free-market pricing process.
- *Realization that politicizing petroleum does not work.* Since the 2008 elections, both the NDC and NPP have learned to withdraw from politicization of petroleum product prices; both parties have basically refrained from campaigning on a reduction of fuel prices.
- *Timing of reform for success.* Ghana deregulated petroleum product prices at a time when world prices were significantly low, helping to reduce the impact of price reforms on the consumer while also helping to communicate to the consumer that local prices will change in the same direction as international prices because the country is a net importer of petroleum products.

Conclusions

Ghana, being a net importer of petroleum products, is susceptible to world price volatilities. Although various subsidy reforms have been implemented since 2001, they have not been sustained because of inconsistency in implementation. Reforms have often been suspended because of executive intervention in the implementation of a full pass-through of world prices to domestic prices. Meanwhile, subsidy programs have caused tremendous fiscal strain on the government.

Other impediments to sustainable subsidy reform included lack of an adequate mitigation strategy that could help sustain automatic price increases in addition to the following four factors:

- Reforms were not timed in such a way that they would be self-sustainable or leave little incentive for government to intervene again. The political will to continue with the reform was lost immediately when world prices began to go up because no system was in place to create a buffer to minimize the social impact of the reform.
- The relevant stakeholders were not adequately consulted and engaged during the planning phase.
- Poor communication strategies generally failed to support the reforms. Although communication worked to some extent in the 2004 reforms, subsequent reforms have had poor communication strategies except for the NPA's media campaign to announce the price changes.
- The lack of clearly defined roles for state agencies to carry along the process contributed to the failure of reforms, given their huge presence in the downstream supply chain.

In contrast, the price deregulation of July 2015 benefited from the lessons of past attempts, incorporating four key strategies:

- Timing of implementation while world prices were favorably low
- Strong stakeholder engagement to get the buy-in of all interested parties
- Effective communication to the general public
- Use of state-owned oil marketers to provide a supply buffer, thus ensuring that product availability would not depend solely on the private sector, especially during the first six months of implementation

Although price deregulation was backed by some civil society organizations, other consumer watch organizations and civil society organizations heavily criticized the concept. Seven months of implementation has shown that market competition has driven local prices to 10 percent below the full cost recovery price.

Despite the success of the latest reforms so far, it is still too early to conclude that this is a sustainable equilibrium. The implementation of the 2015 Energy Levies Act has increased prices by about 30 percent even under currently low world prices, which has sparked unrest.[33] The government is currently bound by its responsibilities in the implementation of the IMF's keenly monitored fiscal consolidation and austerity program and, by extension, might not have the appetite to intervene in prices again. However, political and vote-seeking interests could change things as in the past, particularly in the face of international price hikes.

Annex 3A Political Chronology of Ghana

Table 3A.1 Major Political Events in Ghana, 1843–2013

Year	*Event*
1843–44	British government signs bond of 1844 with Fante chiefs.
1873–74	Last Asante invasion of coast. British capture Kumasi.
1874	Britain establishes Gold Coast Colony.
1896	Anglo-Asante war leads to exile of Asantehene and British protectorate over Asante.
1900	First Africans are appointed to colony's Legislative Council.
1902	Northern territories are proclaimed a British protectorate.
1919	German Togo becomes a mandate under Gold Coast administration.
1925	Constitution of 1925 calls for six chiefs to be elected to Legislative Council.
1947	United Gold Coast Convention is founded.
1949	Kwame Nkrumah breaks with United Gold Coast Convention and forms the Convention People's Party (CPP).
1951	New constitution leads to general elections, and the CPP wins two-thirds majority.
1954	New constitution grants broad powers to Nkrumah's government.
1956	Plebiscite in British Togoland calls for union with Gold Coast. CPP wins 68 percent of seats in legislature and passes an independence motion, which the British Parliament approves.
1957	British colony, the Gold Coast, becomes independent Ghana on March 6.
1958	Entrenched protection clauses of the constitution are repealed, regional assemblies are abolished, and the Preventive Detention Act is passed.
1960	Plebiscite creates a republic on July 1, with Nkrumah as president.
1964	Ghana is declared a one-party state.
1966	While Nkrumah is in China, the army stages a widely popular coup. The National Liberation Council comes to power.
1969	The Progress Party, led by Kofi. A. Busia, wins National Assembly elections.
1972	Lieutenant Colonel Ignatius Acheampong leads a military coup in January that brings the National Redemption Council to power.
1978	Fellow military officers ease Acheampong from power.
1979	Junior officers stage Ghana's first violent coup on June 4. The Armed Forces Revolutionary Council is formed under Flight Lieutenant Jerry John Rawlings. Hilla Liman is elected president in July.
1981	Rawlings stages a second coup on December 31. The Provisional National Defence Council is established, with Rawlings as chairman.
1983	The first phase of the Economic Recovery Program is introduced, with World Bank and International Monetary Fund support.
1985	The National Commission for Democracy is established to plan the democratization of Ghana's political system, officially inaugurated in January.
1988–89	Elections for new district assemblies begin in early December and continue through February 1989.
1990	Various organizations call for the return to civilian government and multiparty politics. The Movement for Freedom and Justice is founded in August.
1991	The Provisional Defence Council announces its acceptance of multiparty politics in May. A June deadline is set for creation of a Consultative Assembly to discuss the nation's new constitution.
1992	A national referendum in April approves the draft of a new democratic constitution. Formation and registration of political parties become legal in May. Rawlings is elected president on November 3. Parliamentary elections are boycotted by major opposition parties on December 29, resulting in a landslide victory for the National Democratic Congress (NDC).

table continues next page

Table 3A.1 Major Political Events in Ghana, 1843–2013 *(continued)*

Year	*Event*
1993	Ghana's Fourth Republic is inaugurated on January 4, swearing in Rawlings as president.
1995	President Rawlings pays official visit to the United States March 8–9, the first U.S. visit by a Ghanaian head of state in more than 30 years.
1996	Rawlings is reelected as president with 57 percent of the votes.
1999	Some members of the ruling NDC break out to form the Reform Movement as a large opposition party.
2000	Rawlings's presidency ends, as the constitution allows only two terms in office. Vice President John Atta Mills is the NDC's new presidential candidate, but the New Patriotic Party's candidate, John Kufuor, wins and becomes the new president.
May 2002	A National Reconciliation Commission starts investigating the occurrence of human rights violations during many years of military rule.
March 2007	Ghana celebrates 50 years of independence as the first Sub-Saharan African nation to gain independence.
Dec 2008	After losing two previous elections to John Kufuor, John Atta Mills wins as president over rival Nana Akuffo Addo of the NPP.
July 2012	President Mills dies. Vice President John Dramani Mahama becomes the interim head of state.
Dec 2012	President John Mahama wins reelection.
Aug 2013	President John Mahama is declared winner of the 2012 elections by the Supreme Court after results were questioned by the opposition and a landmark case was filed before the court.

Source: "History Timeline—Chronology of Important Events," GhanaWeb, accessed Oct. 11, 2016, http://www.ghanaweb.com/GhanaHomePage/history/timeline.php.

Annex 3B Ghana's Poverty Reduction Programs

Since 1957, several policies and programs to accelerate Ghana's economic growth and raise the living standards of its people have been pursued with varying degrees of success. The following summary was developed from NDPC (2010, 2014).

- In 1995, the *Coordinated Programme of Economic and Social Development Policies* was developed with the title, "Ghana: Vision 2020." The ultimate objective was to push the country into middle-income status within 25 years.
- Based on "Vision 2020," *The First Medium-Term Development Plan (1997–2000)* was developed. The agenda prioritized human development, economic growth, rural development, urban development, infrastructure development, and provision of an enabling environment.
- The *Ghana Poverty Reduction Strategy (GPRS I)*, issued in 2003, was developed to reflect a policy framework that was to eradicate extreme poverty and hunger.
- The *Growth and Poverty Reduction Strategy (GPRS II)*, issued in 2007, was directed mainly toward attainment of the United Nations' Millennium Development Goal 1 (reducing extreme poverty by half) and was designed to be implemented during 2006–09, emphasizing growth as the basis for sustained poverty reduction "so that Ghana can achieve middle-income status within a measurable planning period."

- Even though substantial progress was made under GPRS I and GPRS II toward the realization of macroeconomic stability and a shift in strategic focus to achieve poverty reduction goals, there were some structural challenges including large fiscal and balance-of-payment deficits. The successor to GPRS II, the *Ghana Shared Growth and Development Agenda I* (*GSGDA I*), was developed as a medium-term development policy framework to be implemented from 2010 to 2013.
- Despite the significant improvements in the performance of the economy in the past two decades, there remain a number of macroeconomic and structural challenges that limit the capacity of the economy to achieve sustainable improvements in the livelihoods of the people. The *Ghana Shared Growth and Development Agenda II* (*GSGDA II*), with an implementation period of 2014–17, is the latest development policy framework being implemented in Ghana.

Annex 3C Chronology of Energy Subsidy Reform Efforts

Table 3C.1 Events Related to Subsidy Reform in Ghana, 2001–16

Year	*Event*
Pre-2001	Prices set by the Tema Oil Refinery (TOR) based on cost of production or cost of imports
2001	Establishment of an automatic adjustment formula based on import parity and full cost recovery
2002	Inclusion of a debt service charge called the TOR Debt Recovery Levy to pay for the accumulated subsidy debt to TOR
	Abandonment of automatic adjustment by the end of 2002 because of heavy citizen resistance to price hikes
2003	January price increases of 90 percent to achieve full cost recovery, with inclusions of a "k" factor in the reimplementation of the automatic adjustment formula to account for TOR inefficiencies
	Downward price adjustment as government faces public outcry and looks toward 2004 general elections
2004	Completion of Ghana Poverty and Social Impact Analysis (PSIA), resulting in a removal of subsidies, with savings directed into social protection programs such as improved access to quality health care and education for the worse-off in society
2005	Establishment of the National Petroleum Authority (NPA) as the downstream regulator and custodian of the automatic adjustment formula
	Establishment of the Unified Petroleum Price Fund (UPPF) to ensure equal prices of petroleum products throughout the country
2006	Introduction of a price stabilization fund to pay marketers for subsidies on liquefied petroleum gas (LPG), kerosene, and premix fuel
2007	Change in price review frequency, from once a month to twice a month, to reflect more-current international prices
2008	Suspension of further price adjustments between May and November due to the impact of international oil and food price hikes
2009–10	Further reduction in prices as well as taxes
2011–Jan 2012	Beginning of an unreversed process to cut fuel subsidies, resulting in fuel price increase of 20 percent

table continues next page

Table 3C.1 Events Related to Subsidy Reform in Ghana, 2001–16 *(continued)*

Year	*Event*
2012	Establishment of a transport fare formula with transport operators, with a government-negotiated trigger point for fare increases in response to fuel price increases (commercial vehicle transporters to increase transport fares by a third of the fuel price increase, if the cumulative fuel price increase exceeds 10 percent, on the condition that other factors in the fare model have also changed, such as substantial cost increases in insurance and spare parts) Reduction of the January price increase by 20 percent, in response to labor union agitation coupled with anticipation of December general elections
2013	Launch of the Rural LPG Promotion Program to encourage use of LPG as an alternative fuel in rural areas to prevent deforestation
2014	Drastic reduction in subsidy levels Introduction in November of Special Petroleum Tax, a 17.5 percent value added tax (VAT) on petroleum products
2015	Implementation of price deregulation after heavy lobbying from bulk distribution companies (BDCs), oil financing banks, and the NPA due to the heavy government indebtedness to the industry
2016	Implementation in January of the 2015 Energy Levies Act, causing a 28–30 percent price increase Civil society organizations, labor unions, and transport operators protest the price increase while also dialoguing with the government for various compensation Latest reforms unaffected by price increases, as the oil marketers have been allowed to pass through costs fully to the pump

Annex 3D Typical Price Build Up (PBU)

The petroleum product PBU schedule is based on import parity with the following objectives:

- Full cost recovery of all investments
- Revenue generation for government through the imposition of taxes and levies by Parliament
- Ensuring that prices are uniform nationwide through the Unified Petroleum Price Fund (UPPF)

According to the pricing formula, the main factors that affect petroleum products pricing in Ghana are international product prices (FOB), the exchange rate (cedis per U.S. dollar), taxes and levies approved by Parliament, and distribution margins (table 3D.1).

The free on board (FOB) prices used are two-week averages of Platts daily quotes for all products except LPG, for which Argus Media's daily quotes are used. For prices effective on the 1st of the month, two-week quotes from the 12th to the 26th of the previous month are used. For prices effective on the 16th of the month, two-week quotes from 27th of the previous month to the 11th of the current month are used.

The "suppliers' premium" constitutes freight, insurance, and total related charges. The ex-refinery ("ex-ref") price is converted from U.S. dollars per megaton (USD/MT) to U.S. dollars per liter (USD/LT) by dividing it by a conversion

Table 3D.1 Typical Petroleum Product Price Build Up

Pricing variable	*Unit*	*Formula*[a]	*Amount*
FOB price	USD/MT	A	400.00
Suppliers premium	USD/MT	B	112.17
Ex-ref price	USD/MT	C=A+B	512.17
Conversion factor	LT/MT	D	1,342.28
Ex-ref price	USD/LT	E=C/D	0.38
Exchange rate	GHS/USD	F	3.80
Ex-ref price	**GHp/LT**	**G=(E*F)*100**	**145.00**
Excise duty	GHp/LT	H	2.7800
Energy debt recovery levy	GHp/LT	I	41.0000
Road fund levy	GHp/LT	J	40.0000
Energy fund levy	GHp/LT	K	1.0000
Price stabilization and recovery levy	GHp/LT	L	12.0000
Primary distribution margin	GHp/LT	M	4.5000
BOST margin	GHp/LT	N	3.0000
Fuel marking margin	GHp/LT	O	1.5000
Ex-depot	**GHp/LT**	**P=G+...+O**	**250.7755**
Special petroleum tax	GHp/LT	Q=17.5%*R	43.8857
UPPF	GHp/LT	R	9.0000
Marketers margin	GHp/LT	S	20.3374
Dealers (retailers and operators) margin	GHp/LT	T	13.5908
LPG filling plant/premix/MGO local admin costs	GHp/LT	U	
Distribution compensation margin	GHp/LT	V	
EX-PUMP PRICE	**GHp/LT**	**W=Q+...+V**	**337.5894**

Source: NPA 2015.
Note: FOB = free on board (price). USD = U.S. dollar. MT = megaton. LT = liter. GHS = Ghanaian cedi. GHp = Ghanaian pesewa. Ex-ref = ex-refinery. BOST = Bulk Oil Storage and Transportation Company. UPPF = Unified Petroleum Price Fund. LPG = liquefied petroleum gas. MGO = marine gas oil.
a. Formula for the buildup to ex-refinery and ex-pump prices.

factor. Each product has its conversion factor, which is based on the standard pricing density of the product. (For example, the conversion factor for gasoline is 1,342.28 based on a density of 0.745.)

The cedi-to-U.S. dollar exchange rate (a two-week average of daily interbank foreign exchange rates monitored from the BoG) is then multiplied by the ex-refinery price (USD/LT) to bring it to Ghanaian cedis per liter (GHS/LT) or Ghanaian pesewas per liter (GHp/LT).

The approved taxes, levies, and margins are then added to the ex-refinery price (GHp/LT) to arrive at the ex-pump price.

Notes

1. Other reviews of energy subsidies in Ghana include Awafo (2014), Crawford (2012), ESMAP (2005), and Reuters (2015).
2. Current production is about 105,000 barrels a day.

3. Capacity figure from TOR, "Company Profile," http://www.tor.com.gh/about-tor/company-profile/.
4. Interviews and data received from the National Petroleum Authority, which is the petroleum downstream regulator.
5. For more details about the elections since Ghana gained its independence in 1957, see annex 3A, "Political Chronology of Ghana."
6. The World Bank provides an overview of Ghana and its economy on the Bank website: http://www.worldbank.org/en/country/ghana/overview.
7. Const. of Ghana, art. 36, § 5.
8. For descriptions of such social and economic development programs since 1995, see annex 3B, "Ghana's Poverty Reduction Programs."
9. The UNDP provides an overview of Ghana's performance toward the achievement of MDG 1 on its website: http://www.gh.undp.org/content/ghana/en/home/post-2015/mdgoverview/overview/mdg1.html.
10. The average poverty rate in Africa has been calculated using the international poverty line of US$1.25 per person per day.
11. For more information about the locations and characteristics of Ghana's 10 administrative regions, see the "Regions" web page of the Ghana government website: http://www.ghana.gov.gh/index.php/about-ghana/regions.
12. The Jubilee oil field, located off the coast of Ghana in the Atlantic Ocean, was discovered in 2007 by Kosmos Energy (an American international oil company based in Dallas) and developed by Tullow Oil (an Irish multinational oil and gas exploration company). A more detailed description of the Jubilee field is available on the Kosmos Energy website: http://www.kosmosenergy.com/operations-ghana-jubilee-field.php.
13. Interviews with, and data from, the officials of the Ghana National Gas Company, which owns and operates the Ghana Gas Processing Plant, October–December 2015. All interviews were conducted in confidentiality.
14. Interviews with, and data from, officials of the National Petroleum Authority (NPA), the petroleum downstream regulator, October–December 2015. All interviews were conducted in confidentiality.
15. Capacity figure from TOR, "Company Profile," http://www.tor.com.gh/about-tor/company-profile/.
16. Company information available at http://www.platongasoil.com/.
17. Interviews with, and data from, the officials of the Ghana National Gas Company, which owns and operates the Ghana Gas Processing Plant, October–December 2015. All interviews were conducted in confidentiality.
18. Interviews with, and data from, the officials of the Ghana National Gas Company, which owns and operates the Ghana Gas Processing Plant, October–December 2015. All interviews were conducted in confidentiality.
19. Interviews and data from Ghana National Petroleum Corporation.
20. Details of Ghana's power generation mix is explained further on the Volta River Authority website: http://www.vra.com/.
21. Interviews with, and data from, the officials of the Ghana National Gas Company, which owns and operates the Ghana Gas Processing Plant, October–December 2015. All interviews were conducted in confidentiality.

22. Interviews with, and data from, the officials of the Ghana National Gas Company, which owns and operates the Ghana Gas Processing Plant, October–December 2015. All interviews were conducted in confidentiality.
23. Interviews with, and data from, the officials of the Ghana National Gas Company, which owns and operates the Ghana Gas Processing Plant, October–December 2015. All interviews were conducted in confidentiality.
24. According to the NPA Act 691 of 2005, the NPA board is made up of the chairperson, the chief executive officer, a representative of the petroleum workers union, a representative of the Ghana Chamber of Commerce or Ghana Chamber of Mines, and three citizens with specialized knowledge and experience.
25. Data from the foreign exchange loss audit report submitted by Ernst and Young audit firm to the government.
26. The "ex-depot" price refers to the cost plus excise duty, with no additional elements of pricing added.
27. Interviews with, and data from, the officials of the Ghana National Gas Company, which owns and operates the Ghana Gas Processing Plant, October–December 2015. All interviews were conducted in confidentiality.
28. Interviews with, and data from, the officials of the Ghana National Gas Company, which owns and operates the Ghana Gas Processing Plant, October–December 2015. All interviews were conducted in confidentiality.
29. The IMF Extended Credit Facility (ECF) "provides financial assistance to countries with protracted balance of payment problems. The ECF is the Fund's main tool for providing medium-term support to [low-income countries]" (IMF 2016).
30. Interviews with, and data from, the officials of the Ghana National Gas Company, which owns and operates the Ghana Gas Processing Plant, October–December 2015. All interviews were conducted in confidentiality.
31. Interviews with, and data from, the officials of the Ghana National Gas Company, which owns and operates the Ghana Gas Processing Plant, October–December 2015. All interviews were conducted in confidentiality.
32. Based on NPA studies on the direct impact of petroleum subsidies on welfare of consumers, the study used data on expenditure of 16,772 households in Ghana.
33. Interviews with, and data from, the officials of the Ghana National Gas Company, which owns and operates the Ghana Gas Processing Plant, October–December 2015. All interviews were conducted in confidentiality.

References

Abdul -Salam, Y., and E. Phimister. 2016. "The Politico-Economics of Electricity Planning in Developing Countries: A Case Study of Ghana." *Energy Policy* 88 (January): 299–309.

Abdulai, A.-G. 2009. "Political Context Study–Ghana." Human Rights, Power and Civil Action research project of the Universities of Oslo, Leeds, and Ghana.

Ackah, Charles. 2015. "Electricity Insecurity and Its Impact on Micro and Small Businesses in Ghana." Study presented at Institute of Statistical, Social and Economic Research (ISSER) workshop, "Electricity Insecurity and Its Impact on the Economy of Ghana," University of Ghana, Legon, May 14. http://isser.edu.gh/index.php/isser-latest-news/92-workshop-on-electricity-insecurity-and-its-impact-on-the-economy-of-ghana.

AfDB (African Development Bank), OECD (Organisation for Economic Co-operation and Development), and UNDP (United Nations Development Programme). 2016. *African Economic Outlook 15th Edition: Sustainable Cities and Structural Transformation.* Paris: ADB, OECD, UNDP.

Alagidede, P., W. Baah-Boateng, and E. Nketiah-Amponsah. 2013. "The Ghanaian Economy: An Overview." *Ghanaian Journal of Economics* 1 (December): 4–34.

Awafo, Edward A. 2014. "Fuel Subsidies: Ghana—Reforms and Lessons." PowerPoint presentation, The Energy Center, Kwame Nkrumah University of Science and Technology (KNUST), Ghana.

Bacon, R., and M. Kojima. 2006. "Phasing Out Subsidies: Recent Experiences with Fuel in Developing Countries." Public Policy for the Private Sector Note 310, World Bank, Washington, DC.

Bernstein, H. 2015. "Agrarian Political Economy." In *International Encyclopedia of the Social & Behavioral Sciences*, edited by James D. Wright, 456–62. 2nd ed. Oxford: Elsevier.

Bezemer, D., J. Bolt, and R. Lensink. 2014. "Slavery, Statehood, and Economic Development in Sub-Saharan Africa." *World Development* 57 (C): 148–63.

CEPA (Centre for Policy Analysis). 2003. "Pricing Petroleum Products in Ghana—The Automatic Formula." In *Ghana: Selected Economic Issues*, Issues Paper 5. Accra: CEPA.

———. 2007. "The Energy Crisis and Growth Performance of the Economy." In *Ghana: Selected Economic Issues*, Issues Paper 15. Accra: CEPA.

Clementi, F., V. Molini, and F. Schettino. 2016. "Poverty and Social Impact Analysis (PSIA): The Impact of Reductions in Fuel and Electricity Subsidies." Unpublished manuscript, World Bank, Washington, DC.

Coady, D., and D. Newhouse. 2006. "Ghana: Evaluating the Fiscal and Social Costs of Increases in Domestic Fuel Prices." In *Poverty and Social Impact Analysis of Reforms: Lessons and Examples from Implementation*, edited by A. Coudouel, S. Paternostro, and A. A. Dani, 387–412. Washington, DC: World Bank.

Crawford, G. 2012. "Ghana's Fossil-Fuel Subsidy Reform." Case Study 09, Institute of Development Studies, Brighton, U.K.

Energy Commission. 2015. *2015 Energy (Supply and Demand) Outlook for Ghana.* Forecast report, Energy Commission, Accra.

ESMAP (Energy Sector Management Assistance Program). 2005. "Ghana: Poverty and Social Impact Analysis of Electricity Tariffs." ESMAP Technical Paper 088, World Bank, Washington, DC.

Fisher Onar, N., J. H. Liu, and M. Woodward. 2014. "Critical Junctures? Complexity and the Post-Colonial Nation-State." *International Journal of Intercultural Relations* 43 (Part A): 22–34.

Freedom House. 2016. *Freedom of the Press 2016: The Battle for the Dominant Message.* Annual analytical report, Freedom House, Washington, DC.

Frempong, A. K. 2008. "Innovations in Electoral Politics in Ghana's Fourth Republic: An Analysis." In *Democratic Innovation in the South: Participation and Representation in Asia, Africa and Latin America*, edited by Ciska Raventós, 189–210. Buenos Aires: CLACSO.

GRIDCo. 2014. *2014 Electricity Supply Plan.* Tema: Ghana Grid Company (GRIDCo).

GSS (Ghana Statistical Service). 2000. *Ghana Living Standards Survey: Report of the Fourth Round (GLSS 4)*. Report of main results, GSS, Accra.

———. 2014. *Ghana Living Standards Survey Round 6 (GLSS 6): Poverty Profile in Ghana (2005–2013)*. GSS, Accra.

———. 2015. "Revised 2014 Annual Gross Domestic Product." Revised GDP estimates release, GSS, Accra.

Hansen, C. P., and J. F. Lund. 2011. "The Political Economy of Timber Taxation: The Case of Ghana." *Forest Policy and Economics* 13 (8): 630–41.

IMF (International Monetary Fund). 2012. *Ghana: Poverty Reduction Strategy Paper*. Country Report 12/203, IMF, Washington, DC.

———. 2013. *Energy Subsidy Reform in Sub-Saharan Africa: Experiences and Lessons*. Washington, DC: International Monetary Fund.

———. 2015. *Ghana: Request for a Three-Year Arrangement under the Extended Credit Facility; Staff Report; Press Release; and Statement by the Executive Director for Ghana*. Country Report 15/103, IMF, Washington, DC.

———. 2016. "IMF Extended Credit Facility (ECF)." Factsheet, October 3. http://www.imf.org/en/About/Factsheets/Sheets/2016/08/02/21/04/Extended-Credit-Facility.

IMF (International Monetary Fund) and World Bank. 2015. *Ghana: Request for a Three-Year Arrangement under the Extended Credit Facility—Debt Sustainability Analysis*. Section of Country Report 15/103, IMF, Washington, DC.

Kojima, M. 2016. "Fossil Fuel Subsidy and Pricing Policies: Recent Developing Country Experience." Policy Research Working Paper 7531, World Bank, Washington, DC.

Kosmos Energy. 2016. "Kosmos Energy Announces Fourth Quarter and Full Year 2015 Results." News release, February 22. http://investors.kosmosenergy.com/phoenix.zhtml?c=238878&p=irol-newsarticle&ID=2141479.

MoF (Ministry of Finance, Republic of Ghana). 2015. *The Budget Statement and Economic Policy of the Government of Ghana for the 2016 Financial Year*. Report to Parliament, presented November 13, MoF, Accra.

Molini, V., and P. Paci. 2015. *Poverty Reduction in Ghana: Progress and Challenges*. Washington, DC: World Bank.

NDPC (National Development Planning Commission, Republic of Ghana). 1994. "National Development Policy Framework: Vol. I, Long-Term Development Objectives." Framework document, NDPC, Accra. https://s3.amazonaws.com/ndpc-static/pubication/NDP+Framework+Vol+I+LTDO+Feb+1994.pdf.

———. 2010. "Medium-Term National Development Policy Framework: Ghana Shared Growth and Development Agenda (GSGDA), 2010–2013." Framework document, NDPC, Accra.

———. 2014. "Medium-Term National Development Policy Framework: Ghana Shared Growth and Development Agenda (GSGDA) II, 2014–2017." Framework document, NDPC, Accra.

NPA (National Petroleum Authority). 2015. "Petroleum Products Subsidy in Ghana: Do the Poor Benefit More than the Rich?" Unpublished manuscript, NPA, Accra.

Nyame, F. K., and J. A. Grant. 2014. "The Political Economy of Transitory Mining in Ghana: Understanding the Trajectories, Triumphs, and Tribulations of Artisanal and Small-Scale Operators." *The Extractive Industries and Society* 1 (1): 75–85.

Obeng-Odoom, F. 2015. "Global Political Economy and Frontier Economies in Africa: Implications from the Oil and Gas Industry in Ghana." *Energy Research & Social Science* 10 (November): 41–56.

Power, M. 2009. "The Commonwealth, 'Development' and Post-Colonial Responsibility." *Geoforum* 40 (1): 14–24.

Reuters. 2015. "Ghana to Scrap Fossil Fuel Subsidies by Sept—Oil Minister." June 3. http://www.reuters.com/article/ghana-subsidies-idUSL5N0YP4S320150603.

UN (United Nations). 2015. *2014 International Trade Statistics Yearbook*. New York: United Nations, Department of Economic and Social Affairs, Statistics Division.

UNDESA (United Nations, Department of Economic and Social Affairs). 2015. "World Population Prospects: The 2015 Revision, Key Findings and Advance Tables." Working Paper ESA/P/WP.241, UNDESA, New York.

USAID (U.S. Agency for International Development). 2015. "What Power Africa Means for Ghana." Factsheet, USAID, Washington, DC.

WEF (World Economic Forum). 2013. *Lessons Drawn from Reforms of Energy Subsidies*. Davos, Switzerland: World Economic Forum.

Yufanyi Movuh, M. C. 2012. "The Colonial Heritage and Post-Colonial Influence, Entanglements and Implications of the Concept of Community Forestry by the Example of Cameroon." *Forest Policy and Economics* 15 (February): 70–77.

Zounmeou, D. 2009. *Ghana's 2008 Election: Towards a Consolidated Democracy?* Situation Report, Institute for Security Studies, Pretoria, South Africa.

CHAPTER 4

Indonesia: Pricing Reforms, Social Assistance, and the Importance of Perceptions

Christopher Beaton, Lucky Lontoh, and Matthew Wai-Poi

Introduction

For many years, Indonesia has subsidized a range of energy products and services: gasoline, diesel, kerosene, liquefied petroleum gas (LPG), and electricity. These have been costly policies, with Indonesia having spent 1–4 percent of gross domestic product (GDP) on gasoline and diesel subsidies alone every year since the start of the 21st century. This chapter focuses on gasoline and diesel: Indonesia's oldest subsidy policies as well as its most expensive and regressive.

The chapter begins by reviewing the economic, fiscal, and political context surrounding these subsidies. It then places them in their historical context, outlining the history surrounding their creation as well as the six major reform attempts since the 1997–98 Asian Financial Crisis. These attempts include six ad hoc price increases, three ad hoc price decreases, and two periods when prices have been subject to frequent formula-determined adjustments. The chapter focuses in particular on the most recent reforms: a November 2014 price hike and a January 2015 introduction of a new pricing system. It describes the impacts of this period of policy change before identifying some of the major forces that have determined the political viability of gasoline and diesel subsidy reform at different times.

Several themes arise in the course of the discussion. One is the importance of distinguishing between analyzing the political economy of a subsidy policy (how its benefits are distributed) and analyzing the political economy of the *types* of attempted reforms (which typically result in both costs and benefits that may change over time and vary according to their specific design). This latter task—analyzing specific types of reforms—requires some precision in defining "reform." The chapter proposes at least three types of change that could be defined as a

The International Institute for Sustainable Development (IISD) has copyright over this chapter. Notwithstanding, the World Bank has permission to include this chapter in the book and make it publicly available under the CC BY 3.0 IGO license. See the copyright page for more information.

reform, that may or may not be implemented in unison, with each having faced its own political economy challenges in Indonesia: (a) ad hoc price increases, (b) institutional changes to the underlying pricing system, and (c) complementary changes to the government's capacity to target assistance with nonsubsidy policies. A fourth can also be considered for inclusion: informational changes that alter the state of public knowledge about subsidies and reform plans.

Another theme is the importance of social assistance in mitigating the impact of reforms over time and the virtuous circle that can take place between subsidy reforms and investments in social assistance capacity. As countries develop more-sophisticated tools to assist businesses and households, it becomes easier for them to manage some of the negative impacts of higher energy prices through more-effective, more-efficient policy tools. At the same time, subsidy reforms can liberate funding that allows for investments in social assistance capacity. Most of Indonesia's fuel price increases have been coupled with some form of support targeted at the needy, and as this support has improved over time, so too has the likelihood of successful price increases.

Yet a third significant theme is the importance of perceptions when it comes to subsidies that are available to an entire population: Understanding who benefits from such subsidies does matter, because it is natural to assume that benefits will be distributed disproportionately across different segments of the population. But it may be equally important to understand who *thinks* they will benefit, because these perceptions underlie public opinion that enables or obstructs reforms at a popular level. As such, "informational" reforms—interventions intended to improve the state of information about subsidies, designed with knowledge about popular perception in mind—can serve to increase a government's political operating space over time.

Country Economic and Political Context

Economic Growth

Indonesia has a long history of state intervention to circumscribe competition and create large, strong state-owned enterprises. This pattern was cemented into place after independence in the 1940s and a succession of two autocratic governments, and despite the transition to democracy, it is still evident in the economy today. Throughout the country's history, resource wealth has had a significant impact on economic development, with oil price booms in the 1970s and 1980s helping to drive high growth rates, and extractive industries more generally providing a high share of government revenue (see annex 4A for a full list of major political events in Indonesia from 1871 to 2015).

Today, Indonesia is regarded as one of the world's most successful emerging economies. It is part of the MINT group (Mexico, Indonesia, Nigeria, and Turkey)—countries "hot on the heels of the BRICS" (Brazil, the Russian Federation, India, China, and South Africa) (Coface 2014; O'Neill 2013). The country has achieved an average growth rate since 1980 of 5.5 percent (figure 4.1), and with a 2014 GDP of US$889 billion, it is the 16th-largest economy in the world.[1]

Figure 4.1 GDP Growth in Indonesia, 1980–2014

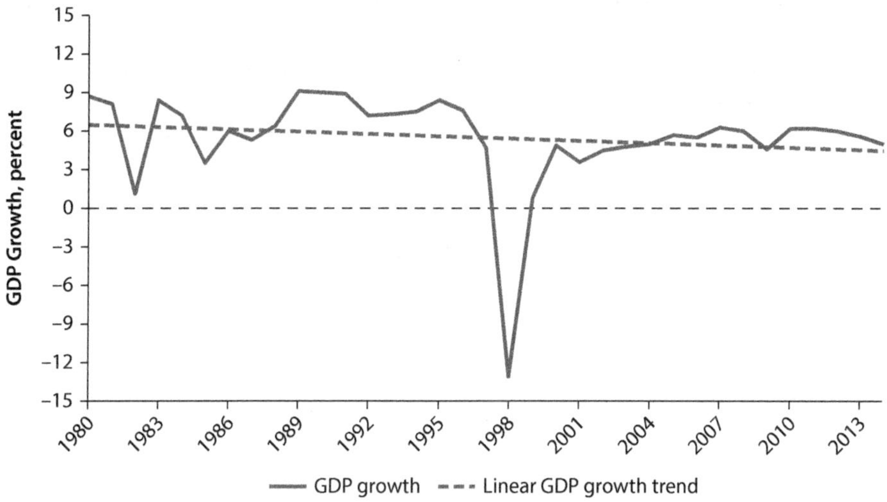

Source: World Development Indicators Database.

The extraordinary pace of Indonesia's development has not been without complications. The 1997–98 Asian Financial Crisis still looms large in recent memory. It caused Indonesia's GDP to contract 13.5 percent in 1998 alone, revealing significant structural and governance problems and triggering the transition to the current democratic regime.

A key concern of current economic policy is to avoid falling into a "middle-income growth trap": an extended period of stagnation that many fast-growing developing countries experience after reaching middle-income status (World Bank 2014b). Typically, this stagnation results from a slowdown in productivity growth as countries exhaust their potential to reallocate workers from low-productivity agricultural sectors to more-productive manufacturing sectors using catch-up technologies imported from abroad. The trap is made worse by failures to invest in the education and infrastructure required to increase competitiveness in high-skilled "innovation" or "design" labor (Agénor, Canuto, and Jelenic 2012).

Mindful of such risks, government priorities today are to maintain high growth rates, ensure that growth is inclusive, and promote further economic diversification and the expansion of domestic capacity in value-added economic activity. Economic policy also emphasizes the importance of exploiting Indonesia's "demographic dividend"—the period in which over half the country's population is under 30, which is due to end in Indonesia around 2025–30 (Bappenas 2015).[2]

Poverty Reduction

Since recovery from the Asian Financial Crisis, poverty has continued to fall in Indonesia, albeit at a slowing rate. On the basis of the national poverty line (Rp 330,776 or US$24.50 per month in March 2015), poverty rates decreased from around 18 percent of the population in 2002 to around 11 percent in

2014 (figure 4.2, panel a). However, the annual reduction in recent years has approached zero (World Bank 2015) alongside a growing gap in the relative wealth of rich and poor (figure 4.2, panel b).

Poverty rates remain higher in rural areas, although the reduction rate has been similar in both rural and urban areas over the past decade. Furthermore, many households remain close to the poverty line. Using a poverty line that

Figure 4.2 Poverty and Equity Trends in Indonesia

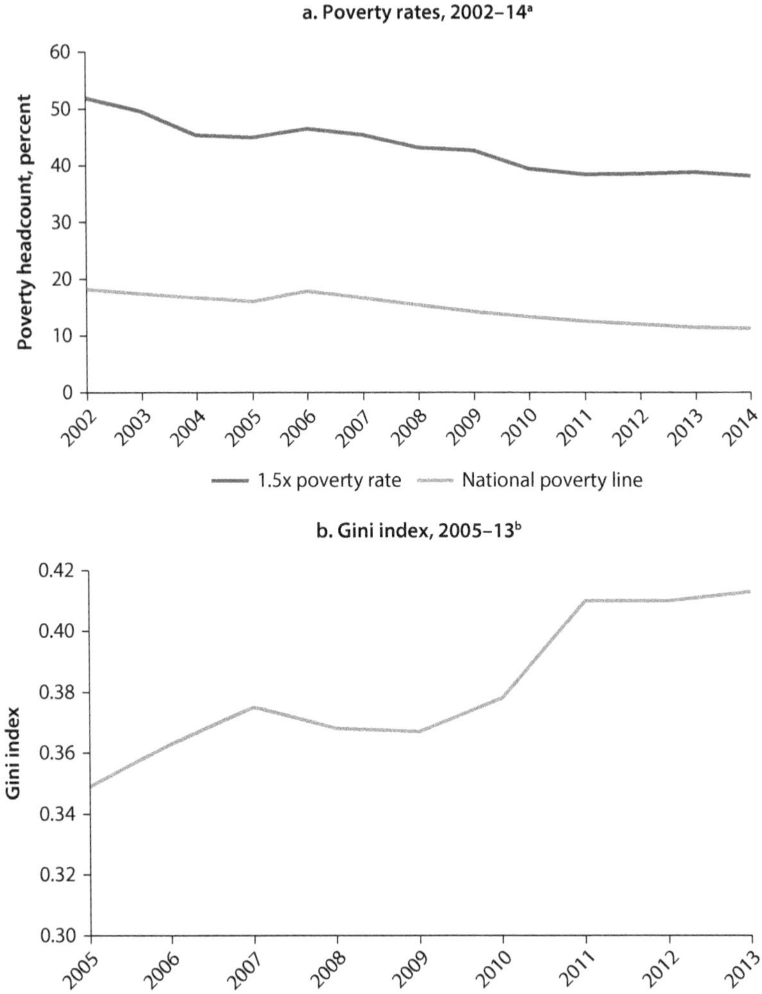

Source: Poverty rate and Gini index based on World Bank calculations using data from the National Socioeconomic Survey (SUSENAS) of the Central Statistics Agency (Badan Pusat Statistik, BPS), http://microdata.bps.go.id/mikrodata/index.php/catalog/SUSENAS.

a. The national poverty line is based on the cost of 2,100 calories per person per day along with a small nonfood allowance for basic necessities. It rose from Rp 108,889 (US$10.89) per month in 2002 to Rp 312,328 (US$26.03) per month in 2014. The poverty "vulnerability" line in Indonesia is defined as 1.5 times the national poverty line.

b. The Gini index measures the inequality of income distribution. A value of 0 indicates full equality, and 1 indicates maximum inequality.

Map 4.1 Poverty Rates in Indonesia, by Province, 2010

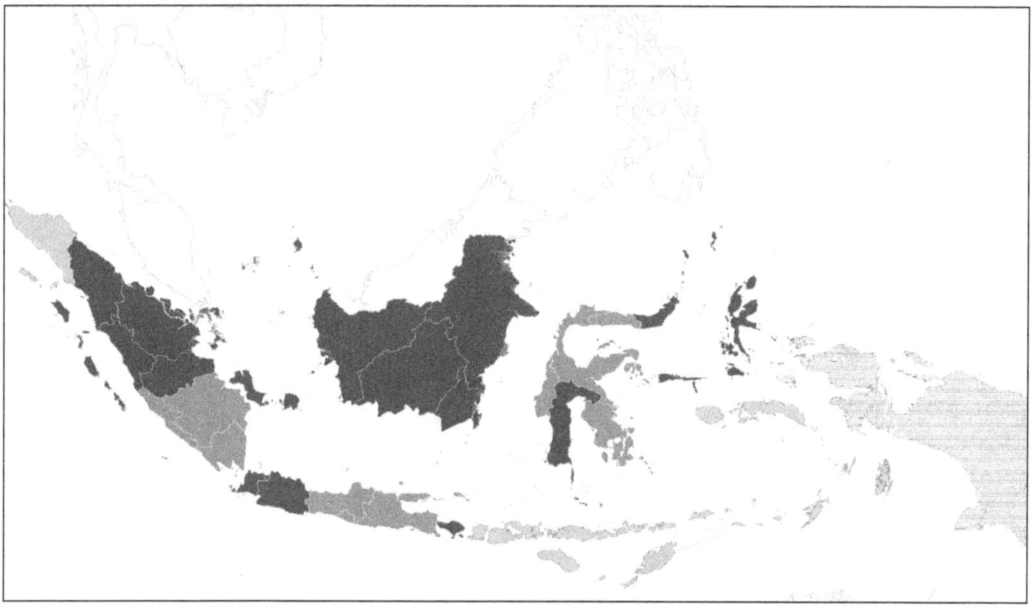

■ Low poverty: 4.15–11.72%
■ Medium-low poverty: 11.72–19.28%
■ Medium-to-high poverty: 19.28–26.85%
▤ High poverty: 26.85–34.42%

Source: SMERU Poverty and Livelihood Map of Indonesia (accessed July 31, 2015), http://www.indonesiapovertymap.org/index.php, ©SMERU Research Institute. Reproduced, with permission, from SMERU Research Institute; further permission required for reuse.
Note: SMERU = Social Monitoring and Early Response Unit. An English-language brochure (SMERU 2014) explains how to access and use the SMERU Poverty and Livelihood Map of Indonesia.

is only slightly higher—1.5 times the official poverty line—would result in 38 percent of households being defined as "poor" (figure 4.2, panel a). This measure is commonly employed as a "vulnerability" line in Indonesia. Households with an income below this line have a 10 percent chance or higher of being poor the following year (World Bank 2012b). Higher poverty benchmarks show similar trends to the official benchmark: poverty reduction has been significant but has slowed over time (figure 4.2, panel a). This large population of the "near-poor" means that even small economic shocks can have a significant impact on vulnerable households.

The rate of poverty is also distributed unevenly geographically: lowest in central, more-populated areas and highest in more-remote, less-populated areas (map 4.1). Consequently, most of the poor (56 percent) live in Java, but the highest percentages of the local population living in poverty are in Eastern Indonesia (World Bank 2006b).

Fiscal Policy

Since 2000, the Indonesian government's revenue has averaged around 17 percent of GDP, but it has been declining in recent times, reaching only 13.4 percent of GDP in 2015—below the averages for lower-middle-income countries

(15.4 percent) and middle-income countries (18.1 percent) and significantly below the average for high-income Organisation for Economic Co-operation and Development (OECD) countries (23.5 percent).[3] Expenditure has consistently exceeded revenue collection (figure 4.4, panel a), but the deficit in all years has remained below 3 percent of GDP, in compliance with a legally binding budgetary rule.

Extractive industries contribute a significant share of revenues. In 2014, the energy and mineral sector accounted for 25 percent of state revenue, with 18 percent contributed by oil and gas and 7 percent by mining (led by coal, tin, and copper) (DEN 2015). This revenue share is 14 percent lower than in 2013 because of declining oil and gas production as well as a ban on mineral exports (DEN 2015), which the government introduced to stimulate businesses to invest in domestic added-value industries in the mineral sector. Falling revenue from energy and minerals has driven efforts to increase revenue collection from other sources and to broaden the tax base.

Subsidy Expenditure

Various categories of subsidies make up a significant share of government expenditure in Indonesia. Before reforms in 2015, the largest among them was "fuel subsidies," a term encompassing subsidies for gasoline and diesel automotive fuels as well as for LPG (a cooking fuel) and, in some parts of the country, kerosene (both a cooking and lighting fuel). This group of "fuel subsidies" sits within the broader category of "energy subsidies," comprising both fuel subsidies and electricity subsidies. In addition, "nonenergy subsidies" include subsidies for rice, fertilizers, some rail and sea transport, and assistance to small and medium enterprises (SMEs).

In 2013, gasoline subsidies made up 6.0 percent of all government expenditure, diesel subsidies 4.4 percent, LPG 1.9 percent, kerosene 0.4 percent, and electricity 6.1 percent, as shown in figure 4.3 (BPK 2014). Nonenergy subsidies made up around 3 percent of government expenditure.

The high cost of energy subsidies has constrained the fiscal resources available for other purposes such as spending on education and health (Bi et al. 2014), as shown in figure 4.4, panel b. Energy subsidy expenditure over the past decade—including subsidies for gasoline, diesel, LPG, kerosene, and electricity—has taken up a large share of public expenditure, in most years around 10–20 percent of all central state expenditure, equivalent to around 3 percent of GDP, as shown in figure 4.4, panel a.

Energy subsidies have also been a source of significant fiscal uncertainty because budgeted subsidy expenditure has been contingent on typically optimistic assumptions about world oil prices, exchange rates, and domestic crude production—assumptions that have required, in most years, significant and politically complex negotiations over midyear budget revisions (Lontoh, Beaton, and Clarke 2015; Lontoh, Clarke, and Beaton 2014).

Figure 4.3 Subsidies as a Share of the Indonesian Budget, by Type, 2013

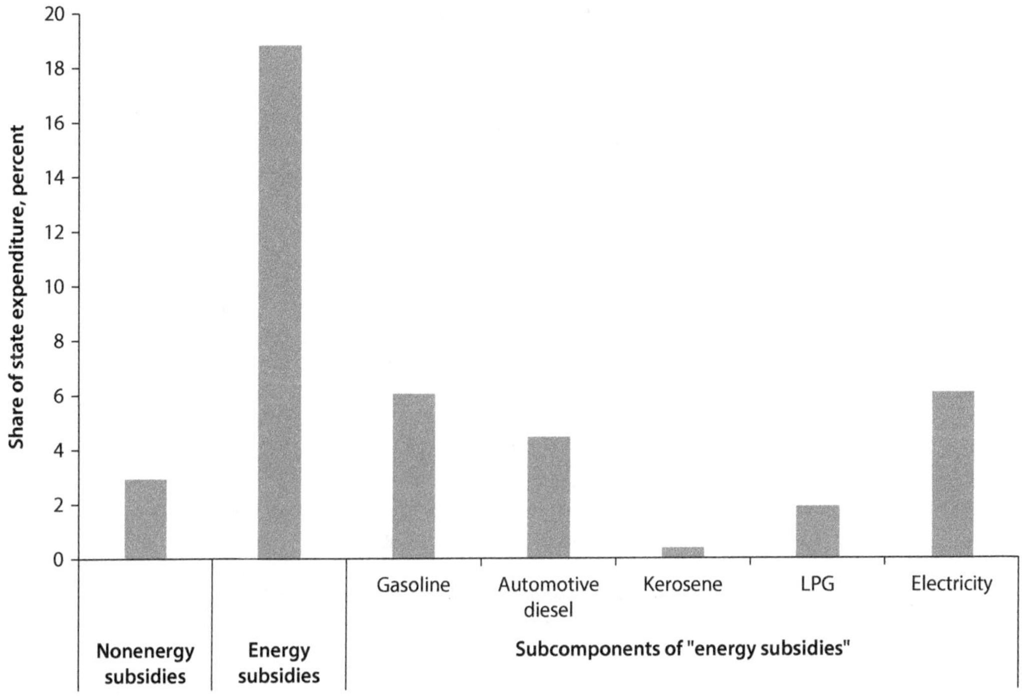

Source: BPK 2014.
Note: LPG = liquefied petroleum gas. "Share of state expenditure" includes transfers to regions. "Energy subsidies" comprise all fuel and electricity subsidies. "Nonenergy subsidies" include subsidies for rice, fertilizer, some rail and sea transport, and assistance to small and medium enterprises.

Other Development Expenditure

Partly because fuel subsidies lock up such a large share of expenditure, the Indonesian government's expenditure on other key areas of development has been low relative to other countries. Various sources calculated the country's 2011 government expenditure on health as being between 1.8 percent of all "central government" expenditure (Bi et al. 2014) and 6.2 percent of "total government" expenditure (WHO 2014). In contrast, the Southeast Asian regional average was 8.7 percent, and lower-middle-income countries' average was 8.1 percent in the same year (WHO 2014).

Indonesia also has ranked among the worst-performing lower-middle-income countries in Southeast Asia on the Asian Development Bank's (ADB) social protection index, based on the country's allocation of only 1.2 percent of GDP for social protection in 2009 (ADB 2013). The average for Asian Pacific economies in the same year was estimated to be about 5 percent of GDP (OECD 2014).

In addition, it is estimated that Indonesia's total infrastructure investment over the past decade—around 3–4 percent of GDP—has been around half of what has been needed, costing the country around 1 percent of economic

Figure 4.4 Government Revenue, Expenditure, and Fuel Subsidy Trends in Indonesia

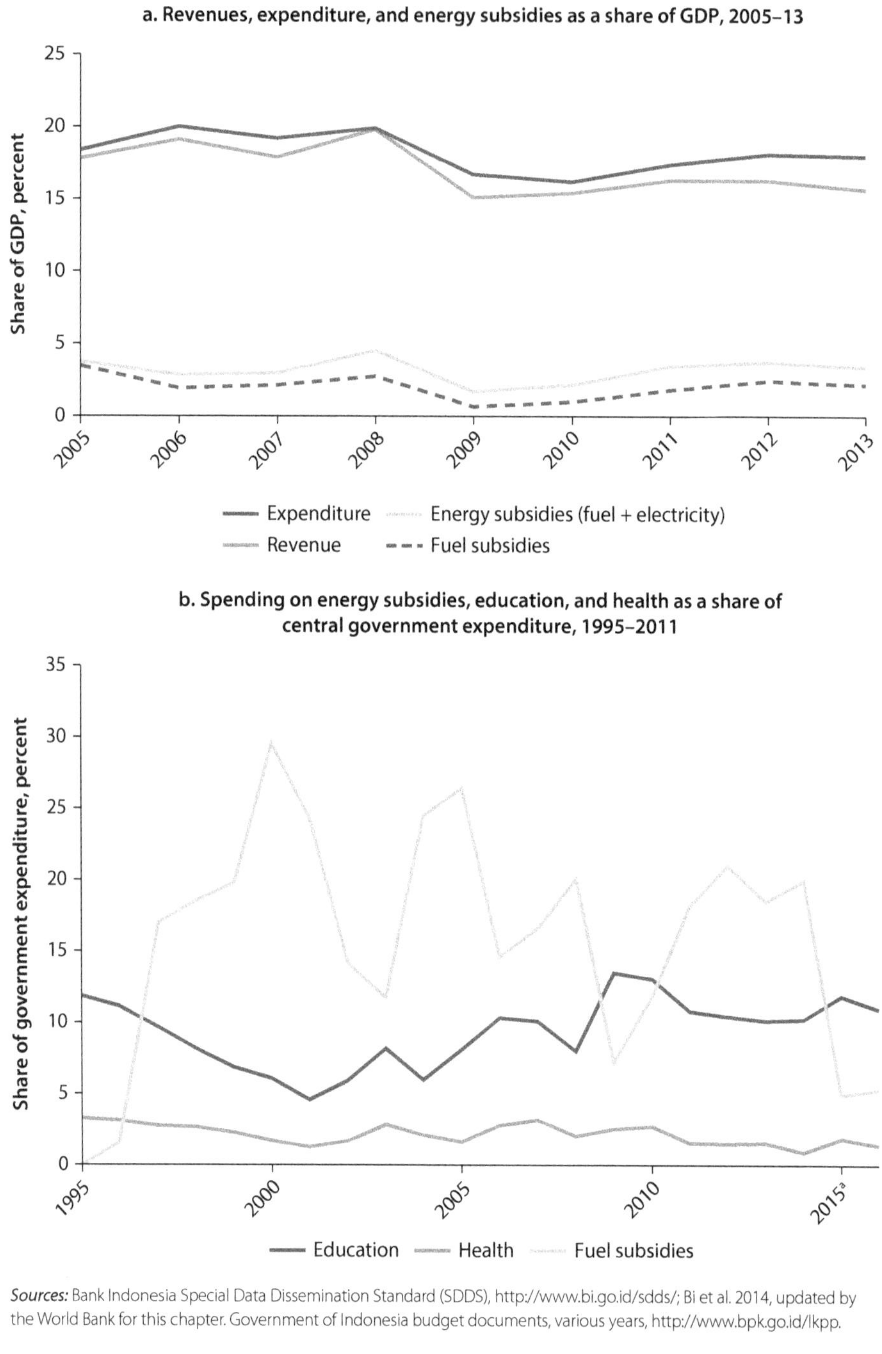

Sources: Bank Indonesia Special Data Dissemination Standard (SDDS), http://www.bi.go.id/sdds/; Bi et al. 2014, updated by the World Bank for this chapter. Government of Indonesia budget documents, various years, http://www.bpk.go.id/lkpp.

growth each year (World Bank 2014a). This contrasts with infrastructure spending of around 7 percent in Thailand and Vietnam and 10 percent in China (World Bank 2014b).

Political System

In its first 50 years following independence, Indonesia was led by two autocratic governments, first by President Sukarno (1947–67) and then by President Suharto (1967–98). Suharto's regime fell in the aftermath of the Asian Financial Crisis, and since then the Indonesian political system has undergone a significant democratic transformation, a period known as Reformasi (Reform). Today, Indonesia is a presidential representative democratic republic. The president has fairly strong executive powers, with the capacity to block legislation and influence the formulation of implementation guidelines (Datta et al. 2011).

The system is nonetheless marked by an uncommonly strong counterbalancing of power in the parliamentary branch of government—the People's Representative Council (DPR), explicitly named the country's lawmaking institution. Both executive agencies and ministers of parliament can draft legislation, and the DPR is expected to play an accountability role with respect to government (Datta et al. 2011). With respect to subsidy policy, the most notable exercise of this accountability function has been in approving the annual state budget. The budget is formulated each year by the government proposing a draft in August and parliamentarians then debating and approving items at a highly detailed level. Parliamentary sectoral commissions have significant influence, with the power to place a "hold" upon disbursements until their concerns have been addressed (Blöndal, Hawkesworth, and Choi 2009). Another key feature of the political system is an ongoing process of decentralization of power to the country's 34 provinces.

This political system reflects not only the country's transition away from decades of rule by two strong military heads of state but also a set of cultural norms that places high value on negotiation and consensus. Some argue that the Suharto regime's oligarchic elites continue to play too strong a role in the political system, engaging in an unacceptable degree of rent-seeking behavior. Others emphasize the significant progress that has been made toward a functioning democratic state while accommodating these elements from the old regime (Datta et al. 2011).

In either case, the shift to democratization appears to have led to a fragmentation of power and the rise of a number of similarly powered political parties. Following the 2014 legislative elections, parliamentary seats were fairly well distributed among Indonesia's 10 major political parties. Four of them—the Indonesian Democratic Party of Struggle (PDI-P), the Party of the Functional Groups (Golkar), the Great Indonesia Movement Party (Gerdindra), and the Democratic Party—each secured more than 60 of the 560 seats in the DPR. The share of electoral votes captured by major parties has, however, consistently declined since 1999, indicative of a gradual diffusion of political power (Datta et al. 2011).

Reform of Gasoline and Diesel Subsidies

Energy Sector Overview

Energy Supply

Indonesia's primary energy supply, from both domestic production and imports, mostly comprises oil (48 percent), coal (31 percent), and gas (17 percent) (DEN 2015). A variety of renewable energy resources contribute what remains (4 percent), as shown in figure 4.5.

Production and Imports. The country has significant fossil and renewable energy resources. Indonesia was once a major oil and gas producer, although crude oil production has been in decline since 1995, while gas production has plateaued in recent years (BP 2015). This has led to increasing reliance on costly imported oil and oil products (figures 4.6 and 4.7). Indeed, the country has become a net oil importer since 2004.

Today, Indonesia is ranked 22nd globally in crude production and 29th in crude reserves.[4] Although it has only a small share of proven coal reserves, it was the world's largest exporter of coal in 2013 (IEA 2014). Policy makers recently curbed the rate of coal extraction as part of a mineral exports ban. That ban was officially intended to control the rate at which reserves are consumed and to promote more added-value extractive industries domestically (ICTSD 2014).

Energy Access. Despite its rich energy resources, Indonesia is one of the poorest-performing nations in Southeast Asia in terms of energy access (IEA 2015). Gasoline and diesel fuel are supplied to most of the population, but subsidies have frequently caused scarcity and shortages, thus (a) reducing the incentive

Figure 4.5 Primary Energy Supply in Indonesia, 2004 and 2014

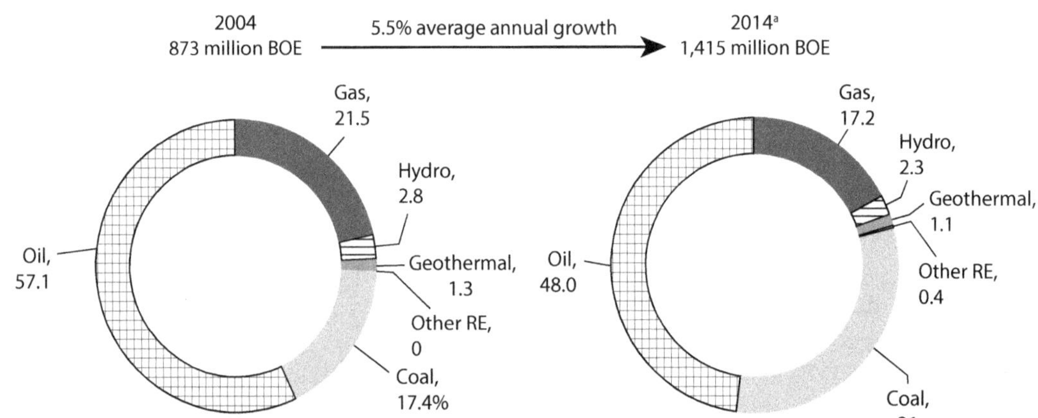

Sources: DEN 2015, ©National Energy Council (DEN). Reproduced, with permission, from DEN; further permission required for reuse.
Note: BOE = barrels of oil equivalent. RE = renewable energy. "Supply" includes both production and imports.
a. Temporary data.

Figure 4.6 Oil Production, Consumption, and Price in Indonesia, 1965–2014

Source: BP 2015.
Note: From 1965 to 1983, spot price is Arabian Light posted at Ras Tanura. From 1984 to 2014, spot price is Brent dated. Spot prices are inflated to 2014 dollars.

Figure 4.7 Fuel Imports in Indonesia, 2005–14

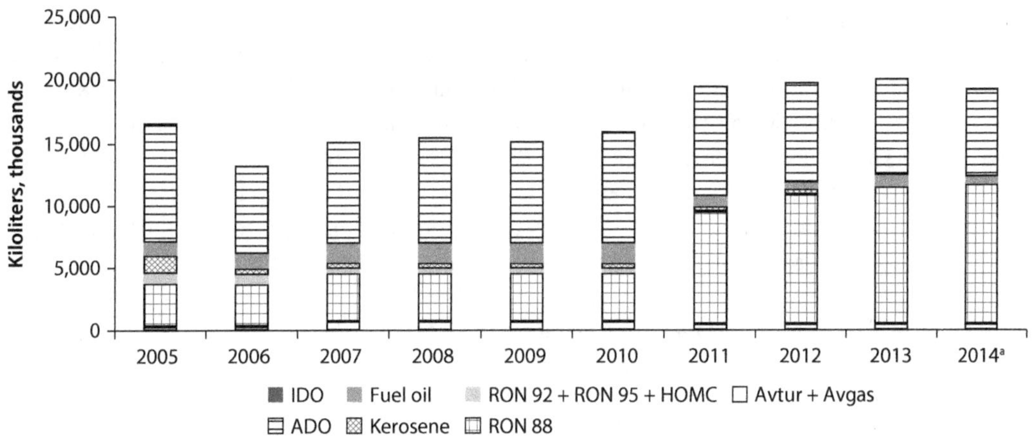

Source: DEN 2015.
Note: Avtur = aviation fuel. Avgas = Aviation gasoline. HOMC = High Octane Mogas (motor fuel) Component. ADO = Automotive diesel oil. IDO = Industrial diesel oil. Gasoline octane ratings are expressed by their Research Octane Number (RON).
a. Temporary data.

for the state-owned oil company, Pertamina, to adequately supply more-remote regions; (b) requiring rationing in some years to avoid exceeding the approved quota for subsidized fuel; (c) causing hoarding in anticipation of price increases; and (d) incentivizing smuggling and illegal marketeering at above-official prices (GSI-IISD and IESR 2012; Harvey 2005; Listy, Kristanto, and Parikesit 2014;

Lontoh, Beaton and Clarke 2015; Sadmoko, Leonal, and Rahadiana 2014; Suherdjoko and Muryanto 2013; Susanto and Suherdjoko 2013).

Similarly, the State Electricity Company (Perusahaan Listrik Negara, or PLN) has for various reasons—including poorly financed electricity subsidies and the challenges of electrification across a large archipelago nation—achieved an electrification rate of 84.4 percent by 2014. However, 32.2 percent of households still cook primarily with firewood (DEN 2015).

Energy Consumption

Energy demand in Indonesia has grown strongly in tandem with economic growth, averaging a 5.5 percent annual increase since 2004 (DEN 2015). In the transportation sector, the consumption of "Premium" brand (88-octane) gasoline—the subsidized grade of gasoline—has more than doubled since 2000, while nonsubsidized 92-octane and 95-octane gasoline[5] remain a small share of overall supply (figure 4.8, panel a).[6]

This growth in fuel demand has been matched by an enormous uptick in vehicles that use this fuel. The number of private vehicles, notably motorcycles, in Indonesia has more than quadrupled between 2000 and 2010 (figure 4.8, panel b).

History of Gasoline and Diesel Subsidies

This subsection reviews, first, the origins of gasoline and diesel subsidies in Indonesia; second, their early history; and third, the major attempted reforms from 2000 to 2013. Because of the complexity of understanding any given period of subsidy reform—ideally including information on the political context, pricing changes, compensation measures, actual economic and social impacts, and public perceptions—this subsection identifies only the most salient aspects of reforms during this period for which information is readily available in existing literature. The next subsection ("The 2014–15 Reform of Gasoline and Diesel Subsidies") then describes Indonesia's most recent policy changes—in November 2014 and January 2015—in greater detail. See annex 4B for a full chronology of events and policies related to energy subsidies from 1956 to 2015.

Birth of the Indonesian Gasoline and Diesel Subsidy

Some form of fuel subsidy has existed in Indonesia since at least the 1960s (Hunter 2007; Woo and Nasution 1989). However, it was not acknowledged officially until the state budget of fiscal year 1977/78.

Fuel subsidies began with support for kerosene, diesel, and fuel oil (Hope and Singh 1995; World Bank 1983). Kerosene was subsidized (a) for economic reasons linked to inflation, and (b) for social and environmental reasons linked to modern energy access and deforestation. In the early 1980s, kerosene accounted for 32 percent of all consumption of commercial energy, so it was feared that price increases would have a significant inflationary impact (World Bank 1983). State-owned electricity company PLN covered only 5.7 percent of the villages in Indonesia; 24.3 percent of the population lived in poverty;[7] 80 percent of kerosene consumption was among households; and 50 percent of total energy consumption came

Figure 4.8 Gasoline Sales and Vehicle Ownership Trends in Indonesia, 2000–13

a. Gasoline sales[a]

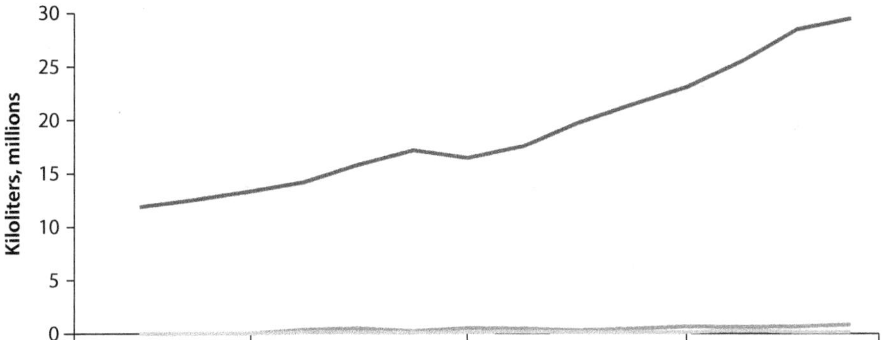

	2000	2004	2008	2012
RON 88	11.9	15.8	19.7	28.5
RON 92	0.0	0.5	0.3	0.7
RON 95	0.0	0.1	0.1	0.1

RON 88 — RON 92 — RON 95

b. Vehicle ownership

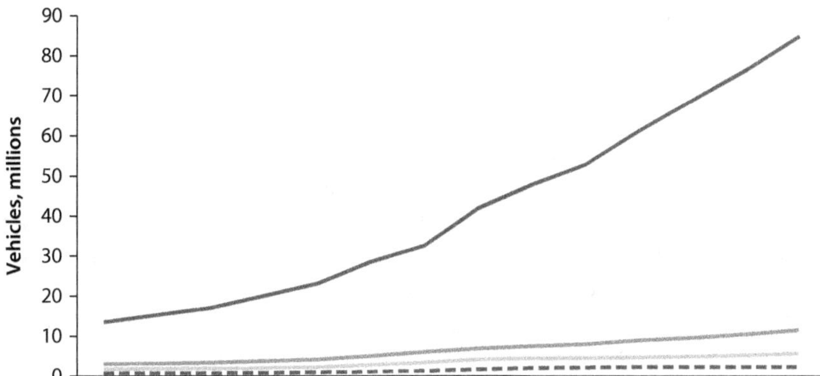

	2000	2001	2002	2003	2004	2005	2006	2007	2008	2009	2010	2011	2012	2013
Motorcycles	13.6	15.3	17.0	20.0	23.1	28.5	32.5	42.0	47.7	52.8	61.1	68.8	76.4	84.7
Passenger car	3.0	3.2	3.4	3.8	4.2	5.1	6.0	6.9	7.5	7.9	8.9	9.5	10.4	11.5
Trucks	1.7	1.8	1.9	2.0	2.3	2.9	3.4	4.2	4.5	4.5	4.7	5.0	5.3	5.6
Buses	0.7	0.7	0.7	0.8	0.9	1.1	1.4	1.7	2.1	2.2	2.3	2.3	2.3	2.3

Motorcycles — Passenger cars — Trucks - - - Buses

Sources: ESDM 2014; Central Statistics Agency (Badan Pusat Statistik, BPS) database, http://www.bps.go.id/linkTabelStatis/view/id/1413.

a. RON = Research Octane Number. The consumption statistics reported here do not include Pertalite, a nonsubsidized 90-octane fuel not introduced until 2015, after the period covered by the figure.

from traditional fuel such as firewood and agricultural waste (World Bank 1983, 1984, 1990). The subsidy was intended to help extend a more convenient, cleaner cooking and lighting fuel to communities with poor energy access.

Diesel was subsidized at the same time as a way to help Indonesian businesses compete internationally. This subsidy policy was poorly targeted, covering all kinds of firms whether or not they contributed to the national goal to boost exports.

By contrast, the price of gasoline was largely higher than its cost, with some exceptions due to sudden international price changes—standing, for example, at 2.6 times more than the border (reference) price in 1986. This arrangement existed to allow a cross-subsidy from gasoline to kerosene, according to Subroto, Indonesia's former minister of energy and natural resources (1978–87) who became secretary-general (1988–94) of the Organization of Petroleum Exporting Countries (OPEC) (Subroto 2005). Gasoline subsidies first became entrenched at some point in the early 1990s, although sources reviewed by this study did not identify precisely when, potentially because of poor budgetary transparency at the time.

The fuel subsidy began to take on additional significance under the "New Order" administration of President Suharto in the latter half of the 1970s.[8] During this period, policy making had become more dependent on Suharto as the ultimate decision maker, and technocratic support was becoming less and less influential. The government shifted toward a more nationalistic development policy, and many factors combined to motivate opposition against the regime (Aspinall 2005; Bourchier and Hadiz 2003; Eklöf 2003; Smith 2005; Tuong 2010; Woo, Glassburner, and Nasution 1994):

- Increasing army domination in virtually every aspect of life
- A surge of foreign investment and imported goods
- Windfall oil profits that were not translated into a better standard of living but *did* increase the costs of living through impacts on exchange rates and food prices
- Blatant mismanagement and corruption
- Efforts to weaken other political parties through constitutional means

That resentment subsequently led to a power struggle, which culminated in an infamous riot in January 1974 known as the Malari Incident ("Malari" being the acronym, in Indonesian, for January Disaster).

According to Chalmers and Hadiz (1997), the New Order's greater emphasis on providing subsidies, including for fuel, was a response to such regime-threatening criticisms (essentially, part of its broader effort to retain its grip on power)—a view also shared by Strand (2013) and Vatikiotis (1998). Commodity subsidies were chosen because the government had limited capacity to provide direct, tangible handouts to citizens in any more targeted way. Robison (1986) goes further, arguing that subsidies were part of a broader swath of policies directly intended to enable capital accumulation, thereby winning support for the government from powerful domestic stakeholders.

The subsidy policy also reflected Indonesia's economic means. As a result of the first two oil price shocks, the income from oil in the 1970s rose from around

5 percent to over 50 percent of total government revenue by the mid-1980s (Ooi 1982; Woo and Nasution 1989). Huge oil revenues allowed the government to finance the subsidies. It also made the protectionist nature of subsidies relatively secure from influence by international powers, given Indonesia's strong balance of payments position (Robison 1986; World Bank 1984).

End of the New Order and Recognition of Need for Reform

Some policy changes did occur under the New Order regime but largely to reduce fiscal expenditure and promote efficiency, without any broader ambition of a need for subsidy removal. For example, fuel price increases took place in 1980 and 1982–86, in response to a decline in international oil prices that saw annual GDP growth fall from 8.7 percent in 1980 to 1.1 percent in 1982.[9] The per-unit subsidy on all fuels increased as a result, with even gasoline briefly being priced at less than its cost (World Bank 1983). The balance of payments over the same period fell from a surplus of 2.9 percent of GDP to a deficit of 4.7 percent of GDP.[10] The government responded by devaluating the rupiah and tightening expenditure, including an increase in fuel prices (Woo and Nasution 1989; World Bank 1985).

In 1980, the adjustments raised gasoline and diesel prices to 50 percent of their 1979 levels; by 1986, gasoline prices had been increased to 260 percent and diesel prices to 440 percent of their 1980 levels[11] (figure 4.9). This left gasoline prices at 1.5 times the border reference price and brought diesel prices above the border reference price briefly before a return to subsidization (Hope and Singh 1995).

Figure 4.9 Gasoline and Diesel Price Adjustments (Nominal) in Indonesia, 1966–2000

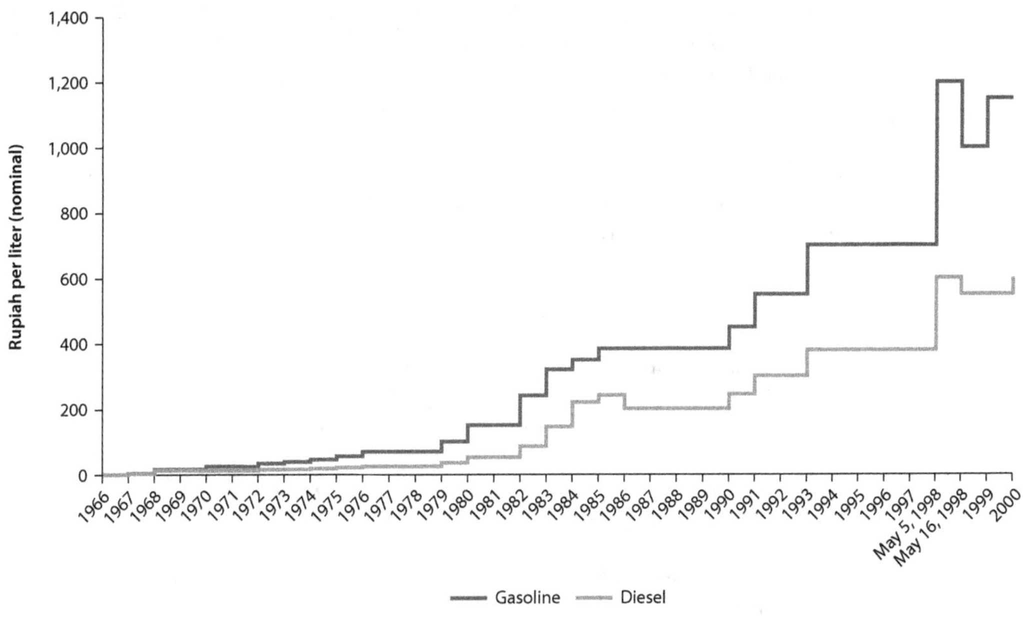

Source: ESDM, n.d.

Note: From 1966 to 1983, spot price is Arabian Light posted at Ras Tanura. From 1984 to 2014, spot price is Brent dated. Spot prices are inflated to 2014 dollars. Data for 1997 and 1998 reflect the period preceding and following the onset of the Asian Financial Crisis in July 1997. In the wake of increased popular unrest, President Suharto resigned on May 21, 1998.

These reforms took place at the peak of the New Order regime, following a maneuver to weaken opposition to the government that was so sweeping that it was described as "the emasculation of the political parties" (Eklöf 2003).[12] The most devastating blow was the introduction of the "floating mass" doctrine, which restricted public political activities outside the general election period and prohibited political activities below the district level (Eklöf 2003). Political parties had to rely on government subsidies to fund their operational activities (Aspinall 2005; Bourchier and Hadiz 2003). As a result, these price increases were implemented without meaningful social or political challenges.

The situation abruptly changed with the onset of the Asian Financial Crisis in 1997. To help survive the crisis—which brought a 13 percent contraction of GDP in 1998 alongside similarly drastic impacts on government deficits, foreign direct investment, and inflation (table 4.1)—Indonesia sought assistance from the International Monetary Fund (IMF). The government promised several major reforms to acquire an SDR 7.3 billion[13] (US$10.07 billion) loan through an IMF Stand-By Arrangement, which, among other things, required the government to remove the fuel and electricity subsidies by the end of March 1998 and provide a transparent record of all subsidies in the state budget (Government of Indonesia 1997; IMF 1997).

Following months of discontent, the government implemented its commitment with a fuel price hike in May 1998, which proved to be the "missing piece" that shifted public opinion away from seeing Suharto as a good leader surrounded by bad advisors and toward viewing him as one of the speculators and corrupt businessmen who had caused the economic disaster. The ensuing protests culminated in his stepping down and the transition to democracy. Subsequent political leaders learned from Suharto's experience that if fuel price hikes lead to protests, the consequences can be politically devastating.

Australian scholar Greg Barton describes this period as follows:

> Tension mounted throughout March and April, but Suharto was still very much in control. Then on 4 May that control began to disintegrate. That day he announced a reduction of subsidies on fuel that would cause a 70 percent price hike for petrol, in line with IMF prescriptions. The announcement met a violent response.

Table 4.1 Indonesia Macroeconomic Indicators, 1996–99

Indicator	*1996*	*1997*	*1998*	*1999*
GDP growth (%)	7.64	4.70	−13.13	0.79
Cash surplus or deficit (current Rp, trillions)	10,557	8,261	−17,610	−40,416
Cash surplus or deficit (% of GDP)	1.98	1.32	−1.84	−3.68
Central government debt, total (% of GDP)	23.91	71.83	53.79	44.62
Foreign direct investment, net inflows (BoP, current US$, billions)	6.19	4.68	−0.24	−1.86
Inflation, consumer prices (%)	7.97	6.23	58.39	20.49

Source: World Development Indicators Database.
Note: Rp = rupiah. BoP = Balance of payments.

> Large-scale riots broke out in Medan, North Sumatra, and students began flooding into the streets throughout Java. (Barton 2002, 235–36)

As writer and journalist Michael R. J. Vatikiotis further explains,

> Then, Suharto blinked. No one quite knows what moved him to increase the price of premium gasoline by 70 percent by removing subsidies on 4 May. The IMF was certainly in no hurry to do so. The IMF team was afraid of sparking further unrest. On cue, that's just what happened. The subsequent rioting in the North Sumatran capital of Medan on 4 and 5 May brought the simmering level of public discontent to the surface. (Vatikiotis 1998, 226)

It was an IMF requirement during the loan payback period (1997–2006) for successive democratic governments—including those of interim President B. J. Habibie, followed by Wahid, Megawati, and the first years of Yudhoyono—to reiterate the commitment to reduce the subsidy and improve transparency. In the first few years of democratic government, little significant progress was made, but some incremental steps were taken. For example, subsidies were entirely removed from aviation fuel on February 1, 1999 (Government of Indonesia 1999). This slow approach reflected more-immediate priorities at the time: rescuing severely damaged banking sectors, resolving the debt problem, and making some other major structural adjustments such as the divestment of state-owned enterprises (IMF 2000). It also reflected anxiety that price hikes might once again trigger mass protests that could topple a government.

Key Attempts to Reform Fuel Subsidies, 2000–13

The Indonesian government has attempted to reform gasoline and diesel subsidies numerous times since the beginning of the 21st century. Key attempts during this period to partially reform fuel subsidies—some successful, some unsuccessful—are summarized below and described briefly in the subsequent sections. They include six major episodes of reform: five ad hoc price increases, three ad hoc price decreases, and two periods of frequent price adjustments following a pricing formula.

In addition to these discrete reform events, two ongoing developments during the 21st century entrenched the recognition that reform would align well with the needs of domestic policy, above and beyond the conditions of the IMF loan. These developments were (a) the increasing fiscal strain from the subsidies; and (b) policy makers' recognition, in the wake of the Asian Financial Crisis, that the country lacked an adequate social safety net for the poor and vulnerable.

Fiscal Strain from Subsidies. Fuel subsidies became increasingly costly, partly because of the ongoing decline in domestic oil production (as shown earlier in figure 4.6). As a result, Indonesia had to purchase fuel internationally at world prices to meet domestic demand rather than relying on domestically produced oil products that it could procure at the cost of production. In turn, the subsidies' affordability became contingent on volatile world oil prices, which significantly appreciated during the first decade of the 2000s (figure 4.10). The costs of

Figure 4.10 Timeline of Gasoline and Diesel Subsidy Cost, World Oil Prices, and Subsidy Reforms in Indonesia, 2000–15

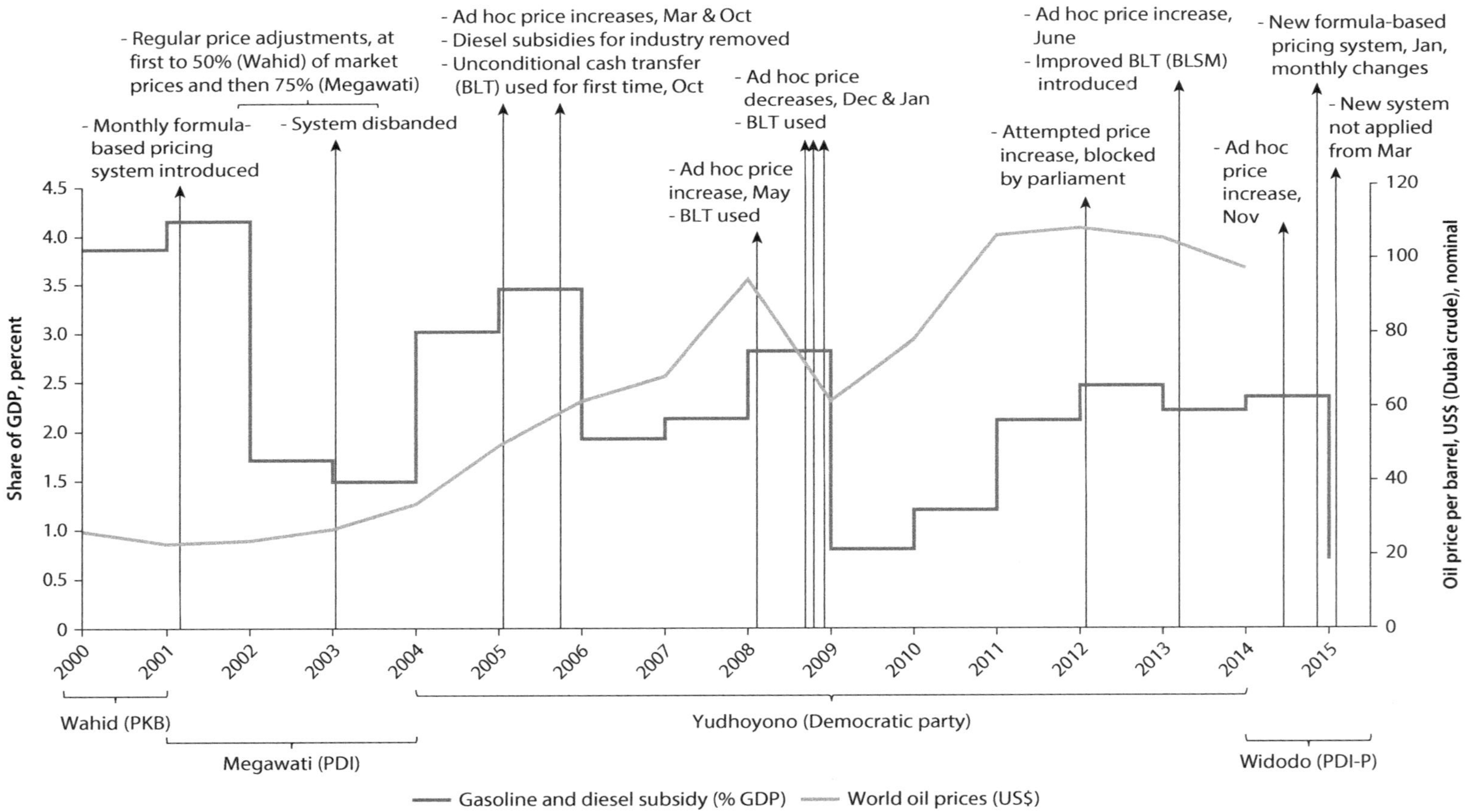

Sources: Subsidy estimates from Government of Indonesia, annual state budget documents, http://www.bpk.go.id/lkpp; GDP data from World Development Indicators Database; oil price data from BP 2015.

Note: BLT = Direct Cash Assistance. BLSM = Temporary Cash Transfer Program. PKB = National Awakening Party. PDI-P = Indonesian Democratic Party of Struggle. Available subsidy data are annual only. This means that subsidies incurred *during* a year are recorded as data points at the beginning of the year in question; for example, the 2001 subsidy expenditure is reported directly above the tick mark for 2001. The exact dates of policy changes are known and therefore indicated more precisely as events that took place during a given year; for example, a 2001 policy change is indicated as taking place at roughly the correct interval between tick marks for 2001 and 2002. A policy change *during* a year is likely to have influenced total subsidy expenditure reported at the *beginning* of that year, taking into account world oil price fluctuations.

importing expensive fuel imports were further exacerbated by Indonesia's increasingly weak foreign exchange rate. These three factors—lower domestic production, higher international prices, and a weakening currency—led to rapidly ballooning subsidy costs. The improved budgetary transparency required by the IMF also furthered recognition of the fiscal problem among policy makers.

Need for Social Safety Net. Policy makers also had realized during the Asian Financial Crisis that they had lacked necessary tools to assist the poor and vulnerable. To manage these impacts, they introduced a set of social safety net programs in 1998 known as the Social Safety Net (Jaring Pengaman Sosial, or JPS), which focused on areas such as in-kind subsidies for rice, health, scholarships, and grants to schools in poor areas (Daly and Fane 2002; Perdana 2014). These tools were, by design, structured according to theories of how best to reduce poverty by targeting benefits to the poor. Although some analysts criticized their initial effectiveness, the programs represented a new model of social assistance in Indonesia (Perdana 2014).

The growth of this administrative capacity over the next decade—and the expenditure required to sustain and expand the social safety net programs—also called in question the significant opportunity cost of the increasingly expensive, untargeted fuel subsidies. Moreover, policy makers increasingly understood that gasoline and diesel subsidies performed badly at supporting poor households, which purchased very small quantities of these fuels and thus benefited only indirectly from the fuel subsidies' impacts on the price of staple goods. Instead, gasoline and diesel subsidies predominantly benefited richer households, which could afford to own vehicles and purchase large quantities of fuel: the richest decile captured over 40 percent of the fuel subsidies (Agustina et al. 2008).

Pricing Formula, 2001–03. In March 2001, President Abdurrahman Wahid ordered the domestic retail prices of five fuel products (88-octane gasoline, kerosene, automotive diesel, industrial diesel, and fuel oil) to be set at 50 percent of the market price, with the option of increasing prices until they reached market levels.[14] At the time this policy was introduced, subsidized gasoline had been 59 percent of market price; automotive diesel, 30 percent; and industrial diesel, 28 percent.[15] This price indexation was seen as the pathway to enacting a mandate to gradually reduce subsidies in the National Development Program (Propenas) 2000–04 (Bappenas 2000).

The stated motivation for the policy change was to reduce the fiscal burden of fuel subsidies. The director of Pertamina was authorized to calculate a price benchmark adjustment every month, but the decision to actually change domestic retail prices rested with the president. Initially, the combination of the new pricing system and the decline of international oil prices reduced fuel subsidy expenditure significantly, from Rp 68.38 trillion (4.2 percent of GDP) in 2001 to Rp 31.62 trillion (1.7 percent of GDP) in 2002, although world oil prices had also fallen slightly from their 2000 levels (figure 4.11).

Wahid's successor, Megawati Sukarnoputri, extended the decree.[16] Her government adjusted the formula to set gasoline prices at market levels and diesel

Figure 4.11 Timeline of Nominal Subsidized Gasoline and Diesel Prices and Subsidy Reforms in Indonesia, 2000–15

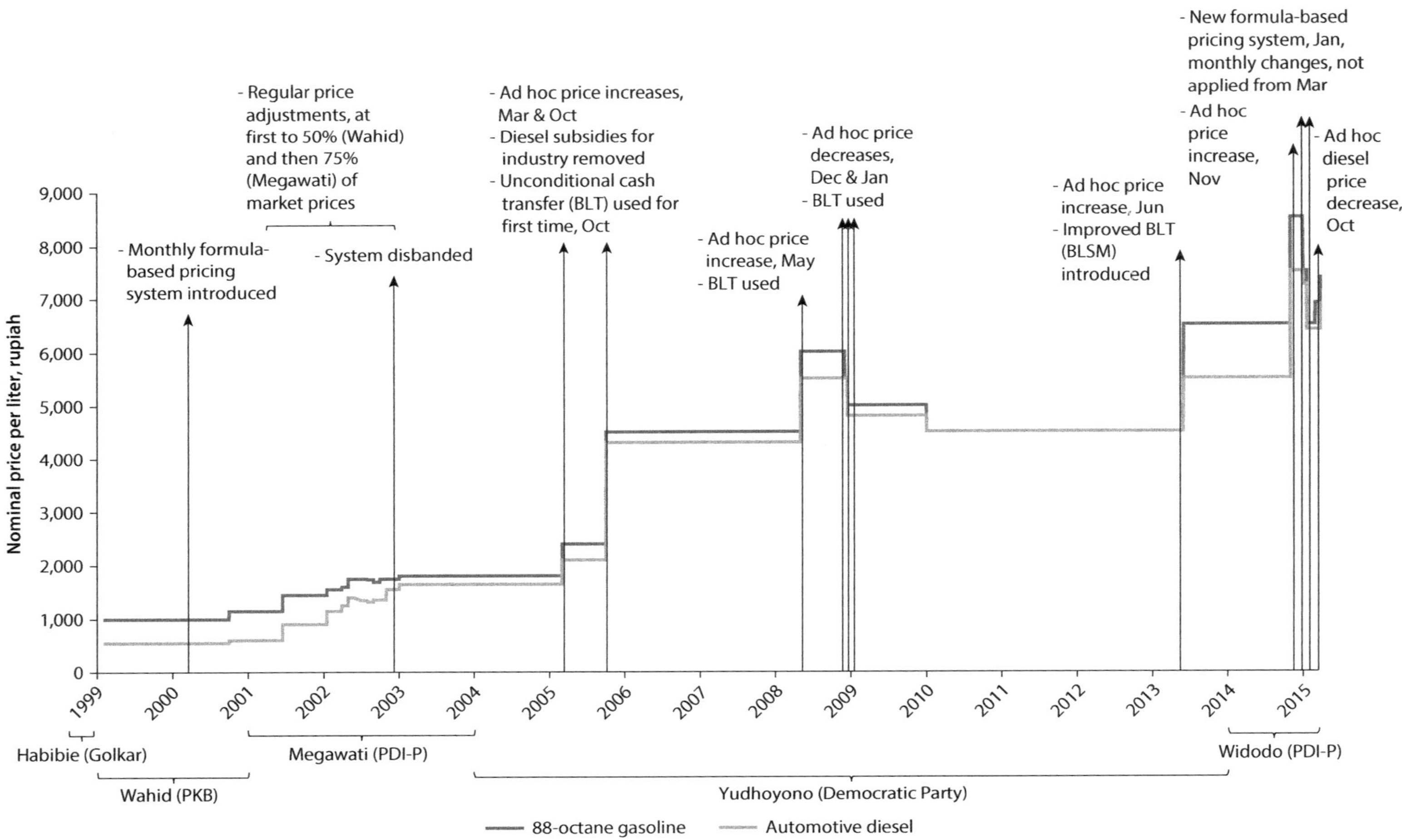

Sources: Based on gasoline and diesel price data from Adamrah 2009; Beaton and Lontoh 2010; GSI-IISD 2013b, 2015a, 2015d; World Bank 2006a.

Note: BLT = Direct Cash Assistance. BLSM = Temporary Cash Transfer Program. PKB = National Awakening Party. PDI-P = Indonesian Democratic Party of Struggle. Gasoline and d esel price data are accurate to day and month and so can be compared directly with changes in policy.

prices at 75 percent of market levels, within minimum and maximum price bands, with adjustments to take place monthly (Beaton, Christensen, and Lontoh 2015). Soon, the system was under pressure from the start of a steady rise in world oil prices that would peak in 2008 and eventually come to be recognized as more than just volatility; rather, it was a structural appreciation in world markets, largely from increased global demand. Monthly fuel price adjustments were implemented as planned, but they were met with ongoing student protests in Makassar, Jakarta, Surabaya, Denpasar, Manado, and Bandung (Beaton and Lontoh 2010). By the end of the year, prices had reached their top bands, and the fuel subsidy expenditure had been reduced by around 50 percent compared with the previous year.

Despite its initial successes, the formula-based system for regularly adjusting prices was abandoned in January 2003 after a strong, widespread set of protests against a fuel price hike that took place at the same time as (a) increases in prices of electricity, sea and train transport, toll roads, LPG, vehicle taxes, and fresh water; and (b) the introduction of a new, higher regional minimum salary (Beaton, Christensen, and Lontoh 2015; Liputan6.com 2002a, 2002b; Nugroho SBM 2003; *Suara Merdeka* 2002; Sumantyo 2003a, 2003b).

Bacon and Kojima (2006) report that a key motivation for the protests was a belief that the government had been favoring powerful interest groups, as well as general dissatisfaction with political corruption and inefficiency. Two major business associations—the Indonesian Entrepreneur Association (Asosiasi Pengusaha Indonesia, or Apindo) and the Indonesian Chamber of Commerce (Kamar Dagang dan Industri Indonesia, or KADIN)—challenged the policy, although they were particularly opposed to the increase in regional minimum salaries (Liputan6.com 2002c, 2003a, 2003b).

In addition, the technocratic planning behind the reforms may have been relatively weak. Shiraishi (2006) argues that the economic ministries that would have been in charge of these reforms were not functioning as a cohesive and coordinated team at the time, largely because of ongoing internal instability while the new democratic governance system found its bearings. Sardini (2003) acknowledges the government's inadequate planning and strategy but argues that the principal problem was insufficient direct communication between Megawati and the public about the rationale for the reforms.

The protests' success in preventing policy change likely stemmed from a combination of different factors, all pointing toward the high value placed on political stability:

- Megawati's decisions were likely influenced by the role that fuel price protests had played in the rapid demise of the Suharto regime.
- Indonesia was still in the midst of its recovery from the Asian Financial Crisis and its transition to democracy.
- The new Indonesian political system placed significant power, including on fiscal decisions, in parliament's hands. Wahid's presidency was cut short directly because of a tense political showdown with parliament, which demonstrated

> its power by removing Wahid (Barton 2002). Subsequent presidents thus took a cautious approach in negotiating sensitive policies with parliament.

And the reforms had indeed caused divisions among political parties. Megawati had failed to gain adequate support from parliament and had not complied with a crucial procedural requirement to consult with parliamentarians on reforms (Isra 2003). Even within Megawati's own party, PDI-P, many members perceived the policy changes as a liberal approach that was against their nationalist principles (*Suara Merdeka* 2003). Moreover, Megawati was due to stand for reelection in 2004. It was good timing for opposition parties to exploit a publicly sensitive issue and so weaken her popular support base.

Throughout the Wahid and Megawati attempts to remove subsidies, a compensation package was provided—the Energy Subsidy Reduction Impact Mitigation Program (Program Penanggulangan Dampak Pengurangan Subsidi Energi, or PPD-PSE), which allocated Rp 2.0 trillion in 2001, Rp 2.9 trillion in 2002, and Rp 3.9 trillion in 2003 (0.1 percent, 0.2 percent, and 0.2 percent of GDP, respectively). According to the Ministry of Finance's state budget proposal in 2005, this "social compensation on fuel and energy price increase" consisted of support for education, health and social welfare, transportation, clean water infrastructure, small enterprises, empowerment of coastal communities, unemployment, provisioning of contraceptive devices, and monitoring and evaluation of public complaints (Government of Indonesia 2004).

It is hard to assess the extent to which this compensation did or did not counteract opposition to reform. The policies were, however, criticized for having a disarrayed design and for not being launched in parallel to price hikes (Liputan6.com 2003a, 2003b).

Constitutional Challenge to 2001 Petroleum and Gas Framework. In November 2001, a few months following her inauguration, Megawati signed into law a new framework for the governance of the oil and gas sector, Law No. 22/2001.[17] One of the law's main objectives was to further liberalize upstream and downstream oil and gas markets. On the upstream side, Pertamina's monopoly was dismantled, and its regulatory function was transferred to twin regulatory agencies that answered to the president: the Executive Agency for Upstream Oil and Gas (BP Migas) and the Regulatory Agency for Downstream Oil and Gas (BPH Migas). On the downstream side, fuel distribution was opened up to private companies, and Article 28 created a legal basis for prices to be "entrusted to the mechanism of fair and reasonable business competition."

This law was intended to establish the legal basis for a gradual transition to market prices, which had already begun during Wahid's presidency in early 2001. But in January 2003, the same month that the formula-based pricing system was disbanded, a challenge was brought against Law No. 22/2001 to the Constitutional Court.[18] The claimants challenged a number of articles, including the Article 28 clause about fuel pricing. Their objections focused on the third clause of Article 33 of the Indonesian Constitution: "The land, the water and the natural resources within them shall be controlled by the State and shall be used for the greatest prosperity of the people." The challenge argued that market pricing would both prevent the government from ensuring the energy supply and make Indonesia vulnerable to price manipulation by foreign powers. In addition, the policy change was accused of being a part of a neoliberal agenda that ran contrary to the values of the constitution (Beaton, Christensen, and Lontoh 2015; Constitutional Court of Indonesia 2004; Mochtar 2015).

The court ruled in December 2004 that Article 28 was unconstitutional, finding that the pricing system could not be completely entrusted to business competition, although the government could make use of competition in determining prices (Constitutional Court of Indonesia 2004; Mochtar 2015). This ruling set a precedent that effectively ruled out reforms that structurally take gasoline and diesel pricing entirely out of the hands of political decision makers, such as through an automatic pricing mechanism administered by an independent body.

As a result of the court decision, the pricing system that the Megawati regime had abandoned—a formula system that would automatically adjust prices to reflect international oil price fluctuations—was viewed as a risky strategy to reenact. Such a strategy would raise the possibility of a legal challenge, and the court had left open a significant gray area as to exactly what degree of government decision making might be required for a pricing system to be deemed constitutional.

2005 Price Hikes under Yudhoyono. A former minister of energy, President Susilo Bambang Yudhoyono took action on fuel prices swiftly after coming into office. He was in a difficult position for several reasons:

- World oil prices had continued to increase since the disbanding of the formula-based pricing system in 2003, but domestic prices had not changed, so subsidy costs were expanding rapidly.
- The pace of change was increasing. The international crude price (West Texas Intermediate) was recorded at US$38 per barrel in June 2004 and rose to US$43 per barrel by December that year; in August of 2005 it had climbed further to US$65 per barrel, while the exchange rate was weakening.[19]
- Yudhoyono had inherited a state budget from Megawati that had based the fuel subsidy on an assumption that the crude price would decline to as low as US$24 per barrel in 2005 (Government of Indonesia 2004). During the previous Megawati presidency, the fuel subsidy was recorded at Rp 31.16 trillion (1.7 percent of GDP) in 2002 and Rp 30.04 trillion in 2003 (1.5 percent of GDP), but by the end of 2004 it had ballooned to Rp 69.02 trillion (3.0 percent of GDP), as shown earlier in figure 4.10.
- Trends in international food prices contributed to the sense of urgency: the cost of purchasing food was increasing for poor and nonpoor Indonesians alike, and technocrats argued that spending on social security was slight compared with the increasingly bloated fuel subsidy.[20]

On March 1, 2005, Yudhoyono increased the gasoline price by 33 percent, automotive diesel by 27 percent, and kerosene by 22 percent. On October 1, 2005, he again increased the gasoline price, this time by 88 percent, and automotive diesel by 105 percent, though reducing the kerosene price by 9 percent. Many external commentators viewed these changes positively (Donnan 2005), which also showed that an Indonesian leader could increase fuel prices without losing office.

In the short term, the 2005 price hikes were a fiscal success, reducing subsidy expenditure by about a third in 2006. They were also a political success, in that they were large price increases that were not immediately reversed. The success of the price hikes reflected several factors related to the broad political context in which they took place:

- *Coalition building.* After winning the election, Yudhoyono had adeptly brought a number of parties into his governing coalition, ultimately securing 59 percent of parliamentary seats and pleasing many of the economic and political forces in the country (von Luebke 2010).
- *Shrewd appointments.* He established a cabinet that reflected not only coalition representatives but also a number of highly skilled technocrats, such as Jusuf Anwar, an executive director of the ADB, as minister of finance; Sri Mulyani, a former executive director on the board of the IMF as the minister of national development planning; and Purnomo Yusgiantoro, former minister of defense and the president-secretary general of OPEC, as minister of energy and mineral resources.
- *Weakened opposition.* Yudhoyono's main opposition, Megawati's PDI-P party, had suffered heavy losses in the 2004 general election and had only recently attempted similar policy reforms, thus reducing its legitimacy in criticizing the reforms. The Indonesian delegation to the European Union at the time opined that opposition forces felt empathy for the government, given their own recent struggles with the fuel subsidy (Osman 2005).
- *Analysis and preparation.* The reforms were built on a great deal of analysis and preparation after the failed reforms of 2001–03. Since then, an informal task force of reform-minded economists and technocrats had been established and analyzed various subsidies, their incidence, possible forms of compensation for households and industry, and the elements of an effective communications strategy. When Yudhoyono was inaugurated, some of these task force members entered the administration in influential positions, carrying forward its thinking into government planning on subsidies.[21]

Yudhoyono's personal approach to implementing subsidy reform also played an important role. A president with a flamboyant, media-conscious character, Yudhoyono understood how to use mass communications to build support for difficult reforms, cultivating the image of a tough-minded reformer. In one speech, delivered at the opening of the Indonesian Capital Market 2005 event in February 2005, he proclaimed, "A leader should be willing to become unpopular. That issue is second or third for me. Significant subsidy reduction resulting from the price increase is for justice. Shame on me if I still want to be popular, but I let the economy fall and business pillars crumble" (Detik.com 2005).

Messaging from the rest of the government was coordinated through a comprehensive public communications strategy crafted by a professional advertising firm. The messaging focused first on fairness, illustrated by the regressive nature of the subsidy and the alternative priorities that could be afforded with the same expenditure. Second, the messaging highlighted the government's compensation measures. A key element of the campaign was a full-page newspaper advertisement signed by a number of prominent economists and public figures. In addition, senior officials received dedicated media training and briefing notes to ensure that government figures would speak confidently and consistently with one unified voice.[22]

Yudhoyono's government also developed a more complex approach to mitigating the impacts of subsidy reform, reflecting the background of the technocrats in his administration. This included the development over only six months of a registry of low-income households to target two unconditional cash transfer payments following price increases.[23] The Bantuan Langsung Tunai (BLT) program—a temporary unconditional cash transfer program also known as Direct Cash Assistance—was specifically developed to help compensate for the fuel subsidy reform. It was first used alongside the October price increase, transferring to poor households a sum worth around US$30. Three more payments were made over the first nine months of 2006 (World Bank 2012b).

On a technical level, the BLT was a solid success. It was costly but less so than the fuel subsidy, particularly given its temporary nature, with the total expenditure reported at Rp 23 trillion (0.8 percent of GDP) (World Bank 2012a). Moreover, it was an administratively and logistically complex policy that had been brought from conception to implementation in only five months.

There was undeniably significant room for improvement. The registry of beneficiaries was identified largely through community-based targeting (asking subvillage heads to identify poor households in their community) without a clear basis for nomination. As a result, only 46 percent of the poorest 30 percent of households received the payments (World Bank 2012b). Nonetheless, it was still the best-targeted of all of Indonesia's major social assistance programs—and significantly better targeted than gasoline and diesel subsidies.

On a political level, the BLT was generally credited with alleviating some of the political opposition to reform, but this did not come without complexities. Attitude surveys conducted as part of a rapid appraisal found, on average, high levels of satisfaction among beneficiaries with targeting, distribution, and the frequency and size of payments (Hastuti et al. 2006). But there were also negative responses to its introduction. Initially, 15.5 million households (about 28 percent of the population) were pronounced eligible for payments. This was met with protests from households who considered themselves to have been unjustly excluded. The government responded by commissioning a second round of surveys after having removed some beneficiaries and adding others, increasing the total registry of eligible households to 19.2 million (around 35 percent of the population) (Bacon and Kojima 2006; Widjaja 2009).

Notably, according to the rapid appraisal, almost all village officials reported negative impacts related to their role in helping to identify eligible households, which in some cases affected their ability to carry out their official duties (Hastuti et al. 2006). As such, it has been hypothesized that the BLT may actually have helped to redirect political dissatisfaction with subsidy reform away from the central government, although this was unlikely to have been a conscious intention of policy design (Beaton and Lontoh 2010).

In addition to the BLT, some smaller compensation policies were also provided, including the following (Beaton and Lontoh 2010):

- *Health Insurance for the Poor* (Asuransi Kesehatan Masyarakat Miskin, abbreviated as Askeskin)
- *School Operational Assistance* (Bantuan Operational Sekolah, or BOS), a program to eliminate fees in primary and junior secondary schools and provide targeted scholarships for senior secondary school students
- *The Rural Infrastructure Program* (Infrastruktur Perdesaan, or IP) to make direct grants for low-income and remote villages to improve infrastructure and generate temporary employment

2008 Price Hikes and Reductions under Yudhoyono. The 2005 price increases significantly reduced subsidy expenditure for only about a year. Rising world oil prices drove expenditure upward again in 2007. By 2008, world spot prices had risen even higher (in retrospect, we now know their peak),[24] and the ballooning subsidy budget was unsustainable.

The Yudhoyono government followed the model it had established in 2005. In May 2008, subsidized gasoline prices were increased by 33 percent and diesel by 28 percent. These hikes were combined with a package of compensation measures, including two payments through the BLT unconditional cash transfer system at a reported cost of US$1.52 billion (Beaton and Lontoh 2010), as well as subsidized rice, loans for small businesses, and educational support for the families of lower-ranking civil servants and the military.

Without the BLT, it was estimated that poverty would have been 1.5 percentage points higher than it was with the BLT in place, when actual poverty fell from 15.4 percent in March 2008 to 14.2 percent in March 2009 (World Bank 2009, 2013a). Compared with 2005, no major public relations effort took place in 2008, likely because of the relatively moderate price changes and the public focus on nascent campaigning for upcoming parliamentary and presidential elections.[25]

The government made announcements at the time about shifting toward a new pricing system that would set fuel prices at market levels within fixed bands rather than relying on one-off price adjustments that would become obsolete as soon as world oil prices changed. However, it reversed the price increases toward the end of 2008. At the start of December, subsidized gasoline prices were reduced by 9 percent. Two weeks later, the price of gasoline was reduced by a further 10 percent and diesel by 15 percent. In addition, a third BLT payment was arranged despite the price decreases (Beaton and Lontoh 2010).

The decision to decrease prices appeared to reflect two external factors: First, world oil prices had begun to fall from their mid-2008 peak, removing the fiscal pressure that was motivating reform. Second, presidential elections were to take place in the first half of 2009. Yudhoyono won reelection, with political advertising in the run-up to elections arguing that the price reductions were an achievement of his presidency.

The BLT program emerged as an issue that contributed to Yudhoyono's popularity, with 84 percent of poll respondents approving of the program (O'Rourke 2009). It was viewed skeptically by opposition parties, who contended that it had been used inappropriately to influence the elections (Adamrah 2009; Antara News 2009; *Kompas* 2009; Sanjaya 2008; Wardany and Hajramurni 2009). Although a complex array of factors can influence approval ratings, a review of such polls for President Yudhoyono found that fuel price hikes were associated with decreased popularity and cash transfers with increasing popularity, particularly after being in place for some time (figure 4.12).

To fully understand the sensitivity of all political parties on this issue, remember that decades of systematic "depoliticization" had taken place during Suharto's presidency, limiting political activities for much of the recent past. Therefore, in this political context, many citizens have weak institutional or ideological ties with political parties; vote buying is a common practice; and many small parties, with little funding, struggle to compete against a ruling party that can develop programs with the state's authority.

Despite the 2008 price increases, total fuel subsidy expenditure grew significantly, from 2.1 percent of GDP in 2007 to 2.8 percent of GDP

Figure 4.12 Indonesian Approval Ratings of President Yudhoyono During Periods of Fuel Price Hikes and Cash Transfers, 2005–09

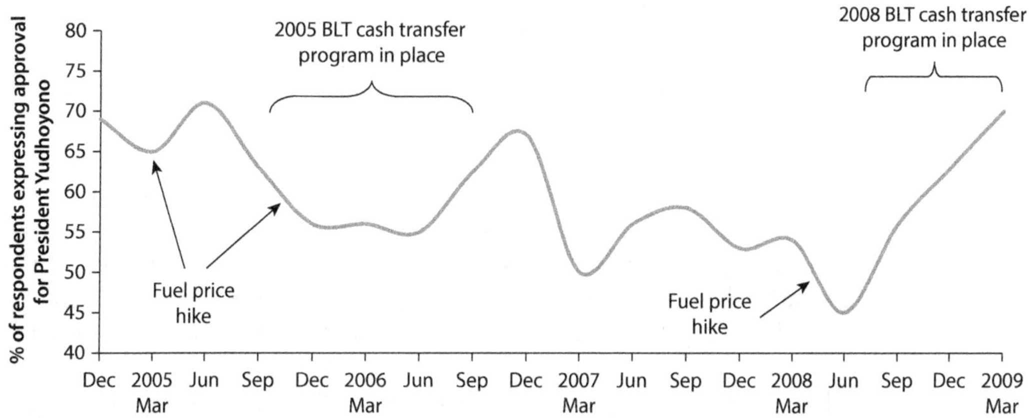

Source: O'Rourke (2009) based on nationwide polls by Lembaga Survei Indonesia.
Note: BLT = Direct Cash Assistance.

(as shown earlier in figure 4.10). Price increases therefore sufficed only to contain growing expenditure, not to reduce it. In 2009, total fuel subsidy expenditure fell dramatically, from 2.8 percent to only 0.8 percent of GDP. Given the December 2008 price reductions (which would ordinarily have increased subsidy expenditure), the fall in subsidy expenditure can be attributed almost entirely to falling world oil prices and, to some extent, ongoing economic growth rather than to government policy. By early 2010, the government had effectively abandoned its plan to shift to a new pricing system (Beaton and Lontoh 2010).

2012 Attempted Price Increase. In early 2012, the government again began to publicly consider raising gasoline prices, this time by around 33 percent. The domestic fuel price had not changed since early 2009, while international crude prices had increased from US$43.91 per barrel in January 2009 to US$106.89 per barrel in January 2012.[26] After the 2009 crude price decline, resulting in a relatively low fuel subsidy bill of Rp 45 trillion (0.8 percent of GDP), the subsidy soared to Rp 165.6 trillion in 2011 (2.1 percent of GDP), as shown earlier in figure 4.10.

This time, Yudhoyono faced different circumstances. Because of a prior budgetary agreement, fuel price increases required parliamentary approval as part of the state budget revision instead of being solely at the president's discretion. Following a plenary and voting session that was televised live and lasted until the early hours of the morning, parliament rejected the option of increasing prices, instead agreeing only to allow the government to increase prices by Rp 1,500 per liter if international crude oil prices rose by 15 percent above the US$105 stated in the budget assumptions. If prices fell by 15 percent below budgetary assumptions, the government would be compelled to reduce domestic prices (Simorangkir 2012). Such a situation did not ultimately materialize.

Several factors worked against the attempted reform. First, the government had changed tactics too quickly: Yudhoyono's second-term electoral campaign had overemphasized the benefits created by the 2009 price reductions, and his administration had made announcements in late 2011 that prices would not rise in 2012, instead emphasizing plans to restrict access to subsidized fuel and promote fuel diversification (Indriyanto et al. 2013). Opposition parties could cite Yudhoyono's own campaign material to argue against his attempted policy change.

Second, the proposal sparked significant public protests. The police reported 1,063 public demonstrations in March 2012 alone, 28 ending in street clashes (Indriyanto et al. 2013). In addition, Dien Syamsudin, the leader of Muhammadiyah (Indonesia's second-largest Islamic mass organization), led a challenge in the Constitutional Court against the initiative—probably in part because some members of the ruling coalition were involved in high-profile corruption scandals (Hafil 2012; *Jakarta Post* 2012a, 2012b; Mishkin 2012).

Third, and most important, Yudhoyono in 2012 seemed to display less prowess in consolidating political support and communicating with the general populace than he had during previous reforms. That parliament had established a requirement that it approve any reform was the most apparent instance of this reduction in presidential power. But even within this framework, some unexpected shifts in alliance took place. For example, days before the parliamentary vote in late March, rumors had spread that the fuel price increase plan had been initiated by the Golkar Party. Aburizal Bakrie, Golkar's chairman, immediately refuted the claim, and subsequently Golkar—one of the five largest parties—ceased its support of the fuel price increase. There was more political capital to be earned from opposing fuel subsidy reforms than from supporting them.

On top of this, the government lacked an effective communications strategy. An independent review of the government's communication strategy, based on interviews with officials, found that the government had conducted a wide range of communications activities in 2012, including interactive dialogues, cultural performances, public seminars, meetings with key interest groups, print and television advertisements, and pamphlets and stickers (Indriyanto et al. 2013). Despite this breadth of activities, the review could not identify an underlying strategy: the communications appeared to have been conducted with no clear objective beyond "awareness raising," no systems for monitoring and evaluation, and no audience research that would allow for audience segmentation and tailored messaging. An intergovernmental team established to coordinate communications activities had been effective in many cases, but it appeared to lose its efficacy in the case of senior government officials, resulting in a lack of coordinated messaging at the ministerial level.

2013 Price Increase. By mid-2013, the Indonesian state budget was once again under significant fiscal pressure: without more fuel subsidy reforms, the deficit would have risen to 3.38 percent of GDP, above its legal limit of 3 percent of GDP (GSI-IISD 2013b). In mid-June, fuel price hikes were announced, with subsidized gasoline prices rising by around 45 percent and diesel by around 21 percent.

Again, the government provided a range of social compensation mechanisms. The unconditional cash transfer previously known as BLT was renamed the Temporary Cash Transfer Program (Bantuan Langsung Sementara Masyarakat, or BLSM). This renaming was intended to help convey the temporary nature of the policy, as it had been criticized in previous years for being short-term and not seeking to promote a long-term exit strategy from poverty. The program was also to be targeted using the new Unified Database (UDB), a targeting registry developed in 2012.

Other social assistance measures—rice subsidies; education subsidies; and an expansion of the country's conditional cash transfer program, the Hopeful Family Program (Program Keluarga Harapan, or PKH)—were distributed through a new social protection identification card, also targeted with the UDB. In addition, a basic infrastructure program was announced, to focus on housing and water infrastructure needs among poor communities.

In total, the subsidy cuts were estimated to save around Rp 40 trillion (0.4 percent of GDP), while the compensation package was reported to cost around Rp 29.1 trillion (0.3 percent of GDP) (GSI-IISD 2013b; Teather 2013). The government launched a mass communications effort in support of the reforms, including television advertisements, text messages to 240 million active mobile phone numbers, social media activity, and a guidebook to explain compensation programs (GSI-IISD 2013b).

After the failed attempt to reform subsidies in 2012, the 2013 price hikes—influenced largely by the need to reduce the budget deficit—took many by surprise. Other drivers may have included the following:

- *Political cycles.* Mid-2013 was likely the last time it would be possible to adjust prices before legislative elections in early 2014 and presidential elections in mid-2014.
- *Presidential term limits.* That Yudhoyono was serving his second term and knew he would be unable to stand again enabled the government to introduce what would otherwise have been a risky policy change.
- *Reduced parliamentary power.* More practically, the clause in the 2012 budget that had required parliamentary approval for price reforms had not been carried over to 2013. Nonetheless, parliamentary approval was required to enable budgetary expenditure on allocation programs.

The impact of the reforms was to reduce fuel subsidy expenditure by a modest degree, down from 2.5 percent of GDP in 2012 to 2.3 percent of GDP in 2013.

The response to the price hikes was, as in previous years, dominated by news reports of public protests and violent clashes with police, including student and labor groups (Cochrane 2013), though some reports indicated a muted response compared with previous years (Einhorn and Ho 2013). Most of the criticism of the social compensation measures focused on the BLSM unconditional cash transfer program, inaccuracies in the register of eligible households, asynchronous delivery of cash transfers to some areas, and particularly governance concerns around providing cash transfers so close to upcoming elections (GSI-IISD 2013a; Muryanto 2014).

The 2014–15 Reform of Gasoline and Diesel Subsidies

In November 2014 and January 2015, the government of Indonesia introduced its most recent attempts at gasoline and diesel subsidy reform. The section here reviews in more detail why and how these latest policy changes took place and identifies some of their economic and social impacts. This complements the previous review of the history of gasoline and subsidy reforms by providing a more in-depth review of experience in one recent period.

The 2014–15 Reforms

On November 17, 2014, Indonesia's new government, led by President Joko Widodo, hiked gasoline prices by around 31 percent and diesel by 36 percent

(GSI-IISD 2015a). Only a month and a half later, on December 31, it announced a second set of reforms:

- Complete removal of gasoline subsidies in the Java-Madura-Bali area (central Indonesia)
- Removal of all gasoline subsidies in other areas of the country, except those related to distribution costs
- Introduction of a "fixed price" diesel subsidy that would set prices at Rp 1,000 (US$0.08) per liter below market prices

Under this new pricing system, the prices of gasoline and diesel were to be adjusted every two weeks to one month, according to a published pricing formula based an international market reference price. The immediate impact was a 12 percent reduction in the price of gasoline and a 3 percent reduction in the price of diesel because of the sudden, sharp declines in world oil prices since late 2014 (GSI-IISD 2015a).

Together, these policy changes amounted to one of the most significant periods of reform in Indonesian fuel subsidy policy, taking prices to their highest nominal levels and attempting to introduce the first structural reform to the underlying pricing mechanism since 2003. What made this shift politically possible?

Lead-Up to the 2014–15 Reforms

Joko Widodo's early signaling during the 2014 general election of his intention to reform subsidies significantly increased the legitimacy of his government in subsequently adjusting prices. Such messaging marked a dramatic departure from previous elections, when references to energy pricing were generally discouraged because of the issue's controversy and divisiveness—even for Widodo's party, PDI-P, which had opposed subsidy reforms during most of Yudhoyono's administration.

In part, such campaign messaging reflected Widodo's political style. As a politician from outside Indonesia's traditional ruling elite—having advanced from humble beginnings as a local furniture businessman—he developed a reputation for taking principled stances on controversial issues. It also reflected his strong popular support base (as evidenced by his decisive victories in mayoral elections in Surakarta and Jakarta), which gave him a buffer against too much dependence on traditional interest groups within his own party.

Being pro-reform was also a position that Widodo had tested publicly over the previous year as governor of Jakarta, when he had announced to much press attention that Jakarta would prefer to have fuel subsidies withdrawn and the funding reallocated for the city to invest in mass urban transport. The stance of his political campaign may also have been based on a perceived shift in public opinion regarding subsidies, as reflected by the relatively muted protests against price rises in 2013.

Being a political outsider may also have made Widodo more capable than his peers in opposing special interest groups, which some media have speculated played a role in the previous government's long-running inability to fully reform the subsidy. Speculation has abounded for many years that an "oil and gas mafia" has profited from slight discrepancies between the government's subsidy payments and the size of the gap between the cost of fuel imports and domestic retail prices (*Asia Sentinel* 2014; Saragih 2014a). It is possible that such leakage could have been taking place because Indonesia's subsidized fuel (88-octane gasoline) is such a low-quality fuel that it is not commonly traded, and therefore no spot price can be used to precisely verify that subsidy payments are the correct size.

Despite these claims—and the fact that illegal and rent-seeking behavior in the energy sector certainly exists—no hard data have ever been produced to prove clear corruption in the subsidy system linked to political elites. Nonetheless, Widodo's willingness to tackle such groups became unambiguously clear by his launch of an oil and gas task force upon coming into office.[27] With a mandate to look into the broad set of governance issues in the sector, the team was popularly dubbed the "energy mafia" task force (Cahyafitri and Widhiarto 2014; Saragih 2014b).

In addition, public opinion may have become better disposed to fuel price increases, having just experienced a fuel scarcity crisis as a result of postponing reforms (Dipa and Fadli 2014; Gideon 2014; Sandi 2014)—a delay caused by the Yudhoyono regime's reluctance to increase fuel prices during an election year. In the face of unsustainable subsidy costs, the civil service had been instructed in August 2014 to constrain fuel subsidy expenditure by restricting the fuel supply—causing panic buying and long queues that led to significant economic disruption and social discontent. The measures were so unpopular that they were reversed by the end of the same month (Lontoh, Beaton, and Clarke 2015).

Widodo also enjoyed the same honeymoon period that Yudhoyono had experienced in 2005, when the Megawati government, after many years of trying to reform subsidies, had limited legitimacy in criticizing the new government. Widodo skillfully exploited this period of goodwill by publicly reaching out to Yudhoyono before the transfer of power and offering an arrangement to jointly share responsibility for price increases between the two governments: Yudhoyono would introduce one set of price hikes before leaving office, and Widodo would complete them once inaugurated. Following an August 27 meeting in Bali, however, Yudhoyono rejected the proposal, diplomatically citing his empathy for the poor and the lack of support he had received from the opposition when he took office as his reasons (*Jakarta Post* 2014; Jong and Erviani 2014; Rahadiana and Chatterjee 2014).

Finally, as in most instances of fuel subsidy reform in Indonesia, budgetary necessity and world oil prices likely played significant roles—the former forcing the government's hand in November, and the latter opening a window of opportunity for structural reforms by the end of December.

Budgetary Issues. Budgetary pressure was strong in November 2014 because the Yudhoyono-negotiated state budget left no space for higher-than-planned expenditure on fuel subsidies. Because attempts to restrict the fuel supply had failed, Widodo's government was on course for a budgetary crisis. In addition, pushing back subsidy reform until 2015 did not seem to offer better prospects. This budget had also been drawn up in negotiations led by the previous administration, so it included a carry-over of subsidy debts from 2014 and, as a "baseline budget," was not structured to allow for mitigation measures related to fuel subsidy reform. This would require an effort to reallocate funds, which parliament could block if it opposed price increases (Antara News 2014; EIU 2014; Sambijantoro and Parlina 2014; Sambijantoro and Saragih 2014).

As a head of the government but leading a minority coalition in parliament, and given the likelihood of strong parliamentary opposition to price reforms, it made sense for the Widodo administration to take bold, decisive steps with whatever operating space was available. Widodo's economic team identified an unspent budgetary line in the 2014 budget worth Rp 5 trillion (around US$0.5 billion), initially allocated for a social risk fund, and used this to finance a social security program on November 3, introducing a new card system to distribute education and health assistance and thereby provide some form of mitigation for the price hikes (Antara News 2014; GSI-IISD 2015a).

World Oil Prices. By late December, however, world oil prices had continued their unanticipated decline to lows not seen for many years. This left Widodo's adjusted November prices in an awkward position—actually above market levels. Like some other fuel-subsidizing nations such as India, the government seized the opportunity to announce subsidy reforms during the time of decreasing prices, which by mid-January returned to nearly pre-November levels. This was a politically popular move, but despite the benefits of changing the pricing system at a structural level, it also put the government back in a position where politically costly price hikes—hard-won in November—would likely be needed again in the future.

2014 Compensation and 2015 Reallocation

On November 3, the government announced the launch of a social assistance scheme titled the Productive Family Program (Program Keluarga Produktif), which introduced four cards—the Indonesia Smart Card (Kartu Indonesia Pintar, or KIP); the Indonesia Healthy Card (Kartu Indonesia Sehat, or KIS); the Prosperous Family Saving Card (Kartu Simpanan Keluarga Sejahtera, or KSKS); and a mobile phone SIM card used for checking an account status—all implemented with a smart card technology called Digital Financial Service (Layanan Keuangan Digital). These were largely renamed versions of existing programs, albeit with improved information technology and in some cases slightly expanded coverage.

Widodo had previously used card systems in 2008 as part of an effort to improve the coverage of health and education assistance during his term as the mayor of Surakarta (Abarwati 2014). Shortly after he took office as president, the combination of this information technology with social protection programs became one of his highest-profile policies, providing the following benefits (GSI-IISD 2015a; TNP2K, n.d.):

- KIP provided payments targeting 152,364 students of ages 7–18 years from elementary to high school.
- KIS expanded the coverage of existing health care insurance from 86.4 million to 88.1 million targeted recipients, with the inclusion of near-poor households and a first payment targeting 432,000 recipients.
- KSKS cards were distributed to 1 million people and provide a monthly digital cash transfer of Rp 200,000 (around US$16), paid as Rp 400,000 for November and December.

Upon launch, the government announced that cards would be distributed to 1 million families, with a further 14.5 million families to receive cards in 2015 (*Jakarta Post* 2014). This meant, however, that the large majority still received cash transfers through post offices.

After the government's second stage of reforms on December 31, no additional mitigation measures were announced, reflecting the decreased prices and the expectation of no negative social impacts. Instead, the Widodo government focused on refining and distributing its social security card program—so that future reforms could be better targeted to the poor—and engaging in parliamentary negotiations over how fuel subsidy savings should be reallocated.[28]

No clear record is available to show exactly how the government used savings from the reforms because Indonesia has no formal system to track reallocation of funds in its budget-making processes. However, the government made numerous public commitments to reinvest the savings in infrastructure; indeed, the Revised State Budget 2015 increased the infrastructure allocation from US$15.2 billion to US$23.2 billion. This increase may have reflected previous criticisms of the BLT and the BLSM policies, which had been decried as wasteful for supporting blanket short-term consumption rather than making strategic investments that would improve households' longer-term capacity and opportunities (World Bank 2012a, 2012b).

Public Response to the Policy Changes

The first reforms in November 2014, which increased gasoline and diesel prices, were met as usual with panic buying (with fuel sales increasing to more than twice their daily average in some areas) and sporadic protests across the country, although it was generally believed that such opposition was less fierce than in previous years (GSI-IISD 2015a). Two student unions—typically in opposition to reform—came out in support of the government's policy, and one of the largest demonstrations, in Makassar, came to a surprising end when locals reportedly fought off the demonstrators, being tired of the prolonged obstruction of roads with rocks and burning tires (GSI-IISD 2015a).

Among workers, the most significant opposition came from the Indonesian Land Transport Operators Association (Organda), which staged a one-day nationwide strike that left crowds of passengers unable to reach their destinations (GSI-IISD 2015a). The strike was incited by a Ministry of Transportation restriction that prevented operators from increasing their fares for the first three months after the introduction of new fuel price—essentially forcing transport operators to absorb the immediate burden of higher prices. The ministry quickly called a negotiation and resolved the crisis by agreeing to let operators raise their fares by 10 percent.

The second reforms—the new pricing system and decrease of gasoline and diesel prices in late December—were met with little public outcry. This is no surprise as price decreases are generally greeted favorably by citizens and could not be decried by opposition parties so soon after their criticism of price hikes only a month and a half before. The one exception focused on concerns around "price stickiness," whereby fuel price reductions did not appear to reduce the cost of living as quickly as the price hikes had increased the cost of living (GSI-IISD 2015a).

Implementing the New Pricing Regime: An Uncertain Future

The history of attempted reforms in Indonesia provides strong reason for caution in assuming that the country's entanglement with fuel subsidies is over. The reform of a consumer product subsidy is not achieved by announcing its removal but by the consistent application of the nonsubsidized pricing regime that takes its place. This, in turn, may depend upon addressing the structural factors that gave rise to the subsidies in the first place.

The early days of Indonesia's new pricing system indicate that the future is uncertain. The immediate impact of implementing subsidy removal in January 2015 was to reduce prices—with further reductions in mid-January taking gasoline prices close to their pre-November levels. The new pricing system was intended to result in price changes every two weeks to one month, but since the end of January 2015 it has in effect developed into a new ad hoc pricing system.

The rest of 2015 proceeded as follows (GSI-IISD 2015a, 2015b), with the specific gasoline price changes shown in table 4.2:

- *February:* No price changes were made.
- *March:* Two price increases were made, but these resulted in protests at the same time that the minority coalition government was facing challenges in other areas.
- *April:* The government announced that it was planning for longer intervals between price adjustments.

Table 4.2 Gasoline Prices in Indonesia (Java, Madura, Bali Areas), 2014–15
rupiah per liter

Fuel type	*Prereform*	*Nov 18, 2014*	*Jan 1, 2015*	*Jan 19, 2015*	*Mar 1, 2015*	*Mar 28, 2015*
Gasoline	6,500	8,500	7,600	6,600	6,800	7,300
Diesel	5,500	7,500	7,250	6,400	6,400	6,900

Sources: GSI-IISD 2015b, 2015d.
Note: Gasoline prices refer to 88-octane gasoline.

- *May:* By the end of the month, the government confirmed that adjustments would take place every three months.
- *June:* By June 1, the government had announced that no price changes would take place going into Ramadan.
- *September:* As of September 1, no new price adjustments had taken place.
- *October:* The government announced a new set of fuel price decreases, alongside a range of other measures to stimulate the economy. The price cuts did not apply to the previously subsidized Premium-brand 88-octane gasoline, but they did apply to Solar-brand diesel (still theoretically subsidized at Rp 1,000 below market prices) and a range of fuels whose prices had not been controlled: aviation fuel (Avtur) and two higher-quality brands of gasoline (Pertalite and Pertamax).

During the course of the year, parliament also began discussing the creation of a "petroleum fund" to smooth prices (by taxing fuels when world prices are low and subsidizing prices when world prices are high), thereby creating price certainty without undue subsidization. Although sound in theory, a significant body of analysis shows that in practice such mechanisms tend to result in a return to large-scale subsidization (Kojima 2013).

Throughout 2015, the international oil price continued to fluctuate despite largely static domestic prices. Already in March, state oil company Pertamina announced that the government's retail prices were Rp 200–750 per liter below the price that should have been determined by the official pricing formula (GSI-IISD 2015b). As of September, the Ministry of Energy and Mineral Resources reported that Pertamina had incurred cumulative associated losses of Rp 6.7 trillion (US$0.5 billion) in September (table 4.3). These losses are low in

Table 4.3 Comparison of Pump and Actual Prices of 88-Octane Gasoline in Indonesia, 2015

Date	*Politically determined (pump) price (Rp per liter)*	*Estimated market price[a] (Rp per liter)*	*Price gap (Rp per liter)*	*Total losses to Pertamina (Rp, billions)*
Jan 1	7,600	7,600	0	0
Jan 19	6,600	6,600	0	0
Feb 1	6,600	6,660	0	0
Mar 1	7,000	6,800	−200	−202.18
Mar 28	7,900	7,300	−600	−596.36
May 1	7,950	7,300	−650	−663.54
June 1	8,950	7,300	−1,650	−1,640.79
July 1	9,100	7,300	−1,800	−2,015.51
Aug 1	8,450	7,300	−1,150	−1,207.70
Sept 1	7,700	7,300	−400	−412.53
Total	n.a.	n.a.	n.a.	−6,738.61

Source: ESDM 2015.
Note: n.a. = not applicable. Rp = rupiah. Pertamina is the state-owned oil company.
a. The "estimated market price" is the estimated cost of bringing fuel all the way to retail, including the international price, import costs, distribution costs, and a small profit margin for the retailer.

historical terms, but this is a function of world oil prices. The risk for Indonesia's pricing system will be whether the political will exists to carry through price increases once world prices increase once again—and having lowered prices for previously unsubsidized fuels is a dangerous precedent in this respect.

Impact of the 2014–15 Reforms

Fiscal Impact

Indonesia's 2014–15 reforms have benefited the country's fiscal situation more than most historical reforms, which have typically kept subsidy expenditure stable in the face of rising world oil prices. Electricity subsidies are still large (budgeted at around 0.6 percent of GDP in 2015), and the country's budget for fuel subsidies still includes a line of expenditure that is linked to some remaining policies—LPG subsidies, kerosene subsidies, gasoline distribution costs outside the Java-Madura-Bali area, and the remaining diesel subsidy of Rp 1,000 per liter (budgeted at around 0.7 percent of GDP in 2015). However, the total combined outlay on energy subsidies has fallen from 3.5 percent of GDP in 2014 to 1.3 percent of GDP in 2015 (figure 4.13).

The total savings associated with the fuel subsidy reforms have been reported at around Rp 195 trillion (US$15.6 billion, or 1.6 percent of GDP) (Lontoh, Beaton, and Clarke 2015). The improved fiscal position was generally seen to have increased investor confidence, with the exchange rate strengthening against major currencies and the stock exchange rising in the days after the

Figure 4.13 Government Expenditure on Energy Subsidies in Indonesia, 2007–15[a]

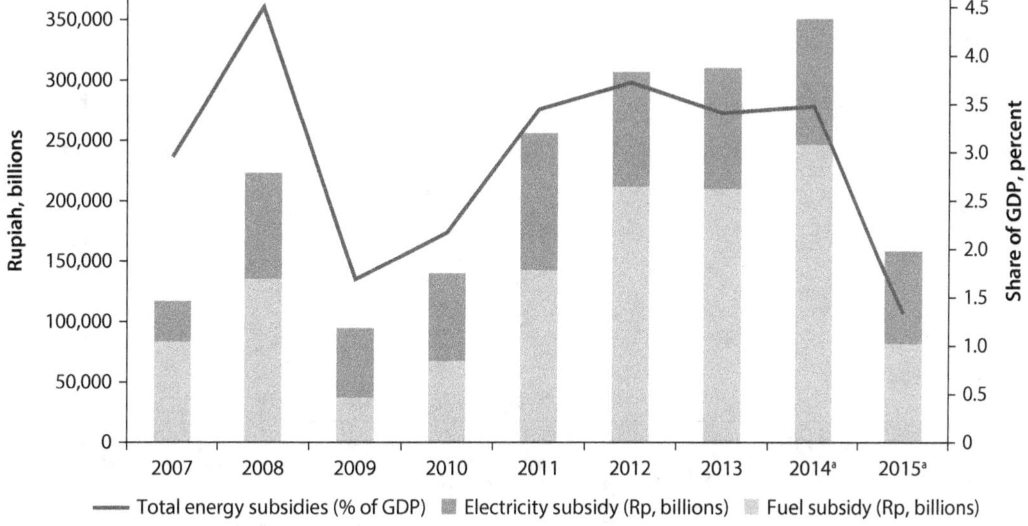

Source: Lontoh, Beaton, and Clarke 2015.
Note: Rp = rupiah.
a. 2014 and 2015 figures based on the revised state budget, not final audited totals.

announcement (Casier and Beaton 2015). Standard & Poor's improved Indonesia's BB+ credit rating from "stable" to "positive"—citing, among other reasons, the improved quality, effectiveness, and predictability of government expenditure (GSI-IISD 2015b).

Inflationary Impact

Fuel price increases generally raise concerns about inflationary impacts. Although reforms usually create only a short-term inflationary effect, large, one-off price increases can have significant impacts that burden low-income households by increasing the cost of living.

The role of inflation in the recent Indonesian reforms is notable, as reflected in the difference in inflationary response between initial price increases in November 2014 and the subsequent price decreases in January 2015. The inflationary response to price hikes in mid-November 2014 accounted for almost half the country's annual inflation for 2014 (figure 4.14). By contrast, only a moderate period of deflation in January and February 2015 followed the price decreases.

This "price stickiness" became a basis for criticizing the government's having entrusted pricing to market forces (Casier and Beaton 2015). It is not possible to assess the possible inflationary impacts of ongoing price volatility because of the lack of price changes after March 2015, although upward price adjustments in March were not associated with any significant increase in inflation beyond the usual trend associated with Ramadan.

Figure 4.14 Inflation and Consumer Price Index in Indonesia, January 2014 to May 2015

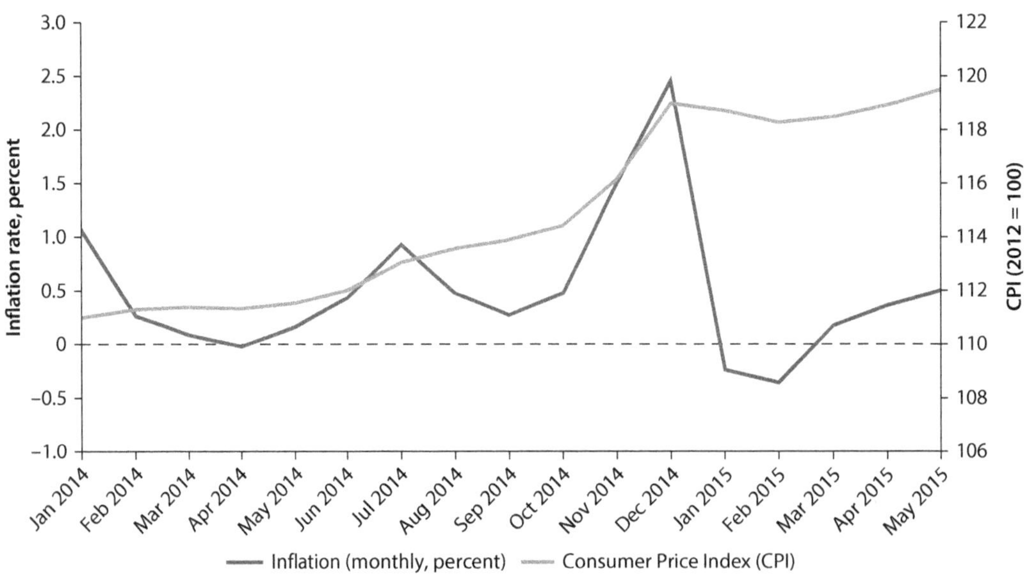

Source: GSI-IISD 2015b.
Note: CPI = Consumer price index. The CPI base year is 2012.

Distributional Impact

Data do not yet exist that would allow for a distributional analysis of Indonesia's reforms in 2014 and 2015, but much can be inferred from the previous decade of subsidy reform, when significant changes occurred in the pattern of gasoline and diesel expenditures across the distribution of Indonesian household consumption.

Gasoline consumption grew fastest among richer households, both in absolute terms and as a percentage of total consumption (figures 4.15 and 4.16). The opposite was true for diesel, where surging demand for generator fuel among poorer households drove higher diesel demand. However, with gasoline consumption far exceeding diesel consumption, aggregate fuel consumption grew faster among richer households (table 4.4).

These consumption patterns determine the extent to which different households benefited from fuel subsidies. In 2004, the poorest half of Indonesians received only a quarter of all subsidy spending on gasoline and diesel; by 2014, this share had fallen to one-fifth (figure 4.17). Conversely, the share of subsidies enjoyed by the richest quintile increased over this period from 44 percent to 50 percent.

Figure 4.15 Gasoline and Diesel Consumption in Indonesia, by Household Consumption Decile, 2004 and 2014

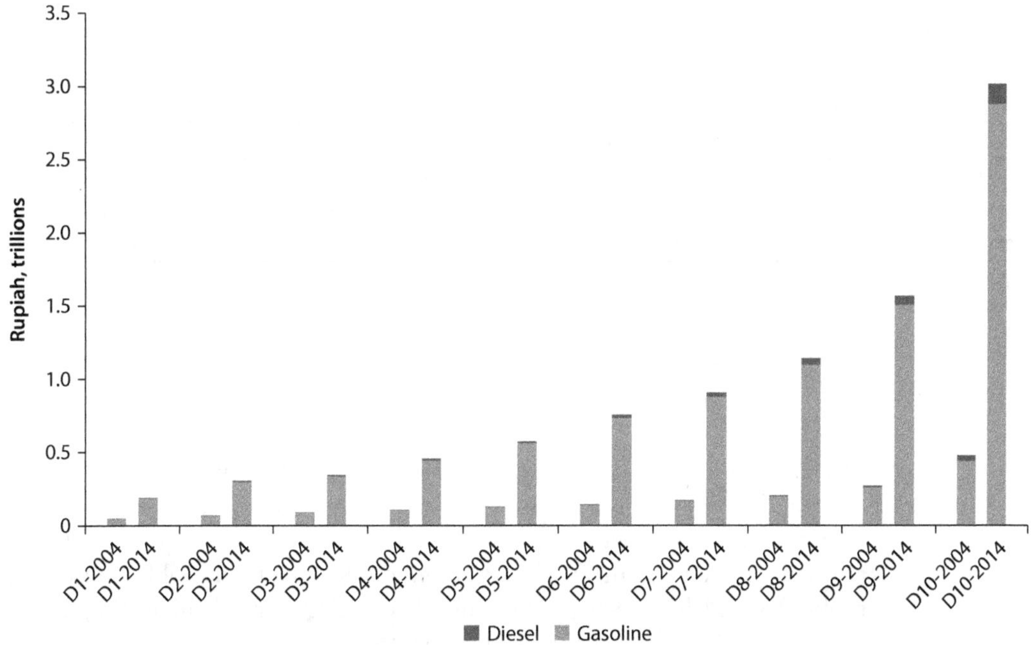

Sources: National Socioeconomic Survey (SUSENAS) of the Central Statistics Agency (Badan Pusat Statistik, BPS), http://microdata.bps.go.id/mikrodata/index.php/catalog/SUSENAS; World Bank calculations.
Note: D = decile of household per capita consumption (1 = poorest, 10 = richest). Household per capita consumption deciles are after spatial adjustments for purchasing power. All fuel consumptions are expressed in nominal rupiah, both spatially and temporally.

Figure 4.16 Gasoline and Diesel Consumption as a Share of Total Consumption in Indonesia, by Household Consumption Decile, 2004 and 2014

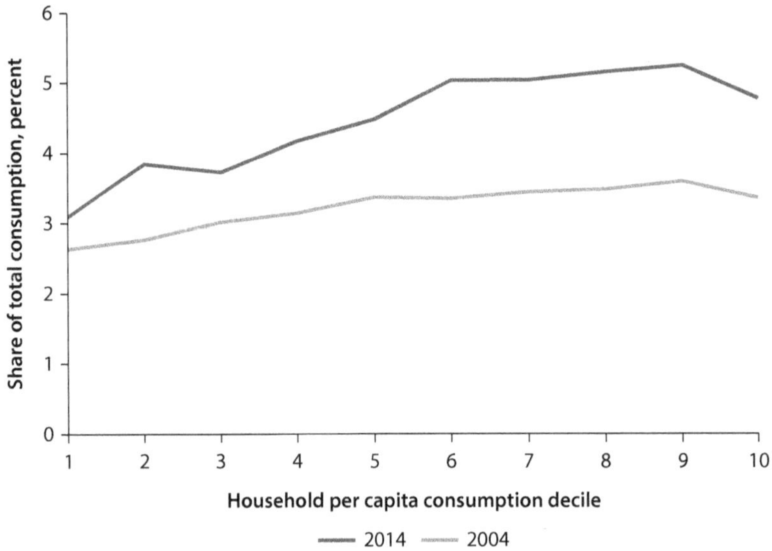

Sources: National Socioeconomic Survey (SUSENAS) of the Central Statistics Agency (Badan Pusat Statistik, BPS), http://microdata.bps.go.id/mikrodata/index.php/catalog/SUSENAS; World Bank calculations.
Note: Household per capita consumption deciles (1 = poorest, 10 = richest) are after spatial adjustments for purchasing power.

Table 4.4 Compound Annual Growth Rate (Nominal) of Household Expenditure on Fuel Consumption in Indonesia, by Decile, 2004–14
Percent

Fuel type	*D1*	*D2*	*D3*	*D4*	*D5*	*D6*	*D7*	*D8*	*D9*	*D10*
Gasoline	14	16	14	16	16	18	18	19	19	21
Diesel	41	35	42	32	25	21	36	19	19	14
Total	15	17	15	16	16	18	18	19	19	20

Sources: National Socioeconomic Survey (SUSENAS) of the Central Statistics Agency (Badan Pusat Statistik, BPS), http://microdata.bps.go.id/mikrodata/index.php/catalog/SUSENAS; World Bank calculations.
Note: D = decile of household per capita consumption (1 = poorest, 10 = richest). Household per capita consumption deciles are after spatial adjustments for purchasing power. Percentages of fuel consumption growth are calculated on the basis of expenditure on fuel in nominal rupiah, both spatially and temporally.

Despite the skewed and increasing share of subsidies going to richer households, the value of energy subsidies is actually greater for poorer households than richer households as a percentage of their income before taxes and transfers (also known as "market income"). That is, although poor and vulnerable households benefited relatively little in absolute subsidy terms, the small benefits they gained meant proportionally slightly more to them than to rich households because the subsidies represented a higher percentage of their incomes (figure 4.18). As a consequence, subsidies have had little impact on inequality (Indonesia MoF and World Bank 2015).

Figure 4.17 Distribution of Gasoline and Diesel Subsidies in Indonesia, by Household Consumption Decile, 2004 and 2014

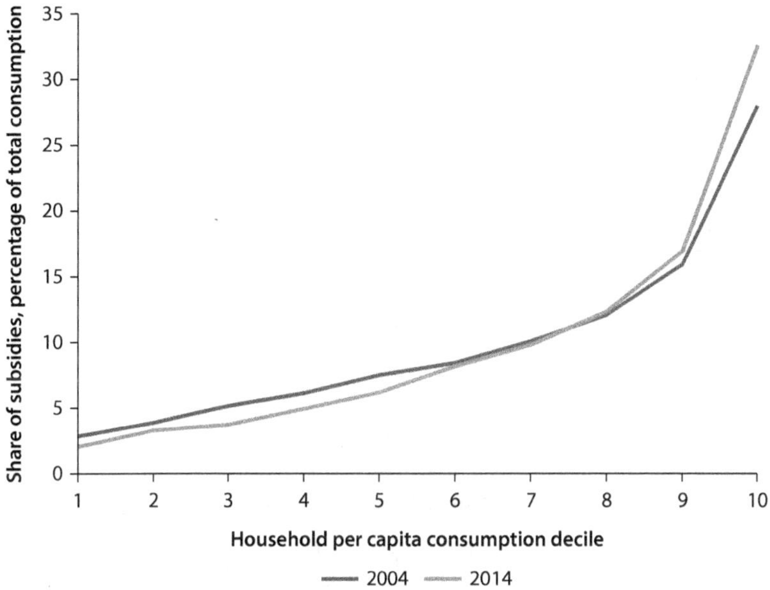

Sources: National Socioeconomic Survey (SUSENAS) of the Central Statistics Agency (Badan Pusat Statistik, BPS), http://microdata.bps.go.id/mikrodata/index.php/catalog/SUSENAS; World Bank calculations.
Note: Household per capita consumption deciles (1 = poorest, 10 = richest) are after spatial adjustments for purchasing power. The subsidy value each year is estimated as the difference between the regulated price of subsidized gasoline and diesel and the retail price of nonsubsidized gasoline and diesel. This subsidy is applied uniformly to each liter of consumption, because the data do not break out household consumption of subsidized and nonsubsidized fuel. This may lead to a slight overstatement of the subsidy for the richest households, which are slightly more likely to use nonsubsidized gasoline because of its higher octane rating.

The removal of subsidies increased inflation directly and indirectly. However, through higher prices for both fuel and other goods and services, the impact of subsidy reform on poverty was minimal in 2008, 2013, and 2014 because of the use of cash compensation targeted at the poorest 25–30 percent of households (World Bank 2012a, 2013b, 2014a, 2015).

Gasoline and Diesel Consumption Impact

The Ministry of Energy and Mineral Resources announced in September 2015 that actual consumption of subsidized gasoline and diesel would likely fall below the allocated yearly quota. The consumption of 88-octane gasoline was reportedly only 7.06 million kiloliters from January to July compared with 7.9 million kiloliters over the same period in 2014—a 9 percent reduction. Diesel consumption was projected to reach around 16.02 million kiloliters by the end of 2015 compared with an allocated yearly quota of 17.05 million, around 6 percent lower than anticipated (*Jakarta Globe* 2015).

Fuel demand typically increases year-on-year in Indonesia, and in most previous years, quotas were set too low and required midyear adjustment.

Figure 4.18 Energy Subsidy Benefit in Indonesia, by Household Market Income Decile, 2012

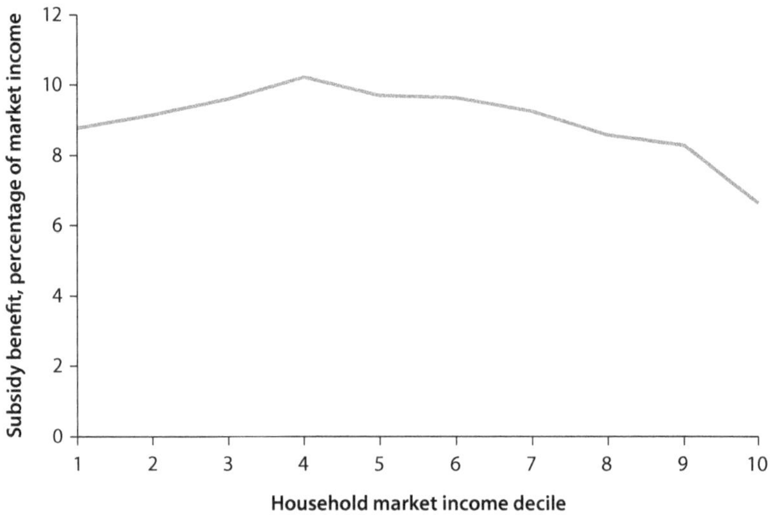

Sources: National Socioeconomic Survey (SUSENAS) of the Central Statistics Agency (Badan Pusat Statistik, BPS), http://microdata.bps.go.id/mikrodata/index.php/catalog/SUSENAS; Indonesia 2012 state budget; and World Bank calculations as reported in Indonesia MoF and World Bank 2015.
Note: Chart includes all energy subsidies (including gasoline, diesel, kerosene, liquefied petroleum gas [LPG], and electricity)—of which gasoline and diesel make up around two-thirds. "Household market income" refers to income before taxes and public transfers.

The decreased consumption in 2015 was likely linked partly to higher prices and partly to a general economic slowdown.

Understanding the Circumstances That Enabled Reform

Characterizing the Reforms

According to the framework for political economy analysis presented in chapter 1, one can categorize different policies according to the size of the benefits they offer to concentrated "special interests" versus the benefits that are more broadly diffused to citizens at large. This characterization provides a starting point for generalizing about the political economy challenges to subsidy reforms.

Until recently, all of Indonesia's gasoline and diesel subsidy policies could be clustered under either Case 1 (large benefits to citizens and special interests alike) or Case 3 (large benefits to citizens and small benefits to special interests), as shown in table 4.5. This uncertainty exists about where to place the policies within the framework because although it is clear that the citizen benefits of Indonesia's universal fossil fuel subsidies are large (around 7–10 percent of a household's total market income in 2014), it is unclear to what extent special interest groups have benefited from the fuel subsidy in Indonesia. This lack of clarity arises from uncertainty about potential governance issues and definitional

Table 4.5 Characterizing Subsidy Policy Benefits in Indonesia

Beneficiary type and benefit size	*Citizen benefits are large*	*Citizen benefits are small*
Special interest benefits are large	**Case 1** Universal subsidies for gasoline and diesel (under high world oil prices)	**Case 2** Universal subsidies for gasoline and diesel (under low world oil prices)
Special interest benefits are small	**Case 3** Universal subsidies for gasoline and diesel (under high world oil prices)	**Case 4** Universal subsidies for gasoline and diesel (under low world oil prices)

questions of whether the political popularity of subsidies could be defined as a "special interest" for ruling parties.

When they first originated, Indonesia's subsidies likely were clustered under either Case 2 (small benefits to citizens and large benefits to special interests) or Case 4 (small benefits to citizens and special interests alike), with benefits from subsidy reform as a share of household income likely lower than their present-day levels. Rather than reflecting any change in policy design, however, the shift westward across the framework for Indonesia has largely been driven by appreciation in international oil prices, although declining oil reserves, increasing consumption, and a weakening exchange rate have also all played a role.

Indonesia's experiences suggest that subsidy policies in either Case 1 or Case 3 are likely to face mass popular opposition to reforms because they involve the transfer of tangible benefits to most citizens, many of whom are likely to resist change unless they are convinced the government will deliver something better. Moreover, in Indonesia specifically, protests were regularly and relatively easily organized in response to broadly unpopular policies. This reflects the country's political context, having transitioned from an autocratic regime that suppressed dissension to a decentralized democracy. In such a context, political organizations, particularly labor and student unions, were well organized and eager to participate in direct action in response to political decision making that affected the general population.

It is harder to draw inferences about the role of special interests in Indonesia's case other than to note that benefits captured by special interests may often be clouded by poor transparency and uncertainty. This makes it harder to appease these interests in order to reform subsidies or to publicize these benefits in order to build popular support for policy change.

It is also clear that when benefits for citizens and special interests are both large, special interests may seek to stoke mass opposition as a strategy to entrench a subsidy policy, making it difficult to untangle one from the other. For example, in one protest in October 2000, news media reported that fuel subsidy protesters had wrecked a car outside parliament, but only because the protest organizer had reneged on a deal to pay them the equivalent of US$6 per person for taking part in the demonstration (AP 2000). Political opposition has typically perpetuated the belief that subsidy reform will harm the poor, despite relatively good awareness among policy makers that low-income households can be better helped through other policies.

Extending the Framework

The framework is helpful in isolating these general patterns that are likely to apply to this theoretical "ideal type" of subsidy policy in other countries. The lessons from the framework can also be further developed in the light of the in-depth review of Indonesia's historical experiences with gasoline and diesel subsidies, which suggest four additional areas that might be relevant for countries to consider when assessing the political economy of subsidy policies.

Nuance in Assessing "Citizen Benefits." First, it can be important to understand the exact distribution of citizen benefits and pathways by which they are delivered. It is common for countries with untargeted and expensive fuel subsidies to have citizen benefits that are on average significant as a share of total income, but "large" benefits do not equate to an equally large distribution of those benefits among different subgroups of citizens. In Indonesia, as in most countries, most of the total expenditure on gasoline and diesel subsidies is clustered among higher-income citizens who own vehicles, have higher purchasing power, and are better organized politically.

Low-income households may use little fuel directly, but it is well established that subsidy benefits can be conferred via direct and indirect pathways, particularly where subsidized fuels are an input in other goods and services (Arze del Granado, Coady, and Gillingham 2012). For example, households living below the poverty line may receive few direct benefits from fuel subsidies because they have little buying power and own no capital that requires fuel. However, they may also receive indirect benefits from consumption of products (food) or services (transport), whose prices are influenced by fuel prices.

Distinguishing between the size of direct and indirect benefits on an absolute basis and as a relative share of total expenditure can help to tease out why subgroups of the population are more or less in support of subsidy policies. In Indonesia, the policies are not only generally highly regressive but also transfer the largest absolute benefit to politically better-organized middle- and upper-income households—at the same time transferring a sufficiently large enough benefit in relative terms to make low-income households view reform attempts with apprehension.

Possible Difficulty in Obtaining Data on "Special Interest" Benefits. Second, Indonesia's experiences are a useful reminder that, in the case of large-scale fossil fuel subsidies, little information may exist about the benefits captured by special interest groups when governance problems are concerned, including data on the magnitude of benefits and the exact special interest groups involved. In Indonesia, no good data exist to prove that political elites have benefited in a concentrated way from the subsidy system despite significant media speculation about the existence of a well-connected "oil mafia." Similarly, businesses that are large fuel consumers could be defined as a special interest, but they are not known to have played any significant role in opposing or supporting reforms.

Distinguishing between Different Types of Reform. Third, it is relatively easy to highlight how subsidy benefits are distributed but more complex to do the same with respect to a subsidy reform plan, particularly given that reforms typically consist of costs as well as benefits and that reforms come in different types (box 4.1), with implications for how impacts are shared among citizens at large and special interest groups.

In Indonesia, citizens have been expected to accept short-term costs with some short-term compensation for a subset of eligible households and otherwise the promise of unspecified medium- to long-term benefits through investments in development. In the context of special interest benefits, one fairly invariable "special interest" related to reform attempts in Indonesia has been the strong political capital that opposition parties can earn by rallying against higher prices and seeing the ruling administration fail at a high-profile policy reform.

Box 4.1 Unpacking the Many Meanings of "Reform"

The literature on fossil fuel subsidy reform commonly refers to "reform" as if it were one coherent concept as opposed to being a broad term that captures various types of policy change, each of which may come with its own political economy challenges.

Price Increases

The most commonly recognized meaning of reform is a "price increase." Even this is not unitary; it can be subdivided into categories of "universal price increase" (for all consumers) or "targeted price increase" (for one or more subgroups of consumers). For example, Indonesia's attempts to increase prices for industry in 2005 faced very different challenges than attempts to increase prices for all consumers. Equally, we may distinguish between "small but frequent" and "large but one-off" price increases, again with their own political and technocratic costs and benefits.

Structural Reforms

If subsidies are to be removed for good, "structural" reforms are also needed. These address the systemic causes of subsidies. As set out in Beaton et al. (2013), structural reforms fall into two broad categories.

The first is "pricing system reform," also referred to in this study as "institutional reform": adjustments to the existing pricing system or the introduction of a lower or nonsubsidy pricing system that is properly regulated and enforced. This system could cause prices to rise or fall in the short term and will certainly introduce greater price volatility and higher average prices. However, without a strong independent pricing system, prices will be subject to political pressures.

box continues next page

Box 4.1 Unpacking the Many Meanings of "Reform" *(continued)*

The second is "targeting assistance reforms," also referred to in this study as "complementary reforms": the improvement or introduction of nonsubsidy mechanisms to assist households or businesses in a targeted way. For households, this reform is likely to involve an increasingly sophisticated social assistance system that can target support to the vulnerable. Without tools that can provide targeted support, governments are more likely to return to highly inefficient policies such as universal energy subsidies when the political need arises.

As Indonesia's experiences show, "institutional" reforms are likely to be discrete events directly linked to attempts to reduce subsidy expenditure, while "complementary" reforms are typically much more diffuse. Complementary reforms can be subcategorized into (a) discrete "tactical" changes in capacity that are directly linked to subsidies (such as Indonesia's BLT unconditional cash transfer); and (b) ongoing "diffuse" changes that are driven by poverty reduction programs and are unrelated to subsidies but have capacity implications in that they can support price increases or supplant subsidization policies. (The latter subcategory includes subsequent improvements to registries of the poor, used by numerous social assistance policies, including the BLSM in 2013.)

Lack of Consideration of Public Perceptions. Fourth—and related to all of the above points—it is necessary to distinguish between reality and perceptions. This point applies to how an *initial subsidy policy* should be characterized: in Indonesia, for example, gasoline and diesel subsidies are commonly described as being in the interests of the poor (when in fact most benefits go to richer households), and the media have speculated that the policy benefits special interest groups (although no hard proof of this exists to date). It also applies to how a *reform attempt* should be characterized: the popular conception of a reform may be quite different from the reform that is attempted, because of misinformation, misunderstanding, or mistrust in the government.

Popular misconceptions about subsidies and reform can even constitute a structural barrier to change, in much the same way that a lack of a pricing system and a lack of targeted assistance capacity are structural barriers (as discussed in box 4.1). In this sense, government and nongovernment communications about reform or simply government delivery of reforms can be tracked as a type of intervention that may alter the available political operating space over time—an "informational reform."

The major difference between this and other types of reform that can be tracked through time is that the state of knowledge about policy and policy delivery is hard to track. Government efforts to alter that state of information are highly diffuse and can only attempt to act as one influence among many, as perceptions are ultimately negotiated through a complex interplay of other actors and contextual variables. Distinguishing between "diffuse" and "tactical" efforts to influence the availability of information and perceptions may help analysts to determine the role being played by informational forces, although a lack of publicly available data on governments' tactical strategies to publish information and change perceptions may well constrain analysis.

An Extended Framework in the Context of Indonesia

Table 4.6 sets out a more complex summary of policy benefits (incorporating differences in perception), and table 4.7 distinguishes between various types of reform in Indonesia since 2001. The subsequent discussion identifies some general lessons from the Indonesian experience with these different types of reform.

"Price Increase" Reform Analysis

In Indonesia, almost all reforms have involved an immediate price increase, many consisting of simple ad hoc price changes that are not coupled with any attempt to alter the underlying pricing system and thereby address the cause of subsidies. The impacts of price increases on citizens are directly linked to the distribution of subsidy benefits: high absolute costs and middling relative costs for richer households, and low absolute costs but significant relative costs for poorer households. Less is known about the impacts on special interest groups, but it is clear that opposition political parties tend to oppose price increases because they can accumulate significant political capital by doing so (Abdulrahim and Kumoro 2015).

Together, these impacts add up to a powerful set of forces opposed to price increases, given that all citizen segments lose benefits that are significant in either absolute or relative terms, with opposition political parties typically poised to exploit the situation (table 4.8).

Three factors appear to have played a primary role in enabling price increases: macroeconomic crises, world oil prices, and windows of opportunity in the political cycle.

Macroeconomic crises. Over the past 15 years in Indonesia, macroeconomic crises have overshadowed most fuel subsidy reforms—from the aftermath of the Asian Financial Crisis to the numerous attempts to avoid large fiscal deficits.

Table 4.6 Framework for Characterizing Benefits of Gasoline and Diesel Subsidies in Indonesia

Beneficiary type	*Data on actual benefits*	*Differences in perception?*
Citizen benefits	Subsidies are highly regressive (most benefits going to the rich) but deliver benefits to lower-income households that are significant in relative terms, particularly diesel subsidies. Over time, the middle classes capture a larger share because of increased vehicle ownership, but subsidies are still highly regressive.	Subsidies are often characterized in some media or by opposition parties as being in the interests of the poor.
Special interest benefits	No data show that special interests benefit from policies aside from large fuel consumers. There is a general lack of transparency around the costs of importing fuel.	Speculation persists that a politically well-connected "oil mafia" benefits from subsidies.

Table 4.7 Different Types of Gasoline and Diesel Subsidy Reform in Indonesia, 2001–15

Reform type[a]		*2001*	*2005*	*2008*	*2013*	*2014*	*2015*
Pricing (increase)		• *All users:* small, monthly, formula-based changes	• *All users:* two large ad hoc increases • *Industry:* market prices hereafter	• *All users:* one large ad hoc increase	• *All users:* one large ad hoc increase	• *All users:* one large ad hoc increase	• *All users:* small fortnightly or monthly, formula-based changes
Institutional		• *Pricing formula:* 50%, then 75%, of market prices, monthly; abandoned in 2003	• *Industrial users:* market pricing used hereafter				• *Pricing formula:* gasoline and diesel prices linked to market prices
Complementary	Tactical	• *Assistance provided or expanded:* using existing capacity	• *Assistance provided or expanded:* using existing capacity • *Cash transfer (BLT):* made to assist price increases; rough but better targeting than any other major program	• *Assistance provided or expanded:* using existing capacity	• *Assistance provided or expanded:* using existing capacity • *Cash transfer (BLSM):* BLT with an updated registry	• *Assistance provided or expanded:* using existing capacity • *Smart card system:* launched but not widely rolled out; largely a recast of existing capacity	
	Diffuse	Following the Asian Financial Crisis, Indonesia made major, ongoing investments to build a comprehensive social welfare system, including the following: (a) a range of welfare programs related to food, health, and education that are used at various times to mitigate impacts of price increases; and (b) increasingly accurate targeting of assistance to low-income households. Gradually, this overall effort reduces the relative importance of fuel subsidization among the government's well-known social assistance policies.					

table continues next page

Table 4.7 Different Types of Gasoline and Diesel Subsidy Reform in Indonesia, 2001–15 *(continued)*

Reform type[a]		*2001*	*2005*	*2008*	*2013*	*2014*	*2015*
Informational	Tactical		• *Strong public relations:* Yudhoyono noted for sudden change in tactical communications compared with previous governments; BLT a part of this			• *Reforms part of preelection campaigning:* high legitimacy • *Efforts to share reforms with outgoing government:* rejected	
	Diffuse	Following the Asian Financial Crisis, the government had good transparency on subsidies through annual budgetary reporting. Generally, government communications efforts around reforms were not well recorded but were clearly ongoing throughout this period. No good data exist on public perceptions over time. Anecdotal reports suggest a gradual reduction in opposition to subsidy reforms, which is substantiated by the increasing acceptability of political parties' proposals for subsidy reforms as part of their 2015 election campaigns.					

Note: BLT = Direct Cash Assistance. BLSM = Bantuan Langsung Sementara Masyarakat, also called the Temporary Cash Transfer Program.

a. "Pricing" reform refers to government regulation of the wholesale or retail prices of energy-related products, including policies that change the size or allocation of a subsidy. "Institutional" reform refers to pricing *mechanisms*, notably the removal of ad hoc government control over prices and shifting to more-automatic pricing mechanisms (such as formulas) or even full reliance on markets for pricing. Institutional reforms have also included reorganization of how subsidies are paid—for example, shifting from systems in which a state-owned enterprise acts as intermediary between imports and in-country sales to one where the government pays direct cash transfers. "Informational" reform refers to active efforts to increase the flow of information to increase interest groups' and citizens' awareness of how a policy change would be beneficial to them. "Complementary" reform refers to reforms that complement or substitute for subsidies in ways that help reformers to reduce the size of subsidies and improve their allocation.

Table 4.8 Costs and Benefits of "Price Increase" Reforms in Indonesia, 2014

Beneficiary type		*Costs*	*Benefits*	*Differences in perception?*
Citizens by income	High (D9–10)	*Absolute:* high, receiving about 50 percent of total subsidy benefits *Relative:* noticeable, as fuel is about 6–8 percent of total expenditure	• Less short-term pressure on other items of expenditure important to citizens	• Subsidies often characterized in media and by opposition political parties as in the interests of the poor
	Middle (D6–8)	*Absolute:* low, receiving about 30 percent of total subsidy benefits *Relative:* noticeable, as fuel is about 9–10 percent of total expenditure	• Short-term opportunity for higher quality of spending in general	• Low trust that tangible benefits will materialize from reallocated expenditure
	Low (D1–5)	*Absolute:* low, receiving about 20 percent of total subsidy benefits *Relative:* noticeable, as fuel is about 9–10 percent of total expenditure		
Political parties		No data show that political parties lose cash benefits from subsidies. Ruling parties can lose political capital to opposition parties	Improved macroeconomic situation for ruling administration	Some speculation that a well-connected "oil mafia" benefits

Note: D = household consumption decile (1 = poorest, 10 = richest).

Other challenges to reforms have included broader concerns about the availability of expenditure for investment in areas such as infrastructure and social protection and how this affects growth.

World oil prices. International oil price increases have driven many of the crises linked to fiscal deficits, in concert with weak domestic exchange rates and falling domestic oil production. Structural obligations (such as the legal requirement not to exceed a deficit of 3 percent of GDP) have contributed to framing the existence of a fiscal crisis, thus preventing political decision makers from postponing subsidy reform indefinitely. Oil prices have, however, also served to entrench subsidies: the government has implemented some domestic price decreases while world oil prices were low, which has prevented the gradual convergence of ad hoc price increases with average world oil prices.

Political cycles. Political windows of opportunity have played a fairly self-evident role that is common to many difficult policy reforms. In the case of subsidy reform, price increases have been (a) easier during the honeymoon period of high legitimacy following an election; (b) easier for an incumbent who knows he or she will not run again in future elections; and (c) effectively ruled out in the run-up to elections. In Indonesia, ex-ruling parties are least able to accumulate political capital by opposing price increases during the year after transition from one administration to another, because it is typically too close in time to their own previous attempts. The shift toward an executive figure outside of the traditional ruling elites may have enabled the 2014 and 2015 subsidy reforms, but the role that this change in political dynamic may have played is highly dependent on unobservable factors related to special interests.

These three drivers—linked either to the need to avert crisis or to the opening of a narrow window of opportunity—help to explain why Indonesia has typically opted for large, one-off, ad hoc price increases rather than a series of small increases. This analysis also explains why price increases have often not been coupled with attempts to address the underlying structural factors that would help to remove subsidies over the longer term.

"Institutional" Reform Analysis

The Indonesian government has made only two attempts to introduce a new "pricing system" in Indonesia—in 2001 and in 2015. Since this kind of institutional reform will lead to higher average prices, its impacts on citizens and political parties are broadly similar to a "price increase," although much of its impact depends upon its precise design.[29] The major difference is that a change in the pricing system will, in most cases, commit a government to regular price adjustments, thus shifting the risk of price volatility from government to household budgets and increasing the number of instances when the opposition may seek to exploit price changes to gain political capital.

Depending on the nature of a pricing system, it might either take away or create opportunities for special interest groups to siphon benefits (table 4.9). If the pricing system aims to help phase out subsidies permanently, it should also place legal and institutional constraints on political decision makers' ability to intervene in energy pricing. This can also be viewed as a political cost, because it removes a powerful tool that government can use to curry political favor.

Institutional reforms have taken place in Indonesia only during periods when world oil prices have been low. In such circumstances, any price adjustments required by the new system can be assumed with some confidence to be within politically acceptable levels. In 2003, Indonesia's pricing system was abandoned as world oil prices continued to climb above preapproved bands; in 2015, the government announced the removal of subsidies at the same time as oil prices were decreasing, but the system ran into difficulties as soon as a series of small price increases were required in the following months.

In Indonesia, pricing system reform likely faces a level of political opposition that is peculiar to the country's specific historical context, as a result of the 2004 Constitutional Court decision that governments must play a role in determining fuel pricing as part of their constitutional social obligations. This has created a

Table 4.9 Costs and Benefits of "Institutional" Reforms in Indonesia

Beneficiary type	*Costs*	*Benefits*	*Differences in perception?*
Citizens	Same as costs of any "price increase" reform plus the following considerations: • The pricing system design may influence distribution of costs across citizens' income groups. • The risks of energy price volatility are shifted to household budgets.	• Less long-term pressure on other expenditures of importance to citizens • Long-term opportunity for higher quality of spending in general	Same as with any "price increase" reform, plus the following: • Citizens may continue associating price changes with political decision makers. • Some (whether citizens or interest groups) may consider fixed prices to be a constitutional right that safeguards the people's social needs.
Political parties	Depending on design, pricing system can • Remove or create opportunities for special interest groups to benefit; • Reduce ruling parties' political capital with each adjustment and remove a powerful tool for currying favor; and • Be vulnerable to legal challenges.	Improved macroeconomic situation for the ruling administration	The new pricing system may be viewed as more or less vulnerable to exploitation by interest groups than it is in reality.

difficult space for policy making. Political opposition can found their arguments on this precedent, and decision makers must choose one of three options:

- Introduce a new pricing system that is highly vulnerable to political intervention
- Introduce a new pricing system that may be ruled illegal by a constitutional challenge
- Begin pricing reforms by challenging the constitutional precedent through legal means

In turn, the ruling reflected and helped to reinforce some popular perceptions that (a) fixed fuel prices are the best way to maximize social welfare, and (b) reforms are part of an external agenda to open up Indonesia to market structures that are against the founding principles of the nation.

"Complementary" Reform Analysis

Most attempted fuel subsidy reforms over the past 15 years in Indonesia have involved the provision of some form of compensation to protect the vulnerable (table 4.10). This compensation has usually depended on the country's evolving

Table 4.10 Subsidy Reform Compensation Packages in Indonesia, 2003–14

2003 Megawati era	*2005 Yudhoyono era*	*2008 Yudhoyono era*	*2013 Yudhoyono era*	*2014 Widodo era*
• Rice subsidies (OPKB) • Health and social welfare • Education • Transportation • Water infrastructure • Revolving fund for small businesses • Direct loans to fishing communities (PEMP)	• Unconditional cash transfer (BLT) • Education • Health insurance (Askeskin) • Rural infrastructure program (IP) • Grants for poor students (BKM) • Operational grants for schools (BOS)	• Unconditional cash transfer (BLT) • Rice subsidies (Raskin) • Low-interest loans for small businesses • Educational support for children of low-ranking civil servants and military men	• Unconditional cash transfer (BLSM) • Conditional cash transfer (PKH) • Rice subsidies (Raskin) • Grants for poor students (BSM) • Infrastructure program	• Indonesia Smart Card (KIP) • Indonesia Healthy Card (KIS) • Prosperous Family Saving Card (KSKS)

Sources: Beaton and Lontoh 2010; Government of Indonesia 2004; GSI-IISD 2013b, 2015a.
Note: Askeskin = Health Insurance for the Poor. BKM = Special Student Assistance. BLSM = Temporary Cash Transfer Program. BLT = Direct Cash Assistance. BOS = School Operational Assistance. BSM = Poor Student Education Support. IP = Rural Infrastructure Program. KIP = Indonesia Smart Card. KIS = Indonesia Healthy Card. KSKS = Prosperous Family Saving Card. OPKB = Rice Special Market Operations. PEMP = Economic Empowerment of Coastal Communities. PKH = Hopeful Family Program. Raskin = Rice for the Poor.

capacity to target assistance to the vulnerable. However, in the case of the BLT unconditional cash transfer, it also required the creation of new capacity specifically to mitigate the impacts of subsidy reforms.

From a citizen's perspective, there are no costs to the reform of a government's capacity to target assistance unless those reforms amount to the restriction of previously enjoyed benefits. Rather, such reforms are designed to improve the effectiveness and efficiency of providing benefits. When targeted assistance mechanisms are linked to fuel subsidy reforms, however, perceptions may play an important role (table 4.11).

In Indonesia, perceptions have differed on the merits of fuel subsidies relative to alternative policies. For example, the BLT and BLSM cash transfer policies were criticized in some quarters for, among other things, (a) errors of exclusion and inclusion in the registry of beneficiaries; (b) the short-term nature of the assistance; and (c) providing cash that might be used for wasteful purposes (Beaton and Lontoh 2010; Kuwado 2014; Shaidra 2014). Such perceptions can undermine the credibility of claims that subsidies are being reformed to allow for better, more-targeted social assistance to take their place.

From the perspective of special interest groups, the costs and benefits of complementary assistance reforms are more complex (table 4.11). For opposition political parties, policies that successfully deliver tangible benefits to

Table 4.11 Costs and Benefits of "Complementary" Reforms in Indonesia, 2014

Beneficiary type		*Costs*	*Benefits*	*Differences in perception?*
Citizens by income	High (D9–10)	Variable, depending on price increases and the removal of other inefficient welfare policies	Low (leakage)	Citizens may perceive new capacity to be • Badly targeted; • Badly designed to address poverty; or • Contributing to lazy or wasteful behaviors.
	Middle (D6–8)		Low (leakage)	
	Low (D1–5)		High	
Political parties		Possibly high for opposition parties if policies significantly increase ruling administration's popularity	Decrease in relative importance of fuel subsidy, easing future government reforms	None

Note: D = household consumption decile (1 = poorest, 10 = richest).

citizens during fuel price increases can be a threat, because they are likely to increase the popularity of the ruling administration. For example, just before the Indonesian general elections in 2009, the BLT cash transfer program was widely considered to have influenced voters to support the incumbent Yudhoyono administration. As a result, opposition increased to future reforms where the BLT might be used again.

At the same time, over the longer term, it is reasonable to conclude that Indonesia's improved capacity to provide targeted, broad-based, nonsubsidy social assistance has significantly altered the relative significance of the fuel subsidy as a social assistance policy. For all political parties, this change has eased future reforms by gradually removing one of the structural causes of fuel subsidies: a lack of alternative policy tools to provide assistance to the needy.

It is hard to identify evidence that can establish authoritatively how reform is affected by the bundling of price increases with complementary measures. There is no way to reliably compare against a counterfactual or to parse out the effect that different elements of policy design have had on overall political acceptability. To some extent, it may be a mistake to attempt generalization: on a case-by-case basis, specific forms of social assistance policy can create political opposition among different groups. For example, in 2001, the opposition of two major business associations was attributed to the introduction of a minimum wage to compensate for a broad set of price increases. A minimum wage, then, may stoke resistance from businesses that might not be witnessed in response to the expanse of a health insurance program.

Literature on the politics of introducing various possible components of a social welfare system may offer more insights here than literature on fuel subsidy reform. Nonetheless, on balance, in Indonesia's case it is reasonable to assert that the bundling of reforms with complementary measures has played an important role in enabling reform, even if it has not always been sufficient to make reform longer-lasting or more ambitious. The frame through which subsidy reform is understood in Indonesia is the removal of a benefit that is one of the government's obligations in protecting social welfare; this leads to the perception that the government must discharge its social obligations by other means if reform is to be acceptable.

"Informational" Reform Analysis

As noted earlier, perceptions related to fuel subsidy reforms can differ substantially from reality, with implications for the political acceptability of policy change. Trends in perceptions are hard to objectively estimate because consistent and objective data on attitudes are lacking; even basic public opinion on higher fuel prices has been difficult to track across years. In addition, little good data exist on government communications strategies and activities, although efforts in 2012 were quite complex, involving interactive dialogues on television and radio, seminars, advertisements, pamphlets, and stickers (Indriyanto et al. 2013).

Media and commentators have observed that public resistance to reform appears to have declined in recent years. This may be the result of successive waves of information campaigns associated with previous attempts at subsidy reform, in addition to the substantial attention focused on the issue during and after 2014 elections.

A nationally representative public survey that took place a few months before the price hikes in November 2014 found that around 79 percent of the population opposed subsidy reform, with opposition highest in central areas and lowest in more-remote areas (map 4.2). The geographical pattern of opposition likely reflected the extent to which different parts of the country could buy fuels at official administered prices (Pradiptyo et al. 2015).[30] These data are useful in stressing the persistence of genuine, broad-based public opposition to higher energy prices, which will continue to play a strong role in preventing policy change.

Despite the long history of government communications about fuel subsidy policies, the same survey found that citizens were often not well informed about such basic facts as the costs of fuel subsidies: only 26 percent of respondents could correctly identify the share of government expenditure on fuel subsidies within a 10 percent standard deviation. It also found that citizens were modestly open to influence by new information: upon being told the costs of the subsidy, an additional 14 percent of respondents changed their responses to support subsidy reform (Pradiptyo et al. 2015).

A separate, nationally representative public opinion survey, which focused on attitudes about social assistance, found that citizens' attitudes might also change depending on the context in which they are asked about subsidy reform (Indrakesuma, Janz, and Wai-Poi 2015). When asked to name their top three priorities for reducing inequality, only 14 percent of respondents selected the option "More subsidies (e.g. for agriculture, fuel etc.)." Subsidies came last, after

Map 4.2 Public Support for Fuel Subsidy Reform in Indonesia, by Region, 2014

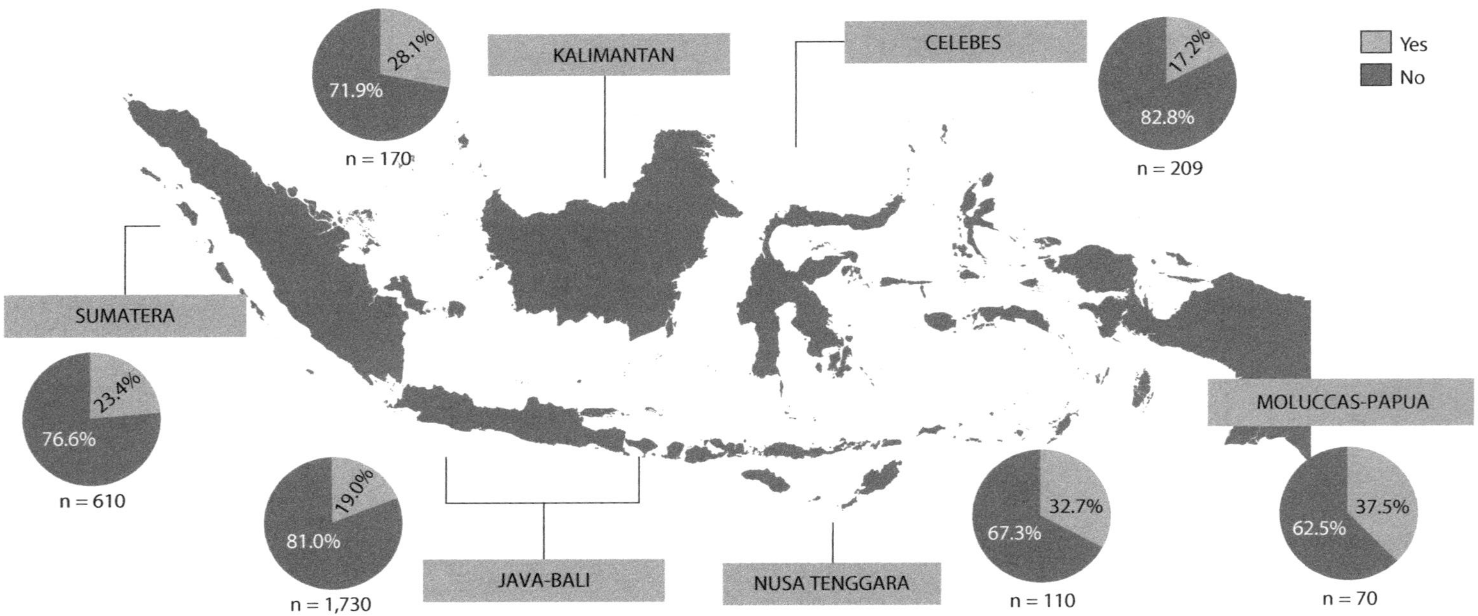

Sources: Pradiptyo et al. 2015, ©International Institute for Sustainable Development (IISD). Reproduced, with permission, from IISD; further permission required for reuse.
Note: n = number of respondents. Percentages equal the share of respondents answering "yes" or "no" to the question, "Do you think that it is better for the government to reduce the fuel subsidy?" Survey conducted by Lembaga Survei Indonesia in August 2014. The region labeled "Celebes" is now called "Sulawesi." "Sumatera" (in Indonesian) is more commonly known as "Sumatra."

Figure 4.19 Citizens' Top Three Priorities for Reducing Inequality in Indonesia, 2014

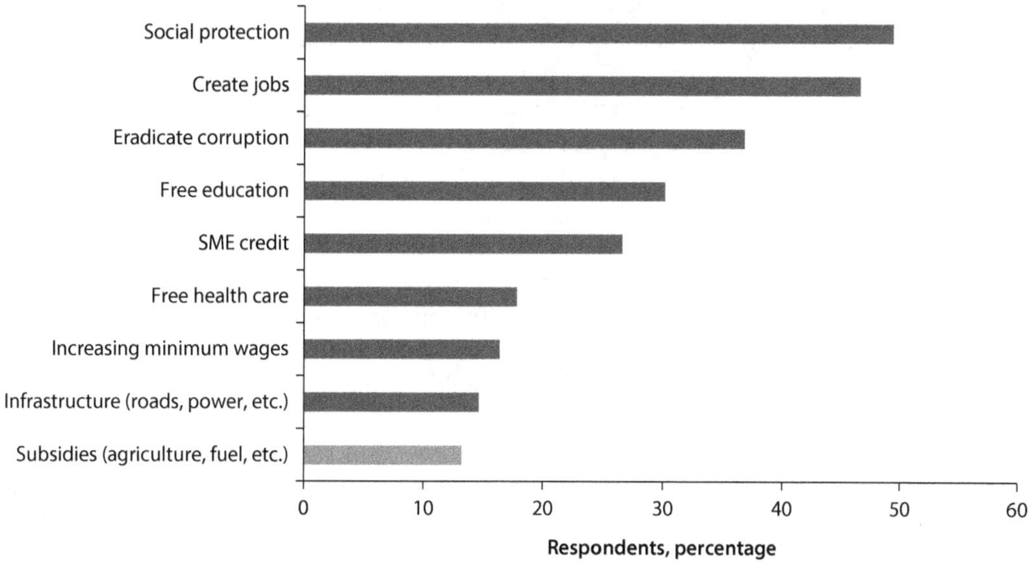

Source: Indrakesuma, Janz, and Wai-Poi 2015.
Note: SME = small and medium enterprise. Survey conducted by Lembaga Survei Indonesia in 2014.

higher priorities such as social protection programs, job creation, and eradicating corruption (figure 4.19).

Although opposition to subsidy reform should not be patronized or dismissed as simply "misunderstanding"—citizens may either have well-justified concerns about policy change or oppose subsidy reform on ideological grounds—these results suggest that efforts to influence perceptions can expand the political space for fossil fuel subsidy reform.

Conclusions

In most countries, policy makers would like to reform fuel subsidies that are inefficient and wasteful. Usually, if reform does not happen, it is because increasing energy prices is politically complex. Analyzing and understanding this complexity can go some way toward helping decision makers identify when to act and how to increase the political operating space for policy change.

In this context, Indonesia's experiences with gasoline and diesel subsidy reforms are an invaluable resource for the international community to learn from. In particular, they emphasize the following principles:

- *Reform is about more than simply increasing prices.* A long-term exit from subsidization requires institutional reforms to the underlying pricing *system* and complementary reforms to develop alternative nonsubsidy mechanisms for targeting assistance. Otherwise, the political pressure to keep domestic fuel prices low will lead to the return of subsidies.

- *Policy makers should prepare for windows of opportunity, likely driven by exogenous factors.* In Indonesia, pricing reforms have been linked to fiscal crises driven by high oil prices or windows of opportunity opened by low oil prices or the political cycle. But often, reforms have simply consisted of ad hoc price changes, and sometimes even price decreases, rather than long-term structural changes. This suggests that policy makers targeting reform should focus on the preparation of more-comprehensive reforms, so they can be quickly implemented when opportunities arise.
- *Reform is both an opportunity and a threat for the political opposition.* Subsidy reform is an opportunity for opposition parties to accumulate political capital by criticizing the government with populist messaging. But it can also pose a threat, particularly if the ruling administration succeeds in transferring tangible benefits to large shares of the population through a more effective, targeted policy alternative.
- *Perceptions often differ from reality.* The problems with fuel subsidies are often not appreciated by the general population in Indonesia, despite over a decade of highly public reform attempts coupled with government communications. Differences in perceptions can reduce political support for reform plans and the alternative assistance policies that have been introduced instead of subsidies. It is necessary to track perceptions to understand how to address them—either by changing policies to account for citizen concerns or by addressing misinformation.
- *Reforming fuel pricing is not an event but a process.* In Indonesia, the reform of gasoline and diesel subsidies has been ongoing for many years. Although this prolonged effort reflects a number of nationally specific challenges, it also reflects the fact that a long-term exit from subsidization requires structural changes that cannot be implemented overnight.

Annex 4A Political Chronology of Indonesia

Table 4A.1 Major Political Events in Indonesia, 1871–2015

Year	*Event*
Preindependence: The Dutch Colonial Period	
1871	The Dutch begin oil drilling in Cirebon.
1899	The Netherlands government issues Indische Mijnwet (Mining Law of Indies), Indisch Staatblad 1899 No. 214, starting the era of mining concessions.
1907	The Royal Dutch Company merges with Shell Transport and Trading Company Ltd., forming the Royal Dutch/Shell Group of Companies, known now as Shell.
1940	Oil production is recorded at 136,000 barrels per day, of which 31 million barrels are exported through Singapore.

table continues next page

Table 4A.1 Major Political Events in Indonesia, 1871–2015 *(continued)*

Year	*Event*
Postindependence: The Sukarno Era	
1945	Indonesia declares independence on August 17, 1945, following the Japanese defeat in World War II.
1957	Dutch petroleum assets in Indonesia are nationalized, from which Permina was founded as a state-owned oil enterprise.
1958	The Indonesian government takes over the Dutch companies operating within Indonesian territory, in the midst of intensifying dispute over West Papua.
1959	With Act No. 10/1959 on the Cancelation of Mining Rights, Indonesia declares the cancellation of mining contracts before 1949.
1960	With Government Regulation in Replacement of Act (Perppu) No. 44/1960 on Oil and Natural Gas Mining, Indonesia establishes new regulations for oil and natural gas mining.
1961	The government creates Permigan and Pertamin, both state-owned oil enterprises.
1965	A political conflict ends with a communist purge and the fall of Sukarno. A military junta, led by Suharto, takes power.
1966	Permigan's assets are absorbed into Pertamin and Permina.
The New Order: The Suharto Era	
1967	Suharto takes over full executive authority as president of the Republic of Indonesia.
1967	With Act No.1/1967 on Foreign Investment, Suharto takes the first step toward restoring Indonesia's relationship with international investors.
1968	Permina merges with Pertamin, creating Pertamina.
1971	Act No. 8/1971 cements Pertamina's role as operator-regulator, starting Pertamina's monopoly over oil and natural gas market.
1973	First world oil price shock occurs, and Indonesia oil boom era begins.
1975	Pertamina scandal reveals large debt caused by malpractices and mismanagement.
1979	Second world oil price shock occurs.
1997–98	The Asian Financial Crisis hits Indonesia hard. On October 31, 1997, Indonesia requests assistance from the International Monetary Fund (IMF) to rescue the country's economy.
May 1998	The May Riot begins when student demonstrators are shot during a riot over fuel price increases. Suharto steps down in the ensuing protests.
Transition to Democracy: B. J. Habibie	
May 21, 1998	B. J. Habibie becomes the president of the Republic of Indonesia, following the resignation of Suharto.
June 1999	After three decades with only three parties in the general election, 48 political parties compete to fill parliamentary seats in the general election.
Abdurrahman Wahid (1999–2000)	
Oct 1999	The People's Consultative Assembly (MPR) appoints Abdurrahman Wahid as the president of the Republic of Indonesia.
Nov 20, 2000	The government issues the National Development Program (Propenas) 2000–04, which declares a thorough evaluation of subsidies, including a gradual reduction of the fuel subsidy.

table continues next page

Table 4A.1 Major Political Events in Indonesia, 1871–2015 *(continued)*

Year	*Event*
Megawati Sukarnoputri (2001–04)	
July 23, 2001	Megawati Sukarnoputri is inaugurated as president of the Republic of Indonesia, following the impeachment of Abdurrahman Wahid by parliament.
Nov 23, 2001	Act No. 22/2001 on Oil and Natural Gas dismantles Pertamina's monopoly and provides the legal ground for a further liberalized oil and gas market.
2003	Under massive public pressure, Megawati cancels an increase of fuel, telephone, and electricity prices on January 1, 2003. The fixed price system for automotive gasoline and diesel is disbanded as international oil prices begin a structural appreciation. The IMF disburses its final assistance to Indonesia in relation to the Asian Financial Crisis.
2004	In Indonesia's first direct presidential election, Susilo Bambang Yudhoyono and Jusuf Kalla defeat Megawati Sukarnoputri and Hasyim Muzadi in the second round.
Susilo Bambang Yudhoyono (2004–14)	
Dec 2004	Jusuf Kalla takes over the leadership of the Golkar Party from Akbar Tanjung. This seals the majority of the Yudhoyono-Kalla coalition in both executive and legislative branches.
2005	Yudhoyono increases the fuel price twice, in May and October. The government introduces the Direct Cash Assistance (BLT) program, a cash transfer scheme to compensate low-income households for fuel price increases.
2006	Presidential Regulation No. 5/2006 sets a goal to overhaul Indonesia's national primary energy mix with significantly reduced dependency on oil. Indonesia settles its debt to the IMF in relation to the Asian Financial Crisis.
2007	Indonesia launches its program for conversion from kerosene to liquefied petroleum gas (LPG) to alter energy consumption in the household sector and slash the kerosene subsidy bill.
2008	Indonesia decides not to extend its membership in the Organization of Petroleum Exporting Countries (OPEC). In June, parliament exercises its right to investigate (*hak angket*) and challenge the fuel price increase. Yudhoyono increases the fuel price before the end of the year, followed by two price reductions. The BLT is used again to provide cash payments to low-income households. The price reductions are hailed as the president's achievement in electoral ads.
Aug 2009	Yudhoyono wins a second term, defeating Megawati Sukarnoputri and Prabowo Subianto, as well as his former vice president Jusuf Kalla and Wiranto, by a steep margin in one round. He picks a senior economic professor, Boediono, as his running mate.
March 2012	Rounds of violent street protests take place to oppose a planned fuel price increase. Kwik Kian Gie, a former minister and senior politician, publishes a controversial calculation to counter the fiscal argument to increase prices. Rumors spread that the price increase plan was initiated by the Golkar Party. Leader Aburizal Bakrie refutes the claim, and by the end of the month Golkar withdraws its support for the reform. A group of opposition figures led by Dien Syamsudin, the leader of Muhammadiyah, Indonesia's second-largest Islamic mass organization, attempt to challenge the price increase through the Constitutional Court. The ruling coalition loses the vote to increase fuel prices in a plenary and voting session that is televised live nationally.

table continues next page

Table 4A.1 Major Political Events in Indonesia, 1871–2015 *(continued)*

Year	*Event*
Nov 13, 2012	The Constitutional Court decides that using the market price to determine domestic fuel prices does not violate the constitution. However, it rules that the upstream regulatory body, BP Migas, is unconstitutional. BP Migas is dissolved. The government creates a replacement agency under the Ministry of Energy and Mineral Resources, SKK Migas, to resume the duty as the regulator of the upstream oil and gas sector.
May 2013	Standard & Poor's downgrades Indonesia's credit rating, citing fuel subsidies as one of its reasons for lack of confidence in the economy.
June 2013	The government increases subsidized fuel prices. It provides a compensation package for poor households, including another unconditional cash transfer, renamed the Temporary Cash Transfer Program (BLSM), to emphasize the temporary nature of the assistance.
Aug 2013	Rudi Rubiandini, head of SKK Migas, is arrested by the Corruption Eradication Commission.
June 17, 2014	Sutan Bhatoegana, chairman of the parliament's Energy Commission, is arrested by the Corruption Eradication Commission over a graft case.
July 2014	Joko Widodo and Jusuf Kalla defeat Prabowo Subianto and Hatta Radjasa in national elections.
Aug 27, 2014	Widodo meets Yudhoyono in Bali to discuss the transition and proposes responsibility sharing over increasing fuel prices. Yudhoyono turns down Widodo's proposal.
Joko Widodo (July 2014–present)	
Oct 20, 2014	Joko Widodo is inaugurated as the seventh president of the Republic of Indonesia.
Nov 16, 2014	The government announces the creation of a task force for National Oil and Natural Gas Management Reform, headed by Faisal Basri. Media dub this "The Team of Anti Oil and Gas Mafia."
Nov 18, 2014	Widodo announces a price increase for subsidized gasoline from Rp 6,500 (US$0.65) to Rp 8,500 (US$0.85) per liter and subsidized diesel from Rp 5,500 (US$0.55) to Rp 7,500 (US$0.75) per liter.
Nov 2014	Violent street protests in response to the price hike break out in several cities. In Makassar, student-led protesters block the main road and disrupt economic activities for more than a week. They are eventually pushed back by citizens of the city.
Dec 31, 2014	With Presidential Regulation No. 191/2014 on Provisioning, Distribution, and the Retail Price of Fuel, the government introduces a new scheme of subsidized fuel and pricing system. Indonesia moves from a fixed price regime to a semiautomatic pricing regime.
May 5, 2015	Jero Wacik, former minister of energy and mineral resources in the Yudhoyono era, is arrested by the Corruption Eradication Commission over a corruption case.
May 13, 2015	Rini Suwandi, minister of state enterprises, announces the liquidation of Pertamina Energy Trading Limited (Petral).

Annex 4B Chronology of Energy Subsidies

Table 4B.1 Energy-Related and Subsidy Reform Efforts in Indonesia, 1956–2015

Year(s)	*Events*
1956–65	Under the Sukarno regime, there is significant government intervention in markets, with Dutch enterprises nationalized in 1957. High levels of government spending that are politically determined contribute to serious problems with inflation.
1966–73	Under the Suharto regime comes a period of stabilization, rehabilitation, partial liberalization, and economic recovery.
1974–82	During the "oil boom," rapid economic growth takes place and government intervention increases.
1983–96	After the oil boom comes a period of deregulation, renewed liberalization (in reaction to falling oil prices), and rapid export-led growth. Corruption at all levels of government bureaucracy is an increasing concern. From 1990, Indonesian fuel demand grows on average by about 7 percent per year.
1997	The Asian Financial Crisis hits Indonesia.
May 1998	The government of Indonesia announces large price increases for fuel and electricity. The price of kerosene is increased by 25 percent, diesel fuel by 60 percent, and gasoline by 71 percent.
	Subsidy cuts trigger protests over the next weeks from thousands of students in the cities of Medan, Bandung, and Yogyakarta, which devolve into general rioting.
Jan 1999	The aviation fuel subsidy is removed.
Oct 2000	The price of gasoline is raised 15 percent, diesel by 9 percent, and kerosene by 25 percent. This is followed by violent demonstrations but not reversed.
2001	A new Oil and Gas Law provides a legal basis for moving away from the subsidy regime, and it abolishes Pertamina's monopoly over the downstream sector, opening it up to entry by other players. Efficient, competitive pricing of petroleum fuels is to be supervised by BPH Migas.
Mar 2001	Subsidies for diesel and marine fuel for the industrial and sea transport sector are removed.
Apr 2001	Fuel prices for large industry, which represented about 23 percent of the market, were increased to 50 percent of the international market price.
June 2001	Indonesia introduces a semiautomatic fuel pricing system for subsidized automotive gasoline and diesel products for industry, transportation, and fishery sectors. Prices for gasoline are raised by 26 percent and diesel by 50 percent.
Jan 2002	A presidential decree reduces fuel subsidies in phases, aiming to set gasoline prices at 100 percent and diesel at 75 percent of the international market price, within certain bounds, for both household and industrial users. Student demonstrations take place in the city of Makassar, with smaller protests also taking place in Jakarta, Surabaya, Denpasar, Manado, and Bandung.
2003	Attempted price increases in 2003 are hotly opposed. Diesel prices are increased by only 6.5 percent, instead of the originally planned 21.9 percent. A case is brought to the Constitutional Court against Oil and Gas Law 22/2001.
2004	Indonesia becomes a net oil importer for the first time in 2004. In December, the Constitutional Court rules that the government cannot rely entirely on business competition to set fuel prices and must continue to play some role in price setting.

table continues next page

Table 4B.1 Energy-Related and Subsidy Reform Efforts in Indonesia, 1956–2015 *(continued)*

Year(s)	*Events*
2005	The government increases fuel prices in March and again in October by an average of 29 percent and 114 percent, respectively, reducing the Indonesian state budget deficit by US$4.5 billion in 2005 and US$10 billion in 2006. A presidential decree announces that the remaining fuel subsidies are to be phased out but does not specify a time frame. In October, prices are raised to international market levels for industry, and the government rolls out the first payment in a cash transfer scheme targeted at poor households (Direct Cash Assistance, or BLT), worth US$30 per household.
2006	The second BLT payment takes place in January.
2007	A National Action Plan for Addressing Climate Change recognizes that fossil fuel subsidies encourage waste and inefficiency and retard alternative energy sources.
2008	International market prices finally peak, with a U.S. light sweet crude price of US$147.27 a barrel, causing subsidy spending to balloon to US$17.6 billion.
	Fuel prices are increased on average by 28.7 percent. The BLT is used again to compensate poor households.
Sep–Nov 2009	The Group of Twenty (G-20) and the Asia-Pacific Economic Cooperation (APEC), both of which count Indonesia as a member, commit to phase out and rationalize inefficient fossil fuel subsidies that lead to wasteful consumption.
2012	The government attempts to increase the prices of subsidized gasoline and diesel, but a parliamentary vote on the issue prevents the increases.
Jan 2013	The government announces that fuel subsidies will no longer be provided for government and government-affiliated vehicles.
June 2013	The price of gasoline is increased from Rp 4,500 (US$0.41) per liter to Rp 6,500 (US$0.59) per liter, a 44 percent increase. The diesel price rises from Rp 4,500 (US$0.41) per liter to Rp 5,500 (US$0.50) per liter, a 22 percent increase. These increases are combined with a Rp 29.1 trillion package of compensation mechanisms targeted at low-income households, including a temporary cash transfer, a basic infrastructure program, and expansions of the Poor Student Education Support (BSM) program, the Hopeful Family Program (PKH) conditional cash transfer, and the subsidized rice program (Raskin).
Oct 2014	Joko Widodo is inaugurated as president.
Nov 2014	Subsidized gasoline prices increase from Rp 6,500 (US$0.52) to Rp 8,500 (US$0.7) per liter. Diesel prices rise from Rp 5,500 (US$0.44) to Rp 7,500 (US$0.62) per liter.
Dec 2014	Widodo announces the removal of subsidized gasoline and the introduction of a "fixed" price for subsidized diesel at Rp 1,000 (US$0.08) below the market price. Because of falling international oil prices, the immediate impact is a decrease in the subsidized gasoline price from Rp 8,500 (US$0.68) to Rp 7,600 (US$0.61) per liter, while the price of subsidized diesel declines from Rp 7,500 (US$0.60) to Rp 7,250 (US$0.58) per liter. In the Revised State Budget 2015, the allocation of state funds to fuel subsidies falls by just over Rp 211 trillion (US$16.9 billion), equal to over 10 percent of all originally planned government expenditure in 2015.
Jan 19, 2015	The price of subsidized gasoline is reduced from Rp 7,500 (US$0.60) to Rp 6,500 (US$0.52), and the price of diesel from Rp 7,250 (US$0.58) to Rp 6,400 (US$0.51).
March 1, 2015	The price of subsidized gasoline is increased from Rp 6,500 (US$0.52) to Rp 6,800 (US$0.54), while the diesel stays the same.
March 28, 2015	The price of subsidized gasoline is increased from Rp 6,800 (US$0.54) to Rp 7,400 (US$0.59), and diesel from Rp 6,400 (US$0.51) to Rp 6,900 (US$0.55). PT Pertamina indicates that the company may suffer losses because of the lower sale price decided by the government.

Notes

1. Indonesia GDP data from the World Development Indicators Database (http://data.worldbank.org/data-catalog/world-development-indicators) and other World Bank databases (http://data.worldbank.org/). For world GDP rankings, see http://data.worldbank.org/data-catalog/GDP-ranking-table.
2. The United Nations Population Fund (UNFPA) defines the "demographic dividend" as "the economic growth potential that can result from shifts in a population's age structure, mainly when the share of the working-age population (15 to 64) is larger than the non-working-age share of the population (14 and younger, and 65 and older)." In other words, it is "a boost in economic productivity that occurs when there are growing numbers of people in the workforce relative to the number of dependents." This period of increased growth usually lasts about 20 to 30 years. For more information, see "Demographic Dividend" on the UNFPA website: http://www.unfpa.org/demographic-dividend.
3. Government revenue and expenditure data from the Bank Indonesia Special Data Dissemination Standard (SDDS), http://www.bi.go.id/sdds/.
4. "Country Comparison: Crude Oil—Proved Reserves," World Factbook Database, CIA (Central Intelligence Agency), https://www.cia.gov/library/publications/the-world-factbook/rankorder/2244rank.html.
5. Gasoline octane ratings throughout the chapter refer to the Research Octane Number (RON).
6. As in many fuel subsidizing countries, the rationale for subsidizing a lower-grade fuel is twofold: First, it is cheaper to procure internationally, reducing overall subsidy costs for any given fixed domestic price. Second, it is an "inferior" good (higher-grade fuels allow vehicles to run better and last longer), and as such, richer households might self-select higher-grade fuels that are unsubsidized. In practice, the use of 88-octane gasoline has actually made full subsidy costs nontransparent because it is of such a low grade that there are no international spot prices to help benchmark the accuracy of costs claimed by fuel importers. (See discussion later in the chapter on alleged corruption linked to the fuel subsidy regime.) The inferiority of the product also appears to have done little to counteract the incentive created by its low cost. In addition to the range of fuels listed above, the government in 2015 introduced Pertalite, a 90-octane fuel that is nonsubsidized but cheaper than 92-octane and 95-octane fuels. Pertalite is not included in consumption statistics presented here because insufficient data are currently available to report on trends.
7. This poverty rate was calculated on the basis of an earlier poverty definition, which used a lower standard of living than the current national poverty line. Therefore, it cannot be compared with more recent poverty data.
8. "New Order" refers to the authoritarian, centralized, military-dominated government built by President Suharto to maintain political and economic stability during his 31-year rule.
9. GDP data from the World Development Indicators Database (http://data.worldbank.org/data-catalog/world-development-indicators).
10. Balance of payments data from the World Economic Outlook Database, International Monetary Fund (http://www.imf.org/external/pubs/ft/weo/2015/02/weodata/index.aspx).

11. "Perkembangan Harga BBM Tahun 1965–2000" dataset, Ministry of Energy and Mineral Resources of the Republic of Indonesia (ESDM), Jakarta (http://www.esdm.go.id/publikasi/harga-energi/harga-bbm-dalam-negeri/doc_download/694-harga-bbm-dalam-negeri-1965-2000.html).
12. The fuel price increases in the 1980s took place in a political space that was already highly constrained for groups outside the ruling regime. After winning the 1971 election, the Suharto government had forced political parties in Indonesia to merge into three parties: the government's party was Golkar; the Islamic parties were merged into the United Development Party (Partai Persatuan Pembangunan, or PPP); and the nationalist and other non-Islamic parties were merged into the Indonesian Democratic Party (Partai Demokrasi Indonesia, or PDI). In addition to the New Order regime's information control and arbitrary use of coercion during election periods, it had no real electoral opposition, winning six consecutive general elections from 1971 to 1997 and never securing less than 60 percent of the vote. Apart from its elected members, the Indonesian parliament at that time also included regional delegations and group delegations, the members of which were appointed by the government. For a further discussion of this period, see Heryanto (2006).
13. Special drawing rights (SDRs) are an international reserve asset created by the IMF in 1969 to supplement its member countries' official reserves based on four key international currencies applied by the IMF (IMF 2015). Concerning SDR valuation, see the IMF's online SDR rate calculator: https://www.imf.org/external/np/fin/data/rms_sdrv.aspx.
14. Presidential Decree No. 45/2001.
15. "Perkembangan Harga BBM Tahun 1965–2000" dataset, Ministry of Energy and Mineral Resources of the Republic of Indonesia (ESDM), Jakarta (http://www.esdm.go.id/publikasi/harga-energi/harga-bbm-dalam-negeri/doc_download/694-harga-bbm-dalam-negeri-1965-2000.html).
16. Presidential Decree No. 9/2002.
17. "Law No.22/2001, dated November 23, 2001, Petroleum and Natural Gas" (accessed February 8, 2006), http://www.eisourcebook.org/cms/Indonesian%20Law%20on%20Petroleum%20and%20Natural%20Gas,%202001.pdf.
18. Claimants included the Association of Legal Counsel and Human Rights of Indonesia (APHI), the Association of Legal Aid and Human Rights of Indonesia (PBHI), and 324 Foundation. For further information on the challenge, see Constitutional Court of Indonesia (2004).
19. Oil price data from the IndexMundi data portal (http://www.indexmundi.com/commodities/?commodity=crude-oil-west-texas-intermediate&months=180).
20. Interviews with World Bank staff knowledgeable about the reforms. All interviews were conducted in confidentiality, and the names of interviewees are withheld by mutual agreement.
21. Interviews with World Bank staff knowledgeable about the reforms. All interviews were conducted in confidentiality, and the names of interviewees are withheld by mutual agreement.
22. Interviews with World Bank staff knowledgeable about the reforms. All interviews were conducted in confidentiality, and the names of interviewees are withheld by mutual agreement.
23. Cash transfer policies can be designed in unconditional or conditional forms. An "unconditional" cash transfer (UCT) is one whereby all recipients receive cash if they

meet the eligibility criteria for inclusion in the scheme, usually related to some benchmark of poverty or vulnerability. A "conditional" cash transfer (CCT) is one whereby eligible recipients must adhere to specific, measurable conditions to receive cash payments. These are typically linked to early physical and mental childhood development, including attendance at prenatal and postnatal clinics and schools. UCTs seek to improve outcomes simply by supplementing household incomes. CCTs seek to improve outcomes by supplementing incomes and incentivizing investments in people that will break intergenerational cycles of poverty. The government chose a UCT in Indonesia because (a) its purpose was to provide short-term compensation for higher prices, and (b) a CCT is significantly more complex to design and implement, requiring not only sophisticated administrative systems but also adequate capacity (such as enough clinics and schools) for conditions to be achievable for the majority of a population. In 2007, a CCT program, the Hopeful Family Program (Program Keluarga Harapan, or PKH) was subsequently developed, using the same essential delivery mechanism as the BLT. It still exists today, but its coverage is much smaller because of the aforementioned capacity constraints (Perdana 2014).

24. West Texas Intermediate (WTI) crude prices peaked at US$147 a barrel on July 11, 2008 (Khan 2009).
25. Interviews with World Bank staff knowledgeable about the reforms. All interviews were conducted in confidentiality, and the names of interviewees are withheld by mutual agreement.
26. Oil price data from the IndexMundi data portal (http://www.indexmundi.com/commodities/?commodity=crude-oil-west-texas-intermediate&months=180).
27. The task force, formally called the Committee for Oil and Gas Management Reform, operates through the Ministry of Energy and Mineral Resources.
28. Pers. comm. with World Bank staff in Jakarta.
29. Market pricing, for example, would raise average prices for all consumers, while a dual pricing system might create different fuel prices for different groups of consumers. Similarly, formal links between a fuel pricing system and social assistance policies might mitigate impacts on certain household groups. For a comprehensive overview of fuel pricing systems, see Kojima (2013). For a review of fuel price system options in the context of Indonesia, see World Bank (2006a) and Beaton, Christensen, and Lontoh (2015).
30. As noted earlier, subsidies have frequently caused scarcity and shortages, particularly in Indonesia's more-remote areas, because they reduce Pertamina's incentives to adequately supply more-remote regions, require occasional rationing to avoid exceeding the approved quota for subsidized fuel, cause hoarding in anticipation of price increases, and incentivize smuggling and illegal marketeering at above-official prices.

References

Abarwati, Ika. 2014. "Rekam Jejak Kartu Sakti Jokowi di Solo dan Jakarta." *Selasar Politik*, November 14. http://slsr.in/politik/rekam-jejak-kartu-sakti-jokowi-di-solo-dan-jakarta.

Adbulrahim, R., and B. Kumoro. 2015. "Fuel Subsidy and Challenges for the New Government." *Indonesia Energy Subsidy Review* 2 (1): 1–18.

Adamrah, Mustaqim. 2009. "Price Cuts: Yudhoyono's Generous Gift Ahead of Polls." *Jakarta Post*, January 13. http://www.thejakartapost.com/news/2009/01/13/price-cuts-yudhoyono039s-generous-gift-ahead-polls.html.

ADB (Asian Development Bank). 2013. *The Social Protection Index: Assessing Results for Asia and the Pacific.* Manila: ADB.

Agénor, P., O. Canuto, and M. Jelenic. 2012. "Avoiding Middle-Income Growth Traps." *Economic Premise* Note 98, Poverty Reduction and Economic Management (PREM) Network, World Bank, Washington, DC.

Agustina, C., J. Arze del Granado, T. Bulman, W. Fengler, and M. Ikhsan. 2008. "Black Hole or Black Gold? The Impact of Oil and Gas Prices on Indonesia's Public Finances." Policy Research Working Paper 4718, World Bank, Washington, DC.

Antara News. 2009. "Penyerahan BLT Bisa Indikasikan Politik Uang." March 18. http://www.antaranews.com/berita/135594/penyerahan-blt-bisa-indikasikan-politik-uang.

———. 2014. "Indonesian Govt Unveils Rp2,019.9 Trillion Budget Plan." August 15. http://www.antaranews.com/en/news/95329/indonesian-govt-unveils-rp20199-trillion-budget-plan.

AP (Associated Press). 2000. "Indonesians Rage over Fuel Prices." *Deseret News*, October 3. http://www.deseretnews.com/article/786180/Indonesians-rage-over-fuel-prices.html.

Arze del Granado, J., D. Coady, and R. Gillingham. 2012. "The Unequal Benefits of Fuel Subsidies: A Review of Evidence for Developing Countries." *World Development* 40 (11): 2234–48.

Asia Sentinel. 2014. "Jokowi Takes On the Oil Mafia." November 19. http://www.asiasentinel.com/politics/jokowi-takes-oil-mafia/.

Aspinall, E. 2005. *Opposing Suharto: Compromise, Resistance, and Regime Change in Indonesia*. Stanford, CA: Stanford University Press.

Bacon, R., and M. Kojima. 2006. "Coping with Higher Oil Prices." Energy Sector Management Assistance Program (ESMAP) Report 323/06, World Bank, Washington, DC.

Bappenas (Ministry of National Government Planning, Republic of Indonesia). 2000. "Program Pembangunan Nasional 2000–2004 (PROPENAS)." National Development Program document, Bappenas, Jakarta. http://bappenas.go.id/id/data-dan-informasi-utama/dokumen-perencanaan-dan-pelaksanaan/program-pembangunan-nasional-2000-2004-propenas/.

———. 2015. "Rancangan Teknokratik. Rencana Pembangunan Jangka Menengah Nasional 2015–2019." Technocratic draft, medium-term development plan, Bappenas, Jakarta. http://www.bappenas.go.id/files/7714/1557/5291/RT_RPJMN.PDF.

Barton, G. 2002. *Abdurrahman Wahid: Muslim Democrat, Indonesian President—A View from the Inside.* Sydney, Australia: University of New South Wales Press.

Beaton, C., I. Gerasimchuk, T. Laan, K. Lang, D. Vis-Dunbar, and P. Wooders. 2013. *A Guidebook to Fossil-Fuel Subsidy Reform for Policy-Makers in Southeast Asia*. Report of the Global Studies Initiative of the International Institute for Sustainable Development, Geneva and Winnipeg.

Beaton, C., and L. Lontoh. 2010. *Lessons Learned from Indonesia's Attempts to Reform Fossil-Fuel Subsidies*. Report of the Global Studies Initiative of the International Institute for Sustainable Development, Geneva and Winnipeg.

Beaton, C., L. Toft Christensen, and L. Lontoh. 2015. *An Input to Indonesian Fuel Price System Reforms: A Review of International Experiences with Fuel Pricing Systems*. Report of the Global Subsidies Initiative of the International Institute for Sustainable Development, Geneva and Winnipeg.

Bi, X., A. Tandon, C. Cashin, P. Harimurti, E. Pambudi, and J. Langenbrunner. 2014. "Fiscal Space for Universal Health Coverage in Indonesia: Lessons from Jamkesmas Financing." East Asia Pacific HNP Policy Brief 90526, World Bank, Washington, DC.

Blöndal, J. R., I. Hawkesworth, and H. Choi. 2009. "Budgeting in Indonesia." *OECD Journal on Budgeting* 2.

Bourchier, D., and V. R. Hadiz, eds. 2003. *Indonesian Politics and Society: A Reader.* London: RoutledgeCurzon.

BP. 2015. "Statistical Review of World Energy June 2015." Annual statistical review, BP, London.

BPK (Audit Board of the Republic of Indonesia). 2014. "Laporan Keuangan Pemerintah Pusat Tahun 2013." Annual audit report, BPK, Jakarta. http://www.bpk.go.id/lkpp.

Cahyafitri, Raras, and Hasyim Widhiarto. 2014. "Big Guns Brought in for Reform." *Jakarta Post,* November 20. http://www.thejakartapost.com/news/2014/11/20/big-guns-brought-reform.html.

Casier, L., and C. Beaton. 2015. "Fossil-Fuel Subsidy Reform and Higher Fuel Prices in Indonesia: Impacts and Expectations." Issue brief, Global Subsidies Initiative of the International Institute for Sustainable Development, Geneva and Winnipeg.

Chalmers, I., and V. R. Hadiz, eds. 1997. *The Politics of Economic Development in Indonesia: Contending Perspectives.* London: Routledge.

Cochrane, J. 2013. "Crowds Protest as Indonesian Lawmakers Raise Fuel Prices." *New York Times,* June 17. http://www.nytimes.com/2013/06/18/business/global/indonesia-budget-fuel-prices.html?_r=0.

Coface. 2014. "Coface Identifies 10 Emerging Countries Hot on the Heels of the BRICS." Press release, March 26. http://www.coface.com/News-Publications/News/Coface-identifies-10-emerging-countries-hot-on-the-heels-of-the-BRICS.

Constitutional Court of Indonesia. 2004. "Putusan Perkara No. 001-021-022/PUU-I/2003." Decision, Constitutional Court of Indonesia, Jakarta. http://www.mahkamahkonstitusi.go.id/public/content/persidangan/putusan/Putusan022PUUI2003.pdf.

Daly, A., and G. Fane. 2002. "Anti-Poverty Programs in Indonesia." *Bulletin of Indonesian Economic Studies* 38 (3): 309–29. doi:10.1080/00074910215535.

Datta, A., H. Jones, V. Febriany, D. Harris, R. K. Dewi, L. Wild, and J. Young. 2011. "The Political Economy of Policy-Making in Indonesia: Opportunities for Improving the Demand For and Use of Knowledge." Working Paper 340, Overseas Development Institute, London.

DEN (National Energy Council). 2015. "Executive Reference Data: National Energy Management." Booklet, DEN, Jakarta. http://www.den.go.id/upload/booklet/file/executivedata-2015.pdf.

Detik.com. 2005. "Naikkan Harga BBM, SBY Siap Tidak Populer." February 25. http://news.detik.com/berita/299641/naikkan-harga-bbm-sby-siap-tidak-populer.

Dipa, A., and Fadli. 2014. "Long Queues Form as Fuel Shortage Threatens." *Jakarta Post,* August 26. http://www.thejakartapost.com/news/2014/08/26/long-queues-form-fuel-shortage-threatens.html.

Donnan, S. 2005. "Indonesia Raises Fuel Prices by 126%." *Financial Times,* October 1. http://www.ft.com/intl/cms/s/0/103aebc0-3219-11da-9c7f-00000e2511c8.html#axzz3giCSPixQ.

Einhorn, B., and Y. Ho. 2013. "Indonesia Cuts Fuel Subsidies, Risking Social Unrest." *Bloomberg Business*, June 27. http://www.bloomberg.com/bw/articles/2013-06-27/indonesia-cuts-fuel-subsidies-risking-social-unrest.

EIU (Economist Intelligence Unit). 2014. "Budget 2015 Gives Jokowi Poisoned Chalice 2014." September 20. http://country.eiu.com/article.aspx?articleid=1942194578&Country=Indonesia&topic=Economy.

Eklöf, S. 2003. *Power and Political Culture in Suharto's Indonesia: The Indonesian Democratic Party (PDI) and Decline of the New Order (1986–98)*. Copenhagen: Nordic Institute of Asian Studies Press.

ESDM (Ministry of Energy and Mineral Resources of the Republic of Indonesia). 2014. *Handbook of Energy & Economic Statistics of Indonesia 2014*. Annual statistical report, Pusdatin ESDM, Jakarta.

———. 2015. "Kebijakan Harga dan Subsidi BBM (untuk peningkatan ketahanan energi)." PowerPoint presentation, Forum Dialog Energi dan Kebijakan Pengurangan Subsidi BBM, Jakarta, October 31.

______. n.d. "Perkembangan Harga BBM Tahun 1965–2000." Dataset, ESDM, Jakarta. http://www.esdm.go.id/publikasi/harga-energi/harga-bbm-dalam-negeri/doc_download/694-harga-bbm-dalam-negeri-1965-2000.html.

Gideon, A. 2014. "Indonesia Darurat BBM." Liputan6.com, September 1. http://news.liputan6.com/read/2096435/indonesia-darurat-bbm?p=1.

Government of Indonesia. 1997. "Indonesia Letter of Intent, October 31, 1997." Policy description supporting request to the International Monetary Fund, Government of Indonesia, Jakarta. https://www.imf.org/external/np/loi/103197.htm.

———. 1999. "Letter of Intent and Supplementary Memorandum of Economic and Financial Policies: Fourth Review under the Extended Arrangement." Government of Indonesia, Jakarta. https: //www.imf.org/external/np/loi/1999/031699.htm.

———. 2004. "Nota Keuangan dan Rencana Anggaran Pendapatan dan Belanja Negara Tahun Angaran 2005." Annual budget document, Government of Indonesia, Jakarta.

GSI-IISD (Global Subsidies Initiative of the International Institute for Sustainable Development). 2013a. "Indonesia Energy Subsidy Briefing August 2013." Issue briefing, GSI of the IISD, Geneva. https: //www.iisd.org/gsi/sites/default/files/ffs_newsbriefing_indonesia_aug2013_eng.pdf.

———. 2013b. "Indonesia Energy Subsidy Briefing July 2013." Issue briefing, GSI of the IISD, Geneva. https: //www.iisd.org/gsi/sites/default/files/ffs_newsbriefing_indonesia_july2013_eng.pdf.

———. 2015a. "Indonesia Energy Subsidy Briefing February 2015." Issue briefing, GSI of the IISD, Geneva. https: //www.iisd.org/gsi/sites/default/files/ffs_newsbriefing_indonesia_feb2015_eng.pdf.

———. 2015b. "Indonesia Energy Subsidy Briefing June 2015." Issue briefing, GSI of the IISD, Geneva. http://www.iisd.org/gsi/sites/default/files/ffs_newsbriefing_indonesia_June2015_eng.pdf.

———. 2015c. "Indonesia Energy Subsidy Briefing September 2015." Issue briefing, GSI of the IISD, Geneva. http://www.iisd.org/gsi/sites/default/files/ffs_indonesia_newsbriefing_Sep2015_eng.pdf.

———. 2015d. "Indonesia Energy Subsidy Briefing. November 2015." Issue briefing, GSI of the IISD, Geneva. https: //www.iisd.org/gsi/sites/default/files/ffs_indonesia_newsbriefing_Nov2015_eng.pdf.

GSI-IISD and IESR (Global Subsidies Initiative of the International Institute for Sustainable Development and the Institute for Essential Services Reform). 2012. "A Citizens' Guide to Energy Subsidies in Indonesia. 2012 Update." Report update, IISD, Geneva.

Hafil, M., 2012. "Anas Terlibat Kasus Hambalang?" *Republika*, April 30. http://www.republika.co.id/berita/nasional/umum/12/04/30/m3awk9-anas-terlibat-kasus-hambalang.

Harvey, R. 2005. "Indonesia Hit By Petrol Shortages." BBC News, July 18. http://news.bbc.co.uk/1/hi/business/4683335.stm.

Hastuti, N. Toyamah, S. Usman, B. Sulaksono, S. Budiyati, W. D. Widyanti, M. Rosfadhila, H. Sadaly, S. Erlita, R. J. Sodo, S. Bazzi, and S. Sumarto. 2006. *A Rapid Appraisal of the Implementation of the 2005 Direct Cash Transfer Program in Indonesia: A Case Study in Five Kabupaten/Kota*. Jakarta: SMERU Research Institute.

Heryanto, A. 2006. *State-Terrorism and Identity Politics in Indonesia: Fatally Belonging.* London: Routledge.

Hope, E., and B. Singh. 1995. "Energy Prices Increases in Developing Countries: Case Studies of Colombia, Ghana, Indonesia, Malaysia, Turkey, and Zimbabwe." Policy Research Working Paper 1442, World Bank, Washington, DC.

Hunter, A. 2007. "The Indonesian Oil Industry." In *The Economy of Indonesia: Selected Readings*, edited by B. Glassburner, 254–314. Singapore: Equinox Publishing.

ICTSD (International Centre for Trade and Sustainable Development). 2014. "Indonesia Enacts Mineral Export Ban." *Bridges* 18 (1), ICTSD, Geneva, January 16. http://www.ictsd.org/bridges-news/bridges/news/indonesia-enacts-mineral-export-ban.

IEA (International Energy Agency). 2014. *2014 Key World Energy Statistics.* Paris: IEA.

———. 2015. *Southeast Asia Energy Outlook 2015.* World Energy Outlook Special Report. Paris: Organisation for Economic Co-operation and Development and IEA.

IMF (International Monetary Fund). 1997. "IMF Approves Stand-By Credit for Indonesia." Press Release 97/50, IMF, Washington, DC.

———. 2000. "Recovery from the Asian Crisis and the Role of the IMF." Issue Brief 00/05, IMF, Washington, DC.

———. 2015. "Special Drawing Right (SDR)." Factsheet, IMF, Washington, DC. http://www.imf.org/external/np/exr/facts/pdf/sdr.pdf.

Indonesia MoF (Ministry of Finance) and World Bank. 2015. "Taxes and Public Spending in Indonesia: Who Pays and Who Benefits?" Working Paper 101667, World Bank, Jakarta.

Indrakesuma, Taufik Ramadhan, Edgar Janz, and Matthew Grant Wai-Poi. 2015. "A Perceived Divide: How Indonesians Perceive Inequality and What They Want Done about It." Working Paper 101664, World Bank, Washington, DC.

Indriyanto, A., L. Lontoh, A. Pusakantara, N. Siahaan, and D. Vis-Dunbar. 2013. "Fossil-Fuel Subsidy Reform in Indonesia: A Review of Government Communications in 2012." Research report, Global Subsidies Initiative of the International Institute for Sustainable Development, Geneva.

Isra, S. 2003. "Menyoal Hubungan DPR-Pemerintah." Article, Social Democratic Union, June 12. http://www.unisosdem.org/article_detail.php?aid=1053&coid=3&caid=3&gid=2.

Jakarta Globe. 2015. "Subsidized Fuel Consumption to Fall Short of Quotas in 2015." September 2. http://jakartaglobe.beritasatu.com/business/subsidized-fuel-consumption-fall-short-quotas-2015/.

Jakarta Post. 2012a. "Nazaruddin Faces His Verdict Today." April 20. http://www.thejakartapost.com/news/2012/04/20/nazaruddin-faces-his-verdict-today.html.

———. 2012b. "KPK Vows to Solve Bank Century Case This Year." February 16. http://www.thejakartapost.com/news/2012/02/16/kpk-vows-solve-bank-century-case-year.html.

———. 2014. "New Cards Are First Steps toward Prosperity for All, Says Jokowi." November 3. http://www.thejakartapost.com/news/2014/11/03/new-cards-are-first-steps-toward-prosperity-all-says-jokowi.html#sthash.As5rKIwv.dpuf.

Jong, H. N., and N. K. Erviani. 2014. "Jokowi Fails to Persuade SBY on Fuel Subsidy." *Jakarta Post*, August 28. http://www.thejakartapost.com/news/2014/08/28/jokowi-fails-persuade-sby-fuel-subsidy.html.

Khan, M. S. 2009. "The 2008 Oil Price 'Bubble.'" Policy Brief PB09-19, Peterson Institute for International Economics, Washington, DC.

Kojima, M. 2013. "Reforming Fuel Pricing in an Age of $100 Oil." Energy study, Report 79284, World Bank, Washington, DC.

Kompas. 2009. "Wapres Bantah Ada Politik Uang dalam Pembagian BLT." March 19. http://sains.kompas.com/read/2009/03/19/21304071/wapres.bantah.ada.politik.uang.dalam.pembagian.blt.

Kuwado, F. J. 2014. "Okky Asokawati Kritik Kartu Indonesia Sehat Jokowi." *Kompas*, November 3. http://nasional.kompas.com/read/2014/11/03/17451971/Okky.Asokawati.Kritik.Kartu.Indonesia.Sehat.Jokowi.

Liputan6.com. 2002a. "Dampak Kenaikan Tarif Komoditi Dasar Tak Signifikan." Liputan 6.com, November 30. http://news.liputan6.com/read/45721/dampak-kenaikan-tarif-komoditi-dasar-tak-signifikan?id=45721.

———. 2002b. "PAM Jaya Menaikkan Tarif Sebesar 25–35 Persen." Liputan 6.com, September 22. http://news.liputan6.com/read/41887/pam-jaya-menaikkan-tarif-sebesar-25-35-persen.

———. 2002c. "Ribuan Massa Berdemonstrasi di Depan Istana Merdeka." Liputan 6.com, January 9. http://news.liputan6.com/read/47704/ribuan-massa-berdemonstrasi-di-depan-istana-merdeka?id=47704.

———. 2003a. "Pengurus Apindo Menemui Komisi V DPR." Liputan 6.com, January 11. http://news.liputan6.com/read/27010/pengurus-apindo-menemui-komisi-v-dpr?id=27010.

———. 2003b. "SPSI Menolak Ikut Demonstrasi Kenaikan BBM." Liputan 6.com, January 8. http://news.liputan6.com/read/47680/spsi-menolak-ikut-demonstrasi-kenaikan-bbm?id=47680.

Listy, L. L., P. H. Kristanto, and G. Parikesit. 2014. "Premium Scarcity Drives Prices Up." Tempo.co, November 14. http://en.tempo.co/read/news/2014/11/14/055622014/Premium-Scarcity-Drives-Prices-Up.

Lontoh, L., C. Beaton, and K. Clarke. 2015. *Indonesia Energy Subsidy Review* 2 (1). Biannual survey of energy subsidy policies, Global Subsidies Initiative of the International Institute for Sustainable Development, Geneva. https: //www.iisd.org/gsi/sites/default/files/ffs_indonesia_reviewi2v1_english.pdf.

Lontoh, L., K. Clarke, and C. Beaton. 2014. *Indonesia Energy Subsidy Review* 1 (1). Biannual survey of energy subsidy policies, Global Subsidies Initiative of the International Institute for Sustainable Development, Geneva. https: //www.iisd.org /gsi/sites/default/files/ffs_indonesia_review_i1v1.pdf.

Mishkin, S. 2012. "Indonesia: Sale of the Century?" *Financial Times, beyondbrics blog,* February 8. http://blogs.ft.com/beyond-brics/2012/02/08/indonesia-sale-of-the-century.

Mochtar, Z. A. 2015. "The Constitutionality of Subsidies and Legal Issues Related to Fossil-Fuel Subsidy Reform in Indonesia." Issue brief, Global Subsidies Initiative of the International Institute for Sustainable Development, Geneva.

Muryanto, Bambang. 2014. "RI's Election System Is Causing Vote-Buying, Warns Expert." *Jakarta Post,* May 28. http://www.thejakartapost.com/news/2014/05/28/ri-s-election -system-causing-vote-buying-warns-expert.html.

Nugroho SBM. 2003. "Kenaikan Harga BBM dan Beban Rakyat." *Suara Merdeka,* January 4. http://www.suaramerdeka.com/harian/0301/04/kha1.htm.

OECD (Organisation for Economic Co-operation and Development). 2014. "Looking at Social Protection Globally, in the OECD and in the Asia/Pacific Region." In *Society at a Glance: Asia/Pacific 2014,* 53–70. Paris: OECD Publishing.

O'Neill, Jim. 2013. "Who You Calling a BRIC?" *Bloomberg View,* November 12. http:// www.bloombergview.com/articles/2013-11-12/who-you-calling-a-bric-.

O'Rourke, K. 2009. "Reformasi Weekly Review." March 20.

Ooi, J. B. 1982. *The Petroleum Resources of Indonesia.* Kuala Lumpur, Malaysia: Oxford University Press.

Osman, S. 2005. "Yudhoyono in Strong Position to Ride Out Crisis." Mission of Indonesia to the European Communities website, March 2. http://www.indonesianmission-eu .org/website/page711875649200503035l0484.asp.

Perdana, A. 2014. "The Future of Social Welfare Programs in Indonesia: From Fossil-Fuel Subsidies to Better Social Protection." Briefing Note, Global Subsidies Initiative of the International Institute for Sustainable Development, Geneva.

Pradiptyo, R., A. Wirotomo, A. Adisasmita, and Y. Permana. 2015. "The Role of Information in Perception of Fossil-Fuel Subsidy Reform: Evidence from Indonesia." *GSI Report* (March 2015), Global Subsidies Initiative of the International Insitute for Sustainable Development, Geneva.

Rahadiana, R., and N. Chatterjee. 2014. "Widodo Fuel-Price Rise Bid Rejected by Indonesia's Yudhoyono." Bloomberg Business, August 28. http://www.bloomberg .com/news/articles/2014-08-28/indonesia-s-yudhoyono-rejects-widodo-s-fuel -price-rise-request.

Robison, R. 1986. *Indonesia: The Rise of Capital.* Singapore: Equinox Publishing.

Sadmoko, D., B. Leonal, and R. Rahadiana. 2014. "Fuel Smugglers Line Up Every Day to Drain Indonesia Economy." Bloomberg Business, October 12. http://www.bloomberg .com/news/articles/2014-10-12/fuel-smugglers-line-up-every-day-to-drain -indonesia-s-economy.

Sambijantoro, S., and Bagus B. T. Saragih. 2014. "SBY Leaves Fiscal Mess for Jokowi." *Jakarta Post,* August 16. http://www.thejakartapost.com/news/2014/08/16 /sby-leaves-fiscal-mess-jokowi.html.

Sambijantoro, S., and I. Parlina. 2014. "SBY Maintains Status Quo in 2015 Budget." *Jakarta Post,* August 18. http://www.thejakartapost.com/news/2014/08/18/sby -maintains-status-quo-2015-budget.html.

Sandi, A. P. 2014. "Pertamina Denies Fuel Shortage." Tempo, August 25. http://en.tempo.co/read/news/2014/08/25/055602171/Pertamina-Denies-Fuel-Shortage.

Sanjaya, Robby. 2008. "Penerima BLT Rentan Dimanfaatkan Pada Pemilu 2009." Okezone, June 18. http://news.okezone.com/read/2008/06/15/1/118877/penerima-blt-rentan-dimanfaatkan-pada-pemilu-2009.

Saragih, Bagus B. T. 2014a. "Jokowi Team Eyes 'Mafia' Crackdown." *Jakarta Post*, August 19. http://www.thejakartapost.com/news/2014/08/19/jokowi-team-eyes-mafia-crackdown.html.

———. 2014b. "Jokowi to Form Task Force on Energy 'Mafia'." *Jakarta Post*, September 23. http://www.thejakartapost.com/news/2014/09/23/jokowi-form-task-force-energy-mafia.html.

Sardini, N. H. 2003. "Persoalan Komunikasi Politik Megawati." *Suara Merdeka*, January 18. http://www.suaramerdeka.com/harian/0301/18/kha2.htm.

Shaidra, A. 2014. "Yusril Ihza Kritik Tiga Kartu Jokowi." Tempo.co Business, November 6. http://bisnis.tempo.co/read/news/2014/11/06/090620150/yusril-ihza-kritik-tiga-kartu-jokowi.

Shiraishi, T. 2006. "Technocracy in Indonesia: A Preliminary Analysis." Discussion Paper 06-E-008, Research Institute of Economy, Trade and Industry (RIETI), Tokyo.

Simorangkir, J. 2012. "Fuel Subsidy Policy Post-2012 State Budget." Secretariat General, People's Representative Council, Republic of Indonesia, Bureau of Budget Analysis and State Budget Implementation, Jakarta. http://www.dpr.go.id/doksetjen/dokumen/apbn_Kebijakan_Subsidi_BBM_pasca_APBN-P_201220130130135951.pdf.

SMERU (SMERU [Social Monitoring and Early Response Unit] Research Institute). 2014. "Poverty and Livelihood Map of Indonesia." Brochure, SMERU Research Institute, Jakarta. http://www.indonesiapovertymap.org/data/brosur/povertymapbrosur_eng.pdf.

Smith, B. 2005. "Life of the Party: The Origins of Regime Breakdown and Persistence under Single-Party Rule." *World Politics* 57 (3), 421–51.

Strand, J. 2013. "Political Economy Aspects of Fuel Subsidies: A Conceptual Framework." Policy Research Working Paper 6392, World Bank, Washington, DC.

Suara Merdeka. 2002. "PDAM Kenakan Biaya Batas Minimum." December 16. http://www.suaramerdeka.com/harian/0212/16/dar20.htm.

———. 2003. "PDI-P Pecah Jadi Dua." January 15. http://www.suaramerdeka.com/harian/0301/15/nas1.htm.

Subroto. 2005. "Subroto." In *Pelaku Berkisah: Ekonomi Indonesia 1950-an sampai 1990-an*, edited by K. W. Thee and translated by K. S. Toer, 232–73. Jakarta: Penerbit Buku Kompas.

Suherdjoko and B. Muryanto. 2013. "Protests against Diesel Fuel Scarcity Continue." *Jakarta Post*, April 26. http://www.thejakartapost.com/news/2013/04/26/protests-against-diesel-fuel-scarcity-continue.html.

Sumantyo, Riwi. 2003a. "'Kado Tahun Baru' untuk Masyarakat." *Suara Merdeka*, January 4. http://www.suaramerdeka.com/harian/0301/04/kha2.htm.

———. 2003b. "Menyikapi Revisi Harga BBM." *Suara Merdeka*, January 23. http://www.suaramerdeka.com/harian/0301/23/kha1.htm.

Susanto, S., and Suherdjoko. 2013. "People Blame Govt. for Diesel Fuel Scarcity." *Jakarta Post*, April 11. http://www.thejakartapost.com/news/2013/04/11/people-blame-govt-diesel-fuel-scarcity.html.

Teather, Edward. 2013. "How to Think about the Fuel Price Hike in Indonesia?" *Jakarta Post*, June 3. http://www.thejakartapost.com/news/2013/06/03/how-think-about-fuel-price-hike-indonesia.html.

TNP2K (National Team to Accelerate Poverty Reduction). n.d. "Saves Family Welfare." Web page, TNP2K, Jakarta. http://www.tnp2k.go.id/id/program/program-membangun-keluarga-produktif/simpanan-keluarga-sejahtera/.

Tuong, V. 2010. *Paths to Development in Asia: South Korea, Vietnam, China, and Indonesia.* Cambridge: Cambridge University Press.

Vatikiotis, M. R. 1998. *Indonesian Politics Under Suharto: The Rise and Fall of the New Order.* London: Routledge.

von Luebke, C. 2010. "The Politics of Reform: Political Scandals, Elite Resistance, and Presidential Leadership in Indonesia." *Journal of Current Southeast Asian Affairs* 29 (1): 79–94.

Wardany, Irawaty, and Andi Hajramurni. 2009. "SBY Counters Megawati's Criticisms of Cash Aid." *Jakarta Post*, March 29. http://www.thejakartapost.com/news/2009/03/29/sby-counters-megawati%E2%80%99s-criticisms-cash-aid.html.

WHO (World Health Organization). 2014. *World Health Statistics 2014.* Geneva: WHO.

Widjaja, M. 2009. "An Economic and Social Review on Indonesian Direct Cash Transfer Program to Poor Families Year 2005." Research paper, Department of Economics, University of Indonesia, Jakarta.

Woo, W. T., B. Glassburner, and A. Nasution. 1994. *Macroeconomic Policies, Crises, and Long-Term Growth in Indonesia, 1965–90.* Washington, DC: World Bank.

Woo, W. T., and A. Nasution. 1989. "Indonesian Economic Policies and Their Relation to External Debt Management." In *Developing Country Debt and Economic Performance, Vol. 3: Country Studies—Indonesia, Korea, Philippines, Turkey*, edited by J. D. Sachs and S. M. Collins, 17–146. Chicago: University of Chicago Press.

World Bank. 1983. *Indonesia—Selected Issues of Energy Pricing Policies: The Main Report.* Report 4285-IND, World Bank, Washington, DC.

———. 1984. *Energy Issues and Options in Thirty Developing Countries.* Report 5230, Report of the Joint United Nations Development Programme (UNDP) and World Bank Energy Sector Management Assessment Program (ESMAP), World Bank, Washington, DC.

———. 1985. *Indonesia—Policies and Prospect for Long Term Financial Development.* Report 5501-IND, World Bank, Washington, DC.

———. 1990. *Indonesia—Strategy for a Sustained Reduction in Poverty.* World Bank Country Study, Report 10009, World Bank, Washington, DC.

———. 2006a. *Fuel Pricing and Subsidies in Indonesia: Reaching an Equitable and Sustainable Policy.* Energy study, Report 70420, World Bank, Washington, DC.

———. 2006b. *Making the New Indonesia Work for the Poor.* Poverty assessment, Report 37349-ID, World Bank, Washington, DC.

———. 2009. "Clearing Skies." *Indonesia Economic Quarterly* (September 2009), World Bank, Jakarta.

———. 2012a. "BLT (Bantuan Langsung Tunai) Temporary Unconditional Cash Transfer: Social Assistance Program and Public Expenditure Review 2." Working Paper 67324, World Bank, Washington, DC.

———. 2012b. *Targeting Poor and Vulnerable Households in Indonesia*. Public Expenditure Review, Report 67217, World Bank, Washington, DC.

———. 2013a. "Adjusting to Pressures." *Indonesia Economic Quarterly* (July 2013), World Bank, Jakarta.

———. 2013b. "Continuing Adjustment." *Indonesia Economic Quarterly* (October 2013), World Bank, Jakarta.

———. 2014a. "Delivering Change." *Indonesia Economic Quarterly* (December 2014), World Bank, Jakarta.

———. 2014b. "Indonesia: Avoiding the Trap." *Development Policy Review 2014*, World Bank, Jakarta.

———. 2015. "In Times of Global Volatility." *Indonesia Economic Quarterly* (October 2015), World Bank, Jakarta.

CHAPTER 5

Jordan: Reform amid Turmoil

Gabriela Inchauste, Yusuf Mansur, and Umar Serajuddin

Introduction

Energy subsidies are an expensive fiscal tool that typically benefits the better-off more than poor households. This is especially true in the Middle East, where many countries have been subsidizing energy for decades. For oil-importing countries such as Jordan, this tradition has been a source of repeated reform efforts because the size of energy subsidies has been a constant source of external and fiscal vulnerability. Despite ample evidence that these subsidies are an inefficient way to deliver benefits to the poor, the technical arguments have often been insufficient to allow reform to take place.

During the 1990s, Jordan went through a period of economic liberalization, abandoning subsidized prices for many commodities in the context of high inflation and unsustainable fiscal and external positions. Nevertheless, energy subsidies persisted well into the 2000s—leading to large fiscal and current account deficits that have been repeatedly funded by foreign grants and loans. Although this assistance sometimes came in the form of cash grants, more often it came as in-kind transfers in the form of crude oil and natural gas at concessional prices from neighboring countries.

In early 2008, to strengthen Jordan's fiscal and external accounts, the government moved to remove fuel subsidies and institute an automatic price adjustment mechanism that would fully pass through increases in world prices to domestic end users. However, lower growth in the context of the 2008–09 international financial crisis, followed by regional turmoil and demands for wider political reform in the wake of the Arab Spring in 2011, put this effort on hold. Subsequently, fuel subsidies quickly grew once more to unsustainable levels as international fuel prices rose.

Given the wider regional tensions and continual protests, the government could not fully reinstate the automatic price adjustment mechanism until late 2012. Between January 2011 and December 2012, five new governments were formed in Jordan, with some lasting no more than six months.

As part of a wider effort to learn from experiences with energy subsidy reforms around the world, this case study aims to document the economic, political, and distributional circumstances that allowed reforms to ultimately take place. In particular, it focuses on the 2012 subsidy reform process—including its design, passage, and implementation—and shows how those policy choices were affected by political economy factors in Jordan. In contrast to other studies that have tended to focus normatively on the need for subsidy reform, the objective is to document *how* reforms took place, thus enabling other countries considering reform to learn from others' experiences. For this purpose, we follow the analytical framework presented in chapter 1 to enable a coherent description of the political economy of reform.

The case study supports the hypotheses that reform is more likely at a time of impending crisis because a crisis allows for a realignment that often includes addressing the status quo, including with regard to benefits afforded to special interest groups. Moreover, the case study supports the notion that reform was enabled by government leaders that communicated and consulted with key stakeholders. Finally, reform was made possible partly thanks to government's ability to establish a cash-transfer targeting mechanism.

The rest of the chapter is structured as follows: The next section describes the country context, including Jordan's political, economic, poverty, and equity context at the time of the reforms. The subsequent section describes the fuel subsidy reforms in detail, including their fiscal and distributional impacts. "Circumstances That Enabled Reform," using the proposed framework, then analyzes the conditions and political dynamics that allowed the reforms to take place, including the roles of different stakeholders. The final section summarizes the findings. Annex 5A provides a chronology of main political events, annex 5B provides a detailed sequence of subsidy reforms, and annex 5C provides a timeline focusing particularly on events between 2011 and 2013.

Country Political and Economic Context

Jordan's Political System[1]

Jordan is a constitutional monarchy that vests executive authority in the King and his Council of Ministers. The Council of Ministers is headed by the prime minister, whom the King appoints upon a recommendation from the Chamber of Deputies (the lower house of Jordan's bicameral legislature).[2] The ministers are also appointed by the King upon the recommendations of the prime minister.

The King signs and executes all laws. His veto power may be overridden by a two-thirds vote of both houses of the National Assembly. He appoints and may dismiss all judges by decree, approves amendments to the constitution, declares war, and commands the armed forces. Cabinet decisions, court judgments, and the national currency are issued in his name.

Legislative power rests in the bicameral national assembly. The King has the power to suspend or dissolve the National Assembly and to shorten or lengthen its term of session. The National Assembly (*Majlis al-Umma*) has two chambers:

- *Chamber of Deputies (Majlis al-Nuwaab)*. This house has 150 members in single-seat constituencies, including 15 seats reserved for women by a special electoral college, 9 seats reserved for Christians, 9 seats reserved for Bedouins, and 3 seats for Chechens or Circassians.[3] The people elect these representatives for four-year terms, although the King has dissolved the entire parliament before the term is completed. The main legislative abilities of the Chamber of Deputies are limited to approving, rejecting, or amending legislation; it has minimal power to initiate laws. Laws and bylaws are initiated primarily by the executive branch (Council of Ministers). The lower house does not initiate new legislation, it only discusses what is presented by the government.
- *Assembly of Senators (Majlis al-Aayan)*. The Senate's 75 members are appointed by the King for four-year terms. (Its number of members may not exceed half that of the Chamber of Deputies.) Although the Senate is primarily limited to discussion of legislation that passes through the Chamber of Deputies, it may suggest legislation if requested by 10 members or more. However, it is rare that the Senate initiates laws.

The judiciary is responsible for interpreting and applying Jordan's laws. The Constitution of the Hashemite Kingdom of Jordan guarantees the independence of courts and judges, who are subject to no authority other than that of the law. Courts are divided into civil, religious, and special courts. Judges of the Civil and Sharia courts are appointed and dismissed by a royal decree, in accordance with the provisions of the law. A Judicial Council is responsible for matters related to civil judges.

In the wake of the Arab Spring, Jordan has gradually been implementing political reforms. The constitution was revised in late 2011 to review the balance of power between the executive, legislative, and judicial branches of the government. In July 2012, parliament approved a new election law, intended to consolidate the move toward a multiparty political system (IMF 2012a).

Between the end of 2010 and late April 2012, Jordan had several changes in government. Since then, parliamentary elections were held in January 2013, which were peaceful although boycotted by the Muslim Brotherhood.

Although the constitution states that the King appoints the prime minister, political reform allowed the newly elected parliament to select the candidates. Thus, after unprecedented consultations between the head of the Royal Court[4] and coalitions of the lower house of parliament, the King reappointed the prime minister in 2012, giving the prime minister greater legitimacy.[5] In 2013, King Abdullah II issued several discussion papers, envisaging the gradual transformation of Jordan into a constitutional monarchy.[6]

Economic Context

History of Fuel Subsidies

Tunisian scholar Larbi Sadiki coined the phrase *dimuqratiyyat al-Khubz* ("democracy of bread") to refer to the implicit social contract between rulers and the ruled in authoritarian states in the Arab world (Sadiki 1997). The state was a central supplier of employment and social welfare programs and was able to provide subsidies on basic consumer goods.

In the case of Jordan, during the 1980s, the Ministry of Supply imported wheat, meat, and other basic foodstuffs, distributing them at subsidized prices (Metz 1989).[7] It also bought crops from Jordanian farmers at above-market prices, thus injecting cash into the incomes of rural and often poor farmers. Fuel, water, and electricity were largely subsidized. At the same time, persistent tax exemptions kept government revenues low. High spending and low taxation meant that budget deficits increased significantly, raising government debt to over 200 percent of gross domestic product (GDP) in 1989. Because the budget deficit was largely monetized, foreign exchange reserves were depleted. Access to external borrowing virtually ceased, and a currency and banking crisis unfolded (Sabha 2014).

In the context of the crisis, Jordan and the International Monetary Fund (IMF) agreed on a Stand-By Arrangement, which granted Jordan US$275 million in funds beginning in 1989 and entailed cuts in public expenditure, removal of food subsidies, an increase in gasoline prices, and higher import duties on luxury goods (Sabha 2014). A combination of higher import prices and a depreciated dinar made inflation soar in 1989, reducing living standards. In response, riots broke out, predominantly in Jordan's southern cities, killing and injuring several people (Cowell 1989).

In the online magazine *Muftah*, writer and aid worker Saleem Haddad (2012) characterized the ensuing situation as follows: "To minimize the damage, the Jordanian regime promised political liberalization. This included moves to rescind martial law [imposed in 1967 following the Arab-Israeli War], end censorship, and legalize political parties, which had been banned since 1957. These gestures of political liberalization were to strengthen the business elite and co-opt the opposition. For instance, the return of parliamentary life gave business owners greater opportunities to influence government policy. Indeed, business people were able to secure their influence and power in Jordan by lobbying members of Parliament and forming strong political coalitions."

In February 1992, following the first Gulf War, Jordan signed a second Stand-By Arrangement with the IMF, initiating another phase of economic reforms that included trade liberalizations and tax restructuring.[8] Most food prices were liberalized except for wheat, which has continued to be subsidized despite occasional attempts at reform.

Nonetheless, the budget deficit, excluding grants, persisted until the late 1990s. One of the main reasons was that certain tax increases and subsidy cuts were never implemented—for instance, when the government's attempt to remove the wheat subsidies (with prices almost tripling) triggered widespread social discontent and the 1996 "bread riots" (Lamis and Schwedler 1996).

The government also undertook important structural reforms, especially through 1997, in financial market development, trade liberalization, and tax reform. As a result, public sector debt declined to just below 100 percent of GDP by 2000, partly on account of grants but also thanks to strong growth, which averaged 4.3 percent a year between 1990 and 1999 (figure 5.1). However, the pace of structural reform slackened, and by the end of the decade, economic reforms had lost pace (IMF 1999; Sabha 2014).

Economic Performance in Early 2000s

In the context of the reforms begun around 1989, the Jordanian economy performed remarkably well—notably during the first part of the 2000s. Real GDP growth accelerated, foreign exchange reserves rose sharply, real interest rates declined, and inflation remained low (IMF 2009).

Despite large negative external shocks (increasing oil prices, uncertainties related to the Iraq War, and volatile foreign grants), growth increased from a low of 2 percent in 1996 to a high of 8.6 percent in 2004 and then remained at 7–8 percent a year through 2008 (figure 5.1). In addition, amid falling deficits, public and publicly guaranteed debt declined from 96 percent of GDP in 2001 to 55 percent of GDP in 2008 (figure 5.2). Although the current account deficit increased from a balanced position in 2004 to a deficit of over 17 percent of GDP, sizable foreign direct investment (FDI) inflows enabled a steady and sizable increase in foreign reserves.[9]

Figure 5.1 GDP Growth in Jordan, 1994–2014

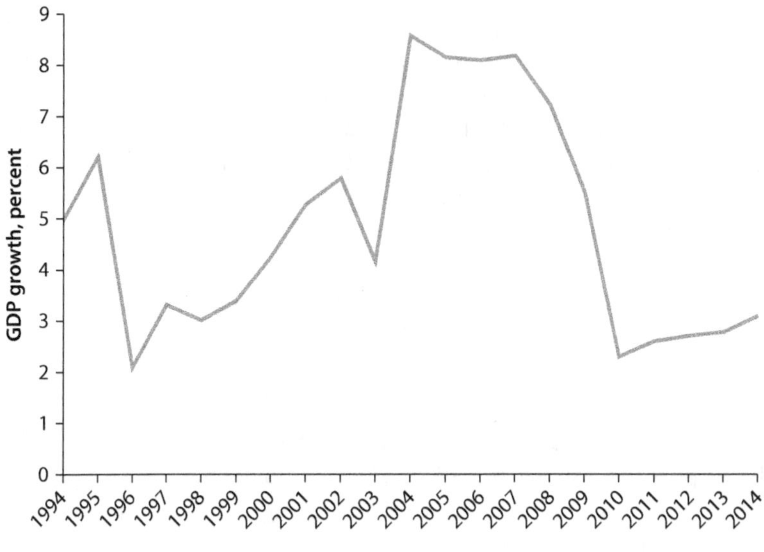

Sources: Jordan Department of Statistics national accounts database, http://web.dos.gov.jo/sectors/national-account/?lang=en, and 2013 and 2014 growth estimates, http://dos.gov.jo/dos_home_e/main/economic/nat_account/sel2/nat_6/4.pdf.

Figure 5.2 Central Government Net Debt including Government Guarantees, as a Share of GDP, Jordan, 1998–2014

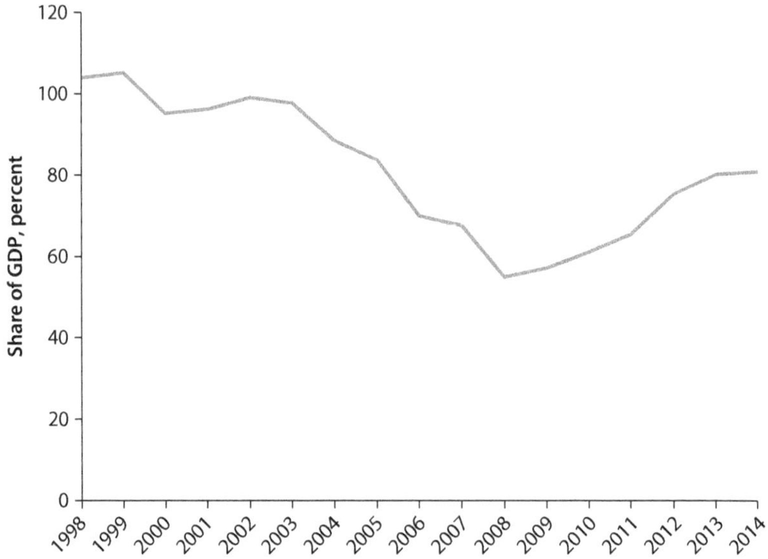

Sources: IMF 1999, 2002, 2005, 2007, 2008, 2009, 2012a, 2012c, 2013a, 2013b, 2014, 2015b, 2015c.

This boom came to a halt with the global economic downturn starting at the end of 2008. Real GDP growth fell from almost 7.2 percent in 2008 to 2.3 percent in 2010 (figure 5.2).

The increased economic activity in the early 2000s led to important social gains. Real GDP per capita grew by 38 percent between 2001 and 2008, while the unemployment rate fell from 14.7 percent to 12.7 percent over the same period (figure 5.3). This improvement in employment and economic activity led to an important decline in poverty. Using the US$2.50 poverty line (at 2005 purchasing power parity [PPP]), the headcount poverty rate declined from 19.9 percent in 2002 to 7.7 percent in 2008. Even in the wake of the global financial crisis, when per capita output growth declined, unemployment remained more or less stable.

Fiscal and External Pressures after the 2008 Financial Crisis

Given the slower growth beginning in the last quarter of 2008, along with an increase in international oil prices, both the fiscal and external accounts came under strain.[10] Aided by large external grants in 2008, fiscal policy initially accommodated the impact of these shocks. However, Jordan's already difficult fiscal position was worsened in 2009 by lower tax revenues that came from a cyclical weakening in the economy along with a dramatic downturn in external grants.

The overall deficit widened by more than 3 percentage points of GDP in a single year, reaching 9 percent of GDP in 2009 (figure 5.4). Tax revenue had

Figure 5.3 GDP Per Capita, Poverty, and Unemployment in Jordan, 2000–14

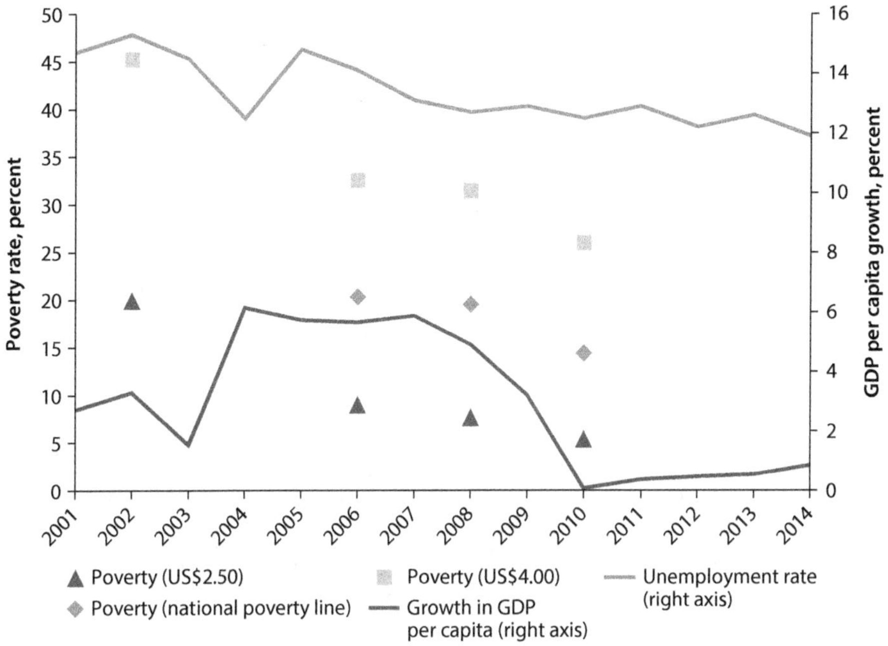

Sources: Poverty and PPP calculations from PovcalNet (http://iresearch.worldbank.org/PovcalNet/index.htm) and Jordan's Household Expenditure and Income Survey (HEIS); GDP and unemployment data from Jordan Department of Statistics national accounts database (http://web.dos.gov.jo/sectors/national-account/?lang=en), 2012–14 growth estimates (http://dos.gov.jo/dos_home_e/main/economic/nat_account/sel2/nat_6/4.pdf), and social sectors database (http://web.dos.gov.jo/sectors/social/social-surveys/?lang=en).

Note: Poverty rates are represented by data points for the years when household survey data are available; there is no yearly monitoring of poverty. The "national poverty line" is determined from the "cost of basic needs," based on a national caloric requirement of 2,347 calories per capita per day and a common food and nonfood basket for all households. The poverty line is based on the consumption and expenditure patterns of the bottom 30 percent of the population (poor or near-poor) as reflected in the 2010 Household Expenditure and Income Survey (Jolliffe and Serajuddin 2015). The estimated poverty line to meet basic needs was set at JD 813.7 per person per day in 2010 (US$3.42 per day at 2005 purchasing power parity [PPP]).

declined from a high of 21 percent of GDP in 2007 to 17 percent of GDP in 2009. Foreign grants also fell by 2.6 percentage points of GDP in 2009. The debt-to-GDP ratio rose to about 56 percent by the end of 2009 (IMF 2010).

The outcome could have been much worse if not for the bold decision in early 2008 to remove fuel subsidies and institute an automatic price adjustment mechanism that fully passed changes in world prices along to the domestic end users (IMF 2009). Until early 2005, Jordan had a tradition of buying crude oil at concessional prices from neighboring countries (originally Iraq, then Saudi Arabia). This oil was refined by the Jordan Petroleum Refinery Company, and the resulting products were then sold on the domestic market at controlled prices, with the government reimbursing the refinery for any losses on a "cost-plus" basis (Coady et al. 2006).

Gasoline has traditionally been taxed and used to cross-subsidize other petroleum products, such as diesel, kerosene, and liquefied petroleum gas (LPG) (Coady et al. 2006). LPG and kerosene are directly consumed by households for

Figure 5.4 Fiscal Operations in Jordan, 2001–14

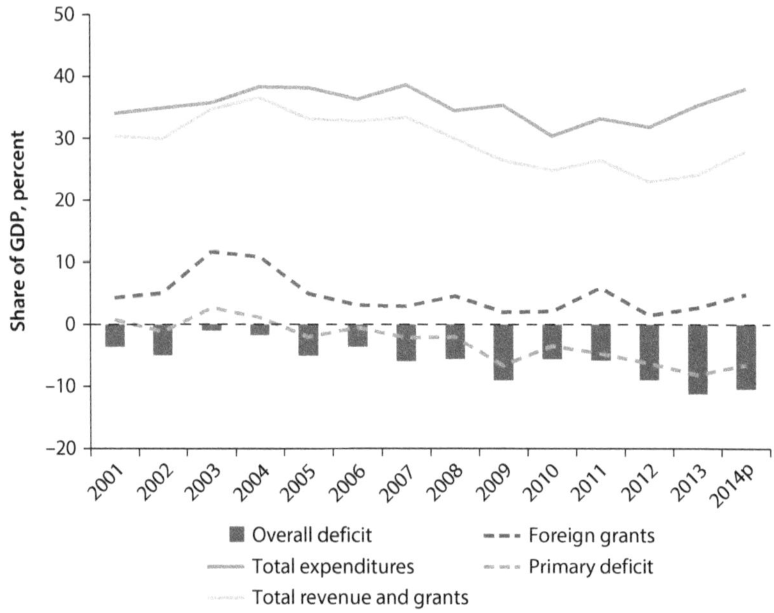

Sources: Ministry of Finance, *General Government Finance Bulletin* 17 (4), May 2015; IMF 1999, 2002, 2005, 2007, 2008, 2009, 2012a, 2012c, 2013a, 2013b, 2014, 2015b, 2015c.
Note: "2014p" designates IMF projections.

cooking and lighting and represent a larger share of the consumption bundle of the poor. As further described in the distributional impact analysis below, poor households' largest form of energy consumption is from LPG, which accounts for nearly 90 percent of the total energy subsidy that the poor receive (Atamanov, Jellema, and Serajuddin 2015). In contrast, diesel is important for transport and industry. Despite several domestic price increases for gasoline and other less socially sensitive fuels, net fuel subsidies reached 5.6 percent of GDP in 2005 (IMF 2008).

The government reduced fuel subsidies gradually, culminating in a full price pass-through in February 2008 when fuel prices were increased by 33–76 percent, depending on the type of fuel. To compensate vulnerable groups, the government introduced several measures (IMF 2008):

- An increase, on a progressive scale, in public sector wages and pensions
- Cash assistance to the poor in the private sector
- An increase in assistance provided by the National Aid Fund (NAF)
- Financial support targeted at small farmers
- Continuation of a low electricity lifeline tariff

At the time of this reform, the Ministry of Finance began to merge several administrative and tax databases to identify the potential beneficiaries. The identified population received cash transfers by way of Treasury-issued checks.

The removal of subsidies in 2008 was part of a longer-term fiscal consolidation strategy to significantly reduce the primary fiscal deficit (excluding grants). King Abdullah dissolved the Jordanian parliament in November 2009, which helped to remove roadblocks that were stalling market reforms. A new government (formed in December 2009 and led by Prime Minister Samir Rifai) supported an ambitious effort that achieved the fiscal consolidation goals, reducing the primary fiscal deficit (excluding grants) from 8.6 percent of GDP in 2009 to 5.6 percent in 2010 (IMF 2010, 2012c). The reforms supporting this effort included a freeze on civil service employment and curtailing of government tenders because of budget shortfalls—measures that hurt the business community and the pool of aspiring job applicants.

Since 2011, Slow Progress amid Regional Turmoil

Following this period of austerity and in the context of broader regional turmoil, the government reversed a rise in fuel prices in mid-January 2011. By February 1, the King had dismissed Prime Minister Rifai and replaced him with Marouf al-Bakhit, a former prime minister and former army general who was instructed to form a new cabinet and given a mandate of reform.

In January 2011, the King also announced a US$500 million package of price cuts in fuel and necessary goods (including some food products) and gave civil servants and military employees a salary increase (Barany 2012). This move froze fuel prices beginning in 2011 (figure 5.5).

Figure 5.5 Domestic Fuel Prices in Jordan, 2008–13

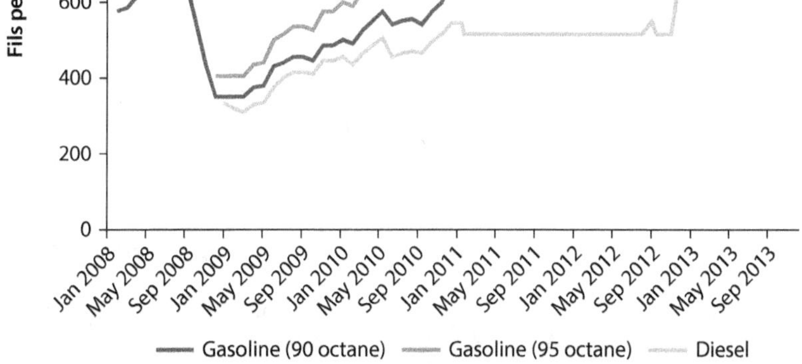

Sources: Ministry of Energy and Mineral Resources (MEMR) annual reports published in 2009, 2010, 2011, 2012, 2013, and 2014.
Note: Data for 95-octane gasoline and diesel were not available until January 2009.

The cost of these subsidies quickly escalated because of a large increase in world oil prices in 2011 (figure 5.6, panel a). Moreover, the decision to freeze fuel prices coincided with a negative shock to Jordan's energy sector from extensive disruptions to the flow of natural gas from the Arab Republic of Egypt, a pipeline repeatedly bombed in 2011, which required Jordan to import more-expensive fuel for electricity generation (IMF 2012a).

Low regulated electricity tariffs had been supported by below-market prices for natural gas imports from Egypt since 2005. Indeed, by 2011, underpriced Egyptian gas had become the main source of fuel for electricity generation (IMF 2012a).[11] Although this strategy had allowed for extensive electrification, it had also created an important external vulnerability: The National Electric Power Company (NEPCO), Jordan's public shareholding and electricity transmission company, purchases all energy from producers and resells it to distributors. Under the existing structure of the electricity system, NEPCO bears all the financial risks from increases in fuel prices. Therefore, when natural gas supplies from Egypt stopped and electricity began to be generated by more-expensive fuels, there was an immediate increase in the subsidy paid to NEPCO, which is the sole importer of crude oil and refined oil products.[12] NEPCO's losses soon mounted because electricity tariffs were not adjusted to reflect the more-expensive fuel mix (Verme 2011). (Producing electricity from fuel oil was about three times more expensive than Egyptian gas at the time.)

The 2011 abandonment of the 2008 automatic price adjustment mechanism thus made Jordan highly vulnerable to external shocks in the oil markets. Energy imports increased from 9 percent of GDP in 2003 to 19 percent of GDP in 2011, largely reflecting higher fuel imports to generate electricity (figure 5.6, panel b).

Figure 5.6 Fuel Subsidies, Oil Imports, and Account Balances as a Share of GDP in Jordan, 2001–14

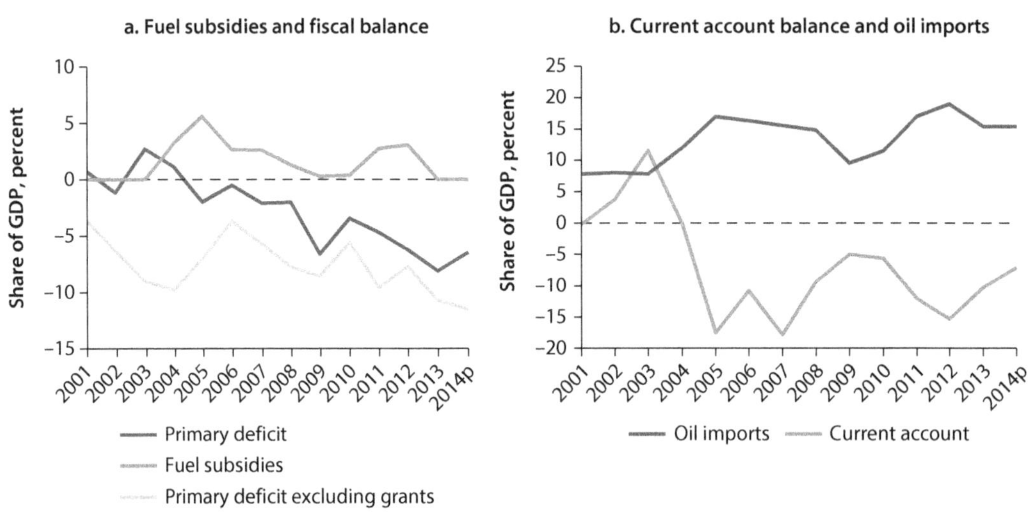

Sources: IMF 2005, 2007, 2008, 2009, 2012a, 2012c, 2013a, 2013b, 2014, 2015b, 2015c.
Note: "2014p" designates IMF projections.

Together with a weakening in domestic revenue, these measures raised the primary fiscal deficit (excluding grants) to 9.6 percent of GDP in 2011 (figure 5.6, panel a). Moreover, the more-expensive fuel imports resulted in a decline in the Central Bank of Jordan's reserves—a decline exacerbated by an increase in deposit dollarization, reflecting depositor nervousness. At the same time, regional tensions adversely affected tourism, remittances, and FDI (IMF 2012a).

Budgetary grants from Saudi Arabia totaling US$1.4 billion (5 percent of GDP) in 2011 helped to fund the cost of fuel subsidies and the current account deficit in 2011 (IMF 2012a). Despite this aid, the external current account deficit (including grants) widened from 7 percent of GDP in 2010 to 12 percent in 2011 (figure 5.6, panel b). To finance the fiscal deficits, the central government increased its borrowing; it also increased government borrowing on behalf of NEPCO to cover the more-costly imported fuel oil used during the long interruptions in the natural gas supply. The result was an increase in the public debt-to-GDP ratio to about 64 percent by the end of 2011 (IMF 2012a).

Changes in Government and Political Reform

This economic strain also coincided with a period of political change. Starting in early 2011, Jordan had frequent changes in government (Mansur 2013a; also see detailed timeline in annex 5C). Between January 2011 and December 2012, five new governments were formed, with some lasting no more than six months.

Political reform was gradually introduced, beginning in March 2011, when King Abdullah II appointed a 53-member National Dialogue Committee including representatives of political parties, professional associations, the economic sector, civil society organizations, and youth and women's societies. The committee was tasked with opening extended dialogue with all citizens to arrive at a consensus over legislation governing political reform, including the elections and the political parties' laws.[13] In April, the King established a Royal Committee to review the constitution, and in May, amendments to the Public Assemblies Law were approved, making it possible for meetings or demonstrations to take place without approval by administrative governors.[14]

By June 2011, commemorating 12 years on the throne, the King said he would relinquish his right to appoint prime ministers and cabinets and would leave it to the elected parliamentary majority to form future cabinets. He also announced that there would be more reform in the future, including new elections and political parties' laws.[15] In September, the constitution was revised to review the balance of power between the executive, legislative, and judicial branches of the government. In December 2011, an independent elections commission was established.[16]

Subsidy Reform

The 2012 Reform Process

A spate of sabotage attacks in early 2012 shut flows on the Arab Gas Pipeline—the long pipeline that carries Egyptian gas to Jordan, Lebanon, and the Syrian

Arab Republic. The result for Jordan was still-higher imports of expensive fuel oil for electricity generation (IMF 2012a).

Moreover, worker demonstrations hit a record high during the first quarter of 2012: 302 protests, a 28.5 percent increase over the same period in 2011. Around 180,000 Jordanian workers participated in these protests, which called for pay raises, changes to labor-related regulations, and new job opportunities (Mansur 2013a). Amid criticism over the slow pace of reform, Prime Minister Awn Shawkat al-Khasawneh submitted his resignation (Mansur 2013a).

By then, the need for corrective action to reduce fuel subsidies became more urgent as the sharp decline in Egypt gas flows led to a growing current account deficit, a loss in reserves, and reduced confidence.

Austerity Measures and Fuel Price Hikes

The new government that came into office in May 2012 embarked on wide-sweeping reforms to reduce public sector financing needs, lower public debt, ease pressures on reserves, and secure fiscal viability (IMF 2012a). In late May 2012, newly appointed Prime Minister Fayez Tarawneh announced a new wave of subsidy reform. The increasing prices for gasoline, asphalt, and fuel oil for power generation resulted in a 26 percent increase in premium gasoline prices (for 95-octane gasoline) and raised electricity tariffs for major industrial and service sectors.[17] The only fuels whose prices did not increase were LPG, diesel, and kerosene because of their potentially large impact on the poor.

In the context of the 2012 IMF Stand-By Arrangement, the government in June 2012 reinstated the monthly fuel price adjustment for less socially sensitive types of fuel (gasoline, jet fuel, and heavy fuel oil) and later increased the price of high-octane gasoline. Beyond the fuel price adjustments, the IMF program envisaged structural reforms, including a comprehensive reform of the electricity tariff structure to ensure the long-run sustainability of NEPCO and diversification of the energy supply (IMF 2012c). As a result of the austerity measures, demonstrators took to the streets (Mansur 2013a).

In early September, continued increases in international oil prices led to a cabinet decision to increase domestic fuel prices by 10 percent across all fuels. More protests followed, including by taxi drivers who brought traffic to a halt in Amman (Trend News Agency 2012). Jordanian lawmakers called on the King to oust Prime Minister Tarawneh for imposing the price rise, threatening to follow through on a vote of no confidence in the premier (Trend News Agency 2012). At that point, the King suspended the new fuel price hike. These events were followed by a new change in government as the King dissolved parliament in early October and Prime Minister Tarawneh and his cabinet resigned (Mansur 2013a).

A New Approach

With growing pressures on both the fiscal and external fronts, newly appointed Prime Minister Abdullah Ensour engaged in an intensive communications and consultation campaign to open up the debate on energy subsidy reforms. The debate was precipitated in late October and early November 2012,

Figure 5.7 Excess Reserves in Jordan, 2008–15

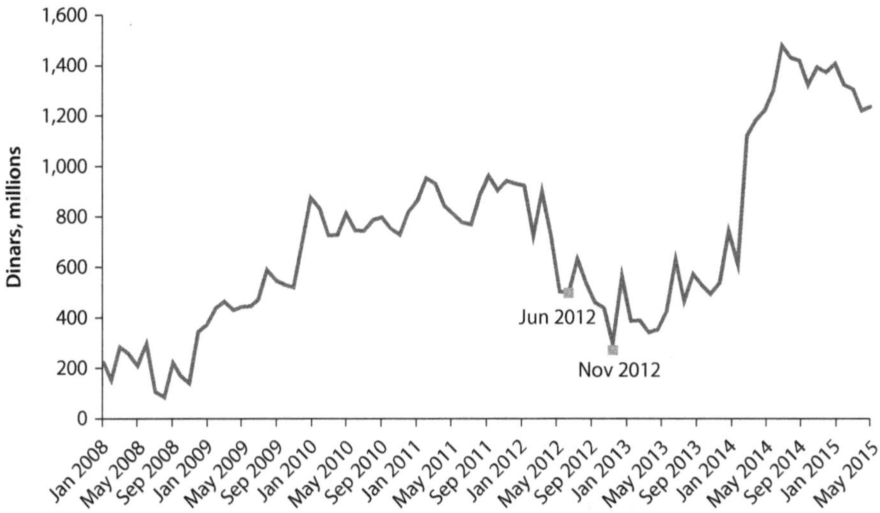

Source: Central Bank of Jordan Statistical Database, Money and Banking Sector, "Reserve Money Component," http://statisticaldb.cbj.gov.jo/index?action=level4&page_no=3.
Note: "Jun 12" designates the low point before the June 13 price hikes. "Nov 12" designates the low point before price increases in November 2012 and resumption of monthly price adjustments in December 2012.

when uncertainty about the macroeconomic situation was followed by a subsequent loss in reserves (figure 5.7).

The government swiftly announced new price increases in November 2012. Although kerosene, diesel, and LPG prices had initially remained unchanged because of their potentially large impact on the poor, the government could no longer shoulder the growing budget deficit (Kojima 2013). Therefore, the government increased the price of LPG in 12.5 kilogram cylinders by 54 percent and increased kerosene and diesel prices by 33 percent (figure 5.8).

In addition, the government began in December 2012 to make monthly price adjustments for all fuels except LPG (Kojima 2013), the fuel with the largest incidence on the poor (as further discussed in the "Distributional Impact" subsection below). The retail price of diesel and other products had been lower than the free on board (FOB) price between 2011 and the November 2012 reforms, signaling a large subsidy (Kojima 2013). The effect of this policy is evident in the huge spike in Jordanian diesel prices at the end of 2012 (figure 5.8).

Compensatory Cash Transfers

Given the potential impact of the fuel price hikes on households, the government concurrently announced and quickly implemented compensation for 70 percent of the population through cash transfers (Araar et al. 2013). These transfers consisted of JD 70 per person per year (for a maximum six people per household), amounting to about 6 percent of the income of the poorest decile. In fact, without these transfers, poverty (as measured by the official estimate) could have increased by 1 percentage point (Araar et al. 2013). Households were

Figure 5.8 Domestic and International Diesel Prices, Jordan, 2008–14

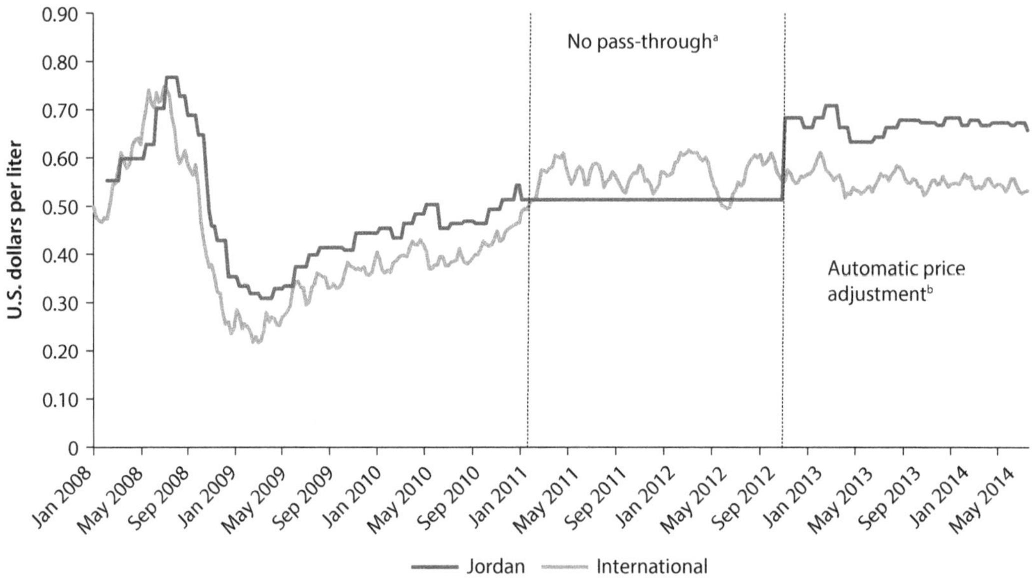

Sources: Ministry of Energy and Mineral Resources (MEMR) annual reports of 2009, 2010, 2011, 2012, 2013, and 2014; U.S. Energy Information Administration "Petroleum & Other Liquids" weekly spot price data, http://www.eia.gov/dnav/pet/hist/LeafHandler.ashx?n=PET&s=EER_EPD2DXL0_PF4_RGC_DPG&f=W.

Note: International prices correspond to the weekly U.S. Gulf Coast Ultra-Low Sulfur No 2 Diesel Spot Price, converted to Jordanian dinars per liter.

a. From January 2011 to November 2012, Jordanian diesel prices remained unchanged; therefore, changes in the international price were not passed through to domestic end users.

b. Beginning in December 2012, the Jordanian government instituted automatic monthly price adjustments for all fuels except liquefied petroleum gas (LPG), resulting in a spike in domestic diesel prices.

selected to receive transfers if they earned less than JD 10,000 (US$14,000) per year, based on self-reported income levels.

The cash transfers began within one week of the removal of subsidies. Public sector employees and pensioners, social security subscribers, and NAF beneficiaries received disbursements automatically through the government payroll.[18] Other applicants received disbursements through branches of the Housing Bank for Trade and Finance, Jordan's second largest commercial bank (Araar et al. 2013). Experience from the 2007–08 subsidy reform enabled the Ministry of Finance to use its consolidated administrative and tax database to identify beneficiaries.

A key ingredient facilitating the distribution of a cash transfer to identified beneficiaries was the fact that all Jordanian households have a unique family identification number that is used across administrative records. Thus, the Ministry of Finance could merge multiple records to construct a single database that enabled highly accurate identification of beneficiaries and administration of the program. In particular, data from the social security administration were merged with (a) wage bill and interest earnings records received by tax administration authorities from private companies and commercial banks; (b) electricity and water consumption information; (c) data from the land department;

(d) automobile ownership data from the police; (e) customs administration records on imports of durables; (f) business partnership information; and (g) data from the border police for nonresidents. This merged database was then used to identify beneficiaries by triangulating its consistency with individuals' reported incomes.[19]

In contrast to the 2007–08 subsidy reforms, the compensatory cash transfer program launched in 2012 was implemented quickly. The Ministry of Finance, learning from the earlier program, also allowed people to complete electronic applications through the Internet, which reduced wait times considerably.

Communication Strategy

In addition to the importance of packaging the reforms—that is, coupling the new price rises with a new scheme to compensate many Jordanians—the communication of this package to the public played a vital role. Prime Minister Abdullah Ensour communicated eloquently, reaching out to the media, civil society, universities, industrial groups, and local community leaders to ensure that the reforms were well understood.[20] He met with every governorate and with stakeholders of every kind. In all of these meetings he was unequivocal about the risks to the economy should these subsidies continue, explaining that the main beneficiaries of subsidies are not necessarily the poorest members of society, and presenting the cash transfer mechanism as a mitigation measure to protect the most vulnerable (Al-Khalidi 2012; *Jordan Times* 2012).

Nevertheless, the fuel price increases triggered protests at first (Halaby 2012). Three deaths resulted from these protests, but tensions did not escalate, and the protests soon ended. Some commentators credited the crisis in Syria and the effects of the Arab Spring across the Middle East for the Jordanian protests' limited violence and duration, claiming that Jordanians preferred to remain calm to ensure continued domestic stability (Mansur 2013b). In various media outlets, civil society representatives called for calm as the Arab Spring eventually generated fear of unrest and violence, all the more so given the experiences of neighboring Egypt and Syria (Atamanov, Jellema, and Serajuddin 2015).

Fiscal Impact

The impact of the subsidy reform on the budget was immediate. Public expenditures on petroleum subsidies declined from JD 674 million (3.1 percent of GDP) in 2012 to zero by 2013 (figure 5.9). In contrast, the cash transfer program cost about JD 193 million in 2013 (0.8 percent of GDP).[21]

The combined result of the subsidy reform and compensatory cash transfer program was a decline in current spending from 28 percent of GDP in 2012 to 25 percent in 2013. However, the country's overall fiscal balance did not improve, mostly because of the large increase in outlays needed to cover NEPCO's operating losses, which amounted to 5.3 percent of GDP in 2012 (IMF 2014), as shown in figure 5.9.

It was clear that the only way to cover NEPCO's losses was to increase electricity tariffs to cost-recovery levels. However, setting tariffs at the cost of

Figure 5.9 Public Expenditures on Subsidies in Jordan as a Share of GDP, 2004–14

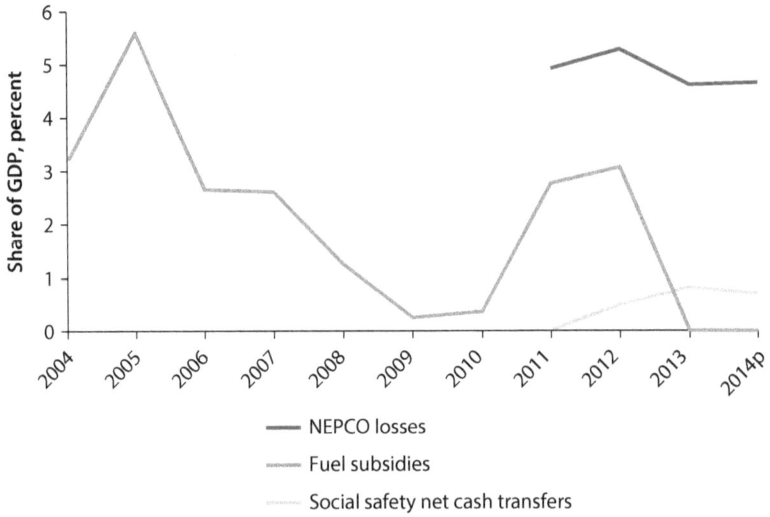

Source: IMF 2005, 2007, 2008, 2009, 2012a, 2012c, 2013a, 2013b, 2014, 2015b, 2015c; Ministry of Finance, *General Government Finance Bulletin* 17 (4), May 2015.
Note: NEPCO = National Electric Power Company. "2014p" designates IMF staff projections. Cash transfers to compensate the poorest households for the loss of subsidies and the consequent rise in fuel prices began in November 2012.

production would have almost doubled the cost of electricity—an outcome that was politically infeasible. The government decided instead to increase these tariffs gradually (Reed 2013). At the same time, Jordan also initiated efforts to diversify its energy sources, with the aim of providing a long-term solution to the problem of dependence on imported gas and fuel oil.[22]

Given the widening NEPCO and central government deficits, gross public and publicly guaranteed debt increased considerably by the end of 2012, to 80.2 percent of GDP (as shown earlier in figure 5.1).

Distributional Impact

As in most countries, wealthier households spend much larger amounts on petroleum products, particularly on gasoline and, to some degree, diesel, while kerosene and LPG are relatively more important for less-affluent households (Atamanov, Jellema, and Serajuddin 2015). The wealthiest quintile spent seven times more on subsidized products than the poorest quintile, and as a result, wealthier households received higher per capita subsidies than poorer households. Indeed, Atamanov, Jellema, and Serajuddin (2015) estimate that the wealthiest quintile on average received three times more in fuel subsidies than the poorest quintile.

In addition to the overall regressive nature of untargeted subsidies, other important patterns are revealed from an examination of particular fuels. For example, gasoline and diesel subsidies were regressive, not only in absolute terms

Figure 5.10 Concentration of Expenditures and Fuel Subsidies before Reform in Jordan, 2010

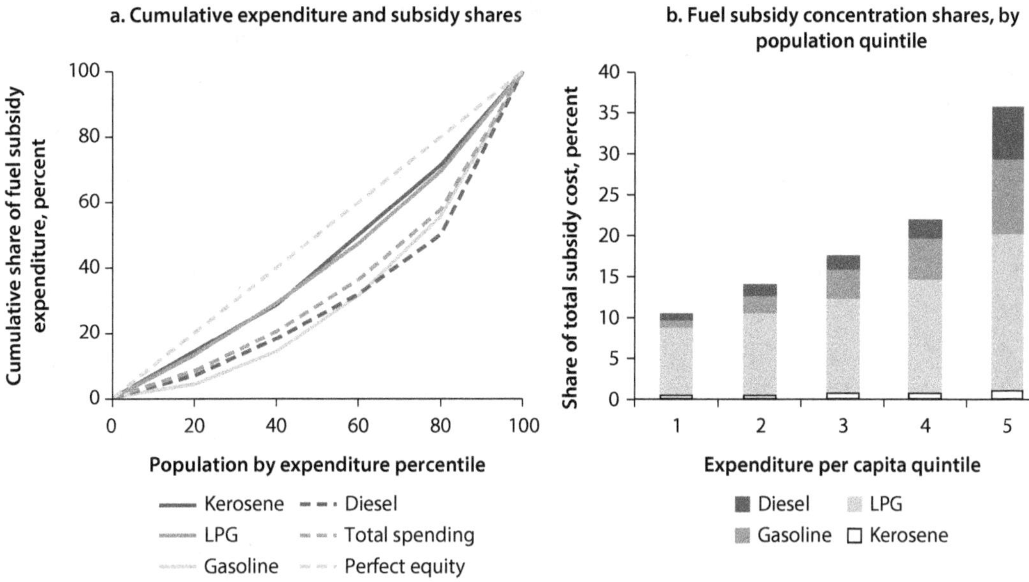

Source: Based on estimates by Atamanov, Jellema, and Serajuddin 2015.
Note: LPG = liquefied petroleum gas. Incidence includes both direct and indirect impacts of subsidies on gasoline and diesel. Figure orders households by their household per capita expenditure.

(as wealthier households consumed a larger amount of the subsidies) but also in relative terms (as subsidies represented a larger relative share of wealthier households' total expenditures). The latter is shown by a concentration curve for subsidies that is below the total spending curve (figure 5.10, panel a).[23]

In contrast, kerosene and LPG subsidies were progressive in relative terms, as the amount of subsidy for poorer income groups was high relative to their share of expenditures. However, it is still true that most of these subsidies benefited higher-income groups—the amount benefiting the richest 20 percent of the population being at least five times that benefiting the poorest 20 percent (figure 5.10, panel b).

These combined results show that the removal of LPG and kerosene subsidies without a mitigating program would be especially hard on the poor because subsidies constitute a larger share of their budgets (figure 5.10, panel a).

When considering the combined effect of subsidy removal and the targeted cash transfers, simulations by Atamanov, Jellema, and Serajuddin (2015) show that removal of these subsidies and compensation through cash transfers implied a net loss of purchasing power for all but the poorest 20 percent of households (table 5.1). This loss was mostly due to the removal of LPG subsidies, with the direct cash transfers able to compensate the bottom 20 percent of the distribution for higher fuel prices.

Together, table 5.1 and figure 5.11 show that, in contrast to the generalized fuel subsidies, the cash transfer was progressive in absolute terms. The transfer is not only a larger share of income for lower-income groups (as shown by a

Table 5.1 Simulated Distributional Impacts of Fuel Subsidy Reforms in Jordan

	Prereform	*Change in monthly consumption (JD per month) due to change in:*					*Postreform*	
Population quintile (by consumption per capita)	*Total expenditures per capita (JD per month)*	*Diesel*[a]	*Gasoline*[a]	*Kerosene*	*LPG*	*Cash transfers*	*Total expenditures per capita (JD per month)*	*Change in per capita consumption (%)*
1	843	−3	−3	−2	−28	46	853	1.2
2	1,240	−5	−7	−2	−34	46	1,238	−0.2
3	1,624	−6	−12	−3	−39	39	1,603	−1.3
4	2,198	−8	−17	−3	−47	33	2,156	−1.9
5	4,336	−22	−31	−4	−65	21	4,235	−2.3
Total	2,048	−9	−14	−3	−42	37	2,017	−1.5

Source: Atamanov, Jellema, and Serajuddin 2015.
Note: LPG = liquefied petroleum gas. JD = Jordanian dinars. Simulations based on data from 2010 Household Expenditure and Income Survey.
a. Includes both (a) direct impacts through spending on these products and (b) indirect effects, estimated using an input-output matrix, to capture increases in transport costs and therefore more generalized increases in prices.

concentration curve above the Lorenz curve of income distribution), but it also lies above the 45-degree perfect equity line, indicating that a larger share of total spending on the cash transfer is directed to the poor (figure 5.11). Not surprisingly, the Lorenz curve for expenditures after the reform is closer to the 45-degree line, indicating that the reform was not only pro-poor but also equalizing.

Simulations of the cash transfer program show that about 50 percent of all cash transfer spending was targeted to the bottom 40 percent of the distribution (table 5.1), in line with the design of these transfers, which were meant to benefit 70 percent of the population.

Circumstances That Enabled Reform

The 2012 subsidy reforms in Jordan reduced total energy subsidies, although the fiscal savings were limited. As shown earlier in figure 5.9, total savings from the reform amounted to about 2.3 percent of GDP in 2013 once the cost of the targeted cash transfer is taken into account. This section examines the circumstances that allowed these reforms to take place.

Two crises drove the reform process: The first was a fiscal crisis caused by higher international oil prices and the loss of external grants. The second was the broader general turmoil in the wake of the Arab Spring. Both crises unfolded at the same time, but they point to different requirements for subsidy reform. The first points to the need to eliminate costly subsidies. The second points to the need to create a mechanism that would protect a larger part of the public (beyond the poor) through cash transfers.

Characterizing the Reforms

Using the framework for political economy analysis of subsidy reforms described in chapter 1, one can roughly characterize energy policies according to the size of

Figure 5.11 Simulated Concentration of Expenditures and Cash Transfers after Subsidy Reform in Jordan

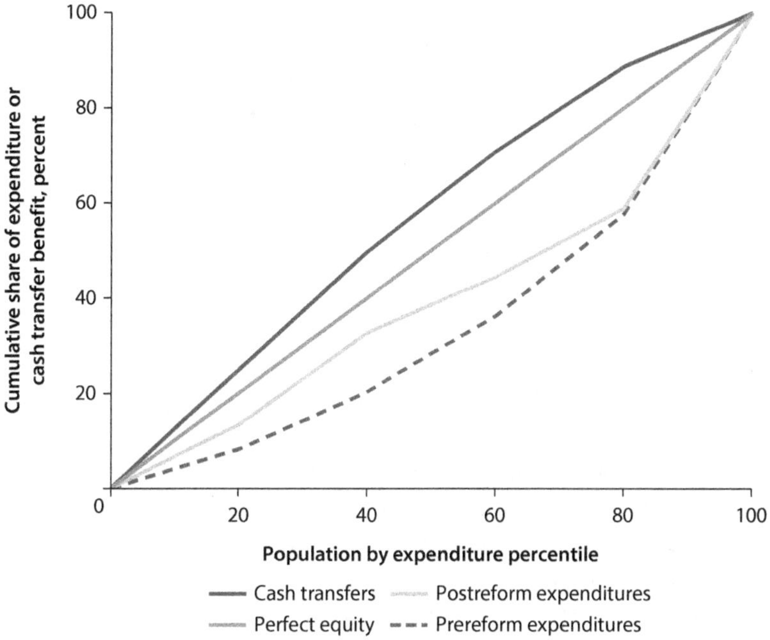

Source: Based on Atamanov, Jellema, and Serajuddin 2015.
Note: "Cash transfers" are those issued to targeted beneficiaries in compensation for the loss of fuel subsidies beginning in November 2012. Simulation based on data from 2010 Household Expenditure and Income Survey.

the benefits they offer to concentrated "special interests" versus the benefits more broadly diffused to citizens at large. This framework yields a range of possibilities—shown in table 5.2 along with a mapping of subsidy policies in Jordan over time. In what follows, we focus on the conditions that enabled the 2012 reforms to take place, following the hypotheses established by the adopted framework.

The prereform case in Jordan had large generalized benefits but no particular targeting of the subsidy to special interests—a scenario closest to Case 1 (upper-left corner) before the reform process (large benefits to special interests and citizens alike), as shown in table 5.2. This equilibrium moved closer to Case 2 after the 2008 reform (large special interest benefits but small citizen benefits) and closer to Case 3 after the 2012 reform (small special interest benefits but large citizen benefits).

Although the reforms of February 2008 involved sharper price hikes (of 33–76 percent on various gasoline products) than the November 2012 reforms (when prices on similar products rose by 14–33 percent), the 2008 reforms occurred at a time when martial law was in place and while the economy had strong growth and household incomes were rising.

Government employees received annual salary increases of JD 540 or JD 600, depending on their income levels. Private sector employees with annual incomes

Table 5.2 Characterizing Subsidy Policy Benefits in Jordan

Beneficiary type and benefit size	*Citizen benefits are large*	*Citizen benefits are small*
Special interest benefits are large	**Case 1** Jordan fuel subsidies before reforms	**Case 2** Jordan cash transfer program after 2008 reform
Special interest benefits are small	**Case 3** Jordan cash transfer program after 2012 reform	**Case 4**

of less than JD 1,000 received one-time cash transfers of JD 10 to JD 25, while families receiving social assistance from the NAF received increases of JD 3 to JD 10 per month. In addition, cattle owners and cereal farmers received assistance. Apart from these targeted transfers, the government took broad measures such as increasing the bread subsidy and removing taxes on a number of basic food items. Most of the budget set aside for compensatory measures (JD 355 million) was allocated for the salary increase of government employees. All other direct transfers amounted to JD 97.5 million (including one-time transfers), and indirect or universal subsidies amounted to JD 40 million.

The 2012 reforms, on the other hand, had more generous benefits for citizens than for special interest groups. Using a simple rule, compensatory transfers targeted all households with an annual income of less than JD 10,000 and aimed to reach a broad swath (70 percent) of the population regardless of employment status. Moreover, compared with the 2008 reforms, the compensation was far more generous for those not in the public sector.

According to the framework, an equilibrium described in Case 3 exists if social solidarity increases and when "social altruism" is inspired by specific, rather than general, consumption needs of the poor (as discussed further in chapter 1). By the end of the 2012 reform process, the political equilibrium around subsidies in Jordan was closer to Case 3, largely because of the economic and political crises, as described below.

The Role of Economic and Political Crises

Energy policies before 2008 in Jordan mostly benefited broad interests: most citizens had access to fuel and electricity at subsidized prices. The result was large subsidies amounting to as much as 5.6 percent of GDP (figure 5.9). The analytical framework described in chapter 1 predicts that reform is more likely at a time of impending crisis because a crisis allows for a realignment that often includes addressing the status quo, including regarding benefits afforded to special interest groups. In particular, subsidy reform is more likely under Case 1 if the following conditions hold:

- The costs of providing benefits rise sharply.
- Governments face general fiscal stringency, *and* energy subsidies are a large fraction of government spending.
- External pressure changes the political equilibrium.

Confronted with fiscal stringency, governments undertake reforms—often under external pressure. Crisis may allow for a political window of opportunity to address the status quo when it comes to benefits afforded to special interests. In the case of Jordan, strong economic growth through 2008 came to an abrupt end in 2009 with the onset of the international financial crisis (as shown earlier in figure 5.1). Despite efforts to reform, regional political tensions, combined with increasing international oil prices and the end of cheap natural gas imports from Egypt, made for an extremely difficult set of circumstances for the country.

In particular, when the government froze the automatic price adjustment mechanism in early 2011, the simultaneous increase in the cost of providing electricity made for an unsustainable economic situation. Together with a weakening in domestic revenue, these measures raised the primary fiscal deficit to 9.6 percent of GDP in 2011. Moreover, the more-expensive fuel imports resulted in a decline in the Central Bank of Jordan's reserves, leading to an external current account deficit of 12 percent of GDP (as shown earlier in figures 5.6 and 5.7).

At the request of government, an IMF Stand-By Arrangement was agreed, which set out conditions that aimed to ensure a return to a sustainable fiscal and external track. This broader effort was conducive to subsidy reform.

The Role of Administrative Feasibility and Competence

The analytical framework presented in chapter 1 predicts that reform is more likely when politicians change their beliefs about the "special" nature of energy and shift redistributive policies to more-efficient transfers. In the case of Jordan, energy subsidies had been broadly available. Thus, the critical ingredient, in addition to the economic and political crises, was a growing consensus (based on analyses by both domestic and international institutions) that untargeted, generalized subsidies were disproportionately benefiting the more-affluent households.

Perhaps more important, however, the availability of an effective targeting mechanism allowed the reform to take place. Specifically, the establishment of a database that allowed the government to identify poor households made the implementation of targeted subsidies feasible.

The Role of Citizen Engagement

Under Case 1 (large subsidy benefits for special interests and citizens alike), reforms are also more likely if citizens develop greater capacity to engage in their own collective interests (see annex 5C).

Although in general the framework predicts that reform is less likely when governments change or elections are introduced, there is one big exception: reform becomes *more* likely when a party or politician reaches out and substantially engages with citizens on reform priorities. To the extent that Prime Minister Ensour was widely seen as having been able to communicate the objectives and the need for reform, his October 2012 appointment was an important step in enabling the reform to take place.

The Role of Communication and Stakeholder Involvement

A perceptions survey was conducted in the spring of 2012 that helps to better explain the population's initial aversion to reform and why the cash transfer program helped to make the reform more palatable. Specifically, the survey found that a large share of Jordanians were not aware of the extent of fuel and electricity subsidies in their country (Silva, Levin, and Morgandi 2013). In particular, only 30 percent of the Jordanian respondents were aware of gasoline subsidies, and only 25 percent were aware of diesel subsidies. However, nearly 50 percent of respondents were aware of LPG subsidies, which, as discussed earlier, were relatively more important for household budgets.

The MENA SPEAKS survey also asked respondents in Egypt, Jordan, Lebanon, and Tunisia a set of questions related to subsidy reform.[24] Specifically, the following two questions were posed: "If the government could not afford to subsidize all of the following products, which product's price would you want the government to stop subsidizing? And what would be your second choice?"

The general acceptance of subsidy reform was relatively low in Egypt and Jordan. Fifty-nine percent of Egyptians and 56 percent of Jordanians refused to accept subsidy reform of any one product on the list, compared with 11 percent of Lebanese and 37 percent of Tunisians. For Jordanians who were willing to accept some reform, the largest share (50 percent) pointed to diesel subsidies, while 25 percent mentioned gasoline, 20 percent mentioned LPG, and 12 percent pointed to electricity subsidies (figure 5.12, panel a). The survey also found that most Jordanians (61 percent) favored targeting any savings from subsidy reform solely to the poor, more so than in Lebanon or Tunisia (figure 5.12, panel b).

The government undertook a series of efforts to ensure the political viability of the reform efforts. This included a communication strategy that centered on the fiscal costs of these subsidies and the fact that they were not reaching the poorest. The existing analytical work helped Prime Minister Ensour to counter criticism and inform the policy debate with an evidence base on both the cost of subsidy policy and who was benefiting.

These communications were coupled with a concerted effort to consult and dialogue with stakeholders. Before and after the November 2012 increase in energy prices, as noted earlier, Prime Minister Ensour met with various stakeholders at all levels, including parliament, local nongovernmental organizations, the business community, and labor representatives.

An Ongoing Agenda

One of the main reforms currently on the agenda is the reform of electricity subsidies. As discussed earlier, these were the most expensive subsidies, making up a large share of the total deficit through NEPCO's losses, which amounted to 4.7 percent of GDP in 2014 (as shown earlier in figure 5.9). Beginning in 2013, the government initiated reforms in the electricity sector as well. This has involved gradual price increases with the aim to achieve full cost recovery by

Figure 5.12 Subsidy Reform Perceptions and Preferences in Jordan, 2012

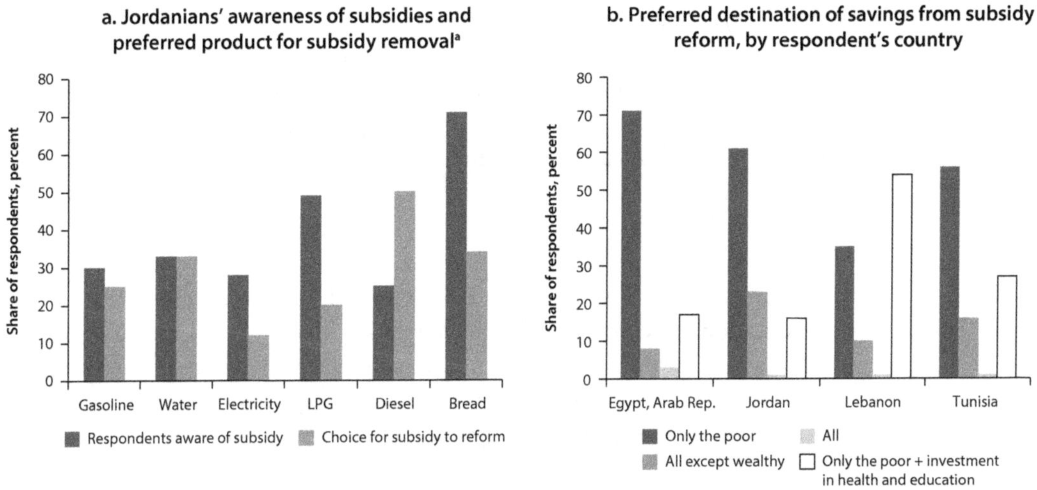

Source: Silva, Levin, and Morgandi 2013, based on MENA SPEAKS surveys in spring 2012.
Note: LPG = liquefied petroleum gas.
a. Regarding subsidy removal, survey respondents were asked, "If the government could not afford to subsidize all of the following products, which product's price would you want the government to stop subsidizing? And what would be your second choice?"

2017 (from a baseline of 56 percent in 2014). Consequently, the government increased electricity tariffs by 15 percent in both 2013 and 2014, and by 7.5 percent in January 2015. (Because of falling oil prices, the January 2015 increase was reduced from 15 percent to 7.5 percent.)[25] The government has been considering reorganizing the tariff structure as well.

As part of a broader reform strategy, the government has also attempted to diversify the country's energy sources. In July 2015 it opened a liquefied natural gas terminal in Aqaba as a fuel supply source, and it has taken longer-term steps to improve the production of renewable energy (with a target of renewable energy making up 10 percent of the overall energy mix by 2020). Similar reforms are planned in the water sector as well.

This is a large agenda, entailing significant distributional impacts. The fall in oil prices has improved the fiscal situation, requiring lower price increases than previously forecasted. Yet, underlying structural weaknesses endure.

More immediately, the government is improving its targeting system for cash transfers. Because households self-report their incomes to the tax authorities, the Ministry of Finance became the de facto administrator of the cash transfer system. The expectation is that improvements in the cash transfer system can also improve the targeting and efficiency of the social safety net. A related ongoing initiative of the government is to develop a National Unified Registry (NUR) to help rank households and target cash compensation schemes to those most affected by price or tariff increases (World Bank 2015).

Conclusions

This chapter has discussed the reforms of energy subsidies in Jordan, focusing on the 2012 reforms of subsidies on gasoline, diesel, LPG, and kerosene. An effort has been made to document the details of the reform process, including its design, passage, and implementation. The chapter has shown how those policy choices were shaped by factors that changed the political economy and therefore allowed the reforms to take place. The framework detailed in chapter 1 has helped to enable a coherent description of the political economy of reform.

The reform effort in Jordan serves as a useful case study for multiple reasons: First, as an oil-importing country, it is extremely vulnerable to international price fluctuations. Second, it faced challenges in the context of the Arab Spring, while at the same time confronting large economic shocks in the forms of higher international fuel prices and interruptions to gas supplies from Egypt.

Under these circumstances, a combination of circumstances made subsidy reforms possible:

- An impending fiscal and current account crisis with the potential to destabilize the currency
- The ability to establish a cash-transfer targeting mechanism by combining multiple databases
- Greater citizen engagement in the policy debate around trade-offs
- Concerted efforts by government leaders to communicate and consult with key stakeholders

Despite the advances in subsidy policy in Jordan, the reform agenda remains ongoing. Reforming the energy subsidies has led to a reduction in total energy subsidies, replacing them with a targeted cash transfer. However, more needs to be done to target electricity subsidies and diversify the country's sources of energy.

Annex 5A Political Chronology of Jordan

Table 5A.1 Major Political Events in Jordan, 1922–2013

Year	*Event(s)*
1922	The Council of the League of Nations recognizes Transjordan as a state under British supervision.
1946	The United Nations recognizes Jordan as an independent sovereign kingdom.
1948	The State of Israel is created under the British mandate in Palestine. Thousands of Palestinians flee Arab-Israeli fighting to the West Bank and Jordan.
1950	Jordan annexes the West Bank.
1951	July: King Abdullah I is assassinated by a Palestinian gunman angry at his apparent collusion with Israel in the carve-up of Palestine.
1952	August: King Hussein is proclaimed King.
1957	British troops complete their withdrawal from Jordan.

table continues next page

Table 5A.1 Major Political Events in Jordan, 1922–2013 *(continued)*

Year	*Event(s)*
1967	Israel takes control of Jerusalem and the West Bank during the Six-Day War, leading to a major influx of refugees into Jordan.
1970	Major clashes break out between government forces and Palestinian guerrillas, resulting in thousands of casualties in the Jordanian Civil War remembered as Black September (September 1970 to July 1971).
1972	An attempted military coup is thwarted.
1974	King Hussein recognizes the Palestine Liberation Organization (PLO) as the sole legitimate representative of the Palestinian people.
1986	King Hussein severs political links with the PLO and orders its main offices in Jordan to shut.
1988	King Hussein publicly backs the Palestinian uprising, or intifada, against Israeli rule.
1989	Jordan holds its first general election since 1967, contested only by independent candidates because of the 1963 ban on political parties.
1990	Jordan comes under severe economic and diplomatic strain as a result of the Persian Gulf crisis following Iraq's invasion of Kuwait.
1994	Jordan signs a peace treaty with Israel, ending a 46-year official state of war.
1997	Parliamentary elections are boycotted by several parties, associations, and leading figures.
1999	King Hussein dies. His eldest son, Crown Prince Abdullah, succeeds to the throne.
2001	King Abdullah II and presidents Bashar al-Assad of the Syrian Arab Republic and Hosni Mubarak of the Arab Republic of Egypt inaugurate a US$300 million (£207 million) electricity line linking the grids of the three countries.
2002	January: Riots erupt in the southern town of Maan, the worst public disturbances in more than three years, following the death of a youth in custody.
	August: A spat erupts with Qatar over a program on Qatar-based Al Jazeera television, which Jordan says insulted its royal family. Jordan shuts down Al Jazeera's office in Amman and recalls its ambassador to Qatar.
	September: Jordan and Israel agree on a plan to pipe water from the Red Sea to the shrinking Dead Sea. The project, costing US$800 million, is the two nations' biggest joint venture to date.
	October: Senior U.S. diplomat Laurence Foley is gunned down outside his home in Amman, in the first assassination of a Western diplomat in Jordan. Scores of political activists are rounded up.
2003	June: First parliamentary elections under King Abdullah II are held. Independent candidates loyal to the King win two-thirds of the seats.
	October: A new cabinet is appointed following the resignation of Prime Minister Ali Abu al-Ragheb. The King appoints Faisal al-Fayez as prime minister and also appoints three female ministers.
2004	Authorities seize cars filled with explosives and arrest several suspects said to be linked to al-Qaeda and planning a chemical bomb attack on the intelligence services headquarters in Amman.
2005	April: A new cabinet is sworn in, led by Prime Minister Adnan Badran, after the previous government resigns amid reports of the King's unhappiness over the pace of reforms.
	August: Three missiles are fired from the port of Aqaba. Two of them miss a U.S. naval vessel; a third one lands in Israel. A Jordanian soldier is killed.
	November: Suicide bombings at three Amman hotels kill 60 people. Al-Qaeda in Iraq claims responsibility. Most of the victims are Jordanians. A day of mourning is declared.
2007	July: The first local elections are held since 1999. The main opposition party, the Islamic Action Front, withdraws after accusing the government of vote rigging.
	November: Parliamentary elections strengthen the position of tribal leaders and other pro-government candidates. The fortunes of the opposition Islamic Action Front decline. Political moderate Nader Dahabi is appointed as prime minister.

table continues next page

Table 5A.1 Major Political Events in Jordan, 1922–2013 *(continued)*

Year	*Event(s)*
2009	November: King Abdullah dissolves parliament halfway through its four-year term.
	December: King Abdullah appoints a new premier, Samir Rifai, to push through economic reform.
2010	May: A new electoral law is introduced. Pro-reform campaigners say it does little to make the system more representational.
	October: The leader of an Islamist militant group is jailed for plotting attacks on the army.
	November: Parliamentary elections are boycotted by the opposition Islamic Action Front. Riots break out after it is announced that pro-government candidates have won a sweeping victory.
2011	January: Tunisian street protests unseat that country's president and encourage similar "Arab Spring" demonstrations in other countries, including Jordan.
	February: Against a background of large-scale street protests, King Abdullah appoints a new prime minister, former army general Marouf Bakhit, and charges him with carrying out political reforms.
	October: Protests continue through the summer, albeit on a smaller scale, prompting King Abdullah to replace Prime Minister Bakhit with Awn al-Khasawneh, a judge at the International Court of Justice.
2012	April: Prime Minister Awn al-Khasawneh resigns abruptly, having been unable to either satisfy demands for reform or allay fears of empowering the Islamist opposition. King Abdullah appoints former Prime Minister Fayez al-Tarawneh to succeed him.
	October: King Abdullah calls early parliamentary elections for January. The Muslim Brotherhood's political wing, the Islamic Action Front, decides to continue to boycott the elections in protest of unequal constituency sizes and a lack of real parliamentary power. The King appoints Abdullah Ensour, a former minister and vocal advocate of democratic reform, as prime minister.
	November: Clashes between protesters and supporters of the King follow mass demonstrations in Amman against the lifting of fuel subsidies, at which calls for the end of the monarchy are heard. Three people are killed.
2013	January: Pro-government candidates are victorious in parliamentary elections, which are boycotted by the main opposition group, the Islamic Action Front.
	March: A new government is sworn in, with incumbent Abdullah Ensour reinstalled as prime minister following unprecedented consultation between the King and parliament.

Source: BBC News 2015.

Annex 5B Chronology of Energy Subsidies in Jordan

Table 5B.1 Energy-Related and Subsidy Reform Efforts in Jordan, 1989–2012

Year	*Event(s)*
1989	• The government tries unsuccessfully to reform subsidies in the late 1980s. The attempts result in large-scale protest and force the government to reverse reform.
	• Jordan imports crude oil to be refined at the Jordan Petroleum Refinery Company and then sold at controlled prices. The losses incurred by the refinery are reimbursed by the government directly from its budget.
1996	• Food price riots follow the removal of subsidies under an economic plan supervised by the International Monetary Fund.
2003	• Following the United States-led invasion of Iraq in 2003, Jordan no longer enjoys a preferential price for oil.
2005	• The government implements a three-year strategy to eliminate energy subsidies starting in 2005.
	• Fuel prices increase dramatically: gasoline prices increase by around 10 percent, while fuel oil for power and industry increase by 33 percent and 59 percent, respectively. These increases, however, do not prevent the subsidies from increasing because oil prices in international markets continue to rise. Consequently, the government decides to raise prices again in the same year.
2006	• More price increases are approved, ranging from 1.3 percent for jet fuel to 65 percent for fuel oil to the power sector.
2007	• The government resists passing the international increase in oil prices to the domestic market.
2008	• The government decides to remove almost all energy subsidies, resulting in price increases ranging from 16 percent for gasoline to 76.5 percent for liquefied petroleum gas (LPG).
	• To ensure that domestic prices are aligned with international markets, the government establishes a committee comprising members from the Ministry of Energy and Mineral Resources, Ministry of Finance, and the Jordan Petroleum Refining Company to set the price on a monthly basis based on a formula to reflect international prices and freight allowance.
	• During this period, the government increases the minimum wage and provides a salary increase as well as a one-time bonus to low-paid government employees.
2010–11	• Popular protests against growing living costs and unemployment arise in parallel to the December 2010 Tunisian uprising.
	• Extensive disruptions affect the flow of gas from Egypt.
	• In December 2011, the government approves a US$230 million package to reduce food and fuel prices and discontinue monthly petroleum price adjustments, freezing retail prices (except for heavy industrial users).
2012	• Faced again with fiscal strain, the government reinstates the monthly fuel price adjustment for gasoline, jet fuel, and heavy fuel oil in June.
	• In September, continued increases in international prices lead to a 10 percent increase in all fuel prices. This move is later reversed by the King.
Nov. 2012	• Prime Minister Ensour announces subsidy reform. Fuel subsidies are fully eliminated, resulting in price increases.

Sources: Coady et al. 2006; Haddad 2012; IMF 1999, 2008, 2009, 2012a, 2012c; Mansur 2013a; Trend News Agency 2012.

Annex 5C Timeline of Events in Jordan, 2011–13

Figure 5C.1 Political Events and Government Actions in Jordan, January 2011 to January 2013

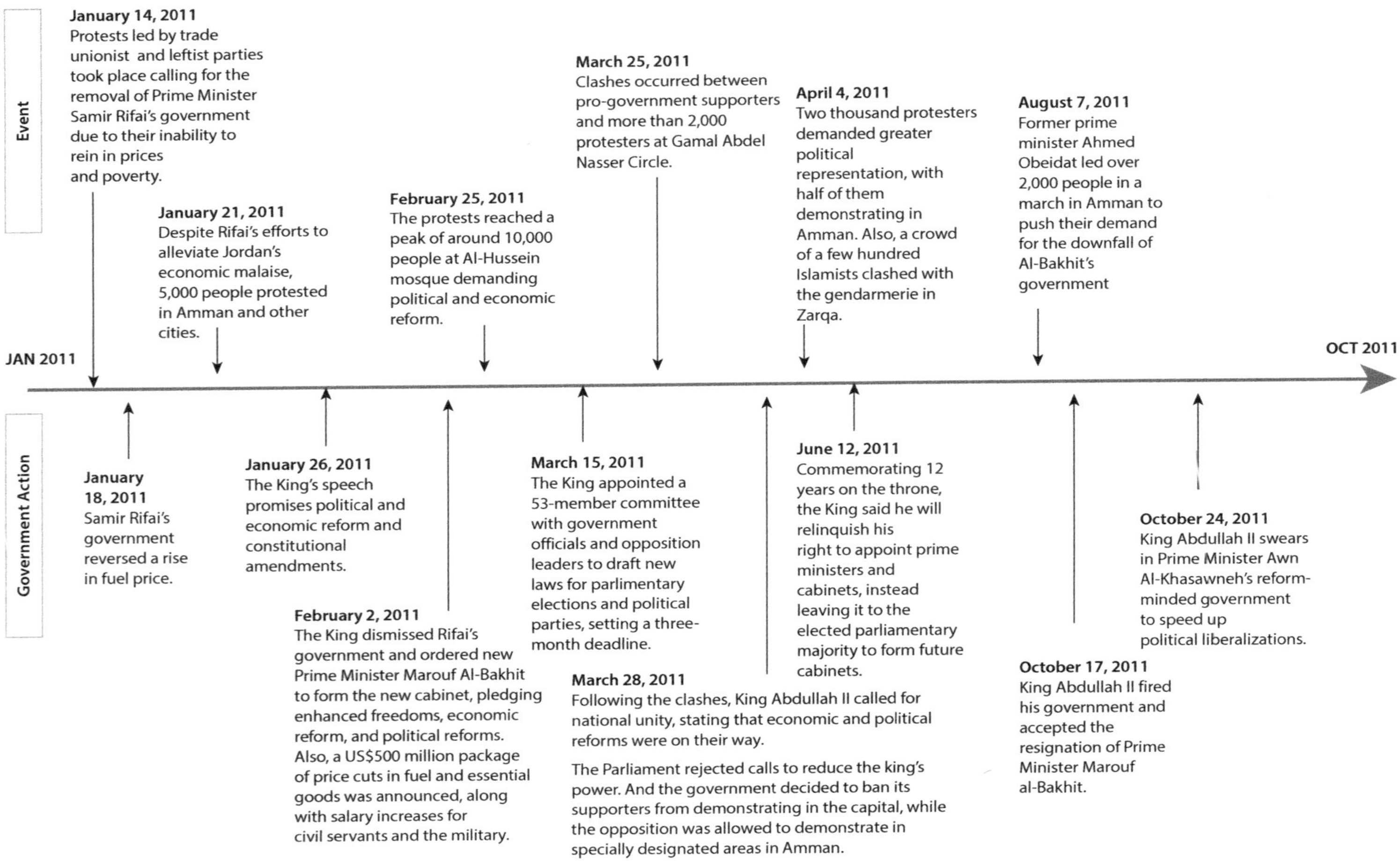

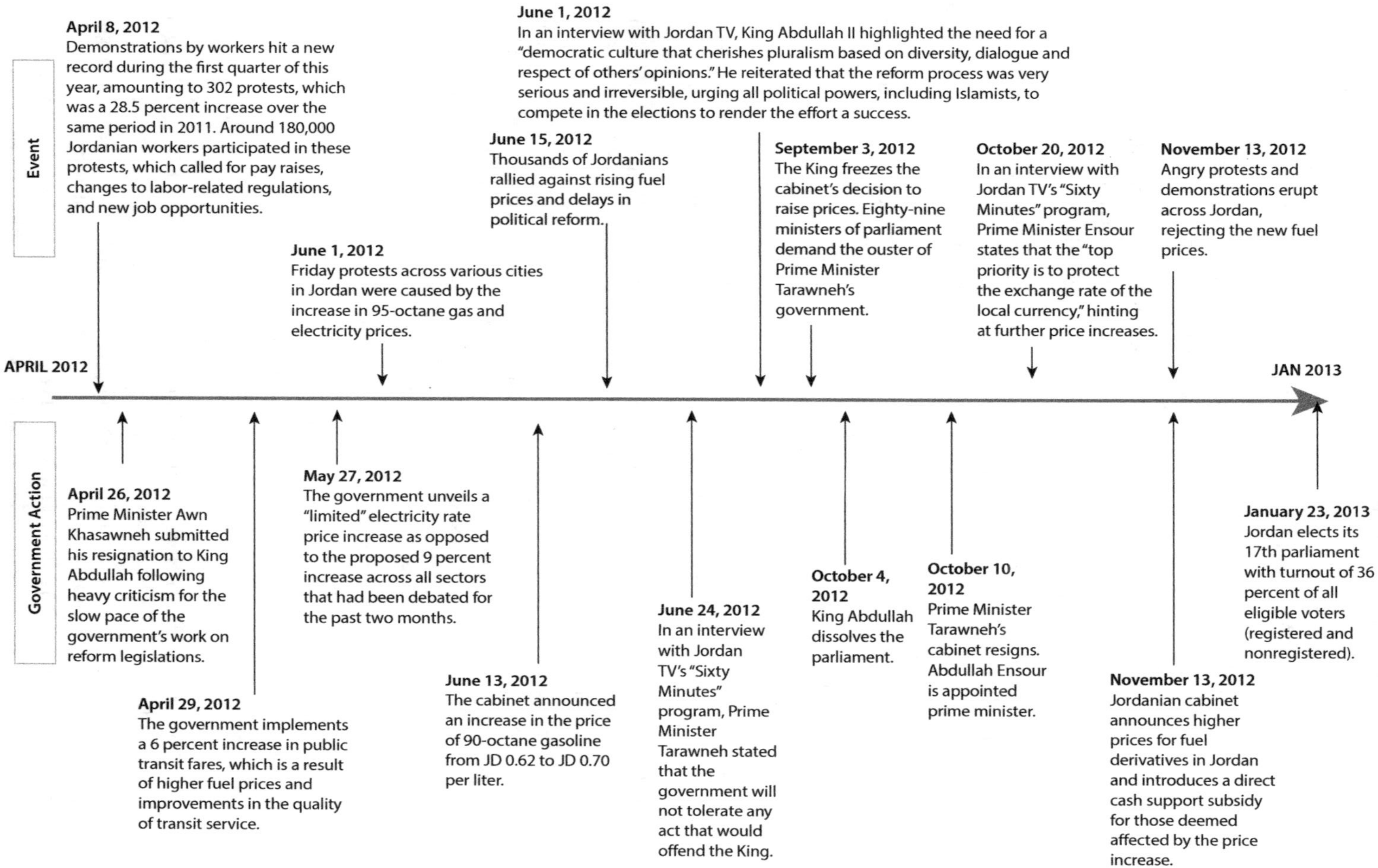

Source: Mansur 2013a, ©Young Entrepreneurs Association and Friedrich Naumann Foundation for Liberty. Reproduced with permission from Friedrich Naumann Foundation for Liberty; further permission required for reuse.

Notes

1. This section was written by Yusuf Mansur (June 2014).
2. This procedure is relatively recent. Until 2000, the King would nominate the prime minister, and the parliament would then approve the King's recommendation or appointment of both the prime minister and the cabinet members.
3. As part of the reform emerging from the Arab Spring, the number of deputies was increased in 2012 from 120 to 150 to accommodate the "national list" (27 representatives) and enable voters to cast two votes instead of one. The first vote is on the constituency level, and the second is for the national level—known as the "national list" ("Timeline of Political Reform," Embassy of Hashemite Kingdom of Jordan, Washington, DC, http://www.jordanembassyus.org/politics/timeline-political-reform).
4. The Royal Hashemite Court serves as the political and administrative link between the King and the central government, the armed forces, and the security forces ("The Royal Court Offices," website of King Hussein, http://www.kinghussein.gov.jo/royal_offices.html).
5. Note that lower-house coalitions could be seen as substitutes for political parties in Jordan, which were formally banned in 1957.
6. See "Discussion Papers" on the website of His Majesty King Abdullah II bin Al-Hussein (accessed Jan. 26, 2016), http://www.kingabdullah.jo/index.php/en_US/pages/view/id/244.html.
7. The Industry and Trade Law of 1998 conveyed the responsibilities of the former Ministry of Supply to the Ministry of Industry and Trade.
8. The IMF's Stand-By Arrangement is its primary lending instrument for emerging and advanced market countries that need financing to help them overcome their balance-of-payments problems during economic crises (IMF 2015a).
9. IMF 2009 and estimates from current account and nominal GDP data, Central Bank of Jordan database, http://statisticaldb.cbj.gov.jo/index?action=level3&cat_id=3&dbName=tab6209.
10. The private sector suffered a significant drop in credit because of a restrictive monetary policy after the 2008 collapse of global financial firm Lehman Brothers and the subsequent unraveling of a domestic Ponzi scheme, known as the Phantom Bourse Crisis. The panic that ensued adversely affected the financial market immediately, and the Central Bank of Jordan adopted a cautionary prudent stance that resulted in reducing liquidity (Al-Rfou 2013).
11. Jordan has consistently bought energy from its neighbors at below-market prices since the 1973 Arab-Israeli War. After the Gulf War, Egyptian gas substituted for relatively inexpensive Iraqi oil.
12. For a more detailed discussion, see Verme (2011).
13. "Timeline of Political Reform," Embassy of Hashemite Kingdom of Jordan, Washington, DC, http://www.jordanembassyus.org/politics/timeline-political-reform.
14. "Timeline of Political Reform," Embassy of Hashemite Kingdom of Jordan, Washington, DC, http://www.jordanembassyus.org/politics/timeline-political-reform.
15. "Timeline of Political Reform," Embassy of Hashemite Kingdom of Jordan, Washington, DC, http://www.jordanembassyus.org/politics/timeline-political-reform.
16. "Timeline of Political Reform," Embassy of Hashemite Kingdom of Jordan, Washington, DC, http://www.jordanembassyus.org/politics/timeline-political-reform.

17. "Annual Report 2012," Ministry of Energy and Mineral Resources (MEMR), Hashemite Kingdom of Jordan, Amman.
18. Jordan's National Aid Fund, established in 1996, functions autonomously under the auspices of the Ministry of Social Development. It administers several means-tested programs, including recurrent cash assistance, emergency aid under specified circumstances, health care benefits, and others ("National Aid Fund," Jordan Scheme Information, International Labour Organization, http://www.ilo.org/dyn/ilossi/ssimain.viewScheme?p_lang=en&p_scheme_id=1665).
19. Author interviews with head of Income and Sales Tax Department, Ministry of Finance, June 2014.
20. Author interviews with officials of the Chamber of Industry, Chamber of Commerce, media organizations, and civil society organizations as well as government officials, June 2014.
21. The government disbursed the cash transfer in three tranches: the first (of about JD 96 million) in November to December 2012 and the next two (totaling JD 193 million) in 2013. Given the timing of the disbursements the actual annual cost of the program was around JD 280 million (Ministry of Finance, *General Government Finance Bulletin* 17 [4], May 2015). Note that the cost of these transfers have substantially come down since then, in line with the decline in the international price of oil.
22. Prominent among these efforts was the opening of the Sheikh Sabah Al Ahmad natural gas terminal in Aqaba, which allowed Jordan to import natural gas by ship and then regasify it for power production in 2015. The terminal was funded in part by the Kuwaiti government (*Jordan Times* 2015).
23. A transfer whose concentration curve lies everywhere below the Lorenz curve is regressive. A transfer whose concentration curve lies everywhere above the Lorenz curve is globally progressive in relative terms. A transfer whose concentration curve lies everywhere above the diagonal "perfect equity" line (that is, the per capita transfer decreases with income) is globally progressive in absolute terms. For a full discussion on defining the progressivity of taxes and transfers, see Duclos and Araar (2006).
24. MENA SPEAKS (Social Protection Evaluation of Attitudes, Knowledge, and Support [SPEAKS] in the Middle East and North Africa [MENA]) refers to a set of nationally representative opinion surveys to collect cross-country data about citizens' perceptions and aspirations concerning social safety nets (Silva, Levin, and Morgandi 2013). The surveys were conducted by the World Bank in partnership with Gallup in Egypt, Jordan, Lebanon, and Tunisia.
25. For a fuller description of the electricity reforms, see World Bank (2015).

References

Al-Khalidi, Suleiman. 2012. "UPDATE 2—Jordan Lifts Fuel Subsidies, Sparks Protests." *Reuters*, November 13. http://www.reuters.com/article/jordan-gasoline-prices-idUSL5E8MDCKK20121113.

Al-Rfou, Ahmad N. 2013. "Awareness of Investors in Phantom Bourses: Financial Sources vs. Investment Results." *International Journal of Business and Management Invention* 2 (5): 39–43.

Araar, A., E. Le Borgne, U. Serajuddin, and P. Verme. 2013. *An Assessment of the Jordan 2012 Petroleum Subsidies Reform and Cash Compensation Program*. Report 79837, World Bank, Washington, DC.

Atamanov, Aziz, Jon Jellema, and Umar Serajuddin. 2015. "Energy Subsidy Reform in Jordan: Welfare Implications of Different Scenarios." Policy Research Working Paper 7313, World Bank, Washington, DC.

Barany, Zoltan. 2012. "The 'Arab Spring' in the Kingdoms." Research paper, Arab Center for Research & Policy Studies, Doha, Qatar.

BBC News. 2015. "Jordan Profile—Timeline." April 29. http://www.bbc.com/news/world-middle-east-14636713.

Coady D., M. El-Said, R. Gillingham, K. Kpodar, P. Medas, and D. Newhouse. 2006. "The Magnitude and Distribution of Fuel Subsidies: Evidence from Bolivia, Ghana, Jordan, Mali, and Sri Lanka." Working Paper 06/247, International Monetary Fund, Washington, DC.

Cowell, Alan. 1989. "5 Are Killed in South Jordan as Rioting Over Food Prices Spreads." *New York Times*, April 20. http://www.nytimes.com/1989/04/20/world/5-are-killed-in-south-jordan-as-rioting-over-food-prices-spreads.html.

Duclos, Jean-Yves, and Abdelkrim Araar. 2006. *Poverty and Equity: Measurement, Policy, and Estimation with DAD*. New York: Springer and International Development Research Centre.

Haddad, Saleem. 2012. "Jordan's Protests: Political Economy, Protest, and Empire." *Muftah*, November 22. http://muftah.org/jordans-protests-political-economy-protest-and-empire/#.VqlVq_krKM9.

Halaby, Jamal. 2012. "Jordan: 1 Gunman Killed in Police Station Attacks." Associated Press, November 14. http://news.yahoo.com/jordan-1-gunman-killed-police-station-attacks-231148272.html.

IMF (International Monetary Fund). 1999. "IMF Approves EFF and CCFF Credits for Jordan." Press Release 99/13, April 16. http://www.imf.org/external/np/sec/pr/1999/pr9913.htm.

———. 2002. "IMF Concludes 2002 Article IV Consultation with Jordan." Public Information Notice 02/51, May 3.

———. 2005. *Jordan: Post-Program Monitoring Discussions—Staff Report; and Public Information Notice on the Executive Board Consideration*. Country Report 05/100, IMF, Washington, DC.

———. 2007. *Jordan: 2006 Article IV Consultation and Fourth Post-Program Monitoring Discussions—Staff Report; and Public Information Notice on the Executive Board Discussion*. Country Report 07/128, IMF, Washington, DC.

———. 2008. *Jordan: 2008 Article IV Consultation—Staff Report; and Public Information Notice on the Executive Board Discussion*. Country Report 08/290, IMF, Washington, DC.

———. 2009. *Jordan: 2009 Article IV Consultation—Staff Report; Public Information Notice on the Executive Board Discussion; and Statement by the Executive Director for Jordan*. Country Report 09/159, IMF, Washington, DC.

———. 2010. *Jordan: 2010 Article IV Consultation—Staff Report and Public Information Notice*. Country Report 10/297, IMF, Washington, DC.

———. 2012a. *Jordan: Request for a Stand-By Arrangement—Staff Report; Staff Supplement; Request for Modification of Performance Criteria; Press Release on the Executive Board Discussion; and Statement by the Executive Director for Jordan*. Country Report 12/343, IMF, Washington, DC.

———. 2012b. *Jordan: Selected Issues*. Country Report 12/120, IMF, Washington, DC.

———. 2012c. *Jordan: Staff Report for the 2012 Article IV Consultation*. Country Report 12/119, IMF, Washington, DC.

———. 2013a. *Jordan: First Review Under the Stand-By Arrangement, Request for Waivers of Nonobservance of Performance Criteria, Modification of Performance Criteria, and Rephasing of Access—Staff Report; Press Release on the Executive Board Discussion; and Statement by the Executive Director for Jordan*. Country Report 13/130, IMF, Washington, DC.

———. 2013b. *Jordan: Second Review Under the Stand-By Arrangement, Request for Waivers of Nonobservance of Performance Criteria, and Modification of Performance Criteria*. Country Report 13/368, IMF, Washington, DC.

———. 2014. *Jordan: 2014 Article IV Consultation, Third and Fourth Reviews Under the Stand-By Arrangement, Request for Waivers of Nonobservance of Performance Criterion and Applicability of Performance Criterion—Staff Report; Press Releases; and Statement by the Executive Director for Jordan*. Country Report 14/152, IMF, Washington, DC.

———. 2015a. "IMF Stand-By Arrangement." Factsheet, IMF, Washington, DC. https://www.imf.org/external/np/exr/facts/sba.htm.

———. 2015b. *Jordan: Seventh and Final Review Under the Stand-By Arrangement and Proposal for Post-Program Monitoring—Press Release; Staff Report; and Statement by the Executive Director for Jordan*. Country Report 15/225, IMF, Washington, DC.

———. 2015c. *Jordan: Sixth Review Under the Stand-By Arrangement, Request for Waivers of Applicability of Performance Criteria, and Rephasing of Access—Staff Report; Press Release; and Statement by the Executive Director for Jordan*. Country Report 15/115, IMF, Washington, DC.

Jolliffe, Dean Mitchell, and Umar Serajuddin. 2015. "Estimating Poverty with Panel Data, Comparably: An Example from Jordan." Policy Research Working Paper 7373, World Bank, Washington, DC.

Jordan Times. 2012. "Is Jordan's PM Ensour Trying to Wriggle out of Subsidies?" October 17. http://www.albawaba.com/business/jordan-ensour-subsidy-446987.

———. 2015. "King Opens Aqaba Gas Terminal." July 31. http://www.jordantimes.com/news/local/king-opens-aqaba-gas-terminal.

Kojima, Masami. 2013. "Petroleum Product Pricing and Complementary Policies: Experience of 65 Developing Countries since 2009." Policy Research Working Paper 6396, World Bank, Washington, DC.

Lamis, A., and J. Schwedler. 1996. "Bread Riots in Jordan." *Middle East Report 201* (October–December): 40–42.

Mansur, Yusuf. 2013a. *Did the Arab Spring Benefit Economic Freedom in Jordan?* Amman, Jordan: Young Entrepreneurs Association and Friedrich Naumann Foundation for Liberty.

———. 2013b. "Impact of Syrian Crisis on Jordan." Presentation, International Conference on the Socio-Economic Dimensions of the Syrian Conflict, Beirut, July 4. http://leb-econ.org/site/wp-content/uploads/2013/07/S2_Jordan_Mansur.pdf.

Metz, Helen Chapin, ed. 1989. *Jordan: A Country Study*. Washington, DC: U.S. Government Publishing Office for the Library of Congress.

Reed, John. 2013. "Jordan Poised to Make Electricity Price Rises after Ramadan." *Financial Times*, July 10. http://www.ft.com/cms/s/0/dc1b1b4a-e95c-11e2-9f11-00144feabdc0.html#axzz3yeW2RQPf.

Sabha, Yassin. 2014. "Growth History of Jordan Part II: The First Growth Interlude (1967–1973)." *YassinSabha: Global Trade and Competitiveness, Italy, Rieti, Jordan and the Middle East* (blog), March 1. https://yassinsabha.wordpress.com/2014/03/01/growth-history-of-jordan-part-ii-the-first-growth-interlude-1967-1973/.

Sadiki, Larbi. 1997. "Towards Arab Liberal Governance: From the Democracy of Bread to the Democracy of the Vote." *Third World Quarterly* 18 (1): 127–48.

Silva, Joana, Victoria Levin, and Matteo Morgandi. 2013. *Inclusion and Resilience: The Way Forward for Safety Nets in the Middle East and North Africa.* Washington, DC: World Bank.

Trend News Agency. 2012. "Jordan's King Suspends Fuel Price Hike after Rising Protests." September 3. http://en.trend.az/world/arab/2061056.html.

Verme, Paolo. 2011. "Electricity Subsidies and Household Welfare in Jordan: Can Households Afford to Pay for the Budget Crisis?" Background paper for the Jordan Poverty Reduction Strategy, World Bank, Washington, DC.

World Bank. 2015. *Jordan—First Programmatic Energy and Water Sector Reforms Development Policy Loan Program Project.* Program document, Report 94786-JO, World Bank, Washington, DC.

APPENDIX A

The Political Economy of Subsidy Reform: Conceptual Framework*

To explain when energy policies change—when governments reduce subsidies or deregulate prices—it is useful to know why the policies were politically desirable to begin with. Two key puzzles are important to unravel. First, as with any government spending program, subsidies have distributional consequences. Why did governments prefer the particular distribution of benefits embedded in the policy? The second question is just as important, but has received far less attention. Why was it politically desirable to achieve these distributional objectives through subsidies as opposed to, for example, cash transfers? Answers to these questions help to identify the characteristics of the political system that should change in order for reform to be possible.

Why did governments prefer the particular distribution of benefits embedded in the policy? One way to organize thinking about this question is to posit that governments care about the welfare of both vested interests[1] and citizens more broadly, but the weight that they put on the welfare of each varies from place to place. Factors that induce politicians to cater more closely to the preferences of special interests than of the general public include the potential for special interests to use violence to insist on policies that benefit them; political institutions that reduce political incentives to favor broad citizen interests (e.g., when governments are not elected); the lack of citizen information about policy actions and consequences; and the inability of citizens to act collectively to demand policies in their interests. The problem of collective action, in turn, emerges when political parties that could mobilize citizens are fragmented and loosely organized; or when society is polarized and divided by exceptionally low trust.

Why deliver government benefits in the form of subsidies rather than something else? This second question is especially important because subsidies—particularly energy subsidies—are notoriously inefficient, not least because they distort production and consumption choices and encourage environmentally

* This framework was developed by Phil Keefer.

damaging externalities. Imperfect citizen information and the lack of government credibility both contribute to a political preference for inefficient subsidies.

Imperfect information might matter, first, because citizens may not know that special interests or elites derive exceptional benefits from energy subsidies. Subsidies that seem to be universal from the point of view of uninformed citizens may, in fact, deliver extraordinary benefits to vested interests. Governments may take advantage of this asymmetry in designing transfer schemes. Cash transfers may be more transparent in this regard, defeating the goals of special interests. Second, if citizens are uninformed about government performance, they may blame government for economic shocks, such as fuel price hikes, that are outside of government control. Faced with the prospect of paying a political price for shocks that are beyond their control, politicians subsidize fuel when prices rise. Cash transfers could also serve this purpose, but a government program to hold energy prices constant masks economic shocks and prevents the political problem from emerging in the first place. Third, though this is perhaps more a question of ideological bias than imperfect information, citizens may simply believe that stable or very low fuel prices are legitimate objectives of government policy. In this case, energy subsidies simply reflect "popular will," though the emergence of such an ideological bias may be linked to imperfect information.

The lack of politician credibility can also explain a political preference for subsidies. First, average citizens and special interests can be concerned that, by themselves, they cannot prevent policies that benefit them from being altered by current or future politicians. Together, though, they can impose large costs on politicians who reverse policies. In these cases, special interests may prefer universal subsidies that give average citizens an incentive to support the policy, while average citizens are willing to tolerate subsidies that disproportionately benefit special interests since only special interests can mobilize average citizens to act collectively in defense of the subsidies. For example, although large Indian farmers are by far the largest beneficiaries of free electricity for agriculture, they can count on small farmers to help protect their interests. Why? Because small farmers, alone, cannot easily mobilize in defense of their small electricity benefits—they need the support of large farmers for this. Larger farmers cannot easily mobilize large groups of citizens in defense of privileges if they alone were to receive the privileges.

Why might energy or other subsidies link special interests and average citizens more closely than cash transfers? First, cash transfers make the disparity in benefits more obvious, making it more difficult for rich beneficiaries to mobilize poor beneficiaries. In contrast, when both groups receive the right to purchase the same product at the same low price, the disparity in benefits depends on individuals' (imperfect) knowledge of the amount purchased by others. Second, governments cannot easily change the distribution of benefits when all individuals have the right to purchase unlimited amounts at the same price. In order to increase the benefits received by some groups, they would have to set a lower price for those groups than for the others, or restrict the quantities that other groups can receive compared to favored groups. If this happens, however, those charged at the lower price, or who are not quantity-limited, can buy larger volumes and resell the product to those who do not. Competition among those who are eligible for the more favorable terms will drive down the resale price, resulting in nonfavored groups receiving nearly the same low price as the favored groups. Cash transfers do not admit this kind of arbitrage. This does not mean that subsidies for particular groups cannot exist. However, the usual reasons for such subsidies—the ability of special interests to exert pressure on policy makers—do not explain broad-based subsidies that offer modest benefits to many citizens and outsized benefits to a few.

Hypotheses

This conceptual framework yields a number of hypotheses. These, in turn, point to the types of information that might be collected in the case studies to better understand the political preconditions for reform.

The starting point for any investigation of the politics of subsidy reform is to understand the distribution of benefits of the energy subsidies. Collecting this information is essential prior to exploring the political roots of energy policy and its potential reform. Are subsidies tilted toward industrial interests, urban residents, or the poor? The main indication of bias would ideally come from the volume of benefits received: the amount of the subsidy per unit of energy consumed by a group, in the aggregate and per capita, times the volume consumed. Of course, this turns out to be a difficult analytical enterprise in and of itself. For example, the benefits of low fuel prices for intracity buses might flow to bus customers or, if there are barriers to entry into the bus market, might stay with the owners of the buses. Volumes consumed are frequently not metered (in the case of electricity) or cannot be metered (in the case of fuel for transport). Prices, though, can be a difficult proxy for subsidy benefits. If the poor are targeted with subsidies, but energy supplies to poor areas are frequently rationed or cut off, then the price the poor are supposed to pay offers no information on the benefits they actually receive. Fortunately, precise calculations of benefits received are not essential to the political economy analysis. Instead, it is enough to collect qualitative information on whether, for example, vested interests are able to gain access to low-price energy and to resell it in higher-priced markets; whether industrialists or large farmers consume roughly as much as they want at low prices; whether poor areas or poor consumers have unrationed access at low prices; and whether, in fact, barriers to entry or collusive pricing behavior might allow bus companies to retain a large share of the benefits from access to cheap fuel.

With this information in hand, one can roughly characterize energy policies in a country as offering substantial or relatively few benefits to special interests and substantial or relatively few benefits to citizens at large. This yields four cases: (1) cases in which both vested interests and citizens derive large benefits from subsidies; (2) cases in which vested interests get most of the benefits and citizen get few; (3) cases in which citizen benefits are large and vested interest benefits are low; and (4) cases in which neither special interests nor general citizens benefit significantly (table A.1.1). For each type of case, the proposed framework provides a hypothesis on the circumstances that could lead to a subsidy reform being more (or less) likely.

Table A.1.1 Characterizing Policy Benefits

	Citizen benefits are large	*Citizen benefits are small*
Special interest benefits are large	Case 1	Case 2
Special interest benefits are small	Case 3	Case 4

Case 1: Both Vested Interests and Citizens Derive Large Benefits

This case implies large fuel subsidies, such as fuel prices in Egypt or Nigeria or electricity prices in Indian agriculture, where prices charged are low for all users. Large users benefit exceptionally, but average citizens also see a significant contribution to their household budget.

Hypothesis: Such a policy exists because neither citizens nor vested interests believe government promises to continue to provide them benefits into the future. In particular, massive energy subsidies persist because citizens cannot act collectively and special interests are concerned about exposure to government predation. Each therefore depends on the support of the other for the benefits and neither will support lowering benefits for the other.

Reform is therefore more likely when:

- citizens develop greater capacity to mobilize in their own collective interests—then they do not need vested interests to defend their interests and will support reducing subsidies to them;
- it becomes more difficult for vested interests to mobilize citizens against the reform, lowering the cost to government of reducing subsidies (e.g., because citizens become more aware of the disproportionate volume of benefits flowing to vested interests; or because, for unrelated reasons, the government has cracked down on consumer demonstrations organized by vested interests, or has made high payments to households to persuade them to stay off the streets);
- the costs of providing benefits rise sharply (world fuel prices skyrocket).
- governments face general fiscal stringency AND energy subsidies are a large fraction of government spending (otherwise, there's no particular reason why energy subsidies would be cut more than any other form of government spending);
- external pressure changes the political equilibrium (donors with exceptional leverage—typically because of fiscal crisis, however; or international NGOs provide information on the distribution of subsidy benefits that average citizens previously did not know).

Reform is *not* more likely when governments change or elections are introduced, because the underlying problem of credible commitment remains the same (unless a more credible party or politician replaces a noncredible incumbent); governments promise to replace energy subsidies with cash transfers to average citizens, since average citizens do not believe that these transfers are credible unless they are supported by special interests.

Case 2: Vested Interests Get Most of the Benefits, and Citizens Get Few Benefits

A situation in which prices are high for households and low for industrial users would be one example of such a case. For example in the Dominican Republic large consumers are able to directly purchase electricity from generators, rather than having to go through the distribution companies, leading to large savings relative to households. However, it is rare to find such a policy. Instead, Case 2 is more typically a variant on Case 1: prices are low for all, but average citizens and businesses confront severe rationing, while special interests have privileged access to supplies.

Hypothesis: Such a policy exists when citizens have no ability to defend their collective interests (cannot act collectively) and special interests have no need to rely on citizens to preserve their own privileges. High subsidies would then flow to vested interests under three conditions: First, vested interests are tightly integrated with the government (e.g., by family or personal ties) and do not need the threat of mobilizing citizens to preserve their privileges; second, they are a particularly small fraction of the population and do not need to internalize the social and economic consequences of failed energy polices; and third, their economic interests are little affected by inefficient energy policies.

Reform is therefore more likely when:

- citizens develop greater capacity to mobilize in their own collective interests; the government changes AND special interests have no leverage over the successor government; the rents that special interests rely on dry up;
- fuel prices skyrocket (though the greater likelihood of repression in this setting means that more stringent rationing of fuels for citizens is another response).
- governments face general fiscal stringency AND energy subsidies are a large fraction of government spending (again, otherwise, there's no reason why energy subsidies would be cut more than any other form of government spending).
- external pressure changes the political equilibrium (donors with exceptional leverage—typically because of fiscal crisis; or international NGOs provide information on the distribution of subsidy benefits that average citizens previously did not know).

Case 3: Special Interests Get Few of the Benefits, and Citizens Get Most of the Benefits

Subsidies that are intended exclusively to benefit households fall into this category. These might be low prices on fuel used predominantly by households and less by firms (e.g., gasoline and not diesel) or, in other sectors, price controls on bread, rice, or other food items. It is hard to identify a case in which universal subsidies to households are not also captured by vested interests—for example, when they divert subsidized products to full-price markets. In a case in which citizens are well-organized enough to demand subsidies from government that benefit only them and not special interests, they should also be well-organized enough to demand that those subsidies be delivered in the most cost-effective way—in the form of cash transfers. That is, cases of universal subsidies—certainly of energy—fall always or nearly always into Case 1. The concern in this case, therefore, is targeted subsidies, aimed at small/poor users (e.g., where the price for the first units of energy consumed is very low). The normative case against such targeted subsidies is less clear—nearly all countries have them, although cash subsidies would be more efficient, strictly speaking.

Hypothesis (targeted subsidies): Such a policy exists when the poor are organized and pivotal voters, when social solidarity is high, and when "social altruism" is inspired by specific, rather than general, consumption needs of the poor.

Reductions in these subsidies are more likely when:

- The poor are no longer pivotal.
- The costs of the subsidies rises, either because of fuel price increases, or significant substitution by the poor into the consumption of energy (though this is hard to imagine).
- Immigration or other forces shift country demographics.
- Parties that oppose redistribution come to power. (Note that when ideological parties are present, citizen mobilization is more likely to be high and Cases 3 and 4 are more likely to prevail. Hence, the ideological shifts associated with changes in government are more likely to matter in these cases.)
- Politicians' beliefs about the "special" nature of energy change and redistributive policies shift to more efficient transfers.
- External pressure changes the political equilibrium (donors with exceptional leverage—typically because of fiscal crisis).

Case 4: Neither Special nor General Citizen Interests Benefit Significantly

No one benefits exceptionally from two classes of energy policies. One is when subsidies are simply low. Another, more interesting and reflective of energy policies in several countries, is that policy is intended to stabilize fuel prices in an "actuarially fair" manner (higher prices charged in "good times" fully offset the costs of subsidies in "bad times"), permitting consumption smoothing by average citizens. These "ideal" stabilization policies have a second-order effect on consumer welfare but will insulate governments against political shocks. Large users, with greater capacity to hedge against fuel price changes, may not even receive second-order benefits.

Such policies leave the domain of Case 4 under two circumstances. First, prices rise more than anticipated, depleting the stabilization fund built up when prices where low. When this effect is large, the other cases are more pertinent, depending on the distribution of benefits. Second, stabilization funds can only survive if no arbitrage between subsidized and full-price markets is allowed. If special interests can manipulate access to the fund when world prices are high and domestic prices, because of the fund, are low, then Case 2 applies.

Hypothesis 1: Stabilization policies persist unless they fall out of the domain of Case 4 and into one of the other cases.

Hypothesis 2: Stabilization policies persist until parties with a pro-market ideology come to power. Note that when ideological parties are present, citizen mobilization is more likely to be high and Cases 3 and 4 are more likely to prevail. Hence, the ideological shifts associated with changes in government are more likely to matter in these cases.

Note

1. Vested interests are narrow groups of citizens, ranging from very narrow—elites and cronies—to less narrow, the workers and employers in particular sectors.

Environmental Benefits Statement

The World Bank Group is committed to reducing its environmental footprint. In support of this commitment, we leverage electronic publishing options and print-on-demand technology, which is located in regional hubs worldwide. Together, these initiatives enable print runs to be lowered and shipping distances decreased, resulting in reduced paper consumption, chemical use, greenhouse gas emissions, and waste.

We follow the recommended standards for paper use set by the Green Press Initiative. The majority of our books are printed on Forest Stewardship Council (FSC)–certified paper, with nearly all containing 50–100 percent recycled content. The recycled fiber in our book paper is either unbleached or bleached using totally chlorine-free (TCF), processed chlorine-free (PCF), or enhanced elemental chlorine-free (EECF) processes.

More information about the Bank's environmental philosophy can be found at http://www.worldbank.org/corporateresponsibility.

green press INITIATIVE

www.ingramcontent.com/pod-product-compliance
Lightning Source LLC
LaVergne TN
LVHW080039210926
848481LV00011B/3236